THE ACHILLES HEEL OF DEMOCRACY

Featuring the first in-depth comparison of the judicial politics of five under-studied Central American countries, *The Achilles Heel of Democracy* offers a novel typology of "judicial regime types" based on the political independence and societal autonomy of the judiciary. This book highlights the under-theorized influences on the justice system – criminals, activists, and other societal actors, and the ways that they intersect with more overtly political influences. Grounded in interviews with judges, lawyers, and activists, it presents the "high politics" of constitutional conflicts in the context of national political conflicts as well as the "low politics" of crime control and the operations of trial-level courts. The book begins in the violent and often authoritarian 1980s in Guatemala, El Salvador, Honduras, and Nicaragua and spans through the tumultuous 2015 "Guatemalan Spring"; the evolution of Costa Rica's robust liberal judicial regime is traced from the 1950s.

Rachel E. Bowen is an assistant professor of political science at The Ohio State University, where she teaches courses on Comparative Politics, American Politics, Constitutional Law, and Gender and Politics on the Mansfield Campus. She has been researching Central America since 2002.

The Achilles Heel of Democracy

JUDICIAL AUTONOMY AND THE RULE OF LAW IN CENTRAL AMERICA

RACHEL E. BOWEN

The Ohio State University

CAMBRIDGE
UNIVERSITY PRESS

CAMBRIDGE
UNIVERSITY PRESS

University Printing House, Cambridge CB2 8BS, United Kingdom

One Liberty Plaza, 20th Floor, New York, NY 10006, USA

477 Williamstown Road, Port Melbourne, VIC 3207, Australia

4843/24, 2nd Floor, Ansari Road, Daryaganj, Delhi - 110002, India

79 Anson Road, #06-04/06, Singapore 079906

Cambridge University Press is part of the University of Cambridge.

It furthers the University's mission by disseminating knowledge in the pursuit of education, learning and research at the highest international levels of excellence.

www.cambridge.org
Information on this title: www.cambridge.org/9781107178328
DOI: 10.1017/9781316823514

First published 2017

Printed in the United States of America by Sheridan Books, Inc.

A catalogue record for this publication is available from the British Library

Library of Congress Cataloging-in-Publication data
Names: Bowen, Rachel E., author.
Title: The achilles heel of democracy : judicial autonomy and the rule of law in Central America / Rachel E. Bowen.
Description: Cambridge [UK] ; New York : Cambridge University Press, 2017.
Identifiers: LCCN 2017005280 | ISBN 9781107178328 (hardback)
Subjects: LCSH: Judicial independence – Central America. | Justice, Administration of – Central America. | Judges – Central America. | Political questions and judicial power – Central America. | Rule of law – Central America. | BISAC: LAW / Comparative.
Classification: LCC KG3495 .B69 2017 | DDC 347.9728/012 – dc23
LC record available at https://lccn.loc.gov/2017005280

ISBN 978-1-107-17832-8 Hardback

Contents

Tables

Figures

Acknowledgments

In the decade and a half I have lived with this project, I and it have enjoyed the support of more people than I could ever list. I regret that I cannot personally thank the individuals who participated in this research because of promises of anonymity. The judges, lawyers, and activists with whom I spoke gave generously of their time, pointed me down fruitful avenues, and offered invaluable perspective. This book would not exist without them. Their thoughtful and passionate dedication to their countries was inspiring. I can thank Jorge Vargas Cullell of Estado de la Nación in Costa Rica for his enthusiasm for my research.

At Georgetown, my adviser, John Bailey, was endlessly patient with me throughout my graduate years. I also owe a debt of gratitude to Douglas Reed for his support. One could have no better cheering section. At Georgetown, I also had the good fortune to be a part of a supportive group of friends interested in questions of constitutionalism, notable among them Matthew Taylor and Susan Alberts. I also owe a debt of gratitude to the late C. Neal Tate. Since coming to Ohio State, my Mansfield Campus colleagues have provided endless support, the most significant manifestation of which has been Write Club and its sometimes-shifting membership. Previous drafts of all or part of this work were generously read by Alexei Trochev, Raul Sanchez Urríbarri, Sarah Brooks, Marcus Kurtz, Susan Delagrange, Cynthia Callahan, and Joseph Fahey. Research assistance was provided by Vittorio Merola, who was instrumental in coding the 2010 questionnaires, and Hannah Chelimsky. At Cambridge University Press, I thank four anonymous reviewers and my editor, John Berger. Any and all errors or omissions in this book, however, are entirely my own.

My earliest travels to Central America came as a part of my dissertation research. At that stage, I was fortunate to receive a field research fellowship from Georgetown University's Center for Latin American Studies in 2003 and a Beinecke Scholarship from the Harry S. Truman Good Neighbor Foundation in 2004. The 2003–2004 Jill Hopper Memorial Fellowship from the Department of Government at Georgetown University provided the invaluable opportunity to retain a stipend while conducting research in Guatemala and Nicaragua. Later rounds of field research in 2009–2010 were made possible by a Seed Grant from the Mansfield Campus of The Ohio State University, which also allowed me to arrange my classes to accommodate another extensive field work year in Guatemala and Costa Rica in 2009 and subsequently awarded me a Special Research Appointment in 2011 to facilitate early drafting of this project. Research assistance for this project was supported by two Faculty Grants from the Mershon Center for International Security Studies of The Ohio State University.

I thank the Latin American Public Opinion Project (LAPOP) and its major supporters (the United States Agency for International Development, the Inter-American Development Bank, and Vanderbilt University) for making available the data used to construct several of the charts in chapters one and three.

Parts of chapters one and two have previously been published in *Political Research Quarterly* in December 2013 under the title "Judicial Autonomy in Central America: A Typological Argument" (Vol. 66. No. 4, pp 830–841). I am indebted to three anonymous reviewers at *Political Research Quarterly* for pushing me to take my thinking about the typological argument and its implications deeper.

I also wish to thank my family. My wife, Jen, has learned more about Central American judicial politics than perhaps any architect before her. My parents, John and Laveta Bowen, provided repeated logistical support for my travels and a great deal of child care for my writing. Until our divorce, Delano Lopez was also an enthusiastic cheerleader for me and this project, including accompanying me on most of my research travels. This book is dedicated to my son, Peregrin.

1

Societally Penetrated Judiciaries and the Democratic Rule of Law

In 2015, Guatemala City was rocked by popular protests. Sparked by an investigation into a customs scandal known as "La Linea," the protests ultimately brought down the Guatemalan president. The "La Linea" investigation was only possible because of an international anti-impunity commission that had been working to strengthen Guatemala's justice sector since 2007. While the "Guatemalan Spring" represents a sea change in institutionalization in Guatemala's justice sector that has also allowed for recent trials for massive human rights violations, it has yet to eliminate corruption and threats affecting police, prosecutors, and judges in an environment of continued criminal violence. Contrast this to the relative comfort with which judges operated in Costa Rica: threats are rare and are usually confined to the drug trafficking affected zones in the Caribbean coast and the border with Panama. Meanwhile, Honduras continues to be affected by the judicial legitimation of a coup against President Zelaya in 2009. To the south, the Nicaraguan Supreme Court has become subject to intensifying partisan influences including stepping into the political debate on reelection to open the door to another term for President Ortega in 2009. Violent crime in El Salvador in 2015 reached levels of violence not seen since the civil war of the 1980s and 1990s. The judiciary there has become increasingly independent – and has also increasingly butted heads with the Legislative Assembly. Clearly, serious threats to the independence of judges exist in Central America. These threats come from above (elected politicians) and below (violent criminals) and, indeed, from nearly every quarter. This kaleidoscope of threat poses substantial challenges to those who would try to improve the quality of justice and strengthen the rule of law in this region.

In this book, I argue that a democracy can function well only when its judges are autonomous from societal forces in addition to political actors. Most scholarship on judicial politics has emphasized the political independence of courts while shortchanging their societal autonomy. Judges who are insulated from societal pressures can better control crime, including organized crime, than can judges who are dependent on or threatened by societal actors such as economic elites or criminal actors. I demonstrate the significance of societal pressures by comparing the levels of judicial political independence and judicial societal autonomy across five countries in Central America since 1980, using a conceptual tool I call the "judicial regime type" to examine the interactions of political independence and societal autonomy. Judicial regimes emerge as a result of the impact of dominant decision rules, or "currencies," of politico-legal conflict resolution – be they official violence, unofficial violence, legislation, or constitutions. Judges in Central America today are threatened by criminals and economic corruption at least as often as they are by governmental actors and political pressure. Conversely, those countries where judges are insulated from societal actors enjoy a more complete rule of law, even where the judiciary is not politically independent. We must understand all of these sources of pressure if we are to understand judicial politics and build better governments.

The judicial regime type approach is novel within the comparative study of judicial politics and can help reformers to craft better reform programs throughout the developing world. The persistent focus on political independence is a legacy of the "third wave of democracy" in which the current wave of judicial reform was born, an era in which military and other dictatorships that had either ignored or manipulated their judiciaries were giving way to democracy. Some three decades on, the problems facing judiciaries have changed. The dominant type of violence in Latin America is now criminal in nature rather than being part of an official (if covert) government policy, although the two are sometimes linked. Governments, including democratic governments, have been largely unable to confront this wave of unofficial violence. Thus, I argue that one reason for the persistent shortcomings of nation-building projects around the world has been the inability or unwillingness to confront societal actors. Societal actors in weak states may be able to capture aspects of the state apparatus, including the judiciary. Even without actual state penetration, a weak state will be unable to give its laws practical effect if the judiciary cannot enforce them because of threats from violent societal actors and enticements from their wealthy counterparts.

Nearly three decades after the dirty wars and civil wars of the 1970s and 1980s ended and democracy was reinstituted in Central America, weak states and weak democracies have become the norm in the isthmus, with the exception of Costa Rica. Drug and gang-related violence and organized crime predominate in Guatemala, Honduras, and El Salvador; traffickers have also infiltrated parts of Nicaragua and Costa Rica. Guatemala's political system significantly overlaps the organized criminal sector; former military men present the major opposition to those groups while sometimes also backing their own illegal organizations. Heavy-handed, militaristic tactics are routinely employed against criminals in the region, raising renewed concerns about human rights. In the late 2000s, both Honduras and Nicaragua experienced significant backsliding in their democratic governance, with a coup in the former and the constitutionally questionable reelection of President Daniel Ortega in the latter. The once-powerful political parties of Costa Rica have decayed and are being pursued by upstarts and recent congresses have been paralyzed by the apparent reluctance of congressmen to appear for votes. Nowhere can politicians be counted on to have the ability – or perhaps even the inclination – to address the changes needed to allow a democratic rule of law to function. Even recent progress in Guatemala, as incomplete as it is, has only been possible because of the involvement of an international anti-impunity commission (Comisión Internacional Contra la Impunidad en Guatemala, CICIG), whose mandate renewals are consistently resisted by the national government.

With the rise of democracy in Latin America in the 1980s and 1990s, attention turned to building strong state institutions, including politically independent judiciaries. Despite extensive international aid to further this goal, four of the five Central American countries have failed to build the kinds of judiciaries usually associated with a liberal democracy. In Guatemala, impunity reigns as drug-trafficking gangs are able to infiltrate politics and threaten judges. In Nicaragua and Honduras, the judiciary is highly partisan and responsive to the interests of elected politicians. El Salvador suffers from a mixture of both of these problems. Costa Rica stands alone as a judiciary that is largely free of political and societal threats. Despite these concerns, it remains encouraging that none of these judiciaries is under the direct control of the government as was typical during authoritarian periods.

More than two decades of judicial reform in the region have not substantially improved the rule of law in these countries. Even the dramatic successes of Guatemala's CICIG have primarily affected only a small number of high-profile cases. Reform efforts, while serving lofty goals including building the rule of law by enhancing access to the legal system for all citizens, protecting judicial independence, and increasing the efficiency of the justice sector, have produced gains in some areas and have stalled or even regressed in others. Part of the problem is in the nature of reforms that have tended to focus – and necessarily so – on discrete projects that dealt with only one small part of the problem. More problematic, however, was the tendency to try to layer reforms onto old institutions, frequently leaving in place the officeholders and giving them the chance to reproduce their power and thus subvert reforms.

Additionally, while incremental improvements were often made in certain justice sector problems, crime and social disorganization exploded in these countries and the demand for justice quickly outpaced these reforms. Where this criminal behavior has been the worst – in Guatemala, El Salvador, and Honduras – security has had to become a top priority, though governments and international reformers have often reacted slowly and inadequately. The frightening levels of criminality that accompanies the often pathological resolutions of politico-juridical conflicts are at the heart of these problems.

THE RULE OF LAW IN CENTRAL AMERICA

At the center of the relationship between legal politics and democratic politics is the democratic rule of law, an important but often poorly conceptualized notion. Academic work on democratic consolidation nearly always includes building the rule of law among its important issues. The rule of law is a crucial component of a consolidated democracy.[1] The democratic rule of law can probably be most intuitively understood as the enforcement of the "rules of the game" of democracy.[2] Scholars writing in the Law and Society tradition have focused on the relative gap between the law as written and the law as lived,[3] alongside a skeptical account of the ways in which law and legality are used for social control.[4] O'Donnell has provided a definition of the rule of law that includes the republican ideas of sacrificing private preferences to public interests and the liberal idea that certain rights should be protected.[5] I define the "democratic rule of law" as a system in which power is exercised through formal laws that have been passed by democratic institutions, is checked by horizontal accountability institutions (including courts), and respects liberal political rights necessary for democratic participation; furthermore, to the extent that social rights are provided in national laws, citizens are able to enjoy

---

[1] Carothers, *Promoting the Rule of Law Abroad: In Search of Knowledge*; Linz and Stepan, *Problems of Democratic Transition and Consolidation: Southern Europe, South America, and Post-Communist Europe*; Diamond, *Developing Democracy: Toward Consolidation*.

[2] Przeworski, "Some Problems in the Study of Transitions to Democracy"; Przeworski, "The Games of Transition."

[3] This view is also reflected in Paulo Sergio Pinheiro's introduction to *The (Un)Rule of Law*, in which he suggests that a fundamental weakness of citizenship in the weak democracies of Latin America allows traditional elites to manipulate state institutions, and produces (or at least tolerates) lawless violence, discrimination, and lack of access to justice. Méndez, O'Donnell, and Pinheiro, *The (Un)Rule of Law & the Underprivileged in Latin America*.

[4] Rose, O'Malley, and Valverde, "Governmentality."

[5] O'Donnell, "Ployarchies and the (Un)Rule of Law in Latin America: A Partial Conclusion."

them equitably.[6] The rule of law is perniciously difficult to measure, as is democracy itself.[7] Measures of judicial independence, commonly linked to the democratic rule of law, do not fare much better; one study of the various measures and indices of judicial independence found that they were all flawed in one manner or another and, furthermore, did not correlate with each other.[8] These measures have been criticized as constituting international norms in their own right, imbuing them with the power to regulate developing country governments.[9]

Nonetheless, even imperfect indicators can help to provide a picture of the state of the democratic rule of law in the region. The World Justice Program Rule of Law Index is composed of 47 sub-factors grouped into eight primary indicators, scored from 0 to 1, with 1 representing strongest rule of law. A selection of these sub-factor scores is presented in Table 1.1. Not surprisingly, Costa Rica scores the highest overall, but the differences between the other four are striking. Honduras and Nicaragua score especially poorly on the measures of government influence on both civil and criminal justice as well as "government powers are effectively limited by the judiciary," although Nicaragua scores highest for timely and effective criminal adjudication. Guatemala scores especially low for access to civil justice. Additionally, all but Costa Rica score quite poorly on the sub-factor "government officials are sanctioned for misconduct," suggesting that official impunity is high. Guatemala, Honduras, and El Salvador also all fared very poorly in the World Economic Forum's 2013–2014 ratings for the business costs of crime and violence, efficacy of the courts, and organized crime.[10] Meanwhile, legitimacy of the justice system had gone down and approval of vigilantism had increased, according to one 2011 World Bank report.[11] Despite the presence of formal democracy, it appears that the rule of law was weak in the region.

Crime statistics can provide a partial picture of changes in the rule of law over time. Figure 1.1 provides the Homicide rates per 100,000 residents from 2000 to 2014, according to the United Nations Office on Drugs and Crime. As is evident, there is considerable variation and volatility in homicide rates. Honduras had in the early 2000s the unfortunate distinction of being the most dangerous country in the world. By contrast, Nicaragua and Costa Rica closely

---

[6] Møller and Skaaning, *The Rule of Law: Definitions, Measures, Patterns and Causes*, 25.
[7] Møller and Skaaning, *The Rule of Law*.
[8] Ríos Figueroa and Staton, "Unpacking the Rule of Law: A Review of Judicial Independence Measures."
[9] Urueña, "Indicators and the Law: A Case Study of the Rule of Law Index."
[10] World Economic Forum, "Global Competitiveness Report 2013–2014."
[11] The World Bank, "Crime and Violence in Central America: A Development Challenge," 10.

TABLE 1.1 *Selected World Justice Program Indicators, 2015*

	Costa Rica	El Salvador	Guatemala	Honduras	Nicaragua
Overall score	0.68	0.51	0.44	0.42	0.43
Government powers are effectively limited by the judiciary	0.70	0.45	0.42	0.31	0.29
Government officials in the judicial branch do not use public office for private gain	0.77	0.43	0.36	0.37	0.27
People have access to affordable civil justice	0.69	0.56	0.35	0.52	0.40
Civil justice is free of corruption	0.74	0.42	0.44	0.42	0.34
Civil justice is free of improper government influence	0.77	0.39	0.35	0.26	0.17
Civil justice is not subject to unreasonable delays	0.31	0.46	0.19	0.36	0.31
Criminal investigation system is effective	0.47	0.24	0.24	0.14	0.36
Criminal adjudication system is timely and effective	0.43	0.26	0.24	0.19	0.52
Criminal system is free of corruption	0.68	0.45	0.34	0.34	0.43
Criminal system is free of improper government influence	0.79	0.45	0.31	0.13	0.08
Due process of law and rights of the accused	0.74	0.42	0.47	0.28	0.35
Government officials are sanctioned for misconduct	0.63	0.30	0.31	0.39	0.26
Crime is effectively controlled	0.69	0.58	0.45	0.41	0.67

Source: World Justice Project.[12]

track each other with homicide rates close to 10 per 100,000. Surveys conducted by Vanderbilt University's Latin American Public Opinion Project between

[12] World Justice Project, "WJP Rule of Law Index® 2015."

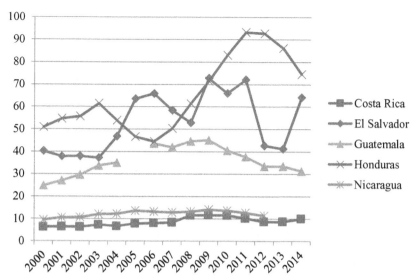

FIGURE 1.1 Homicide Rates per 100,000 (2000–2014).
Source: United Nations Office on Drugs and Crime.[13]

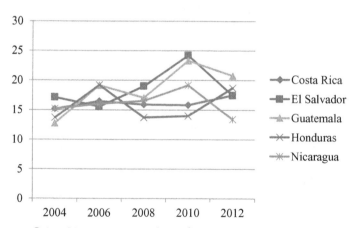

FIGURE 1.2 Crime Victimization in Central America (2004–2012).
Source: The AmericasBarometer by the Latin American Public Opinion Project (LAPOP), www.LapopSurveys.org.

2004 and 2012 suggest that self-reported criminal victimization was somewhat less volatile, as depicted in Figure 1.2. Guatemala saw the lowest figure

---

[13] United Nations Office on Drugs and Crime, "UNODC Statistics Online – Homicide Counts and Rates (2000–2014)."

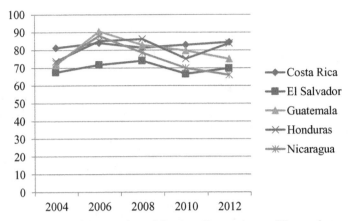

FIGURE 1.3 Percent of Respondents Viewing Corruption as "Somewhat or Very Generalized" (2004–2012).
Source: The AmericasBarometer by the Latin American Public Opinion Project (LAPOP), www.LapopSurveys.org.

(12.76 percent) in 2004 but then had the highest rate (20.78 percent) in 2012. More surprising, perhaps, is the similarly high rates of criminal victimization in Costa Rica (between 15.2 percent in 2004 and 17.49 percent in 2012) and Nicaragua (15.19 percent in 2004, peaking at 19.17 percent in 2010 and then dropping to 13.41 in 2012), given their low homicide rates. The World Bank further reported in 2011 that their own surveys suggested that crime was among the top five impediments to development everywhere in Central America except for Costa Rica.[14]

An additional helpful measure of the democratic rule of law is corruption. Corruption is notoriously difficult to measure and most indicators are based on either expert opinion or public opinion. Transparency International scores and ranks most of the world's countries from least corrupt to most corrupt. Central America sees considerable variation, although only Costa Rica, ranked at 40 in the world, has a relatively controlled corruption problem. El Salvador is in the middle of the rankings in place 72, with Honduras (112), Guatemala (123), and Nicaragua (130) all being scored quite poorly.[15] Notably, these scores have been quite stable, suggesting that little progress is really being made. LAPOP data also includes a question about how generalized respondents believe public corruption to be. Figure 1.3 tracks the percentage of people responding that corruption is somewhat or very generalized. Surprisingly, all countries have

[14] The World Bank, "Crime and Violence in Central America," 8.
[15] Transparency International, "Corruption Perceptions Index 2015."

very high scores on this measure, with El Salvador being the lowest until 2012, Costa Rica tying with Honduras for highest in 2012, and Nicaragua showing the most improvement. Although perceptions of corruption can be sticky, with people continuing to view a government as highly corrupt even after efforts are underway to combat that corruption, these indicators suggest that corruption remains a significant problem throughout the region.

This weakness of the rule of law persists despite decades of judicial reforms. Judicial reform created additional changes in both the opportunities available to activists and the role-orientations of judges. As a part of democratic consolidation, Latin American countries undertook a large number of judicial reform programs, sponsored by international aid and development agencies.[16] Central America was no exception to this trend. Indeed, international penetration of the justice sectors of these countries has been quite high.[17] These reform efforts have focused on building the rule of law by increasing access to justice for citizens, efficiency of the judicial system, and independence of the judiciary.[18] In justifying these projects, scholars tend to focus on the "rule of law" as the important contribution of the judiciary to democracy.[19] The rule of law has provided an important theoretical concept and goal, which changes the way judges perceive their roles in the constitutional order. As judges are exposed to international norms of independence and impartiality, international training programs, and new ways of doing justice, they may become more likely to shed traditional civil law deference and adopt activist approaches.

Changing norms and role-orientations can have a variety of effects on judicial politics. The experiences of a variety of countries indicate that judiciaries do not simply become more independent or activist in a linear fashion. In Eastern Europe, some Constitutional Courts were initially very activist, but have since become relatively deferential in the wake of significant incursions on their independence.[20] The Nigerian Supreme Court has had periods

---

[16] Dakolias, "A Strategy for Judicial Reform: The Experience in Latin America."

[17] Bowen, "International Imposition and Transmission of Democracy and the Rule of Law: Lessons from Central America."

[18] Carothers, *Promoting the Rule of Law Abroad*; Carothers, "The Rule of Law Revival"; Domingo and Sieder, *Rule of Law in Latin America: The International Promotion of Judicial Reform*; Hammergren, *Envisioning Reform: Improving Judicial Performance in Latin America*; Hammergren, *The Politics of Justice and Justice Reform in Latin America: The Peruvian Case in Comparative Perspective*; Ungar, *Elusive Reform: Democracy and the Rule of Law in Latin America*.

[19] Carothers, "The End of the Transition Paradigm."

[20] Epstein, Knight, and Shvetsova, "The Role of Constitutional Courts in the Establishment and Maintenance of Democratic Systems of Government"; Scheppele, "Constitutional Negotiations: Political Contexts of Judicial Activism in Post-Soviet Europe"; Trochev, *Judging Russia: The Role of the Constitutional Court in Russian Politics 1990–2006*.

of extreme independence, including trying to hold a military government accountable to the constitution, but has seen its fortunes rise and fall with different regimes.[21] The Taiwanese Supreme Court was riding a wave of support and activism in the years after democratization, but saw more restraintist judges appointed after the Court began to deal with sensitive issues of identity politics.[22] Even the well-insulated Israeli High Court of Justice saw its prestige drop once its judicial review role was publicly institutionalized.[23] Moments of activism – or even lengthy periods – at one time do not imply widespread or growing activism in the future. Activism or restraint are always the outcome of contestation between different groups trying to influence judicial outcomes. That contestation may be peaceful or it may include violence directed at judges themselves. The specific characteristics of particular groups and the institutional features often understood collectively as "judicial independence" will facilitate or inhibit this contestation by elites of the judicial role.

This book is primarily concerned with the question of how weak democracies can build courts and other justice sector institutions that can exercise autonomous power and contribute to building the rule of law. This question becomes especially important in environments in which some aspects of the rule of law is severely lacking, either because of prevalent partisan favoritism or because of pervasive social violence that persists in impunity. Comparative judicial politics scholarship has delved extensively into the dynamics of overcoming partisanship, but has reflected much less on the influence of criminality on justice sector institutions. I argue that the question of how to build strong, independent institutions can only be understood if we understand political influence in a broad fashion, extending not only to partisan politicians but also to criminals, businessmen, and other social actors who have an eye toward disrupting public policy and governance.

WHY WOULD POLITICIANS BUILD INDEPENDENT INSTITUTIONS?

The larger question of institution building implies another question: how does the judiciary get empowered by politicians in the first place, given that politicians are giving up some of their own power by doing so? The late twentieth century witnessed the rise of judiciaries as political actors in much of the globe, usually – but not exclusively – in the context of democratization or democratic constitutional reform. This judicialization of politics

---

[21] Okere, "Judicial Activism or Passivity in Interpreting the Nigerian Constitution."
[22] Chu, "Global Constitutionalism and Judicial Activism in Taiwan."
[23] Hofnung, "The Unintended Consequences of Unplanned Constitutional Reform: Constitutional Politics in Israel."

corresponded with an increasing emphasis internationally on human rights and legal protections for the rights and lives of citizens. In Latin America, repressive authoritarian regimes of the 1970s and 1980s were subject to global campaigns against them, citing their use of torture, forced disappearance, and extrajudicial killings. Lawyer-activists brought challenges to these actions in both national and international courts.[24] These efforts largely failed to change government behavior in their own time, but they did change some of the rhetoric and expectations in the region around the role of courts. In general, other forces would be necessary to encourage authoritarian and democratizing regimes to empower their courts.

One such force is the need to attract investment or other positive international attention, which requires "credible commitments" to potential economic partners, both foreign and domestic. North and Weingast argue for the usefulness of an independent judiciary for creating the necessary credibility. As opposed to more absolutist ages, seventeenth-century England saw the empowerment of a judiciary that could enforce contracts (notably, for international credit) against the crown.[25] That these developments coincided with the resolution of political coordination problems in favor of limited government and citizen liberties also aided the evolution of English democracy.[26] Although these concepts are based on the English experience, North and Weingast have made some efforts to apply this analysis to the developing world, but their conclusions are likely to disappoint most reformers: Weingast suggests that developing countries are unlikely to transition to "open access orders" (i.e., democracies with the rule of law) through international imposition but instead must evolve on their own paths.[27] While it is not clear whether Weingast, et al, believe these evolutions to be ultimately inevitable, it is clear that developing countries face difficult challenges in transiting from "limited access orders" due to the prevalence of rent-seeking.[28] In his 2007 study of Egypt, Moustafa suggests an alternative answer: governments, even authoritarian governments, will empower courts to control rent-seeking in order to entice foreign investment.[29] This ability to police lower-level bureaucrats is encouraged so long as it does not rise to attacks against the higher-level

---

[24] Sikkink, *The Justice Cascade*.
[25] North and Weingast, "Constitutions and Commitment: The Evolution of Institutions Governing Public Choice in Seventeenth-Century England."
[26] Weingast, "The Political Foundations of Democracy and the Rule of Law."
[27] Weingast, "Why Developing Countries Prove So Resistant to the Rule of Law."
[28] North et al., "Lessons: In the Shadow of Violence."
[29] Moustafa, *The Struggle for Constitutional Power: Law, Politics, and Economic Development in Egypt*.

government actors.[30] Judges then have the ability to engage in a kind of bounded activism that may expand beyond the relatively narrow confines of enforcing the economic rules, especially if it has the support of a network of opposition parties, human rights activists, and professional lawyers' groups. Authoritarian regimes who empower independent judiciaries to remedy pathologies within their own regimes are thus faced with the unintended consequence of creating a judicial avenue for opposition activities.

The functional utility of an independent judiciary is insufficient to convince many elected or unelected politicians to reduce their own power voluntarily. Alternatively, citizen demand for rights may produce what Epp calls "rights revolutions." A rights revolution occurs when citizen rights and liberties are enforced and expanded in the courts as a result of pressure on the courts from a "legal support network" of activists and legal professionals and their organizations. These support networks not only provide the demand for judicial enforcement of rights, they also provide a societal buffer for judges against political retribution. In this way, independence accrues to courts in a gradual way through the expansion and assertion of judicial power, one major decision at a time.[31] Notably, this method of judicial empowerment is most likely to be successful in a democracy that allows those support networks to punish politicians who would seek to rein in the courts, although Widner has chronicled a similar phenomenon in Tanzania.[32] It is also more likely to be successful in the Anglo-American common law systems that elevate court decisions as precedent, but the experience of Costa Rica discussed in chapter three suggests that rights revolutions can happen in civil law countries as well. This account may be too optimistic, however. The rights revolution argument implies that judicial decisions to protect rights will be intended to aid (and will actually aid) the societal have-nots, but the reality may be more complicated, requiring political will on top of judicial action.[33]

Rights revolutions are only as strong as their constitutions and the elites that enforce them, however. Hirschl questions whether bills of rights and judicial empowerment were even intended to aid the have-nots. Parliaments, he argues, enact bills of rights not to bind their own hands and protect the have-nots but rather to bind the hands of a future government that might be swayed by surging radical interests. For Hirschl, it should thus be unsurprising

---

[30] McCubbins and Schwartz, "Congressional Oversight Overlooked: Police Patrols versus Fire Alarms."

[31] Epp, *The Rights Revolution: Lawyers, Activists, and Supreme Courts in Comparative Perspective.*

[32] Widner, *Building The Rule of Law: Francis Nyalali and the Road to Judicial Independence in Africa.*

[33] Rosenberg, *The Hollow Hope: Can Courts Bring About Social Change?*

that courts tend to protect economic rights and basic political rights more than social rights.[34] In a larger sense, however, it may not be valid to segregate policy preferences and interests in the legitimation and strengthening of the judiciary. The wave of "judicialization of politics" that has swept over much of the world, including both authoritarian and democratic developing countries, continues to be controversial.[35] Latin American judges are trained to believe in a minimal role for judicial interpretation; legal and judicial education generally focuses instead on memorization of laws and their strict application, leading many judges to adopt a conservative stance regarding the role of the judiciary in politics.[36] The belief that the judiciary should adopt an activist stance is a policy preference, which is in turn intertwined with other policy preferences regarding the nature of democracy, rights protections, and accountability for other government actors.

Institutional rules may also encourage citizen demands. Wilson's work on the rights revolutions in Costa Rica and Colombia begins with the existence of "rights-rich constitutions" in these two countries alongside already empowered judiciaries. However, he argues, there were not deep-pocketed judicial support networks or organizations that sought to fight for legal rights through the court system. What there was instead was incredible ease of litigant access brought about by a relaxation of judicial formality; litigants could easily fight for their own rights without the need for an interceding organization to help them. In essence, the court itself becomes the support system for the litigant.[37] Costa Rican judges, at least, are thus able to maintain their power without relying on institutionalized societal support, although the constitutional chamber has enjoyed considerable diffuse public support. In both Costa Rica and Colombia, the judicial reforms that allowed these rights revolutions to occur were done as a part of international rule of law reform efforts. While these

---

[34] Hirschl, "The Political Origins of Judicial Empowerment Through Constitutionalization: Lessons from Four Constitutional Revolutions"; Hirschl, *Towards Juristocracy: The Origins and Consequences of the New Constitutionalism.*

[35] Tate and Vallinder, *The Global Expansion of Judicial Power*; Clayton, "The Supply and Demand Side of Judicial Policy-Making (Or, Why Be so Positive about Judicialization of Politics?)"; Ferejohn, "Judicializing Politics, Politicizing Law"; Domingo, "Judicialization of Politics or Politicization of the Judiciary? Recent Trends in Latin America"; Domingo, "Judicialization of Politics: The Changing Political Role of the Judiciary in Mexico"; Seider, Angell, and Shjolden, *The Judicialization of Politics in Latin America*; Ginsburg and Moustafa, *Rule by Law: The Politics of Courts in Authoritarian Regimes.*

[36] Hilbink, *Judges Beyond Politics in Democracy and Dictatorship: Lessons from Chile*; Hilbink, "The Constituted Nature of Constituents' Interest: Historical and Ideational Factors in Judicial Empowerment"; See also Hirschl, "The Realist Turn in Comparative Constitutional Politics."

[37] Wilson, "Institutional Reform and Rights Revolutions in Latin America: The Cases of Costa Rica and Colombia."

countries could be framed as examples of unintended consequences, Wilson focuses instead on the rights revolution idea. Similarly, Wilson's account of Costa Rica and Colombia could be held up as optimistic rejoinders to the pessimism of most accounts of judicial reform in Latin America (see below), but Wilson also declines to frame his work as such. These two judiciaries are, for our purposes, allowed by judicial reforms to empower themselves in response to popular demands.[38]

Citizen demand alone is also unlikely to be sufficient. A third possible explanation for the empowerment of independent judiciaries flows from the presence and competitiveness of elections; politicians may insulate judges from political pressure as a form of "political insurance" that the next government does not tear down all of the accomplishments of the current government.[39] In his 1994 comparative study of the United States and Japan, Ramseyer observes that democratic Japanese politicians engaged in frequent, if subtle, manipulation of the judiciary through their ability to control the assignments of judges to more or less desirable posts according to their orthodoxy. As Ramseyer argues, "If rational politicians face significant odds of being in the minority party, however, they will try to reduce the variance to their political returns. In part, they can do this by insulating the judicial system from political control."[40] Politicians must engage in an "intertemporal calculus" to determine whether it is preferable to give up some control over the judiciary in the present in order to exert some control into the future through secure, persisting judicial tenures or to maintain control in the present at the expense of control in the future. Thus politicians who expect to win in the future will retain current control over the judiciary while politicians who expect to lose in the future will insulate the judiciary from contemporary control; notably, politicians in fear of a military takeover also lack incentives to insulate the judiciary from political control.[41]

Turning to Latin America, Finkel argues that judicial reform (the usual context for judicial empowerment in Latin America for the past three decades)

---

[38] Chapter 3 will discuss some of the political backlash against the highly empowered constitutional chamber in Costa Rica.

[39] Landes and Posner, "The Independent Judiciary in an Interest-Group Perspective"; See also Ginsburg, *Judicial Review in New Democracies*.

[40] Ramseyer, "The Puzzling (In)Dependence of Courts: A Comparative Approach," 741.

[41] This latter point is complimentary to Helmke's strategic defection argument discussed below. Helmke's argument is focused on the judge's calculus while Ramseyer focuses on the politician's calculus, but taken together they suggest that the rational choices of both types of actors might intersect in ways that compound political interference in the courts in at least some settings.

is often initiated somewhat superficially and even disingenuously, with politicians accepting benefits from international financial institutions (IFIs) for such actions as passing constitutional measures that would reform the judiciary. Actual implementation of that reform often lags considerably until the party in power sees that a likely opposition win is on the horizon, when implementing legislation and other features of a robust reform program will be initiated. It is precisely this ability to delay actual reform that allows dominant parties to accept reform initiatives in the first place.[42] Implementation thus varies dramatically from country to country and can best be explained through domestic political dynamics, which, for Finkel, most closely follow the political insurance thesis.[43] Countering the political insurance thesis in the case of Mexico, Inclán Osegura highlights the significance of the electoral calculus and the need for legitimacy. As corruption, including judicial corruption, became more widely recognized and reviled in Mexico, reform became a matter of attracting voters.[44] Empowering the judiciary thus was done not as political insurance that the PRI programs would not be dismantled following an electoral loss, but rather to reassure voters of the legitimacy of the PRI programs themselves.

If the study of judicial empowerment contributes to an understanding of "one of the most important questions of sociolegal studies, namely how a political system can transform itself from one governed by paternalistic forms of authority toward one in which the rule of law prevails,"[45] we will need to understand more than just the dynamics of partisan, electoral politics. As this book will describe, Central America holds a variety of electoral and governing dynamics. Understanding those dynamics presents only a limited view if we do not also understand the role of other actors such as international donors, international courts, nongovernmental organizations, and organized criminal organizations, among others. Indeed, as Ginsburg argues, politics matters for understanding the development of judicial power. However, the politics that matter should not be too closely cabined. In Central America, elements of paternalistic and authoritarian rule persist and defy the rule of law alongside the efforts of some political actors, both domestic and international, to construct it. Where elites are closed, seemingly robust electoral competition may not lead to an independent judiciary due to collusion. Where political parties are

---

[42] Finkel, "Judicial Reform in Argentina in the 1990s: How Electoral Initiatives Shape Institutional Change."
[43] Finkel, *Judicial Reform as Political Insurance: Argentina, Peru, and Mexico in the 1990s.*
[44] Inclán Oseguera, "Judicial Reform in Mexico: Political Insurance or the Search for Political Legitimacy?"
[45] Ginsburg, *Judicial Review in New Democracies,* 20.

weaker – and thus less able to collude effectively – judicial actors may be able to carve out some operational space. Also significant are state strength and capacity; strong parties that nonetheless cannot command a strong state are likely to produce yet different judicial politics as societal actors challenge the rule of law more directly.

HOW DOES AN EMPOWERED JUDICIARY INSTITUTIONALIZE THE RULE OF LAW?

Whether judges are empowered because of a need to produce economic development, to respond to citizen demands, or to protect policy interests, their empowerment only begins the process of institutionalizing the rule of law. Much of contemporary judicial politics scholarship has been focused on how to understand what judges do when faced with political opponents. The "legal school," which is not treated in depth in this section, would suggest that judges would enforce the law as is their duty. The first major departure from the legal school is the "attitudinal model" of Segal and Spaeth that has its origins in the United States and argues that independent judges will generally follow their sincere preferences.[46] With its origins in the North American Legal Realism theories of the 1920s, the attitudinal model of judicial decision-making suggests that judges will not necessarily simply apply the law as written, but will instead rule according to their own preferences whenever possible. In essence, conservative judges will vote in conservative ways and liberal judges will vote in liberal ways. If we assume that all judges must engage in some amount of legal interpretation because laws cannot be perfectly precise, then the attitudinal model seems self-evident. For traditionalists, believers in the legal model or the bureaucratic model, the attitudinal model may seem like a nightmare – or fighting words. A judge who rules according to her preferences – some would say despite how the law is written – may be viewed as a threat to the legal order and even to democratic governance. Despite the apparent weaknesses of judiciaries that have neither the purse nor the sword,[47] many politicians and committed democrats fear that the unelected judiciary will overrule the elected legislature and president. When judges make law, regulate other government actors, and otherwise act beyond the scope of deferential judging, especially in invalidating legislation, politicians are often quick to charge them with "judicial activism."[48]

[46] Segal and Spaeth, *The Supreme Court and the Attitudinal Model Revisited*.
[47] Bickel, *The Least Dangerous Branch, The Supreme Court at the Bar of Politics*.
[48] Wenzel, Bowler, and Lanoue, "Legislating From the State Bench: A Comparative Analysis of Judicial Activism"; Kmiec, "The Origin and Current Meanings of 'Judicial Activism.'"

Judicial activism across the world has contributed to the judicialization of politics as a global phenomenon.[49] The judicialization of politics consequently produced the need to understand "judicial politics" as a previously insignificant aspect of national political life in both democracies and authoritarian systems.[50] While judicial activism is frequently criticized in the American context as being countermajoritarian or extending the power of judges beyond what the constitution provides, many scholars of the developing world plead for more judicial activism in the face of abusive policies, following the model of "Public Interest Litigation" seen in India or the use of the Direct Action of Inconstitutionality as used by the Brazilian bar association.[51] An activist judiciary, understood as one that invalidates laws and other government actions, may be "transformative" in a newly established democracy.[52] If, as Arjomand argues, many late-twentieth century constitutions are intended to remake the political order, then it becomes necessary that a vigilant court helps to ensure that the promises of those constitutions are made real.[53] Because political elites will change over time, judges may be more likely to protect hegemonic interests in general, which may involve exercising both activism and restraint,[54] but may also fight for the underprivileged when a sufficiently large and powerful coalition supports them in this.[55]

Even so, judges are rarely wholly free to pursue their own political interests. Epstein and Knight summarize the "Separation of Powers" model in opposition to the attitudinal model thus: "Rather, justices are strategic actors who realize that their ability to achieve their goals depends on a consideration of

---

49 Tate and Vallinder, *The Global Expansion of Judicial Power.*
50 Ginsburg and Moustafa, *Rule by Law*; Stone Sweet, *The Birth of Judicial Politics in France: The Constitutional Council in Comparative Perspective*; Sieder, Rachel, Line Schjolden, and Angell, "Introduction"; Clayton, "The Supply and Demand Side of Judicial Policy-Making (Or, Why Be so Positive about Judicialization of Politics?)"; Domingo, "Judicialization of Politics or Politicization of the Judiciary? Recent Trends in Latin America"; Huneeas, Couso, and Sieder, "Cultures of Legality: Judicialization and Political Activism in Contemporary Latin America"; Carothers, "The Rule of Law Revival."
51 D'Souza, "The 'Third World' and Socio-Legal Studies: Neo-Liberalism and Lessons from India's Legal Innovations"; Hoque, "Taking Justice Seriously: Judicial Public Interest and Constitutional Activism in Bangladesh"; Moog, "Judicial Activism in the Cause of Judicial Independence: The Indian Supreme Court in the 1990s"; Taylor, *Judging Policy: Courts and Policy Reform in Democratic Brazil.*
52 Dugard, "Judging the Judges: Towards an Appropriate Role for the Judiciary in South Africa's Transformation."
53 Arjomand, "Law, Political Reconstruction and Constitutional Politics."
54 Keck, "Activism and Restraint on the Rehnquist Court: Timing, Sequence, and Conjuncture in Constitutional Development."
55 Erdos, "Postmaterialist Social Constituencies and Political Triggers: Explaining Bill of Right Genesis in Internally Stable, Advanced Democracies"; Tezcür, "Judicial Activism in Perilous Times: The Turkish Case."

the preferences of other actors, the choices they expect others to make, and the institutional context in which they act."[56] This insight represents a significant advance over the attitudinal model, which focuses on the policy preferences of judges without allowance for variation in the strategic environment in which judges operate. The core idea of the separation of powers model that judges must act strategically and consider the actions of other actors is especially relevant when applied to weak democracies in which tenure is insecure and judges may be subject to threats from a variety of sources. Judges facing short terms with no likelihood of reappointment are unlikely to be motivated as strongly by preserving the strength and legitimacy of judicial institutions. Those short tenures may actually create an incentive to sell judicial decisions to wealthy and powerful patrons who can secure a post-judicial future for a judge or magistrate.

This thin strategic model has been influential among scholars of comparative judicial politics, especially when considering the development of new constitutional structures in post-communist countries and in Africa.[57] In Latin America, it has been modified somewhat and applied as Helmke's "strategic defection" hypothesis: judges will be more likely to rule against governments (democratic or authoritarian) who appear to be near the end of their tenure, essentially currying favor with the perceived successor.[58] While Helmke's insight has not traveled from Argentina as smoothly as might be hoped, it has nonetheless been influential.[59] Flowing from Helmke's work, efforts have been made to incorporate historical and contextual elements to strategic accounts, but such work remains merely promising.[60] This model would need to be further modified to apply in environments of compromised citizen security. Where judges experience credible threats in the course of their work, they are likely to reconsider their priorities. Effective judicial security, of course,

[56] Epstein and Knight, *The Choices Justices Make*, 10.

[57] Epstein, Knight, and Shvetsova, "The Role of Constitutional Courts in the Establishment and Maintenance of Democratic Systems of Government"; Solomon, Jr., "Judicial Power in Authoritarian States: The Russian Experience"; Herron and Randazzo, "The Relationship Between Independence and Judicial Review in Post-Communist Courts"; Vondoepp, "Politics and Judicial Assertiveness in Emerging Democracies: High Court Behavior in Malawi and Zimbabwe."

[58] Helmke, "Checks and Balances By Other Means: Strategic Defection and Argentina's Supreme Court in the 1990s"; Helmke, *Courts under Constraints: Judges, Generals, and Presidents in Argentina*.

[59] Sanchez Urribarri and Songer, *A Cross-National Examination of the "Strategic Defection" Theory*.

[60] Hilbink, "The Constituted Nature of Constituents' Interest"; Girod, Krasner, and Stoner-Weiss, "Governance and Foreign Assistance: The Imperfect Translation of of Ideas into Outcomes"; McCann, "Interests, Ideas, and Institutions in Comparative Analysis of Judicial Power."

may make these quandaries easier for judges. Widner, writing about African judiciaries, has highlighted the importance of a sufficient support network to allow judges to be independent even in semi-democracies.[61] Trochev's book on courts in post-communist Russia presents a similar, but markedly more pessimistic, account of a strategic court that was unable to produce the rule of law in a context of extreme institutional uncertainty.[62]

History, institutions, and governance models may affect judicial behavior as surely as judges' attitudes or strategic calculi. In an analysis of the United States Supreme Court, Whittington chronicles a variety of governance models between the president and the Supreme Court. Constitutional authority is, according to Whittington, fluid rather than fixed and varies with presidential leadership skills and presidential power. While there is a clear accrual of judicial power in the historical narrative, Whittington is not arguing for path dependence. Rather, he presents competing approaches to the integration of the judiciary into constitutional governance as ebbing and flowing with the ideologies and power of particular presidents.[63] Hilbink takes a similarly historical approach to explain why the Chilean judiciary was so passive in accepting authoritarian rule, failing to defend liberal democracy and in some cases actively supporting the military regime of General Pinochet, by tracing the influence of institutional structure and ideology. Specifically, Chilean judicial training was steeped in nineteenth-century ideas of legal positivism that encouraged judges to serve the law as written without concern for more political or philosophical ideas about justice, equity, or constitutional liberties. This training produced judges who valued an apolitical role-orientation, understanding the rule of law to mean that judges should scrupulously enforce the laws without consideration of their political content.[64] Hilbink's institutionalist analysis thus takes seriously the ways that institutions can constrain attitudes by shaping the ways that judges understand not just what they want to do but also what they believe they ought to do. We should also remember that institutions such as these are "sticky," persisting beyond their original purposes and sometimes having unintended consequences, including increasing judicial activism.[65]

---

[61] Widner, *Building The Rule of Law*; Widner and Scher, "Building Judicial Independence in Semi-Democracies: Uganda and Zimbabwe."

[62] Trochev, *Judging Russia*.

[63] Whittington, *Political Foundations of Judicial Supremacy: The Presidency, The Supreme Court, and Constitutional Leadership in U.S. History*.

[64] Hilbink, *Judges Beyond Politics in Democracy and Dictatorship*.

[65] Chu, "Global Constitutionalism and Judicial Activism in Taiwan."

Institutionalist norms and role-orientations may also facilitate some kinds of judicial empowerment. Shambayati and Kirdis have argued that the Turkish government expanded the powers of the Turkish Constitutional Court in part in reliance on the bureaucratic role-orientation of Turkish judges.[66] By contrast, the judicialization of politics in Israel was driven by judges who sought to treat the Basic Laws as a true constitution, feeding the fears of some politicians about activist courts.[67] These role-orientations can change, however, as political and elite attitudes change.[68] Even in Chile, the judiciary in the 2000s and beyond has become much more supportive of civil liberties and has even been willing to prosecute former members of the military for human rights violations during the Pinochet government.[69] Kapiszewski's "court character thesis" suggests that judges' decisions about issues of political significance – and politicians' responses to those decisions – will be shaped by the accrued informal institutional elements that comprise the high court's character. Her account thus straddles some of the different themes addressed in the literature in that it looks backward to see the ways in which historical interactions have produced the contemporary context for juridico-political conflicts, and then looks forward to examine the way in which the conduct of these conflicts reshapes those informal institutions going forward in a cyclical fashion.[70]

A flaw in the institutionalist scholarship, however, is the tendency to view institutional ideology and role-orientations as monolithic and as being imposed by an elite as the price of admission to the judicial profession. The reality, however, is likely to be more varied; political elites are rarely unified in their own views of controversial issues related to democracy, human rights, the rule of law, and the role of the judiciary. In the contemporary era, a fractured elite is likely to put sometime competing pressures on individual judges, the judiciary as an institution, and even on the training schools that reproduce judicial ideology. The judicial regime approach that drives this book shares Kapiszewski's cyclical temporal orientation. The judicial regime approach also echoes Wittington's dynamic take on path dependence as a back and forth between competing forces. These forces compete not just over the institutional power of the judiciary, but also over the institutional ideology of the judiciary and the bounds of acceptable political attitudes of individual judges. As will

---

[66] Shambayati and Kirdis, "In Pursuit of 'Contemporary Civilization': Judicial Empowerment in Turkey."
[67] Woods, "The Ideational Foundations of Israel's 'Constitutional Revolution.'"
[68] Erdos, "Postmaterialist Social Constituencies and Political Triggers."
[69] Collins, *Post-Transitional Justice: Human Rights Trials in Chile and El Salvador.*
[70] Kapiszewski, *High Courts and Economic Governance in Argentina and Brazil.*

be seen in subsequent chapters, I understand these forces broadly to include many actors beyond just politicians.

Efforts to change institutional power, ideology, and attitudes have faltered against these forces. A primary finding of much writing about the judicial reform movement has been the observation that many judges – and even lawyers – actively resist reform. Early work on the wave of judicial reform that began in the early 1980s in Latin America was largely done by professionals within the legal reform sector who sought to rationalize reform projects through comparative analysis and theory-building exercises. In 1995, Dakolias wrote an early retrospective on the reform movement, in which she identified the reform movement squarely with the need to modernize the judicial system in order to promote economic development on both the micro-economic level and the international level. She diagnosed the most significant threat to reform as the rent-seeking behavior of judges, other justice sector functionaries, and lawyers – all of whom were seen as resisting reforms that might limit their ability to profit off of their positions. Although most of the reforms advocated in her article are suggestive of the legal school (the right rules will create the right outcomes), she nonetheless is highly concerned with the problem of vested interests that resist reforms.[71] In her 1998 book on Peru, Hammergren, like Dakolias, situates judicial reform's origins in the need to couple political and economic reform efforts. Latin American judiciaries of the 1980s were ill-equipped to aid in either economic development or political modernization and democratization. An early adopter of the typical menu of reform options, Peru initially was viewed as a success story in the region, but by 1997, President Alberto Fujimori had already begun to politicize the reform process in order to better control the judiciary itself.[72]

By 2000, pessimism was becoming the dominant strain in academic writing on rule of law reforms, especially from authors with backgrounds in human rights. Popkin's 2000 book on El Salvador detailed extensively the failure to adequately reform a judiciary or protect human rights. El Salvador had many factors that could have favored a positive reform experience, most notably an extensive international presence as the United Nations oversaw the peace process and maintained an interest in the country (including a peace monitoring agency) for many years. However, the international attention was not matched by indigenous efforts; El Salvador's civil society was too weak and focused on non-judicial issues while the major political changes brought by the peace process largely involved the formal incorporation of the FMLN

---

[71] Dakolias, "A Strategy for Judicial Reform."
[72] Hammergren, *The Politics of Justice and Justice Reform in Latin America.*

guerilla force as a political party rather any attempt to truly change the people in power. Similarly, the truth commission, while not originally intended as a replacement for trials for human rights violations, came to be one as an amnesty was soon passed. Ultimately, Popkin argues, the Salvadoran judiciary became the national institution most resistant to reform, even as the military and police underwent substantial reforms. Popkin's analysis is primarily historical-institutional, based on her vast knowledge of El Salvador. As such, El Salvador's sorrowful past informs a rather dismal view of the possibilities for reform. If the United Nations is no match for El Salvador's justice problems, then what could be?[73]

Prillaman argued in 2000 that the reform program was deeply flawed, in large part because of its failure to account for the need to reform all parts of the judiciary together as well as the highly political nature of any useful judicial reforms – an almost direct contradiction of Dakolias' prescriptions. At the heart of Prillaman's book is his argument that the failure to produce a sufficiently accessible, effective, and accountable judiciary has harmed the ability of Latin American countries to deepen or consolidate their relatively young democracies. Prillaman argued that the failures of the justice sector to provide effective justice to ordinary citizens significantly harmed popular support for democracy as a form of government.[74] Writing in 2002, Ungar echoed some of the same themes as Prillaman. He argued that the rule of law is an essential element in the consolidation of democracy and that Latin American countries were, by and large, failing to provide it. He took on, in large part, the myriad of domestic institutional actors that play a role in the justice sector, identifying failures and corruption at every level. In arguing that executive meddling in an often disorganized judiciary prevents the effective rule of law, he echoes older writing on Latin American judiciaries and their lack of power. In some sense, the cases he studied represent the reverse of Whittington's narrative; rather than a court growing in strength as (some) presidents empower it, Latin American courts have repeatedly lost strength as presidents have undercut them for a variety of reasons.[75] Prillaman's and Ungar's accounts, while discouraging, remain important for highlighting the relationship between democracy and the rule of law, as well as the failures of the reform movement's first two decades to advance either in a lasting way.

---

[73] Popkin, *Peace without Justice: Obstacles to Building the Rule of Law in El Salvador.*
[74] Prillaman, *The Judiciary and Democratic Delay in Latin America: Declining Confidence in the Rule of Law.*
[75] Ungar, *Elusive Reform.*

By the late 2000s, Hammergren continued to give mixed assessments of the reform programs to which she has devoted her career. While justice sector reforms have done too little in too little time, they have nonetheless created an institutional and political environment in which the judiciary could become a politically salient actor. This development has allowed a previously dependent branch of government to become largely independent and empowered; unfortunately, increasingly strong judiciaries have attracted the attention of a new generation of politicians who have frequently sought to re-politicize these judiciaries. One result has been the increasing willingness of judiciaries to engage with high politics, often at the invitation of elected politicians.[76] Thus, politicians may empower courts because of domestic legal pressure backed by international donors and the (seemingly unintended) consequences may be that politicians create a powerful potential ally in partisan gamesmanship.

While many comparative judicial politics scholars have elaborated on law as a site of political contestation, too few have connected that analysis to the social contestation that also occurs through the law. Insights from legal culture and socio-legal studies approaches can help to expand and deepen our understanding of the political and social contexts in which law is embedded. By "legal culture," we should not understand an explanatory variable that can be understood monolithically within one society or even one institution; Huneeus, Couso, and Seider helpfully highlight the significance of the pluralist view of "legal cultures" that are in contention with each other within each society.[77] While these legal cultures can be understood as present in the daily lives and understanding of all members of a society,[78] they should also be understood as present in contested forms in legal institutions themselves[79] – as well as in the shifting relations between the courts, political actors, and citizens.[80] In order to take account of the context of social violence and legal contestation in much of Central America, we need to use "thicker" understandings of rationality, strategies, and context. Political opposition to the CICIG in Guatemala, for example, is not merely about maintaining policy programs or establishing partisan dominance; it is also about shielding politicians and their friends from prosecution for criminal activities. Cross-partisan collusion in Nicaragua and Honduras is rarely about political attitudes and much more fundamentally

---

[76] Hammergren, "Twenty-Five Years of Latin American Judicial Reforms: Achievements, Disappointments, and Emerging Issues"; Hammergren, *Envisioning Reform.*
[77] Huneeas, Couso, and Sieder, "Cultures of Legality," 7.
[78] Ewick and Silbey, *The Common Place of Law: Stories from Everyday Life.*
[79] Kapiszewski, "How Courts Work: Institutions, Culture, and the Brazilian Supremo Tribunal Federal."
[80] Ansolabehere, "More Power, More Rights?: The Supreme Court and Society in Mexico."

about persistence in power and proximity to the benefits that accrue to the people who have it. The inability of El Salvador's justice sector to control criminal violence is rapidly becoming the single most salient political issue in that country. Costa Rica's rights revolution has transformed the distribution of political power primarily through highly individualized litigation.

At the same time, we cannot ignore that the legal system is a site of social and political control. Even as litigants voice their rights claims, they must shape those claims into the forms the courts will recognize; this is as true for civil litigants as it is for criminal defendants.[81] In Valverde's language, "Critical studies, in the sociology of law as in other fields, expose the myth of legal neutrality by revealing the extent to which legal operations uphold and simultaneously conceal relations of power."[82] The discourses and practices of crime control, both governmental and societal, have become means by which society is governed, enforcing both control of some segments of society by others and also the neoliberalization of these societies.[83] These insights help to reveal the contending legal cultures that are the subject of much of this book. On the one hand, social groups that might at one time have defined themselves around notions of community, solidarity, or revolution are now more inclined to use the language of rights. There is thus common ground between those ideas once suspected of subversion and those that now support a stronger state. At the same time, the genuinely high threat of criminality dovetails with persistent inequalities and oppressions that have outlived the civil wars of the region to create support for a stronger state, albeit one that emphasizes the legality of its actions.

Folding these insights into the idea of political insurance yields fruitful avenues for investigations of societal influence on rule of law construction and specifically institution building. If we accept the idea that institutions are never merely political – or, alternatively, that politics should be defined more broadly to include actors who are not partisan politicians – we can begin to see new pathways for influence on institutions. Many kinds of actors have an interest in influencing public policies and their enforcement. These actors do not necessarily have an interest in a strong rule of law and may actually benefit from criminal impunity and lax regulatory enforcement. Democratization and peace processes that sought to increase civil society influence in and access to the justice sector has, in some cases, created pathways through which criminal

---

[81] Feeley, *The Process Is the Punishment: Handling Cases in a Lower Criminal Court.*
[82] Valverde, *Law's Dream of a Common Knowledge*, 11.
[83] Simon, *Governing Through Crime: How the War on Crime Transformed American Democracy and Created a Culture of Fear*; Super, *Governing Through Crime in South Africa: The Politics of Race and Class in Neoliberalizing Regimes.*

and other corrupt influences may enter into the selection of justice sector actors, while also often falling short on their efforts to reduce the possibility of bribery and threats. At the same time, efforts to depoliticize the judiciary by reducing partisan influence have in some countries been frustrated as partisan politicians have consolidated their dominance over appointment and retention procedures. We cannot understand judicial politics if we confine our understandings of "politics" too narrowly.

THE JUDICIAL REGIME TYPE APPROACH

Since (re)democratization in Central America in the 1980s and 1990s, the politics of law have begun to attain priority over the politics of official force. It is no longer sufficient or legitimate for a government to eliminate opponents. Instead, they must be challenged in the polling place, the legislature, and the courtroom. Democratization has thus made Central American judiciaries politically relevant in ways that they had never been before. High courts now rule on the constitutionality of statutes, budgets, and other government actions. Lower courts now extend their power over high-ranking politicians, including even presidents past and present. Courts at all levels must consider the rights and wrongs of the wealthy and powerful. With increasing relevance and power for the judiciary come concerns about who is able to influence judges. Most of the scholarly literature on judicial politics imagines a scenario in which judges' freedom is primarily threatened by the actions of other governmental actors, such as presidents or generals. A focus on the democratic rule of law requires us to look beyond the high politics of inter-branch conflicts in the high courts to also include the low politics of the ordinary lower courts and the influences of unofficial actors.

As discussed in greater depth in chapter two, a great deal has been written on the importance of "judicial political independence," understood to mean the ability of judges to rule unfettered by pressures from other government actors. The presence of judicial independence may be most clear when a court invalidates a statute that has had the support of both the president and the legislature. We can see its absence in political retaliation against judges, such as the removal of a court who has created problems for powerful politicians. This perspective has shaped scholarly studies and reform programs alike, with at least some successes. I argue, however, that this focus ignores the need for judges to be also free from pressures from powerful societal actors, or what I call "judicial societal autonomy." Judicial societal autonomy is reflected in an effectively operating judiciary whose judges are able to administer justice for the powerful and the powerless equally. Judicial autonomy is perhaps most clear in its absence rather than its presence: bribes and threats against judges that induce a judge to ignore legal and constitutional dictates in order to do the bidding of those with influence.

From these two related concepts, I derive four different "judicial regime types." A judicial regime includes the patterns of relations with a variety of powerful actors, the ability and willingness of the judiciary to exercise its authority, and the ways in which politico-legal conflicts are resolved both within and without the courts. Judicial regimes, like political regimes, set the rules of the game, in this case the legal-political game. The judicial regime concept is distinct from the more general concept of judicial politics in that it focuses on the formal and informal decision rules that structure legal-political conflicts. I describe these predominant decision rules as "currencies" of conflict resolution in chapter two; each judicial regime type has a predominant currency, be it official violence, unofficial violence, legislation, or constitutions. The heuristic tool of "judicial regime types" is a holistic approach to the judiciary; a judicial regime includes more than just isolated decisions or interactions, in the same way that a political regime includes more than just specific presidential actions or legislative votes. A judicial regime type is essentially a shorthand description of both the standard operating procedure of a judiciary as well as the decision rule of last resort for judges and litigants. Chapter two lays out the four judicial regime types, their predominant currencies, and their consequences.

Bringing judicial autonomy into the analysis helps to suggest explanations of why efforts to improve judicial independence may not necessarily produce the rule of law. The most pressing problem in Guatemala, for example, is not that judges are frequently the subjects of political pressure, but rather that they are under attack from powerful societal actors such as organized criminal actors. By contrast, Nicaragua has a highly partisan and dependent judiciary that generally manages to avoid major societal pressures. Judicial independence on its own is not a sufficient condition for the development of a democratic rule of law. Indeed, I argue that in at least some areas of politics and policy, judicial autonomy from society may be more important than inter-branch judicial independence. Where the illegal activity to be controlled is primarily conducted by governmental actors (e.g., massive human rights violations or corruption), judicial independence will be more important. Where the illegal activity in question is predominately private in nature (e.g., economic or violent crime), judicial autonomy becomes more important. This book will help to broaden our understanding of judicial politics by applying these concepts to five Central American countries.

This book argues that the shape of the rule of law is a product of the type of judicial regime. These judicial regimes, in turn, develop over time as a result of the accrued consequences of the currencies used in conflict resolution, in combination with state strength; while some reforms may be able to change these currencies, those that fail to do so will fail to change the judicial regime as well. Judicial regimes are defined by their combination of political independence and societal autonomy, two distinct but related concepts. Inter-branch judicial political independence is a function of the institutional environment created by both constitutional structures and informal political institutions, which include the legacies of struggles over judicial empowerment. Judicial societal autonomy is a product of the security, both professional and personal, of judges, which is contingent on state strength, as well as their insulation from corruption. When judges are autonomous from society and thus more able to be impartial, citizens are more likely to bring their conflicts to the courts, thus helping to build the rule of law.

The judicial regime approach provides complex answers to the puzzles of building the rule of law. Politicians will empower judges when they believe that it is in their interest to do so, relying on a calculus that includes their ideological concerns, concerns over political legitimacy, international pressures to reform, the impact on their personal futures in politics and business, and their perceived vulnerability to an empowered justice sector. Many politicians will seek to exploit negotiated reform processes to maintain personal power, privilege, and impunity. Once officially empowered, judges must navigate a dynamic environment in order to pursue their ideological, institutional, and professional interests. Those interests are constructed in part based on this dynamic environment, in which short tenures in most Central American countries make a lifelong judicial career unlikely, in which personal security and the threat of criminal or political retaliation must be central considerations, and in which appointment and promotion processes broaden the types of actors that can influence the justice sector. Judges facing constitutional decisions may stand up for the rule of law, as happened in Guatemala in 1993, but may pay the ultimate price for doing so, as also happened following that stand. An individual judge may also stand up for the rule of law in one decision and undercut the rule of law in the next by engaging in corruption. The rule of law is institutionalized or diminished through the back and forth of judicial and political responses to this environment.

The institutional environment, at the heart of judicial political independence, is discerned through an analysis of constitutional provisions and subconstitutional codes governing the justice sector. Informal political institutions are largely revealed through the answers of interview subjects and survey responses in Guatemala and Costa Rica. Special attention is paid to issues of budget security, appointment procedures, and contacts between politicians and judges. The personal security of judges is at the heart of judicial societal autonomy; its absence is the major cause of impunity. Survey and interview responses concerning threats and bribery are reported along with recorded cases of violence against judges in national and international media. The provision of security details for judges is also discussed. Judges' professional security is also an important consideration and is defined herein by judges' official tenure in office, the frequency of reappointment or promotion, and judges' perceptions of abusive disciplinary processes and transfers, as reported in surveys and interviews.

STUDYING THE JUDICIARY IN CENTRAL AMERICA

This book provides a structured comparison of five Central American countries from 1979 to 2015. Chapter two presents the typology of judicial regime types that will guide the outline of the core of the book. The four empirical chapters are thus presented not country-by-country; rather, they are organized according to the judicial regime type represented. As such, chapter three discusses the politically independent and societally autonomous liberal judicial regime that emerged in Costa Rica after 1989. Chapter four includes Guatemala, Honduras, El Salvador, and Nicaragua during periods of authoritarian or quasi-authoritarian rule. Chapter five covers the impunity and clandestine control of the Guatemalan judiciary after the return to democracy and the end of the internal armed conflict. Chapter six treats contemporary Honduras, El Salvador, and Nicaragua, which share a tendency toward a partisan judiciary. Finally, a conclusion turns to questions of judicial reforms from the point of view of the judicial regime approach and returns to the democratic rule of law.

Central America is a prime candidate for a study of the development of judicial politics in weak democracies and may shed light on other types of systems around the world as well. Within the isthmus, we can see many issues common to developing democracies around the world, including economic deprivation, corruption, dominant executives, semi-dependent judiciaries, coups, and an increasing relevance for judicial bodies. Focusing on Central America allows us to study the relationships between these varied phenomena while holding constant many geographical, historical, and cultural influences:

The civil law system: All five countries under study belong to the continental or civil law tradition, which has its origins in Roman Law and in the Napoleonic Codes of the nineteenth century that were imposed in Spain during French occupation prior to Latin American independence. There are several important differences between the civil law system, which is found in most of the non-Anglophone world, and the common law system, which is found in the Anglophone world including the United States. First, there is great emphasis placed on fidelity to rational codes of law at the expense of judicial reasoning. Traditionally, precedent (previously decided cases) has no role in judging, although many civil law countries around the world have modified this approach. This change is most striking in Costa Rica. Second, as a consequence of the first point, the perceived role of the judge is very different. Whereas common law judges are highly respected and expected to act as wise deciders who balance various interests to produce equitable outcomes, the civil law judge is generally viewed more as a bureaucrat who applies the law without considering her own wise interpretations. There is some evidence that this is also changing as judges interact with their counterparts in other countries more frequently. Third, the career path is entirely different. In the United States, an individual must first distinguish herself as a lawyer before becoming a judge through a highly selective process. In Latin America, law school graduates apply directly to judicial training schools, from which the top students will then pass into the judicial profession. Rather than using a career as an attorney as a stepping stone to a career as a judge, some judges use judicial experience to win lucrative positions as private attorneys. Promotion to the intermediate appellate level is typically done through a bureaucratic mechanism rather than political appointment or election. Judicial elections as are common in some parts of the United States are unheard of in Central America.

Novelty of constitutional review: Historically, constitutional review is not a part of the civil law system and was not known in Central America. However, between the 1980s and 1990s, all of these countries formally wrote into their constitutions that there would be a chamber of the Supreme Court – or, as in Guatemala, a specialized court – to hear constitutional disputes. These typically include both general constitutionality challenges as well as the region-wide action known as *amparo*, which allows an individual to challenge the application of a law or any other governmental action to his specific circumstances. As a general rule, a successful *amparo* challenge does not reduce the validity of a specific law or even a government policy; it only applies to the individual who brought the suit.

Recency of democratic transition: With the exception of Costa Rica, which has enjoyed its present form of democracy since 1949, Central American countries became democracies in the 1980s.[84] Political arrangements are only recently institutionalized, if they are. Partisanship remains strong in Honduras,

---

[84] Nicaragua is not generally recognized as having become a democracy until the election of Violeta Chamorro in 1990.

El Salvador, and Nicaragua. Guatemala's party system is best understood as feckless and Costa Rica's party system is in a period of transition. Honduras has well-institutionalized political parties, but the political dispute underlying the 2009 coup was rooted in the feeling that these long-standing parties represent the elites and not the people. Nicaragua's party system has coalesced for the most part around two parties, but those parties are heavily dominated by their personalist leaders who collude with each other to further a variety of goals political, personal, and corrupt. Guatemala has only one genuinely institutionalized and stable political party, the Guatemalan Republican Front, while other parties come and go and most presidents are elected as the standard-bearers of short-lived coalitions. El Salvador, by contrast, has two relatively strong and representative parties, while Costa Rica's two traditionally dominant parties have been competing recently with a new third party. Up until approximately 2006, all five countries appeared to be moving in the direction of consolidating democracy, but Nicaragua has been backsliding since the election of Daniel Ortega and Honduras took a very large step away from consolidating democracy with the 2009 coup.

History of repressive rule: Guatemala, El Salvador, Honduras, and Nicaragua all have very recent experiences of repressive rule in the 1970s and 1980s and even lasting into the 1990s in Guatemala and El Salvador. The civil wars of Guatemala and El Salvador saw the worst of this violence, which lasted beyond the formal handover of power to civilian politicians. Revolutionary violence in Nicaragua differs in two important ways: the government in the 1980s was leftist in contrast to the right-wing governments to the north, and the violence of the Contra War was much less pervasive. While Honduras did not live through an actual revolution or civil war, the military's fear that one would happen led to repressive actions, including torture, extra-judicial killings, and forced disappearances. There is particular overlap between the techniques and strategies of the militaries of the northern three countries because they were all recipients of training and other assistance from the United States military. All four countries have since had to address questions of truth, reconciliation, and impunity for human rights violations both during the 1980s and today. While the era of dominating military rule and repression has passed, violence continues to be committed in these countries by security forces with impunity. The history of repressive rule and its legacies are the subject of chapter four.

Problems of violence and contraband: The Central American isthmus connects the coca-producing Andean region with the voracious North American cocaine market. All five countries thus find themselves in the middle of a critical trans-shipment route, with all of the accordant violent criminality. The problem has only grown more acute as improvements in monitoring of air and sea routes have driven more of the shipments into the national territories of these countries.[85] Narcotrafficking has attracted many to extremely violent criminal gangs, emanating first from Colombia and more recently from El Salvador and Mexico. No country is untouched by this violence, although Costa Rica has been most able to control it. Honduras, Guatemala, and El Salvador joined the ranks of the most violent parts of the world in the 2000s. Another facet of this phenomenon is that it has created a new role for the military in many countries, where soldiers are being assigned to work either directly with police or in new specialized anti-drug and anti-gang units with police-like powers. Allegations of human rights violations by the military are again commonplace, alongside fears about a growing role for the military in setting civilian policies.

Economic underdevelopment: Of the five countries, only Costa Rica enjoys the relatively comfortable status of being a middle-income country with moderate levels of poverty and inequality. At the other extreme lies Nicaragua, second poorest country in the hemisphere (after Haiti), with extreme poverty, although its socialist legacy of improvements in literacy and health allow its citizens to enjoy a somewhat better quality of life than the per capita income would suggest. Guatemala, while somewhat less poor, is beset with a great deal of poverty and extreme inequalities. Honduras also has a very poor population, while El Salvador's population enjoys some degree of prosperity largely because of the remittances sent back by Salvadorans who have immigrated to the United States and elsewhere in the face of violence and lack of opportunity in their own country.

Cultural similarities: While it is perilous to look to cultural explanations for political phenomena, studying the various countries of Central America allow us to hold constant many of these cultural factors. All of these countries have Catholic religious backgrounds, with a growing Evangelical Christian sector. The Catholic Church has been, among other things, an important political resource with prominent church leaders backing one side or the other in some countries, while lower-level priests during the 1980s often supported radical egalitarianism. Most countries have some history of personalist leaders, with Nicaragua having the strongest such tradition. Clientelism has also been an important part of the political culture of all of these countries, although less so in Costa Rica. Even in Costa Rica, however, a certain hierarchical obsequy permeates the legal society.

Research for this book was conducted in four research trips to Guatemala and Costa Rica in 2009 and 2010. In-country research focused on primary

---

[85] Brands, *Crime, Violence, and the Crisis in Guatemala: A Case Study in the Erosion of the State.*

legal sources; interviews with activists, judges, and lawyers; and an in-depth survey of judges conducted in Guatemala and Costa Rica in 2010. In 2009–2010, 50 structured interviews were conducted, primarily in Guatemala City, Guatemala, and San José and Puerto Limón, Costa Rica. Structured interviews focused on questions about influence on the judiciary from the political sector, organized crime, NGOs, and the media. Lawyers and judges were also asked about any threats or bribery they had experienced, along with open-ended questions about their work, education, fields of specialization, and relationships with clients and/ or litigants. Interviews ranged in length from approximately thirty minutes to two hours. All efforts were made to maintain the confidentiality of the interviews. As a consequence, unless a source chose to speak on the record, I refer to all lawyers as male and all judges as female. I consider this a necessity, especially for sources in Guatemala with direct experience with organized crime. Additionally, some background information comes from five research trips to Guatemala and Nicaragua conducted between 2002 and 2004; interviews conducted during this period are cited with the interviewee's name and do not appear in Appendix A. While the chapters on Guatemala and Costa Rica are based extensively on original research, the discussion of Nicaragua, Honduras, and El Salvador are based primarily on secondary research. Appendix A provides more details on the methodology used in this study.

"THE ACHILLES HEEL OF DEMOCRACY"

The title for this book comes from the response of one Guatemalan judge to my 2010 survey questionnaire. One question asked the respondent to describe the role of the judiciary in the political system of her country.[86] While most respondents provided answers that referred to providing swift and proper justice or other positive ideas, one Guatemalan judge answered simply: "¡Es el talón de Aquiles de la democracia!" ("It is the Achilles Heel of democracy!"). The vehemence and pessimism of this response was striking, especially coming from a member of the judiciary itself. Indeed, much of this book will catalog ways in which the judiciary either fails to contribute to democracy or detracts from it. The partisan judiciary of Honduras legitimated a coup in 2009. Nicaragua's similarly partisan judiciary essentially handed a previously unconstitutional second consecutive term to President Daniel Ortega in

---

[86] Question 37: "¿Qué considera ser el papel principal de la judicatura dentro del sistema político de su país?" (translation: What do you consider to be the principal role of the judiciary in the political system of your country?)

2009. Official and criminal impunity in Guatemala threatens the legitimacy of the entire democratic system. Similarly, El Salvador's judiciary increasingly subverts its institutional obligations under partisan political pressure. Finally, Costa Rica's activist and generally popular constitutional chamber politicizes rights in a way that might be seen as actually hurting their own institutional cause. Indeed, there is reason to believe that the judiciary is the weakest point of democracy in at least some parts of Central America and may be a source of vulnerability everywhere.

Nonetheless, even where the judiciary may in some ways be the Achilles Heel of democracy, it also contains potential to contribute to stronger and better institutionalized democratic governments that protect human rights and promote development. If judiciaries are ever going to contribute to stronger democracies, we must first understand the pathologies that plague them. Where societal forces have penetrated the judiciary and captured judges and magistrates, reforms should be geared to protect judges from threats and bribes. Where political interests influence judicial decisions, a different set of reforms will be needed – ones that must be tailored to the particular party systems and institutional arrangements of that country. Not all judicial differences should be considered pathological. Nor should all political conflicts over the judiciary. Inter-institutional conflicts and negotiations should be understood as a normal part of a robust democracy; we should not imagine that all constitutional reforms are negative just because some – especially in Latin America in recent years – have been designed to aggrandize power. Judiciaries are a necessary part of democratic commitments, including the protection of rights and the enforcement of a rule of law. Judiciaries allow right to have might.

2

The Evolution of Judicial Regimes

A society emerging from civil war and government repression faces a different set of challenges than does an established democracy that is expanding the powers of its judiciary. This contrast is evident in Central America. The Costa Rican legislature empowered its judiciary peacefully by creating a constitutional chamber of its Supreme Court in 1989, even if they did not anticipate the extent to which that new chamber would ultimately come to influence political and social life. Constitutional chambers have also been empowered in El Salvador, Honduras, and Nicaragua, since the 1980s, but none of these three chambers has the power, independence, or societal autonomy that their Costa Rican counterpart enjoys. Guatemala has had a separate Constitutional Court since it was established in the 1985 constitution as their Civil War continued. Indeed, the most famous action by that Court – the rejection of an *autogolpe* (presidential "self-coup") in 1993 – likely led to the assassination of the Constitutional Court president the following year. Major changes have happened to and through the courts of Central America in the past four decades, but they have not all shared a common trajectory. These differences are the result not just of different political pressures, but also of societal pressures.

BRINGING SOCIETY BACK INTO RULE OF LAW RESEARCH

A common thread in the literature discussed in the first chapter is a focus on the political independence of judges, often at the expense of considering judges' insulation from societal influences. This trend is clearest in strategic accounts based on the separation-of-powers model, which are framed as a means of understanding the relationships between (usually) elected politicians (i.e., presidents and legislatures) and the judiciary. Similarly framed dynamics delineate historical-institutional accounts. Theories about the judiciary as a source of "political insurance" are inherently biased toward inter-branch relations. Indeed, arguably the very idea of judicial empowerment implies that the important questions relate to the elected or unelected politicians who allow the judiciary to take on broader powers. Some exceptions exist to this tendency: writing on "rights revolutions" give prominence to the role of societal actors, be they litigants or civil society actors; most reformers were concerned about the relationship between citizen experiences of the justice system and democratic quality and persistence; and Widner's work on Tanzania recognizes that societal actors can be a source of political strength for judges under at least some circumstances. Additionally, Inclán Oseguera's account of Mexico takes seriously the intermingled relationships between elected politicians, voters, and the judiciary when considering issues of judicial reform and legitimacy. Even these exceptions, however, do not do more than hint at a theory of judicial autonomy from society. We thus need a theory of judiciary autonomy from society as distinct from the political independence of the judiciary. The theory outlined in this chapter builds on insights from studies of law and society as well as comparative judicial politics. Understanding the importance of judicial societal autonomy and securing it is essential for building a democratic rule of law.

Political Independence

In the abstract, judicial independence and judicial autonomy may seem like interchangeable terms. Indeed, some authors and a number of the subjects interviewed for this study have used them that way. Despite their linguistic similarities, these terms are distinct in important ways. Primarily, they may be distinguished on the basis of the source of the infringement on judicial prerogative: attacks on judicial political independence generally originate with other political actors, while infringements on judicial societal autonomy come from societal actors. The political definition of judicial independence undelays most of the literature discussed in chapter one. Hilbink, for example, defines "achieving judicial independence" as "find[ing] ways of preventing executive or legislative interference with or manipulation of courts."[1] In an analytically rich account of judicial independence and judicial power, Ríos-Figueroa defines judicial independence as "[i]ndependence of constitutional judges from undue political pressures, especially from the executive and legislative branches . . . "[2]; the five-part index he creates to assess judicial independence not surprisingly includes only entry points for influence from explicitly

---

[1] Hilbink, *Judges Beyond Politics in Democracy and Dictatorship*, 241.
[2] Ríos-Figueroa, "Institutions for Constitutional Justice in Latin America," 28.

political actors.[3] Similarly, the volume *Consequential Courts* focuses on an inter-branch account of judicial activity, although there is included an awareness of the role of judicial support networks.[4] Similarly, Moustafa's account of judicial politics in Egypt focuses on the need for courts to be "perceived to be independent *from the government*,"[5] albeit alongside an extensive account of the interplay between a briefly powerful court and an activist sector seeking legal room to maneuver. Some authors decline to provide an analytical definition of judicial independence, while using the term to refer to judicial action and political reaction in inter-branch interactions.[6] Indeed, a recent analysis of de facto and de jure judicial independence uses the following definition: "it involves the ability and willingness of courts to decide cases in light of the law without undue regard to the views of other governmental actors."[7]

As should be clear, the term *judicial independence* is typically focused on the independence of the judiciary as an institution and this study seeks to limit it to just that. It is worth drawing a further distinction concerning the identity of those who infringe on judicial independence: typically, attacks on the independence of the judiciary are done by other institutional actors, such as the Congress or the President. These infringements might include attacks on the judiciary's budget, "court-packing" plans to fill the courts (especially the high courts) with supporters of the elected branches of government as Menem did in Argentina in 1989 and Franklin Roosevelt threatened to do in the United States in 1937, or even such extreme acts as abolishing a court and rewriting the Constitution to limit the new court's powers as Yeltsin did in Russia in 1993.[8] Other government actors may be able to restrict judicial independence fairly subtly by intervening in the appointment processes.[9]

The exercise or exertion of judicial independence would be expected to happen in the context of litigation between or against institutions of the state. As such, they tend to occur primarily in constitutional courts, especially in

---

[3] Ibid., 29.
[4] Kapiszewski, Silverstein, and Kagan, "Introduction."
[5] Moustafa, "Law versus the State: The Judicialization of Politics in Egypt," 41 emphasis added.
[6] Helmke, *Courts under Constraints*; Ginsburg, *Judicial Review in New Democracies*; Whittington, *Political Foundations of Judicial Supremacy*.
[7] Melton and Ginsburg, "Does De Jure Judicial Independence Really Matter?," 190.
[8] Trochev, *Judging Russia*.
[9] Most constitutions give the president, the congress, or both some influence over the appointment of judges to the high courts and sometimes to inferior courts as well. The American practice of political influence in the appointment of all federal (and most state) judges is not typical of Central America, where most inferior judges enjoy a bureaucratic career path that begins with a judicial training school.

countries where concentrated review is the norm.[10] Courts are also more likely to assert their independence in the context of explicitly constitutional cases. Those typically include the invalidation of laws or other major government actions. In rare cases, we may also see courts participate in extra-constitutional actions, such as the coups in Guatemala in 1993 and in Honduras in 2009. Such participation may reflect a strong statement of judicial independence or a situation in which a subordinated court is being used as a shield to legitimate the actions of the military or one political party; in all cases, they warrant special attention.

Societal Autonomy

In much of the judicial politics literature, the issue of judicial autonomy from society is largely left out. When it is discussed, there is some conceptual blurring between political independence and societal autonomy. Domingo refers to "political autonomy" alongside a concern that judges "do not collude with attempts by rulers or powerful groups in society to favor certain outcomes (political, social, economic)."[11] Couso has highlighted the significance of judicial "impartiality," but has not given it prominence in his scholarship.[12] Others address autonomy as a broad concept encompassing all forms of judicial independence without adequate specification.[13] It is preferable to parse out the two concepts of political independence and societal autonomy. Political independence should be reserved for discussions of inter-branch relations. Societal autonomy, by contrast, would then be a much broader term encompassing relations between societal actors and judges. Judicial political independence largely refers to the judiciary as an institution while judicial societal autonomy refers to the conditions of individual judges. It is possible, then, for a judiciary to be either politically independent but not societally autonomous or societally autonomous but not politically independent. We can get a much fuller picture

---

[10] The American and German practice of diffuse review, where any court can invalidate a law or government action is relatively rare in the world. Newer constitutions, especially, have assigned constitutional review powers primarily to a country's highest court. In some countries, such as Guatemala, there is a specialized constitutional court that is not a part of the general judiciary and which possesses the exclusive power of constitutional review.

[11] Pilar Domingo, "Judicialization of Politics," in *The Judicialization of Politics in Latin America*, ed. Sieder, Rachel, Line Schjolden and Alan Angell (New York: Palgrave MacMillan, 2005), 21–46 at 24.

[12] Couso, "Judicial Independence in Latin America: The Lessons of History in the Search for an Always Elusive Ideal."

[13] Arjomand, "Law, Political Reconstruction and Constitutional Politics."

of the relationship between the judiciary and powerful actors if we consider these two concepts separately.

A handful of judicial politics scholars have taken societal actors seriously. Trochev's definition of judicial independence includes "government and private pressures,"[14] although much of his discussion of judicial power focuses on inter-branch relations. Baum, in a study of the United States Supreme Court, has highlighted a large number of influences on judicial decision-making and opinion-shaping, including the media and social contacts.[15] Some earlier works on democratic consolidation highlighted the role of the judiciary in achieving justice for the socially and politically marginalized; the authors in the wide-ranging volume *The (Un)Rule of Law & the Underprivileged in Latin America* give express recognition of the need for the judiciary to be open to all and to limit the power of traditional and wealthy elites.[16] With their discussion of judicialization strategies as a form of societal accountability primarily used by nongovernmental organizations, Peruzzotti and Smulovitz recognize the significance of one kind of societal actor in coaxing judiciaries to act to constrain government actors to more closely follow the constitution and respect citizen rights.[17]

In a study of police killings, Brinks has provided one of the more extensive accounts of the relationship between the judiciary and society:

> More broadly, this book reveals how deeply embedded the legal system is in its social and political context, even when it is specifically designed to have considerable autonomy. That embeddedness is both vice and virtue. More embedding – that is, more numerous and more effective institutional ties between the legal system and society – makes the system more aware of social needs, and open to information about the situations that come before it. It allows the legal order to evolve in harmony with its social, economic, and political order. At the same time, unless they are consciously designed otherwise, more often than not these social ties import social inequalities into the system and reinforce social hierarchies instead of promoting universal citizenship. On the other hand, then, the analysis in this book exposes the manifold mechanisms that cause legal outcomes to reflect deeper social structures more faithfully than they reflect the pattern of legal rights lightly etched onto the surface of society. On the other, it shows that establishing

---

14 Trochev, *Judging Russia*, 32.
15 Baum, *Judges and Their Audiences: A Perspective on Judicial Behavior*.
16 Méndez, O'Donnell, and Pinheiro, *The (Un)Rule of Law & the Underprivileged in Latin America*.
17 Peruzzotti and Smulovitz, "Social Accountability: An Introduction."

and nurturing the right institutional connections can facilitate the task of using legal rights to overcome social inequalities.[18]

My focus on judicial societal autonomy seeks to put these concerns at the center of our analysis of judicial politics.

Judicial societal autonomy is best understood as referring to the ability of individual judges to rule on cases without interference from private parties. Private individuals, such as litigants or people with a stake in the litigation, are the most likely to infringe on judicial societal autonomy. As such, we expect to see societal autonomy operate primarily within the context of ordinary criminal or civil litigation in ordinary courts. Official actors are typically only involved in infringements of judicial societal autonomy when there are abuses of judicial discipline or impeachment procedures. However, official actors are not irrelevant because governmental commitment to provide protections to judges may be a functional prerequisite to societal autonomy. The most significant infringement on judicial societal autonomy is the threat of violence to individual judges. Here I differ with Garoupa and Ginsburg's discussion of courts and judges as "agents" and society as their proper "principals" because that analysis assumes an identifiable whole of society that can and does direct the courts and the law.[19] The problem with this assumption becomes all the more clear when that analysis is transported to dangerous, unequal, and contentious environments such as are the subject of this study. While different groups in many societies interact with and through the courts to pursue their own advantage, the stakes are raised when those interactions are backed with threats and bribery.

There are many sources of infringements on judicial autonomy. Judges may be subject to supervision or discipline from the judicial hierarchy. Judges may be subject to disciplinary procedures through another body, possibly including an independent judicial council or a legislature that has impeachment power. Judges may also be sensitive to the monitoring of the press; negative (or positive) reporting could influence the way a judge chooses to handle a case. Judges may also be sensitive to the concerns of their social and professional circles.[20] Judges' societal autonomy may also be compromised by their staff; one common type of judicial corruption happens without the judge's knowledge when a clerk accepts a bribe (or responds to a threat) and "loses" a case file or an important document. NGOs may also seek to put pressure

---

[18] Brinks, *The Judicial Response to Police Killings in Latin America: Inequality and the Rule of Law*, 8.
[19] Garoupa and Ginsburg, *Judicial Reputation: A Comparative Theory*.
[20] Baum, *Judges and Their Audiences: A Perspective on Judicial Behavior*.

TABLE 2.1 *Judicial Political Independence vs. Judicial Societal Autonomy*

Political Independence	Overlap	Societal Autonomy
Attacks on the institution *qua* institution, including budget	Attacks on constitutional magistrates	Attacks on individual judges
Attacks by institutional actors (the president, the congress, the military)	Attacks by politicians acting "unofficially."	Attacks by private individuals
Invalidation of laws (pre or post promulgation), extra-ordinary or even extra-constitutional special actions	Some amparos	Ordinary litigation, criminal cases, most amparos
State actors as litigants	Politicians as litigants	Private litigants
Constitutional courts		Ordinary courts
Appointments, esp. of constitutional magistrates		Discipline

on judges through public statements, monitoring, and direct appeals. Finally, clandestine groups also put pressure on judges, often through violent threats.

Political Independence and Societal Autonomy: Distinct but Overlapping

Thus far, this section has been devoted to distinguishing between these two concepts, but there are also some areas of overlap. These overlaps are especially pronounced in settings where economic and political elites are closely aligned or where organized criminal actors have penetrated the political sector. Probing these areas of overlap will help us to understand the distinctions between the two concepts. Table 2.1 summarizes the essential differences between the two concepts of judicial political independence and judicial societal autonomy. These differences can be distilled into four main components: the primary site of conflict, the subject of the attacks, the stage of the judicial career with which infringements are often associated, and some emblematic types of attacks.

Several examples can illustrate the grey areas or areas of overlap between these two concepts. First, when constitutional magistrates are attacked or threatened, both the societal autonomy of that individual magistrate and the political independence of the high court (and perhaps the judiciary itself) are implicated. Second, a politician acting unofficially who publicly attacks or surreptitiously undermines the courts may have an impact on either political independence or societal autonomy or both, depending on the specific details of that situation. If a politician draws on his institutional affiliation to give explicit weight to the attack, then it is better to consider it as an attack on political independence. In this second example, we can begin to see the grey pathways through which influence can come from unofficial actors who are acting on behalf of official actors – or vice versa – and observers cannot always identify the originators of threats, violence, or other influences.

The example of corruption trials may help to illuminate this distinction. Imagine a scenario in which a former president is put on trial for corruption. When the defendant's political party uses its power in the legislature to lash out at the judiciary, there is an infringement on judicial political independence. If a conspirator of the defendant then tries to threaten or bribe the judge, the judge's societal autonomy is being threatened. However, when a sitting president is charged with corruption and must stand trial, it is an exertion of judicial political independence. The president's actions to either cooperate or try to stymie the court's actions may infringe on the court's political independence. It is only when the individual judge comes under attack that societal autonomy is under attack. In practice, of course, corruption cases can be the hardest to parse given that most high-profile defendants continue to have allies in the other branches of the government. High-profile corruption cases also have such high stakes that politically-influenced criminals likely have strong incentives to use violence to try to put pressure on judges.

The trials of former Guatemalan President Efraín Ríos Montt (1982–1983) for genocide and crimes against humanity committed while he was in office provide an interesting lens through which to view these grey areas. Although proceedings against him had been attempted previously, including in Spain, a trial in Guatemala did not begin until he left the Congress and lost his immunity from prosecution in 2012. This trial was the result of significant pressure from societal groups and indigenous activists, including Nobel Laureate Rigoberta Menchú, the Center for Legal Action on Human Rights (CALDH), and a survivors' organization. Ríos Montt was tried in a "high risk" criminal tribunal, created on the recommendation of the CICIG international Anti-Impunity Commission, with the substantial oversight from then-Attorney General Claudia Paz y Paz. Although he was initially convicted, the Constitutional Court annulled the trial on technical grounds; a new trial began in Spring 2016. In this case, then, Ríos Montt was the outgoing head of Guatemala's most stable political party (the Guatemalan Republican Front, FRG) and a former general. He retained significant political and military support. He also had family ties, as discussed in chapter five, to organized crime operators who are believed to have widespread influence in the Guatemalan judiciary. Given that we don't know what truly motivated the Constitutional Court to annul the trial, it is easy to imagine threats coming from criminal actors tied to Ríos Montt or political influence coming through the FRG's share of the Congress. Indeed, the Constitutional Court is the most politically appointed of any of Guatemala's courts. Clearly, there is significant overlap between societal and political influences, although it is notable that overt political measures such as court-packing, budget cuts, or similar institutional attacks were apparently not attempted.

When a judge has routinely taken on highly politicized and highly publicized cases that may have made him politically unpopular, a disciplinary case against him may again blur the lines between judicial societal autonomy and judicial political independence. Spanish Judge Baltasar Garzon became a hero to human rights advocates, especially in Latin America, in the 1990s and 2000s for his repeated investigations[21] and attempts to try former dictators for human rights abuses during the dirty wars of the 1970s and 1980s. His 1998 attempt to have General Pinochet extradited from England to stand trial in Spain on charges of violating the human rights of Chileans who had since become Spanish citizens garnered global attention. Garzon received considerable criticism for his 2008 order to exhume 19 mass graves from the Franco era and was charged with abuse of authority in 2010 at the instigation of a far-right advocacy group.[22] While Garzon was ultimately acquitted by Spain's high court,[23] an attack on a judge as well-known as Garzon must be understood to send a message to other judges. Thus, the attack on that individual judge's autonomy becomes a threat to the independence of the judiciary as a whole.

Another very complicated issue for which it is difficult to parse the relationship between judicial independence and judicial autonomy is that of the causes of action known as the amparo in Latin America. The amparo varies somewhat but follows the basic pattern of allowing an individual litigant (usually a private citizen) to ask the court to invalidate a law or government action as it applies to the petitioner.[24] For our purposes here, it is helpful to

---

[21] In Spanish practice, the trial judge has significant control over the investigation and prosecution of a crime.

[22] Marinero, "JURIST – Paper Chase: Spain Judge Garzon Defends 2008 Franco Probe."

[23] Bottorff, "JURIST – Paper Chase: Spain High Court Acquits Judge Garzon in Abuse of Power Case."

[24] Amparos are most similar to requests for injunctions in the United States or, in rare cases, the writ of *mandamus*. The major difference is that in U.S. law, all law must have *ergo omnes* effects. As such, an injunction against the application of a law in one place will enjoin the authorities throughout the jurisdiction of the court. An amparo, by contrast, applies only to the individual litigant. Given that the countries of Central America generally do not recognize

distinguish between the object of the amparo. When a litigant asks to be relieved of the effect of a decision by a minor governmental official, such as a denial of a business license, it likely does not implicate judicial political independence but rather judicial societal autonomy. When an amparo is brought against a very high official or a major government institution, then judicial political independence may come into play. In rare cases, amparo petitions may instigate major battles over the jurisdiction of the courts and even provoke or threaten to provoke a constitutional crisis. The crisis over the inscription of General Rios Montt as a presidential candidate in 2003 in Guatemala involved a series of competing amparo filings in both the Constitutional Court and the Supreme Court, as is described in Chapter 5. At an extreme, amparos may also be used by lower court judges to question the actions of their superiors; one such incident that happened in Costa Rica in 2010 is described in Chapter 3.

Due and Undue Influences: Situating the Judiciary in Democratic Politics

Pilar Domingo asked in 2000, "... how much independence is considered due, and from whom?"[25] It is also worth asking how autonomous judges should be and from whom. Brinks rightly points out that some limits on the autonomy of judges may be necessary for carrying out democratic will.[26] He has gone on to highlight an "autonomy dimension" in which judges are free to act,[27] assuming also that they have some power to act or what he calls the authority dimension.[28] There are few who would argue that judges should not be autonomous from clandestine groups, but most other infringements on societal autonomy are more debatable. Hierarchical control may be necessary to ensure that judges conform to the law, but can also be used to police unpopular or impolitic decisions by judges. Similarly, monitoring of judicial corruption by the press and NGOs can be very valuable for building a democratic judiciary, but unfavorable press coverage may inhibit the freedom of

class actions, an amparo will not change the law for more than a few people at a time. Where restrictions on amparos are fairly loose, as in Costa Rica, this can mean a very high number of petitions being filed to accomplish essentially the same thing. Variations in the applicability of legal precedent also affect the influence of individual amparos.

[25] Domingo, "Judicial Independence: The Politics of the Supreme Court of Mexico."

[26] Brinks, *The Judicial Response to Police Killings in Latin America: Inequality and the Rule of Law.*

[27] Note that this is a different use of the term "autonomy" from that which is the focus of this book.

[28] Brinks, "'Faithful Servants of the Regime': The Brazilian Constitutional Court's Role under the 1988 Constitution."

judges to make unpopular decisions. Whether or not a particular type of influence is "due" is highly contingent on the specific political and social structure of a given country and is liable to change as that structure evolves.

Thus far, these definitions have presented all influences on judicial independence and autonomy as infringements. For clarity's sake, I have used the language of infringements to refer to all influences, but I wish to now pause to consider the question of how much influence is due. Some influences are clearly due. When a judge oversteps the law, she should be overruled on appeal or even disciplined, whichever is appropriate under the circumstances. However, both of those actions can be applied abusively; I thus choose to lump them all in together. Similarly, most constitutions expect to see some political influence in the appointment of constitutional magistrates, which does not necessarily rise to an anti-democratic level or threaten the rule of law. Choices about how much influence is due are necessarily political and should be decided by each country according to its own processes. Most countries have made these decisions at constitutional moments or when writing their judicial codes. While these codes may be incomplete or vague, it is necessary for there to be allowable international variation in these value judgments.[29]

The focus on judicial independence has clouded our understanding of "how much influence is due." It is possible that the second part of Domingo's question is more important: ". . . and from whom?" When a scholar limits her consideration to only the other branches of government or other elected politicians, it is simple to say that there should be no – or *de minimus* – influence. When one begins to consider a broader array of actors – judicial superiors, the press, nongovernmental organizations, activists, etc. – it is possible to imagine some people who should perhaps have influence, at least at some times. This observation highlights a third question that should be appended to Domingo's artful phrase: *and at what time?* Even overtly political influence by elected politicians may be due at the time of appointment, especially for constitutional magistrates (as is common practice in many systems), but influence from the same actors may not be desirable at the time of deciding a particular case, at reappointment, or at discipline and removal. On the other hand, nongovernmental organizations may have pertinent input (a form of influence) that judges should consider when reaching a decision in a specific case and many systems have institutions designed to allow that to happen.

---

[29] For example, many Latin Americans would be appalled to learn that trial judges are elected in many states, just as many Americans would be shocked to learn that investigation and prosecution are closely tied in most civil law countries.

The theories of democracy that have dominated both the academic and diplomatic communities in recent decades contribute to the tendency to over-look the significance of judicial societal autonomy. Highly individualistic theories have, in particular, tended to view judges in isolation from society. Accounts of democracy as a game played by rational actors all too often leave out the social context of the actors. The game is played primarily by elites who are often considered in the abstract and in isolation from the voters (or of ordinary litigants). Election-focused accounts of democracy have also left out the social context, often with conscious deliberation. In the Latin American context, even some scholars who once felt it important to define democracy "deeply" found themselves conceding that "shallow" democracy was good enough – either for now, or forever.[30] The shallow view of democracy that has predominated since the 1980s defined democracy by the existence of fair elections; the development of adequate rights protection was considered a secondary concern and explicit attention to social justice was sometimes dismissed as dangerous.[31] While many within new democracies continued to fight for social justice or even just to respond to the decaying social environment in which they found themselves, international organizations and leaders focused instead on fostering political liberalism and economic neo-liberalism. An increasing segment of society was marginalized both in the political science literature and in reality.

How, then, should we think about the role of the judiciary in a democracy? Although it is true that unelected judiciaries have potential to usurp democratic policy making processes, it is also true that democratically-enacted

---

[30] O'Donnell and Schmitter, *Transitions from Authoritarian Rule: Tentative Conclusions about Uncertain Democracies.*

[31] This shallow view is essentially Schumpeterian, holding that democracy (and capitalism) are ultimately about competing for the votes (or dollars) of individuals; first-generation rights need to be protected, but later generations of rights are seen as endangering the essential harmony between capitalism and democracy. While this view is clear in the "transitions" literature, it can also be seen in the triumphalist assertions of the permanent ascendance of democracy and the collapse of the communist alternative. In no one person can this trajectory be seen than in the eminent Argentine scholar Guillermo O'Donnell, whose thinking evolved with the changing realities in Latin America from a concern with rights, to a focus on achieving a transition to shallow democracy, to then come back again to a focus on rights and the rule of law. When Carothers declared the "end of the transition paradigm," it was not because of a failure to understand later generations of rights, but because of the empirical failure of so many countries to "complete" a transition. Schumpeter, *Capitalism, Socialism, and Democracy*; Fukuyama, *The End of History and the Last Man*; Huntington, *The Third Wave: Democratization in the Late Twentieth Century*; Carothers, "The End of the Transition Paradigm"; O'Donnell and Schmitter, *Transitions from Authoritarian Rule*; O'Donnell, "Ployarchies and the (Un)Rule of Law in Latin America: A Partial Conclusion"; O'Donnell, "Delegative Democracy"; O'Donnell, "Horizontal Accountability in New Democracies."

policies will be considerably weaker without a strong judiciary to give them life. In many areas of the law, the judiciary's primary role is to ensure that lower-level government officials are administering government policies appropriately. In economic disputes, however, judges have the opportunity to decide whose claims to property and livelihood merit greater respect. In conflicts over violations of human rights, judges have the ability to uphold the dignity of ordinary citizens – or to allow government officials to violate it. Finally, and perhaps most powerfully, in the area of criminal law, the judiciary has the power to deprive defendants of their liberty or to restore it to them; at the same time, judges also have the power to assign value to the lives and injuries of victims – or to allow them to languish unanswered. In all of these ways, the judiciary has an important share of the power to make democratic enactments real – even if that power is shared with (and can at times be abusively usurped by) the police and other justice system actors. Judges have tremendous social power alongside their growing political power.

The democratic rule of law requires more than just accountability for government actors, although that must play a part. The democratic rule of law also requires that private, societal actors accept democratically-enacted legal norms and agree to be subject to them. A judiciary that holds all actors accountable under the same standards and process will contribute to the strengthening of democracy and the state itself. A judiciary, on the other hand, that can be bribed or threatened by the wealthy, the powerful, and the criminal, will contribute to a system of impunity and help to create a hollow democracy in a weak state – even if it remains relatively free of political pressure. Similarly, the judiciary that is highly politicized or rules according to partisan loyalties presents its own problems with impunity for not just governmental actors but also, often, their loyal followers and friends. Impunity is the enemy of democracy because it erodes public trust in the law and hobbles the state. Without enforcement, laws mean little; democracy requires a judiciary that is not just independent from political influences but also free of societal pressures.

JUDICIAL REGIME TYPES

Understanding judicial politics more fully requires us to consider societal autonomy as well as political independence and how these two concepts interact. Considerable effort has been expended in recent decades in Central America and around the world in the service of increasing political independence and, although rarely explicitly or to the same extent, societal autonomy.

TABLE 2.2 *Judicial Regime Types*

	High/Moderate Societal Autonomy	Low/No Societal Autonomy
High/ Moderate Political Independence	**Liberal:** Little political influence on judging. Little societal influence on judging. Past decisions are respected, may be more or less activist, and provide a reservoir of legitimacy to the judiciary.	**Clandestine Control:** Little political influence on judging. Significant societal influence on judging, typically corrupt. Past decisions are likely to be ignored to accommodate corruption; what legitimacy they provide to the judiciary is likely to be squandered.
Low/No Political Independence	**Partisan Control:** Significant political influence on judging. Little societal influence on judging. Past decisions may be disturbed, especially if they are activist, and may not provide legitimacy to the judiciary.	**Government Control:** Massive political influence on judging. May be significant societal influence on judging through corruption. Past decisions are typically ignored or disturbed, especially if they are activist, and provide no legitimacy to the judiciary.

A simple matrix of the interaction of political independence and societal autonomy produces a typology of judicial regime types. These interactions correspond to particular patterns of internal and external constraints on judicial decision-making, including those produced by accrued past judging choices. This section defines four "judicial regime types" that represent different patterns of judicial independence and autonomy. Table 2.2 summarizes this typology.

The four cells of this typology produce four distinct judicial regime types. Before introducing the consequences of these judicial regimes, let us first turn to the basic outlines of how these institutions tend to operate. From the North American perspective, it is easy to assume that the liberal judicial regime would be the most desirable, but there are ways in which a Partisan regime may also be more suitable for some polities. As will be discussed in the next section of this chapter, each of these judicial regime types has some potentially pathological consequences for erstwhile democracies. However, with the exception of the government control judicial regime, each of these judicial regime types may have particular benefits for some polities as well. Crucially, these judicial regime types must be understood on their own merits. While a polity may transit from one to another, these should not be understood as teleological nor unidirectional. Not all judicial regimes are evolving toward being liberal judicial regimes; neither should we believe that liberal judicial regimes will never evolve away from that pattern. Judicial regimes should be understood as stable, but not static.

A liberal judicial regime is both politically independent and autonomous from society, while also enjoying a reservoir of legitimacy based on its past decisions. These systems are also typically associated with the heavy reliance on recourse to constitutional standards to resolve major conflicts, with these constitutional resolutions frequently having precedential effect on future conflicts. In other words, as will be discussed later in this chapter, liberal judicial regimes rely heavily on the constitutional currency. Judicial reform efforts have generally tried to establish a liberal judicial regime, although few successful reform projects can be identified; the difficulty in creating a liberal judicial regime through reform is likely related to the role of the accrual of past decisions to evolve a powerful and legitimate judiciary. In such a system, we should expect to see provision of judicial (and prosecutorial) security services, stability of judicial budgets, lengthy tenures, and a transparent and closely monitored disciplinary system that may or may not be located in the judiciary itself. This regime type has many positives, but any student of the American system can tell you that this judicial independence and empowerment may lead to pathological judicial activism, or at least the perception of it, which may reduce the overall legitimacy of the court within the society. Highly autonomous judges may also be free to make capricious decisions without any accountability for them.

Low judicial independence alongside high autonomy produces what I am calling a partisan control judicial regime. Because judging is subject to significant political influence, past judging choices are likely to be disturbed or ignored by later judges even in substantially similar conflicts. Individual litigants may still be treated fairly and cases may be prosecuted effectively even if there is not likely to be effective horizontal accountability. However, the judiciary in such regimes is limited in its ability to perform horizontal accountability in the face of a dominant legislature (and/ or president). Partisan judiciaries may enjoy considerable legitimacy based on appropriate resolution of ordinary conflicts, but may be just as likely to have their legitimacy suffer based on partisan decisions. In these regimes, judges and prosecutors may have adequate security provisions and stable budgets but be easily subject to politicization in the appointment and reappointment procedures, with short tenures and politicized or partisan disciplinary systems. This regime type is not necessarily pathological if one subscribes to parliamentary-dominant understandings of democracy. However, it can be a concern in a weak democracy where the executive is dominant and judicial appointments are highly partisan, as in Honduras or Nicaragua. Since the Honduran Supreme Court legalized the 2009 coup against President Zelaya, questions have persisted over the partisan nature of constitutional law in that country.

Turning now to the judicial regimes typified by the absence of societal autonomy, we see that largely independent but not autonomous judges produce a situation of clandestine control. In a clandestine control judicial regime, judges are not free from outside influence and are thus likely to be limited in their ability to control crime and provide equal justice. Judges who are subject to threats, bribery, and undue influence (understanding that this begs the question of how much influence is "due") are unlikely to be able to provide the equal application of the laws to all, which is necessary for the rule of law. While the moderate or even high level of judicial independence makes effective judicial review possible, the probability of it is dependent on how autonomous constitutional judges are from the influences of powerful actors with interests in the outcomes of these conflicts. In Guatemala, the judiciary was the site of highly contested human rights trials in the 1990s and into the 2000s, with many judges facing threats for their participation in these trials; as impunity became entrenched, such threats became commonplace. Clandestine control systems may include inadequate security services for justice sector employees, stable but inadequate budgetary resources, short tenures, and a disciplinary system that is not transparent and easily abused by disgruntled litigants. Past decisions may sometimes be respected, at least formally, but the dominance of corruption makes it likely that past decisions will be ignored in future conflicts. Thus, while occasional exercises of political independence may raise the stature of the judiciary, it is unlikely that such acts of judicial boldness will create a reservoir of judicial legitimacy. Over the long term, the probable corrupt influence will lead to judges ignoring such prior acts; any legitimacy gained through judicial boldness is often quickly squandered.

When there is low judicial independence and low autonomy, the government and other powerful actors are able to wield considerable control over both the judiciary as an institution and individual judges in a government control judicial regime. This judicial regime type is usually associated with authoritarian regimes. There is typically a limited rule of law as enemies of the government rarely get fair treatment in the courts, even for ostensibly apolitical conflicts. It should not be surprising given the wide variation in authoritarian institutions that government control regimes may be quite inconsistent. Favored judges, for instance, may have ample security provided by friends in the government or military while troublesome judges may find that their security detail conveniently disappears at the worst moment or participates in actions against them. Budgets may be adequate or inadequate, depending on whether the ruling group chooses to work through the law or outside of it. In any case, judicial tenure is often insecure and disciplinary, appointment, and reappointment procedures are highly politicized. It is unlikely that a judiciary that is complicit in a government control regime could develop popular legitimacy, although it may be possible under certain circumstances that a rebellious judiciary could contribute to a political transition. Under those circumstances, we might expect to see the judiciary obtain considerable legitimacy. Examples of this are considerably rare, but may include Ukraine in 2004 and Thailand in 2008; the actions of Guatemala's Constitutional Court to reverse an *autogolpe* in 1993 do not actually fit this scenario given that the *autogolpe* sought to create a government control or partisan judicial regime (it is not clear which) rather than to maintain one.

Consequences of Judicial Regime Types for Democracy and the Rule of Law

In addressing the consequences of judicial regime types, it is beneficial to revisit the idea of appropriateness implied in this typological theory. Each of these judicial regime types presents its own challenges for reform and contains within it the possibility of specific pathologies. The mythically ideal judiciary may not only be unattainable for most, but may also be variable depending on the ideological trends found in different political environments. For example, the British and European judiciaries have historically subscribed to the theory of parliamentary supremacy, often explicit in European constitutions. Under this theory, the statutes or at least the constitutionally-recognized code laws as passed by the parliament should not be challengeable in court except on technical grounds. This tradition of parliamentary supremacy has come into question with the rise of the European Court of Human Rights' efforts to enforce European human rights law against European Union member countries whose own judiciaries will not act against governmental infringements on human rights. The United Kingdom has been targeted most frequently by the European Court owing to the absence of a constitutional adjudicator in that country; the European Court has in many cases become the court of last resort for British citizens. Even with this skepticism regarding judicial independence, these countries have simultaneously tried to preserve judicial autonomy.[32]

Contrast this to the United States and Canada, where the high courts have frequently made a significant impact on highly salient political issues. Both countries initially empowered their high courts primarily to deal with issues related to the powers of government, including the division of powers under federalism. With the growing significance of the Bill of Rights and its incorporation in the Fourteenth Amendment, the United States Supreme Court became much more active – some might say activist – in the twentieth century. The adoption of Canada's Charter of Rights and Freedoms in 1982 empowered the Supreme Court of Canada to oversee a dramatic reshaping of the Canadian social and political landscape. Neither country had a history of grossly inequitable behavior against the majority of the population by the courts and in both the growing powers of the courts have been embraced by many, though by no means all.[33] If such substantial differences can be permitted between established democracies, why then should one judicial regime type be preferred by reformers in weak democracies?

A judiciary that is institutionally independent and individually autonomous (i.e., a liberal judicial regime) is seen as the most conducive for liberal democracy, especially for reformers coming from the American separation-of-powers system. Such a judicial regime makes it possible for an empowered judiciary to conduct constitutional oversight of the president and legislature as well as to protect the rights of individuals who come before them. These qualities are especially attractive in contexts wherein the prior (or even current) political regime has violated human rights, as is the situation in many weak democracies. Unfortunately, the overwhelming focus on political independence of the judiciary at the expense of building up societal autonomy for judges has obscured the genuine differences between different constellations of judicial institutions. As such, avoiding the assumption that the liberal judicial regime

---

[32] Waltman, "Judicial Activism in England"; Stevens, "The Independence of the Judiciary: The Case of England"; Keller and Stone Sweet, *A Europe of Rights: The Impact of the ECHR on National Legal Systems*; Stone Sweet, *The Birth of Judicial Politics in France: The Constitutional Council in Comparative Perspective*. Among European countries, Italy has struggled profoundly to preserve and expand judicial autonomy in the face of organized criminal organizations. The costs of this struggle have been quite high.

[33] Hirschl, "The Political Origins of Judicial Empowerment Through Constitutionalization: Lessons from Four Constitutional Revolutions"; Hirschl, *Towards Juristocracy: The Origins and Consequences of the New Constitutionalism*; Rosenberg, *The Hollow Hope: Can Courts Bring About Social Change?*; Rosenberg, "Judicial Independence and the Reality of Political Power"; Baar, "Judicial Activism in Canada"; Miller, "Judicial Activism in Canada and the United States"; Halpern, Stephen C. and Lamb, *Supreme Court Activism and Restraint*.

TABLE 2.3 *Consequences of Judicial Regime Types*

	High/Moderate Societal Autonomy	Low/No Societal Autonomy
High/Moderate Political Independence	**Liberal:** Effective crime control. Both private and official abusers can be prosecuted. Horizontal accountability is routine.	**Clandestine Control:** Crime control heavily compromised by corruption. Official abusers may be prosecuted, but private abusers likely will not be. Horizontal accountability is possible, but difficult.
Low/No Political Independence	**Partisan Control:** Effective crime control. Private abusers likely to be prosecuted, but only some official abusers will be. Horizontal accountability is rare.	**Government Control:** Brutal crime control that may or may not be effective. Neither official nor private abusers likely to be prosecuted. Horizontal accountability is rare.

type is always preferable (or even attainable), let us revisit the matrix of judicial regime types and reflect on the consequences of each for the rule of law in the areas of crime control, prosecution of human rights abusers, and horizontal accountability. Table 2.3 summarizes these issues.

Liberal judicial regimes are generally effective at crime control, human rights protections, and horizontal accountability, as is largely true in Costa Rica. As the liberal judicial regime is the typical goal of most judicial reform programs, there should be no need to recount the virtues of this judicial regime type for democracy and the rule of law. What do bear mentioning are the potential areas of inappropriateness. Promoting the liberal judicial regime also implies promoting a certain model of democracy, one that includes a separation of powers model typical of presidential democracies and that also gives a high prominence to a robust constitution including a bill of rights that is enforced through judicial actions. While these may be good ways to organize a democracy, they are by no means the only ways. Parliamentary democracies, especially those following the Westminster model, eschew the separation of powers and until relatively recently have not had strongly empowered judiciaries capable of constitutional review. Although there is considerable convergence around those ideas now, there is no reason to believe that such convergence will always be present. Similarly, effective crime control is closely tied to the rule of law, but there are many approaches in the world to achieve that. Even leaving aside differences in policing strategies, there is considerable variation in criminal trial prosecution and procedure around the world. Whether a jury of one's peers is preferable to an investigating judge is a question generally only answerable through an examination of legal culture and local institutions. Subscribers to some variations on the democratic rule of law may find some aspects or implications of liberal judicial regimes to be pathological or dangerous to democracy even while others do not.

Because partisan control regimes typically do not include horizontal accountability functions, it is easy for some scholars and practitioners to dismiss this regime type as undemocratic or inimical to the rule of law. Such a characterization is quite common when developing democracies are the subject of the scrutiny; when a polity is emerging from a history of dictatorial presidential excess, it is easy to argue that the judiciary should be able to enforce the constitution against the president. While Nicaragua is some decades removed from the Somoza dictatorship, some of these same concerns are evoked by the Supreme Court's decision in 2009 to allow President Daniel Ortega to run for reelection in contradiction of the constitution. However, when one looks at European parliamentary systems that come out of the tradition of parliamentary supremacy, the notion that elected officials can be the guardians of the constitution seems more acceptable, as is the notion of multiple reelection. More concerning in the partisan control regime type is that partisan governments are unlikely to hold partisan allies to account for human rights violations. It is possible to have some trials of public officials, including some high profile or even transitional trials, so long as those facing prosecution can be somehow distanced from those in government. The prosecution and conviction of former President Arnoldo Alemán for corruption in Nicaragua in the 2000s should be understood as such an example, given that President Enrique Bolaños was from a rival Liberal faction. We rarely see partisan judiciaries prosecute co-partisans of the sitting government. Nonetheless, these judiciaries might be quite able to maintain crime control, including the possibility of enforcing human rights against private actors and even some public actors.

Clandestine control judicial regimes often have possibilities of supporting a democratic polity, but are held back by the corruption, often including violence, that permeates them. Because measures have usually been taken to establish at least formal political independence, horizontal accountability is sometimes realized. Similarly, at least some official human rights violations may be prosecuted. Both of these types of exercises of judicial power may meet with significant resistance from official quarters, but political officials will rarely take overt action against the judiciary over them. Guatemala's extremely tense human rights prosecutions in the 1990s and 2000s were an example of this phenomenon, with many threats coming from outside of the elected branches of government (most came from unknown sources). At the same time, it will be much more difficult to prosecute private violators, whether they are guilty of high profile abuses of human rights or basic criminal offences. The intrusion of corruption and threats emanates primarily from the private sector rather than other parts of the government. Consequently, the judiciary is not able to enforce the rule of law, even though there may be significant political independence. The rule of law in these societies is likely to decay as organized crime is able to proliferate and corruption increasingly enters into state institutions. State strength similarly declines. Democratic governance is liable to decompose as rising crime levels lead governments to respond with harsh, even authoritarian strategies to regain control of the society, often with the support of large numbers of the citizens. A judicial regime may be able to exist between the clandestine control and partisan control types, struggling against infringements on societal autonomy just as they build up their political independence, or vice versa. El Salvador is one such judicial regime, with gangs increasingly asserting political power and a somewhat politically empowered judiciary struggling at times to assert its partisan independence.

Government control regimes are creatures of authoritarianism and thus incompatible with democracy. There is typically no horizontal accountability; where some begins to emerge, we should understand that a liberalization may be imminent. Official violations of human rights are often the norm and these violations are unlikely to be prosecuted. The authoritarian atmosphere can also provide cover for private actors who are viewed as being on the side of the government to violate human rights unofficially without fear of prosecution. At the same time, common crime is often viewed as part of the problem that authoritarian governments are to remedy, leading to frequently brutal approaches to crime control. These approaches may be effective in terms of making the streets safer as large numbers of suspects are imprisoned, perhaps without even a trial. However, they may also be ineffective when organized crime is active because the low-level criminals are imprisoned but powerful mafiosos or traffickers are too powerful or too well-connected to control in the absence of open warfare between the state and organized crime. While government control regimes are incompatible with democracy, they may be supportive of a form of the rule of law. In the best of authoritarian circumstances, the laws may be generally enforced against most violators and an atmosphere of social peace may exist even without horizontal accountability or democratic governance. Indeed, political and social nostalgia for authoritarian governance largely stems from the memory of this social peace. However, the incentive to engage in bribery and other forms of corruption is strong when no functional official avenues to free oneself exist. This incentive to corruption can lead to a decay of even authoritarian rule of law.

Taken together, these observations lead to a general conclusion that judicial autonomy is at least as important for the development of a democratic rule of law as is judicial independence. When we consider the possibility for grey pathways between official political actors and unofficial societal, even criminal, actors, the significance of societal autonomy becomes clearer yet. Unfortunately, societal autonomy may be harder to achieve than political independence. Where judicial independence as traditionally conceived requires primarily that the behavior of a small group of people (politicians), albeit very powerful people, be monitored and regulated, judicial autonomy requires that judges be protected from the rest of society as well, including those elements of society that definitionally disregard the rules and laws, criminal organizations. Providing such protections is necessarily in tension with maintaining the accessibility of the justice system for ordinary citizens. It may be undesirable to create a situation in which justice maintains such a distance from citizens that it appears as a distant monolith, meting out punishment from on high. Such a situation is incompatible with a vision of justice as an extension of democracy, of the enforcement of the promise of equality and participation to all.[34]

The following chapters will reveal several observations that support the importance of judicial autonomy. First, length and security of tenure matter more for the creation of judicial independence than does the method of appointment, although other, more idiosyncratic institutional features such as the organization of judicial training schools may also play a significant role. Second, in Central America at least, attacks on the judiciary tend to target specific judges rather that the judiciary as an institution. As such, we see very few attacks on the judicial budget, due in part to the common constitutional provisions guaranteeing a certain minimum percent of the national

---

[34] Consider, for example, the difference between the Nicaraguan Supreme Court's compound, located on the far outskirts of Managua with strong gates guarded by officials with automatic weaponry who vet any potential entrants, with Costa Rica's downtown San Jose Supreme Court building, whose lobby and library are open to the public and often host school tours and whose upper floor offices are guarded under ordinary circumstances by a lone security guard. Not surprisingly, these images correspond to the relative ease or difficulty for citizens of seeking the high courts' aid. Nicaraguans face many obstacles to get any complaint to the Supreme Court which Costa Ricans may make any complaint in any form at any time on any day of the year.

budget for the justice sector and in part to the vigilance of judges at the top of the hierarchy who guard their budgets jealously. Third, disciplinary processes are an understudied yet vitally important feature in how the public, even more than politicians, interact with and try to punish judges. Fourth, threats to judges come from many corners; those emanating from criminal organizations may be the most dangerous and also the most difficult to eradicate.

Mapping Judicial Regime Types in Central America

These judicial regime types are, as with all typologies, ideal types. As we move from the abstract to the concrete, actual judicial institutions and behavior are likely to be considerably more complex. El Salvador, Guatemala, Nicaragua, and Honduras were all clear examples of government control regimes in the 1980s, although there was variation among them, but all had transited to another regime type by the 2000s. In all three cases, however, that transition has not been to the liberal judicial regime. Rather, each has moved to either a partisan regime or a clandestine control regime. Only Costa Rica sits within the typological space for liberal judicial regimes, having transitioned from a partisan judicial regime after the 1989 constitutional reform. The case of El Salvador remains somewhat enigmatic, primarily because it has undergone so much change. It was host to the most extensive judicial reform program in the region prior to the CICIG in Guatemala. Those reforms were initially quite successful in creating a relatively independent and professional judiciary, but there has since been considerable backsliding as the judiciary has been once again increasingly politicized and crime has skyrocketed.

Within the region, Costa Rica is the only example of a liberal judicial regime, despite the strong and persistent efforts of judicial reformers to help the other countries transition to a similar regime. That Costa Rica presents the sole example is problematic given that Costa Rica is so widely viewed as atypical for the region; it is difficult to take "lessons learned" and other helpful developments from an outlier, especially one that is also viewed as a cultural rival by some of her neighbors (Nicaragua, most notably). Additionally, Costa Rica's long and mostly peaceful history of democratic political evolution makes her a "most likely case" to have developed a liberal judicial regime. However, it is important not to treat exceptions as inevitable, unrepeatable, or exemplary of where all countries can and should strive to be. Tracing the initiation and evolution of Costa Rica's constitutional chamber, as well as recent developments in the judiciary more generally, we can begin to see how this exception is built on the accumulation of the same kinds of conflicts that all polities face and the way the path was laid through the responses to all of these conflicts. Moreover, understanding Costa Rica through the lens of judicial regime types also provides a valuable example of transition away from a partisan judicial regime.

Nicaragua, Honduras, and El Salvador have existed primarily within the category of the partisan judicial regime since the late 1980s or early 1990s. In Nicaragua, the partisan nature of the judiciary has its roots in the purges of the *Somocista* judiciary after the 1979 revolution and subsequent replacement of those judges and officials with *Sandinista* loyalists. Following the 1990 transition to liberal democracy, a series of pacts between the dominant political party leaders has divided the available appointments between these parties, solidifying the partisan nature of the judiciary. What distinguishes this from a government control regime, in which government loyalists are appointed to the judiciary, are the guaranteed presence of judges from both government and opposition and the use of democratic, constitutional practices for appointment and removal of judges. Honduras has similarly seen its judiciary divided between dominant political parties through pact-making that has its roots in the hybrid regime of the 1980s. Finally, El Salvador has, since at least the Supreme Court appointment process in 2000, had its Supreme Court divided between dominant political parties as well – although that partisan influence is somewhat muted by the reappointment of only one-third of the Supreme Court every three years. Because the appointment of lower court judges and appellate magistrates is ultimately done by the partisan Supreme Court, this partisan influence filters through the entire judiciary.

Guatemala after 1986 is the primary example of the clandestine control judicial regime type. In the wake of democratization in 1985–1986 and the peace process that concluded in 1996, the role and size of the military were substantially scaled back. At the same time, a large number of reform projects affecting the judiciary and policing were initiated. Unfortunately, the retraction of the repressive state apparatus left a power vacuum that the government failed to fill in timely fashion. Consequently, networks of contraband smuggling that had roots in the civil war years flourished. Street gangs also proliferated, fed by the massive migration of the poor from the rural countryside to the capital city and other cities. As corruption became entrenched, most attempted solutions were superficial and failed to solve the problem even when they were implemented. Rampant crime magnified corruption and reinforced it with violence. At the same time, however, the judiciary attempted to perform horizontal accountability on a number of occasions and held some official violators of human rights accountable under the protective shade of moderate political independence. Crime and corruption reached levels by the mid-2000s that an international commission was created to aid in prosecution alongside increasingly brutal policing. El Salvador also has elements of a clandestine control judicial regime, including corruption and criminal intimidation of judges and leading to brutal policing efforts; she has not been the beneficiary of a similar level of international efforts in the 2000s.

The regional upheaval and violence of the 1970s and 1980s (reaching far earlier and somewhat later in some countries) produced government control judicial regimes in Guatemala, Honduras, El Salvador, and Nicaragua during most of the 1980s. In all of these countries, authoritarian or semi-authoritarian governments were embroiled in violent civil conflicts and counter-insurgency campaigns. In all of these cases, the judiciaries contributed to the enforcement of authoritarian goals. In Guatemala, sensitive cases were largely removed to the military courts if they were even resolved institutionally. For the most part, the judiciary functioned to maintain social order through a façade rule of law that did not touch the military governments. Honduras remained technically democratic during this period, but the influence of the military was so dramatic that it should be understood as a hybrid regime engaged in a "dirty war" against purportedly communist activists. These conflicts rarely went to the courts and even more rarely found resolution there; however, the democratic elements of the political regime did allow for cases to be pursued in the courts. In El Salvador, like in Guatemala, many cases were removed to the military courts or the suspects were simply tortured and killed without recourse to a judge. When the judiciary was involved, it was possible to protect some suspects primarily through bribery. Even when international pressure obliged the government to permit a trial for a human rights violation, as with the infamous murder of six Jesuits in 1989, the higher level intellectual authors of abusive policies and acts were not placed on trial. Finally, in Nicaragua, the socialist Sandinista government increasingly packed the judiciary with ideological loyalists while conducting a war against counter-revolutionaries backed by the United States government. Individuals suspected of being with the *contras* were typically not afforded fair trials. Sandinista officials increasingly enjoyed impunity in their own human rights violations.

A benefit of this typological theory of judicial regimes is that it reveals some of the often-overlooked differences between those judiciaries often deemed disappointing, undemocratic, or deficient. Applying it to these five Central American countries over a thirty-five-year period will help to reveal the ways that these judiciaries have evolved by tracing their transitions from one judicial regime type to another. While political regime transitions may produce a great deal of legal, constitutional, and even judicial change in a short period of time, those changes are often resisted by the institutions who are the objects of those reform efforts. Just as comparative political scholars have problematized the finality of a political transition, so must we not assume the finality of any of these judicial changes – and for similar reasons. Choices made in a period of major upheaval can lay a path for the future, but many will try to venture off that path or to build an entirely different path. As a consequence, we must consider these transitional reforms as simply the initiation of an institutionalization process that reveals little about the likelihood that those institutional arrangements and processes will become routinized in a way that even resembles the goals of those same transitional reformers.

ELITES AND SOCIAL UPHEAVAL

How, then, does a country develop one of these judicial regime types? And how would it shift from one to another, either deliberately or not? Politicians in developing countries in the past few decades have not had as much autonomy as the constitution-writers that most people imagine. Most countries of the developing world have found themselves under significant influence of the international community at any point when they have considered reforms – and at times they have not initiated that consideration. The "law and develop-ment" movement of the 1970s sought to bring rationality to the legal systems of the developing world through the assistance of Western legal experts, but then fizzled.[35] The economic and political upheaval of the 1980s, however, rekindled the interest of the international donor agencies in "building the rule of law" (the jargon of choice at the time) in all countries. Many of the international funding agencies such as the World Bank, the Inter-American Development Bank, and many bilateral aid organizations have devoted consid-erable time and money in the past three decades to "Rule of Law Reforms."[36] These reforms have involved re-writing laws in order to promote economic development and protect individual rights, introduce technical innovations designed to improve the functioning of legal institutions, and, in many cases, oversee broad re-organization of judicial institutions.[37] Policy analysts involved in rule of law reform projects have tended to focus their definitions of the rule of law on the more practical issues of access to justice for the bulk of the

---

[35] Salas, "From Law and Development to the Rule of Law: New and Old Issues in Justice Reform in Latin America."

[36] Domingo and Sieder, *Rule of Law in Latin America.*

[37] In Guatemala, for instance, numerous laws have been re-written, the courts have been equipped with computerized case-tracking systems, and adversarial jury trials have been instituted in the past fifteen years.

population (especially the underprivileged), efficiency of legal institutions, and judicial independence from political influence or pressure.[38] The Central American countries in this study were not alone in dramatically altering their constitutional arrangements since the 1980s to include, among other things, a significantly empowered judiciary, (on paper, at least). The current era of intervention in Latin American reforms dates to the mid-1980s.[39] Although it has attracted numerous donors, participants, and critics, the justice reform movement in Latin America has not satisfied many citizens. Longtime reformer Linn Hammergren reports that major changes were made to internal structure, the reach of the justice sector in terms of both population and territory, and better resources, but that these changes have not necessarily produced better outcomes; at the same time, citizen expectations have expanded.[40] Rule of law promoters were especially active globally in the period immediately following the 1989 fall of communism, as many countries rewrote their constitutions, most aiming for democracy either nominally or substantially and many employing experts from Western Europe. Indeed, the European Union had an official project to help with the creation of new democratic constitutions in its neighbor countries, many of whom have now become its new members.

An important but often overlooked feature of this period in Central America and around the world is the confluence of international pressure with at least some domestic political pressures. If judicial empowerment is often undertaken largely to please donor groups, it may expand in unexpected ways. Arjomand has observed that the constitutions of the late Twentieth Century, especially those in the post-communist and developing worlds in moments of transitions away from authoritarianism, have been intended to explicitly break with the authoritarian past.[41] He argues, "Constitutional politics, when successful, typically result in compromises, in written constitutions and in constitutional legislation and jurisprudence, that can be explained by the relative strength of social and institutional forces and interests behind the constellations of value-ideas, on the one hand, and by the procedural rules and the dynamics of constitutional debates on heterogeneous principles of order, on the other."[42] The constitutional texts and compromises that are the product of these debates – which should be understood to include international pressures, I would add – may provide important signaling and framing about "value-ideas"

[38] Ungar, *Elusive Reform*; Prillaman, *The Judiciary and Democratic Decay in Latin America*.

[39] Seider, Angell, and Shjolden, *The Judicialization of Politics in Latin America*.

[40] Hammergren, *Envisioning Reform*.

[41] Arjomand, "Law, Political Reconstruction and Constitutional Politics."   [42] Ibid., 23.

and about the resolution of future disputes. However, constitutions, however conservative or radical, should never be assumed to be the final word on judicial or even constitutional politics. Indeed, courts around the world have taken up the challenge of ensuring the provision of socio-economic rights, among other things.[43]

Judicial empowerment moments are usually understood to be the critical juncture *par excellence* in the development of a new judicial regime. A court is empowered when it either is invited to play a role in political decision-making or when it inserts itself uninvited into political decision-making. These moments often take place within the context of amending a constitution or writing a new one, often due to a regime change. It is crucial to understand who thinks they will win by empowering the judiciary, even if they do not turn out to be who actually wins. Politicians will only empower the judiciary if they believe that it will help them, although this help may not always be conservative (or even reactionary or counter-revolutionary) in the way that Hirschl identifies. As Arjomand points out that constitutional politics (including judicial empowerment) necessarily includes "the pressure to disguise self-interest as public interest" alongside group interests and institutional interests.[44] What both Hirschl and Arjomand overlook, however, is that decreasing public scrutiny following an empowerment moment or constitutional amendment will allow self-interest to operate more nakedly, albeit in a somewhat changed environment.

The extent of actual judicial empowerment that follows an empowerment moment will likely depend on who is doing the empowerment and to what purpose. While the basic dynamics may be similar, as will be seen, it is simpler to consider constitutional reform or amendment and constitutional revision or regime change separately. The case of reform or amendment would be expected to follow Hirschl's observations, wherein people in power seek to empower a constitutional adjudicator because they believe (whether correctly or not) that this newly empowered body will protect today's winners against tomorrow's political winners.[45] In essence, this kind of constitutionalism makes the political compromise at time n (i.e., a law or policy) subject to the political compromise made at time n-1 (i.e., the constitution). Today's political leaders appoint their friends to the courts with the mission of tying the hands of tomorrow's political leaders. While this may be true, it need not be as

---

[43] Brinks and Gauri, "A New Policy Landscape: Legalizing Social and Economic Rights in the Developing World."

[44] Arjomand, "Law, Political Reconstruction and Constitutional Politics," 23.

[45] Hirschl, *Towards Juristocracy.*

substantively liberal as Hirschl suggests; many left-wing politicians, including the Nicaraguan Sandinistas, have enshrined lengthy bills or rights to try to preserve or establish social or cultural rights against an increasingly liberal economic and political elite, both at home and globally.[46]

Continuity and Change in Judicial Politics

If the impulse to empower the judiciary often comes from abroad, the actual contours of that empowerment typically have more local roots. In short, the patterns of judicial politics that can be seen today are a product of the conflicts and compromises that came before. This statement is not merely an acknowledgment of the influence of path dependence. That notion of following established patterns is not enough, of course. It is especially not enough when considering legal and political actors in unstable political environments. All players in the politico-legal scene in fact make choices and exert power, even if they do so within a constrained environment. In order to understand the development of these judicial regime types – and, thus, how it may be possible to move beyond some of the pathologies within them – it is necessary to consider the patterns of judicial politics prior to empowerment, the specific contingent compromises involved in the moment(s) of empowerment, and the ongoing contingent struggles that may allow for modifications to or evolution of those contingent compromises. At any time, some will win and others will lose and those victories will be accomplished by a variety of means. Which groups or types of actors win *and how they do it* will set the patterns to be followed in at least the next several conflicts.

Few reforms, regime changes, constitutional moments, or even revolutions are so radical as to do away with the influence of the regime that came before in less than a generation and perhaps not even then. As a case in point, the French have not ruled Latin America for over two centuries, but the civil code system imposed during the Napoleonic wars remains the basis of Latin American legal systems. Colonialism casts a long shadow over any now-independent country, of course. As the judicial regimes of Central America are not yet a generation old, the previous judicial regime is an especially important consideration. As Chapter 4 details, the pre-empowerment judicial regime in the four northern countries is a government control regime. Costa

---

[46] There is some argument to be made that this precisely what has happened in Costa Rica since the establishment of the constitutional chamber of the Supreme Court. It is certainly clear that that chamber has been asked to resolve a large number of disputes around those extra-liberal rights.

Rica's pre-empowerment (1949–1989) judicial regime is that of an increasingly independent and autonomous judiciary that did not exert substantial power over the constitution despite having the explicit constitutional authority to perform judicial review – in essence, a weakly partisan regime.

The important thing to understand is that the previous regime of concern is not necessarily independent, democratic, dependent, authoritarian, politicized, apolitical, or militarized. It may be any of those things and more, but it must by definition be not empowered. The unempowered court does not participate in political decision-making and typically does not question decisions made by the government or the military. An unempowered court may question the government within its limited constitutional purview, which usually focuses primarily on deciding legal disputes of a private or criminal nature. An unempowered court may be able to assert itself against the government by acquitting the innocent (or even by acquitting the guilty) or by allowing civil suits against government officials, military officers, or other powerful individuals. An unempowered court, thus, is not necessarily *disempowered*. A disempowered court is one whose power is actively taken away or deliberately suppressed. A disempowered court may be so cowed or compromised that it is not willing to take even perfunctory steps against the government.

The extent to which a judiciary is unempowered, disempowered, or perhaps even mildly empowered and its behavior in light of its opportunity structure in the prior period establishes the point of departure for the shape and success or failure of future reforms. The French judiciary under the *ancien regime* famously so colluded with the aristocracy that anti-judicial sentiment and efforts to institutionally restrain the courts have persisted ever since.[47] Pinochet's constitution in Chile provides another side of that dynamic: Chilean judges in the 1970s and 1980s were so passive in the face of government abuses that his government saw fit to empower them somewhat as he made his very slow exit from the political scene.[48] The development of partisan judicial regimes in Honduras, El Salvador, and Nicaragua should be understood as originating from a similar impulse: politicians have granted some degree

---

[47] Stone Sweet, *The Birth of Judicial Politics in France.*
[48] Pereira, "Of Judges and Generals: Security Courts under Authoritarian Regimes in Argentina, Brazil, and Chile"; Hilbink, "Agents of Anti-Politics: Courts in Pinochet's Chile"; Hilbink, *Judges Beyond Politics in Democracy and Dictatorship*; Barros, "Courts Out of Context: Authoritarian Sources of Judicial Failure in Chile (1973–1990) and Argentina (1976–1983)"; Couso, "The Politics of Judicial Review in Chile in an Era of Democratic Trasition, 1990–2002"; Couso, "The Judicialization of Chilean Politics: The Rights Revolution That Never Was"; Pereira, *Political (In)justice: Authoritarianism and the Rule of Law in Brazil, Chile, and Argentina*; Scribner, "Courts, Power, and Rights in Argentina and Chile."

of formal independence and have protected societal autonomy to some extent because they can maintain political control over judges through appointment processes, short tenures, and reappointment processes.

The development of judicial regimes does not end with the negotiation of constitutional moments, of course. Periods of "ordinary politics" will be punctuated by monumental legal or constitutional conflicts. These conflicts will often take the form of a constitutional crisis, such as the 1993 coup and the 2003 electoral dispute in Guatemala or the 2009 coup in Honduras. Some are merely highly political salient judicial rulings, such as the 2003 decision by Costa Rica's constitutional chamber to allow presidential reelection. More subtle events, happening relatively far from the judiciary, may also have a profound effect on constitutional politics when viewed in retrospect. The political pact-making of the 2000s in Nicaragua provides an excellent example of this. Following a pact between the Liberal and Sandinista leaders, the two parties were able to each claim half of the judicial appointments – along with all other political appointments – for their own. Thus, a partisan judiciary was predictable. These crises should be understood as moments of greater prominence within a period of constitutional evolution.

Evolutionary models are especially important for understanding the processes of change and continuity that have occurred in Central America since the 1980s. Political actors and reformers, coming from both within and without the region, have endeavored to take advantage of the perceived "critical juncture" of the transitions to democracy and the related peace processes. The amount of international penetration of the legal reform communities in these countries, especially Guatemala and El Salvador, is staggering. However, it is not satisfactory to explain all of the constitutional and judicial conflicts of the past three decades through the lens of the bargains made in the 1980s or the 1990s. To do so would be to ignore the substantial changes that have swept the region. At the same time, neither is it satisfying to examine every major conflict of the past three decades as a "critical juncture" in the development of the judicial regimes of these countries. To do that would be to obscure the signs of progress and normalcy that do exist. I propose instead an evolutionary approach that weighs different dynamics of continuity and change interacting with each other and reflecting larger patterns of reform and resistance.

In taking an evolutionary view, I do not wish to ignore the significance of some dramatic moments of change, which may be understood to initiate an institutional pattern. However, taking seriously the idea that an institution is a social and cultural practice,[49] we must look beyond the initiation of these

---

[49] Kenny, "Gender, Institutions and Power: A Critical Review."

practices to see their habituation as well. Just as someone developing any habit such as diet or exercise may perfectly follow a model at the beginning only to slowly degrade her form or "cheat" on her diet from time to time as the habit becomes more ingrained, so do social and institutional actors drift away – sometimes quickly – from the original form of their practices. Whereas drift in individual habits may be explainable through individual psychology, institutional drift is often a result of conflict between the different constituents of the institutions. For example, the relative numbers and power of anti-corruption and pro-corruption members of an institution will have a similar impact on the actual prevalence of corrupt practices within that institution. At the same time, external conflict will play a role as well. Any political or ostensibly apolitical state institution is subject to pressures from different parts of the polity, including users of the institution's services, voters whose taxes fund the institution, other institutional actors who may be competitors for funding or power, and politicians who may make use of the institution's power – or become subject to it. These processes are ongoing and must be understood as being conflictual, cyclical, and evolutionary.

Causal Mechanisms in Conflict

Institutionalist scholars who focus on path dependence debate the relative significance between continuity and change in the contexts of various institutions, systems, and regimes. Various mechanisms for both change and continuity have been proposed and outlined; I will focus herein only on a pertinent selection. When considered together, many of these mechanisms can be easily understood to be in remarkable conflict with one another. For example, the idea that institutions change through replacement of incumbents must be weighed against the tendency of incumbents to reproduce their power whenever possible by selecting successors who share their interests and ideologies. Similarly, elite efforts to frame certain political conflicts in particular ways can be frustrated by processes of political learning when the frame diverges too far from reality. Efforts to convert an institution to another model often becomes a layering process instead when vestiges of the old institution underpin the newly reformed one – or when reform efforts are only partially successful in the first place. Along similar lines, notions of positive feedback, in which an institution is strengthened by the support of its blossoming constituency, should be countered by a notion of negative feedback in which a new institution is sabotaged by people who perceive themselves as harmed by it. Similarly, positive returns, wherein positive externalities enhance the longevity and strength of an institution, should be balanced against negative returns given the theoretically

TABLE 2.4 *Mechanisms for Change and Continuity in Reform Processes*

Mechanisms for Change	Reform Issues	Mechanisms for Continuity
Replacement	Lustration (Re)Training Personnel decisions	Power reproduction
Framing	Public awareness campaigns	Political learning
Conversion	Extent & efficacy of reforms	Layering
Positive feedback	Policy effects on different groups Access to justice	Negative feedback
Increasing returns	Increasing efficiency & legitimacy	Decreasing returns
Brokerage	Creation of new, often liminal, institutions	Brokerage

equal likelihood that externalities will be negative as that they will be positive. In all of these considerations, scholars must also consider Skocpol's question of *for whom* externalities are positive or negative and *for whom* returns are positive or negative; in other words, who stands to lose and who stands to win from institutional continuity and change?[50] These conflicting mechanisms are summarized in Table 2.4 along with some of the reform issues that relate to these different mechanisms.

Aligning these causal mechanisms against each other in this way around specific reform problems begins to hint at the role of power in reform processes. Reform processes, by their nature, seek to change many elements, including fundamental elements, of an institution, system, or regime. Typically, institutional incumbents will see themselves as losing from reforms and will seek to maintain as much continuity as possible. This resistance can be overcome by removing or otherwise neutralizing incumbents or by making the change attractive to those incumbents. As such, we see reformers seeking to engage in replacement, framing, and conversion projects whenever possible, in the hopes that positive feedback and increasing returns will help those new or newly reformed institutions flourish. However, these moves are actively resisted by incumbents and by others who stand to lose from these reforms (negative feedback and decreasing returns). Whenever possible, incumbents will attempt to reproduce (and continue) their power and to force processes of conversion into processes of layering. Additionally, events both within and

---

[50] Skocpol, *Protecting Soldiers and Mothers: The Political Origins of Social Policy in the United States.*

surrounding an institution may frustrate framing efforts by producing conflict, even lethal conflict, that produces significant political learning among institutional incumbents. Brokerage, in which new institutional coordination is created through reform processes, may also create conflict between reformers and incumbents or between different power groups over who will control that coordination.

To put these abstractions in the context of judicial reform, let us consider a few examples. While adjustments or modernizations to training programs (including retraining for incumbents) was a commonly accepted set of reforms, Central American judiciaries almost uniformly resisted lustration processes that would have removed problematic incumbents.[51] Many reformers and reform-minded NGOs have engaged with the public and the media to frame the conversation around justice and judicial reforms, but increasing criminal violence and corruption in the region have negated most of those messages, especially in the Northern Triangle. Even where whole new institutions were created, such as in the police forces of Guatemala and El Salvador, they were layered, operating alongside (in Guatemala) or grafted on top of (in El Salvador) the old institutions. Even the groundbreaking creation of the constitutional chamber in Costa Rica is an example of layering, albeit a dramatic one; the constitutional chamber is simply a fourth chamber of the already subdivided Supreme Court. There has been considerable need to create "buy in" among judicial incumbents in these reform processes to encourage them to use their considerable institutional power – which was being increased in some cases through reforms – to support reforms. Members of the Nicaraguan Supreme Court, for example, personally oversaw the implementation of various judicial reform projects, including the distribution of the budget. Brokerage has been perhaps underutilized because of the multiplicity of reformers on the ground in most countries, often working on overlapping projects with sometimes conflicting aims. However, a few projects have created novel pathways through the creation of new institutions that can negotiate between various institutions as well as political actors; the *Comisión Internacional Contra la Impunidad en Guatemala* (International Commission Against Impunity in Guatemala, or CICIG) in Guatemala is one such brokerage institution, as are the various NGO forums that bring together different justice-oriented watchdog groups in each of these countries.

---

[51] Nicaragua's purges of the Somocista jurists following the 1979 revolution is the only major example of lustration, although a limited purge was carried out in Guatemala following the 1993 autogolpe by President Serrano.

Together, the push and pull of reform and resistance produce the evolution of judicial regimes. Change is likely to happen only through the efforts
of reformers either inside or outside of judiciaries, but powerful actors both
inside and outside of those judiciaries are likely to resist change. The success or
failure of those reforms depends in large part on their ability to overcome that
resistance. Reformers of all types have been disappointingly limited in their
foresight about resistance to reforms and other challenges on the horizon,
such as organized crime and social violence. Reformers and many observers of
Central America can be faulted for failing to recognize both the changes that
have occurred with the genuine transitions away from military authoritarianism and for failing to recognize the continuity of some trends that have their
roots in those transitions if not even earlier. These trends include different
means of resolving conflict that play a major role in supporting different institutional practices. Some of these practices are more concordant with some
judicial regime types than others. As such, we can see the predominant means
of resolving conflict, or what I call "currencies," as a major indicator of the
judicial regime type in a given polity at a given time.

The "Currencies" of Justice

When a party to a conflict finds himself in the courts, he has a variety of options
to call upon to try to get his way. Primarily, he may draw on constitutional law,
statutory law, money, or violence. He will likely choose which to use based on
what has worked for others in the past, depending as well on his capabilities.
He will learn what has worked for others in the past largely through media
accounts of high profile cases and less so through official rules or norms
and the framing that accompanies them, in other words, judicial practices of
power. If we assume a risk-averse litigant, he is likely to prefer legal means
over illegal means because of the risk of facing consequences for engaging in
violence or bribery. However, a risk-averse litigant also typically wishes to see
a clear resolution (and preferably in his favor) within a reasonable amount of
time. Thus, when conditions are right, even a risk-averse litigant may rely on
corruption or violence. These litigant currencies and the judging decisions in
response to them constitute the day to day practices of judicial institutions.
Even if we cannot always identify the initiation of these practices, we can
usually witness their habituation.

A reliance on constitutional law as the ultimate arbiter of conflicts – even
when statutory law may resolve the vast majority of conflicts – is the hallmark
of a liberal regime. The use of the constitutional currency is a requirement
for the judiciary to be able to police the actions of the elected branches. The
constitutional currency is unlikely to guide judicial practice in the absence of

judicial empowerment, although it may lay dormant for long periods.[52] Constitutional conflicts are typically quite high profile and lend greater publicity to the judiciary. Public controversies encourage others, primarily those with less politically salient conflicts, to also employ constitutional strategies. This pattern is clearly evident in Costa Rica, where the number of constitutional claims being filed with the constitutional chamber has grown exponentially since its inception. However, as Arjomand has pointed out, "Radical political change may occur in the context of constitutional continuity or major changes in constitutional law may occur without any political upheaval. Different institutions can become engines of constitutional politics; and the distinction between routine and constitutional politics is frequently blurred."[53] The constitutional currency gives a certain political and social status to the empowered judiciary that an unempowered judiciary cannot have. That the constitutional currency is typically invoked by legal activist organizations suggests that the complex of alliances described by Epp and others as judicial support networks that support judicial activism may be primarily creatures of liberal judicial regimes.[54]

When statutory law – not constitutional law – is the final arbiter of these conflicts, a partisan judicial regime is likely to develop. Statutory law is inherently political law, able to be changed easily by each new president and legislature. Even the legal codes that are prominent in Latin America may be modified by legislatures with greater ease than a constitution. The reliance on statutory law amounts to a presumption that political decisions trump the constitution. The reliance on statutory law is also common in many government control regimes, but there government violence serves as the true final arbiter. The courts in the Northern four countries continued to operate and apply the laws during the government control periods, but did not typically question the actions of their governments. In the partisan regime of contemporary Nicaragua, the decision to allow President Ortega to run for a second consecutive term in 2011 despite the constitutional prohibition reflects the heavy influence of Ortega's Sandinista party on the Supreme Court. Note that the prominence of the currency of statutory law does not erase practices of lawfulness. Partisan regimes are not lawless; their statutes are still enforced even as their constitutions may be enforced only partially.[55]

---

[52] In several European countries, it has been the pattern that a constitutional arbiter was created in the constitutional moment but remained passive or even dormant before stepping into significant political conflicts years later. Jackson and Tushnet, *Comparative Constitutional Law*.

[53] Arjomand, "Law, Political Reconstruction and Constitutional Politics," 27.

[54] Epp, *The Rights Revolution*.

[55] It bears noting that the practice of constitutional review does not respect the value of statutory law and, as such, creates its own uncertainty and lack of reality to the law.

Clandestine control judicial regimes operate a large part of the time on corrupt practices involving the currencies of money and violence. Violence is a prominent feature as the final arbiter of both government control regimes and clandestine control regimes. The major difference is the nature of the violence; government control regimes are backed by the use of official (if often clandestine) government violence, while private, unofficial violence is the driving force in an impunity regime. One may lend itself to the development of the other: Guatemala's widespread private violence has its origins in significant part in the covert official violence of the government control regime that preceded it. As will be discussed in Chapter 5, many of the major organized crime groups are led by individuals and groups that had their formation in the military conflict during the civil war years. The currency of violence is as persistent as it is pernicious; even broad and deep reforms to judicial institutions will do little to change these clandestine practices unless criminal violence can be controlled.

It may seem like a paradox to discuss the nature of judicial practices in government control regimes given that the judiciary is often a smokescreen for government violence. However, there has been considerable variation in the nature of those judicial practices, as is recently becoming widely recognized.[56] In some systems, judicial practices in most circumstances will mirror those in liberal judicial regimes with only certain, sensitive conflicts removed from the ordinary courts; this was the norm in Guatemala under military rule. In other systems, judges may be ideological servants of the political regime and may rule along with the government's wishes whether specifically ordered to or not; this was the norm in communist polities, although it was only somewhat true of Sandinista Nicaragua in the 1980s. Of course, corruption may exist alongside these government controls and provide an escape hatch from them; bribery provided a means by which some political detainees were able to be freed in El Salvador in the 1980s. Nonetheless, the dominant practice of conflict resolution in government control regimes is the deployment of government violence.[57]

---

[56] E.g., Ginsburg and Moustafa, *Rule by Law*.
[57] At this point, I wish to recognize that all judicial actions in all systems are in fact exercises of state violence. Judges either condemn men to suffer state violence through imprisonment or other legal penalty or withdraw from them the exercise of state violence on some basis, which may be exoneration but could also be bribery, favoritism, or orders from political or social masters. Civil litigation includes its share of state violence, as well: a litigant or witness can be condemned to prison for failure to appear, courts can seize a man's property if he does not pay a judgment (to say nothing of debtor's prisons where they still exist), and the triumphant plaintiff can essentially commandeer the apparatus of state violence to enforce his own contracts, property rights, or personal integrity. While these practices should all be understood as state

The currency of money may be found in all judicial regime types, but it is only a prominent component in clandestine control regimes. Bribery is rarely the subject of high-profile judicial disputes; more often, it is commonly known as a widespread phenomenon without necessarily being publicly acknowledged. Bribery may be a magnifier of impunity, essentially making it easier for more and more people to evade or take advantage of the justice system. While not everyone has the stomach or the capacity for violence, a bribe is within the reach of many litigants. Many judges are willing to accept bribes, but for those who aren't, there are many judicial employees who will accept an even smaller bribe to "lose" a case file, rendering justice impossible. Money and violence are not unconnected, however; violently inclined litigants may attempt a bribe before trying to threaten a judge. Perhaps high-profile prosecutions of bribery could help reverse the kindling of impunity. Widespread efforts to clamp down on the routinized but more modest bribery may do more but requires the commitment of substantially more resources; bribery is an extraordinarily sticky institutional practice.

The currencies discussed above are one way of understanding practices of power. When reformers seek to change judicial institutions, they are also trying to change practices of power. Understanding that a liberal judicial regime is beneficial for democracy implies understanding that using the constitution as the primary currency for conflict resolution is a democratic way to use power. Notably, from this perspective, using statutory law as a primary practice of power – in other words, building a partisan control judicial regime – may be helpful for democracy, even if it may be a form of electoral democracy that may not include features such as horizontal accountability. This analysis further explicates the harm that flows from government control and clandestine control judicial regimes: power is practiced predominantly and ultimately through violence. That violence may be mediated through state institutions such as courts, but it should not be understood as being controlled by them; on the contrary, that violence controls them.

LOOKING AHEAD: COUNTRY STUDIES OF EVOLVING JUDICIAL REGIMES

The chapters that follow are organized according to the typological theory laid out above. These chapters employ a process tracing method that seeks to elucidate the causal pathways that allow for stasis or change within

---

violence, their recognition as such does little to help us differentiate practices of violence between political and judicial regimes.

countries across time periods representing different judicial regimes. The identification of these pathways is reinforced through comparison across different country cases. Thus, the analysis reaches back to find causes, forward to find consequences, and across to confirm those causal pathways. The case study analysis found herein should be best understood as a theory generating typological exercise. The case studies of Guatemala, Honduras, El Salvador, and Nicaragua provide a "most similar cases" analysis. Additionally, within those four, Guatemala and El Salvador are cases that should be success stories, given the tremendous enthusiasm and commitment of the international community as well as (at least initially) their national governments to the project of judicial reform. How they came to be currently in a different place from where many hoped they would be is an important puzzle. The inclusion of Costa Rica includes a "most likely case" to analyze for comparison. Although Costa Rica has long been considered an outlier in Central America, it is important to understand the way that its judicial regime, too, has evolved and continues to evolve.[58] In this discussion, the focus is on how the evolving judicial regimes in each country affect the rule of law, seeking to identify the different influences of the judicial regimes and to illuminate the interplay between political independence and societal accountability. The contrary mechanisms of path dependent continuity and change form the architecture of this discussion.

[58] George and Bennett, *Case Studies and Theory Development.*

3

Costa Rica

A Liberal Judicial Regime

I think that a certain credibility endures [in the judiciary] and I give you two indicators: increasingly the people turn to the courts, every year there are more lawsuits before the courts. What this means, I think, I could be mistaken in my reading, is that if you go with a lawsuit before a judge it is because you believe that something can be gotten fair and square.

Then that is an indicator that the people increasingly bring their issues before the courts and after, surveys also reveal that when a person has not had a lawsuit, he has a worse opinion [of the judiciary] than when a person has had a lawsuit and you ask yourself how the service appears to him, then we rise a little, that is also a universal phenomenon but it is confirmed here. That is to say, not only do more people come to the courts every year, but the people that come to the courts have a relatively favorable opinion.[1]

– (CR2009–10)

In Chapter 2, a "liberal judicial regime" was defined as one in which there is both high independence of the judiciary as an institution and high autonomy of judges as individual actors. Costa Rica represents a liberal judicial regime. Institutionally, its judiciary is quite independent. Individually, judges

---

[1] Original: Yo creo que se guarda cierta credibilidad y le voy a dar dos indicadores, cada vez la gente acude más a los estrados judiciales, cada año hay más pleitos ante los tribunales. Lo que significa, creo yo, puedo estar equivocado en la lectura, que si usted va con un pleito ante un juez es porque cree que algo puede obtener en buena lid.
   Entonces eso es un indicador de que la gente cada vez más lleva los asuntos ante los tribunales y después, también las encuestas revelen que cuando una persona no ha tenido un pleito judicial, tiene una opinión menos buena que la persona que ha tenido el pleito judicial y se le pregunta qué le pareció el servicio, ahí subimos un poco, eso también es un fenómeno universal pero aquí se confirma. Es decir, no sólo cada año más gente llega a los tribunales sino que la gente que llega a los tribunales tiene una opinión relativamente favorable.

are generally protected in their prerogatives, their salaries, and their careers. This liberal judicial regime evolved out of a partisan judicial regime, with the most dramatic change occurring when the constitution was amended in 1989 to create a constitutional chamber of the Supreme Court, opening the door for an expansion of the constitutional currency. Additionally, it has not been untouched by violence related to the international drug trade. In some parts of the country, threats against judges have become a concern and criminality is on the rise. These problems are especially acute in the Caribbean coast and the border region with Panama, the areas most affected by drug trafficking. While I would not argue that even the most lawless (or, perhaps more accurately, the least lawful) parts of Costa Rica amount to an impunity judicial regime, there is a threat of movement in that direction. There has been and continues to be significant change in Costa Rica's judicial regime over time.

At the same time that Costa Rica has faced growing difficulties flowing from its geo-political position vis-à-vis the drug trade and related organized criminal activity, it has also experienced an impressive rights revolution. While the Costa Rican government has built a reputation for many years of respecting the rights of its citizens, the ability and willingness of citizens to demand enforcement of those rights in court skyrocketed after the 1989 creation of the constitutional chamber (Sala IV) of the Supreme Court. The constitutional chamber hears complaints regarding a wide array of constitutional rights. Furthermore, barriers to access this tribunal are very low; citizens do not need lawyers, fees, or even a properly written complaint. In this regard Costa Rica's constitutional chamber resembles the Supreme Court of India, with its aggressive receptiveness to public interest litigation.[2] Not surprisingly, Costa Rican citizens can far more easily protect their rights in court and expect to have those protections make a concrete impact on their lives than in any other Central American country. Indeed, in terms of rights protection, Costa Rica's Sala IV rivals any tribunal in the world.

Applying the judicial regime approach to Costa Rica also helps to frame the significance of the creation of the Sala IV and the rise of the consti-tutional currency. Prior to the creation of the Sala IV in 1989, Costa Rica should be understood to have had a partisan judicial regime because the pri-mary currency of conflict resolution was political legislation. Even though constitutional review was possible, it was rare. Costa Rica is thus a useful example of a country whose judicial regime has transitioned from a partisan

---

[2] Moog, "Judicial Activism in the Cause of Judicial Independence: The Indian Supreme Court in the 1990s"; Epp, *The Rights Revolution*; Hoque, "Taking Justice Seriously: Judicial Public Interest and Constitutional Activism in Bangladesh."

regime to a liberal regime. This example is notable in Latin America because it took place without a political regime transition, but rather in the context of a structural adjustment program. Furthermore, the empowerment of the Costa Rican judiciary more broadly was done largely at the instigation and through the long-term militancy of the judiciary itself, which resulted in more budget security and better career protections for all aspects of the judiciary. Even before the constitutional chamber expanded the role of the Supreme Court, the judiciary as a whole was seeing improving political independence and societal autonomy.

INCREASING POLITICAL INDEPENDENCE AND THE CREATION OF THE CONSTITUTIONAL CHAMBER

Costa Rica's judiciary did not go through a period of governmental control in the twentieth century, as Costa Rica did not experience a significant period of military rule during the Cold War. Following its brief civil war (1948), a new liberal democratic constitution was adopted and the armed forces were disbanded. Consequently, since that time a military authoritarian takeover has simply not been possible. Another result of the absence of a military is that Costa Rica has not resorted to the use of military police in basic crime control (especially anti-gang activity), as has happened in many countries, including El Salvador, Guatemala, and Honduras. Without the availability of a large cadre of military police, the *mano dura* approach to crime control remains difficult in Costa Rica. Even before the military was abolished, officers generally left the judiciary and most of political life alone, creating an environment of institutional stability that allowed successive generations of increasingly independent magistrates and other judicial officials to push the country toward a stronger and more liberal judicial regime.

Costa Ricans enjoy a number of myths about their own country, which together contribute to a notion that, within Central America at least, Costa Rica is uniquely suited to democracy. Costa Rica was a relatively resource-poor region at the far-reaches of the Spanish colonial empire, hundreds of miles from the imperial apparatus, with a sparse population whether we consider the indigenous people or the settlers. According to the popular narrative, this history, especially when extended through the absence of large landholdings in the independence period, produced a population almost naturally bred for democracy. A supreme court magistrate quoted this narrative to me almost verbatim in 2009. Wilson[3] has suitably and thoroughly questioned the

---

[3] *Costa Rica.*

ubiquity and inevitability of the democratic development that followed, given that undemocratic transfers of power, coups and attempted coups, and even military rule remained somewhat common through the period that ended with the 1948 civil war. Nonetheless, it is significant that Costa Ricans themselves appreciate these myths, as it suggests that they typically accept a self-identification as democratic.

The correct birthdate of Costa Rican democracy is not universally accepted, as Costa Ricans prefer to date it to the late nineteenth century. However, the end of the 1948 civil war and the adoption of the 1949 constitution provide the clearest foundational moment for present purposes. The compromises that resulted from the brief civil war led to full inclusion of the middle and lower classes in what had previously been primarily an elite democracy. The civil war and the attendant political compromises also led to the creation of a social democracy and the abolition of the military, two factors that helped to direct Costa Rica's democratic path even farther from her neighbors. Since the civil war, Costa Rica has enjoyed freedom from the possibility of military rule and a relative social peace with lower levels of inequality than are typically seen in Latin America.[4]

The judicial regime between 1948 and 1989 should be understood as a primarily partisan one. Constitutional challenges were available to litigants, but were rarely used; the prevailing currency of conflict resolution was in fact statutory law. The development of a partisan judicial regime is not surprising, given the relative stability of the mostly-elitist political parties of the day. The 1948 civil war established the basic cleavages that would define the politcal party system for decades afterward. In essence, there have been two tendencies, one represented by the National Liberation Party (*Partido Liberación Nacional* – PLN) and one by the opponents of the PLN, who were not consistently unified under a single party mantle. The PLN was founded by the victorious rebels following the civil war and represented for many years the social democratic state, although they did not embrace trade unionism. The PLN's opponents have been successful routinely when they are able to unify behind a single candidate; they coalesced most successfully from 1983 in the Social Christian Union Party (*Partido Unión Socialcristiano* – PUSC). The PUSC largely represents the commercial and agricultural elite and is closely associated with neoliberal reforms.[5]

Although the primary character of the judicial regime between 1949 and 1989 was partisan, significant conflicts between the judiciary and the

---

[4] Booth, *Costa Rica: Quest for Democracy*; Wilson, *Costa Rica*.
[5] Booth, *Costa Rica*; Wilson, *Costa Rica*.

legislature occurred in that period, the outcomes of which helped to expand the judiciary's political independence. A recent history of the Costa Rican judiciary produced by the Costa Rican think tank Estado de la Nación highlighted especially the significance of the protracted struggle for a guaranteed judicial budget. In the mid-1950s, judicial employees agitated for increases in compensation.[6] In response, the legislature asked the Supreme Court as head of the judiciary to propose a law to govern judicial salaries, a project that led to the guarantee that the judiciary would receive 6 percent of the national budget. The reforms of the 1950s also contributed to strengthening the hierarchical control of the magistrates of the Supreme Court both by recognizing them as appropriate inter-institutional negotiators and by giving them oversight over the salaries and careers of judicial employees, including lower-court judges.[7] Even so, the 6 percent "guarantee" would not result in a consistent budget of 6 percent until 1991.[8] Additional important changes include the generational shift from magistrates whose backgrounds were in politics to magistrates whose backgrounds were in the judicial career by the 1990s and the professionalization and bureaucratization of the judiciary as a whole following the 1973 Judicial Service Statute (*Estatuto del Servicio Judicial, Ley* 5155).

Since 1989, The Supreme Court's already tremendous independence under the Costa Rican constitution has expanded. The clout of the Supreme Court grew significantly when the constitution was amended in 1989 to create a fourth chamber of the Court that would hear constitutional claims. Although the Supreme Court has had the authority to hear constitutional challenges since 1938 (reaffirmed in the 1949 constitution still in force), such challenges were rare before the creation of the fourth chamber. Although the creation of the fourth chamber was a layering reform, the introduction of new magistrates made it very assertive. The Sala IV or constitutional chamber has become extremely active in the years since its creation, reviewing thousands of claims every year. In recent years, those claims have involved increasingly significant issues. They invalidated a constitutional amendment barring reelection in 2003, allowing Oscar Arias Sánchez to make a successful bid for reelection in 2006. They also ruled on the free trade agreement with the United States (CAFTA-DR), finding it constitutional in a split decision. They have also ruled on a number of significant smaller government policies, including the provision of anti-retroviral drugs for HIV-positive patients through the Social Security system, discrimination against gays and lesbians, and numerous

[6] Programa Estado de la Nación, *I Informe Estado de la Justicia*, 95.
[7] Ibid., 96.   [8] Ibid., 97.

environmental decisions.[9] The judicialization of politics in Costa Rica suggests that the existence of a specialized constitutional court (or chamber) can be a significant driver of a politically active judiciary, even in the absence of a large NGO sector.[10]

The transition to a liberal judicial regime was sped along by the decline of the traditional party system, which limited the ability of the parties to collude to control the judiciary. Although there was substantial partisan bargaining[11] in the initial appointment of magistrates to the Sala IV in 1989, there has not again been the opportunity to name multiple magistrates in the same vote. Since approximately 1990, the traditional two-party system has deteriorated; by 2002, the effective number of parties in the National Assembly had risen to 3.7 from a nearly-five-decade average of 2.5.[12] In the 2006 elections, the PUSC had dropped to only eight percent of the votes for the National Assembly deputies, while "others" won nineteen percent.[13] In the February 2010 elections, the PUSC continued to fare so poorly as to be almost a non-contender, winning only 8.16 percent of votes for Deputies, coming in fourth behind the PLN (37.3 percent) , Citizen's Action Party (17.6 percent), and the Libertarian Movement Party (14.5 percent).[14] Most notable among these statistics, aside from the tenacity of the PLN, is the fact that the majority of voters now do not prefer the two "main" parties.

A major cause of the fracturing of the traditional party system has to do with the decline in Costa Rica's social welfare state in the wake of 1980s Structural Adjustment Programs. Lehoucq has argued that the roots of these problems date to President Rodrigo Carazo's (1978–1982, Unity Party) decision to default on the national debt in 1982, which set in motion the need for structural adjustment programs and pushed the economic policies of the PLN and PUSC into near-alignment.[15] Wilson has further pointed out that structural adjustment was initiated by the PUSC, but was continued and deepened during the first presidency of the PLN's Oscar Arias Sánchez (1986–1990, 2006–2010).[16] President José Maria Figueres Olsen (1994–1998,

---

9 Wilson, "Claiming Constitutional Rights through a Constitutional Court: The Example of Gays in Costa Rica."

10 Barker, *Constitutional Adjudication: The Costa Rican Experience.*

11 There was also inter-institutional bargaining, such that three magistrates were chosen by the PLN, two by the PUSC, and two by the judiciary. Programa Estado de la Nación, *I Informe Estado de la Justicia,* 102.

12 Lehoucq, "Costa Rica: Paradise in Doubt," 142.

13 Lehoucq, "Political Competition, Constitutional Arrangements, and the Quality of Public Policies in Costa Rica," 68.

14 Tribunal Supremo de Elecciones, "Elecciones, Estadísticas de Procesos Electorales."

15 Lehoucq, "Costa Rica: Paradise in Doubt."   16 Wilson, *Costa Rica.*

PLN), whose party did not enjoy a majority (by one seat) in the National Assembly, had an especially difficult time dealing with implementing the economic reforms that were being pushed on Costa Rica by the international financial institutions. The right-of-center PUSC opposition held up the implementation by refusing to approve tax cuts until an accord was passed.[17] The consequence of these developments, according to Lehoucq, is that the parties have too much incentive to collude and too little accountability, especially in light of the constitutional prohibition on reelection.[18] Former President Miguel Ángel Rodríguez (1998–2002, PUSC), in a response to Lehoucq in the *Journal of Democracy*, argued to the contrary that Costa Rica's problem is that politicians are no longer willing to cooperate with each other across party lines.[19]

The creation of the constitutional chamber is thus an important marker in the transformation of Costa Rica's judicial regime from a partisan one to a liberal one, although this shift cannot be understood without also noting the significant changes that were happening in Costa Rica's party system. At the same time that the new Sala IV opened up paths to resolve political conflicts through recourse to the constitutional currency, political parties were losing their abilities to forge and enforce partisan agreements. The rising power of the judiciary coincided with a decreasingly effective legislature. One does not appear to have caused the other – both appear to be the result of the political and economic crises of the 1980s – but the two phenomena reinforced each other. Voters, investors, and politicians who could not achieve their goals in a fracturing legislature turned to the Sala IV for satisfaction. Meanwhile, the protective shade of the Sala IV allowed elected politicians to indulge in intransigence, knowing that the Sala IV would resolve whatever they failed to. The weakened legislature is not a requirement for a liberal judicial regime to exist, but it played a role in fostering the establishment of one in Costa Rica.

INCREASING SALIENCE OF THE LIBERAL JUDICIARY

Popular demand for the services of the constitutional chamber has helped to increase the political salience of the Sala IV and the Supreme Court as a whole. Human rights are widely respected by the government and enforced in the courts. The 2011 United States Department of State human rights report for Costa Rica identifies a large number of cases involving the rights of workers, criminal defendants, women, migrants, LGBT individuals, and other

---

[17] Booth, *Costa Rica*, 165.   [18] Lehoucq, "Costa Rica: Paradise in Doubt."
[19] Rodriguez, "Getting Costa Rica Right."

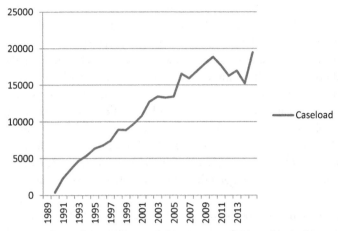

FIGURE 3.1 Caseload of the Costa Rica Constitutional Chamber (1989–2014).
Source: Sala Constitucional – Corte Suprema de Justicia.[20]

potentially marginalized litigants where claims of discrimination and other violations were recognized.[21] Neither Human Rights Watch nor Amnesty International include Costa Rica in their recent annual reports. The pending question in Costa Rica is the effect that rising organized crime will have. The Costa Rican think tank Estado de la Nación has pushed a debate over the "hard" anti-drug state or the "intelligent" anti-drug state. Violent crime is rising in Costa Rica, but remains much lower than the rest of the region, as discussed in Chapter 1. Thus far, Costa Rica has been able to survive using primarily intelligence as it enjoys a much stronger and more capable state and lower incidence of drug trafficking-related organized crime than many of its neighbors.

While the causes of political and official adherence to legal and constitutional norms around rights protections are complex and include the influence of local history and political culture, the accessibility and responsiveness of the constitutional chamber has played a very important role in Costa Rica's rights revolution. As depicted in Figure 3.1, the caseload of the constitutional chamber has grown dramatically since its inception. In 1989, it received 365 cases and in 2014, that number had grown to 19,470. The vast majority of that growth has been in amparos, with the numbers of habeas corpus petitions and actions of inconstitutionality remaining relatively stable. In 2014, 89.36 percent of all

[20] Ibid.
[21] Bureau of Democracy, Human Rights, and Labor, United States Department of State, "Country Reports on Human Rights Practices for 2011: Costa Rica."

constitutional cases were amparos, 9.55 percent were habeas corpus petitions, and only 1.5 percent were actions of inconstitutionality.[22] The constitutional chamber has been able to slow the rate of growth of new cases by insisting that some cases are within the exclusive jurisdiction of the criminal chamber (Sala III) and the administrative chamber (Sala I). While this does not amount to full control over their docket, it allows the constitutional magistrates to narrow the focus of their work somewhat.

The decay of the Costa Rican party system has had significant implications for the judiciary. Partisan politicians in the National Assembly seem to be trying, with minimal success, to resurrect partisan control of the judiciary. In addition to the problems that party system decay has caused for governance as a whole – although Lehoucq has argued elsewhere for the generally good quality of Costa Rican policy making[23] – the inability of the political parties to make effective deals has made it difficult to appoint new magistrates to the Supreme Court. The lack of general accountability (through roll call votes or through reelection) has made legislative intransigence relatively cost-free. One might suspect that this lack of political coherence would also provide some breathing space for the Supreme Court, and it appears that the attempt to prevent the reappointment of constitutional magistrate Fernando Cruz Castro in 2012 was stymied by that very legislative decay. Former president Rodríguez also identified the relationship between the National Assembly and the Supreme Court as a part of the logjam in Costa Rican politics since the Supreme Court in the 1980s began to require the National Assembly to adhere to its own procedures and by-laws. By 2012, Costa Rica was faced with a National Assembly with no majority party, whose Deputies essentially could not be held accountable, and who were angry with at least some of the magistrates of the Supreme Court.

Magistrates are appointed by the National Assembly with a super-majority; the president does not participate in the appointment process. Magistrates enjoy an eight-year term and are eligible for indefinite reappointments. In order to deny reappointment, a super-majority of the National Assembly must vote against the magistrate; this happened for the first time in 2012. As the party system has fractured, however, it has become more difficult to find the super-majorities required to appoint magistrates. Furthering this problem is the tendency for deputies to not attend votes. The difficulty in appointing a

---

[22] Sala Constitucional, Corte Suprema de Justicia, "La Sala Constitucional en números 1989–2014."

[23] Lehoucq, "Political Competition, Constitutional Arrangements, and the Quality of Public Policies in Costa Rica."

replacement for Magistrate Luis Fernando Solano Carrera provides an excellent illustration. Solano retired in January 2008 and was not replaced on the court until December 2009, despite a constitutional limit of thirty days. During this period, numerous candidates were vetted and voted on but could not gain the requisite thirty-eight votes, in part because numerous deputies failed to appear for votes. At one vote, only forty deputies were present. Whether these absences were politically motivated, given an increasingly politicized and controversial Sala IV, or simply the result of laziness, as some suggest, is unclear. With the decline of the traditional parties, there is also a crisis of partisan discipline, which in turns makes bargaining and governing difficult.

Nested within the problem of the failure to appoint a new constitutional magistrate in 2009 was a minor crisis involving the appointment of new substitute magistrates (*magistrados suplentes*). Since the retirement of Magistrate Luis Fernando Solano Carrera in January 2008, the constitutional chamber had been operating only because of the availability of these substitute magistrates; without at least one, there could not be a quorum. In December 2009, the two-year term for the substitute magistrates was set to expire without any indication from the Congress that they would appoint new ones. Editorials suggested that this was indicative of a major showdown between the legislature and the constitutional magistrates. Failure to appoint new substitute magistrates in the absence of a new titular magistrate would have caused the constitutional chamber to close its doors. At the eleventh hour, the legislature did approve new substitute magistrates, not long before approving a new titular magistrate. Opposition parties also balked at reappointing constitutional magistrate Ernesto Jinesta, citing his politics in deciding a variety of cases, although they did not have sufficient votes to actually block his reappointment (*La Nación* September 14, 2010).

In November 2012, the National Assembly did organize sufficient support from the deputies to deny reappointment to constitutional magistrate Fernando Cruz Castro, the first time a constitutional magistrate had been rejected and the first time any supreme court magistrate had been rejected since a Sala III (criminal chamber) magistrate had been denied reappointment in 1993. Cruz Castro was known to be a sometimes dissident member of the court, voting against the majority in a number of important cases, but members of the National Assembly stated that this vote was intended to get the attention of the constitutional chamber as a whole.[24] In the case of the Cruz Castro vote, the fragmentation of Costa Rican political parties appeared to play a role: the traditionally dominant party, the PLN, was able to gain support

---

[24] Oviedo, "Jefe de PLN Afirma Que Es Una 'llamada de Atención' a La Corte."

of the Libertarian Party and a sector of the PLN's traditional opponents, the PUSC. With the political parties in flux, the two-thirds super-majority required to unseat a magistrate may no longer be enough to protect the tenures of the magistrates as it had been in the old two-party system. The immediate reaction from the President of the Supreme Court as well as the Fiscal General was extremely negative and a Sala IV panel composed of substitute magistrates soon overturned the National Assembly's vote.[25]

While it is too soon to know how this conflict will affect the long-term behavior of the constitutional magistrates, their initial reaction was swift and sweeping: a constitutional decision vindicating Cruz Castro and his continuance on the Sala, self-consciously declaring the strength and independence of the judiciary. In a decision dated May 9, 2013, the substitute magistrates ruled that the attempt to remove Cruz Castro was invalid because the National Assembly had taken the fateful vote too late. In the absence of a vote for or against reappointment on the eight-year anniversary of Cruz Castro's appointment, his reappointment was deemed automatic; the vote taken later by the National Assembly was thus out of turn and without effect. Although the decision rested on this fairly specific, technical issue, the opinion went on to include a lengthy discourse on the significance of judicial independence in a democracy. The seminal United States decision in *Marbury v. Madison* was quoted and discussed at length, alongside more succinct discussion of cases from the Spanish Constitutional Court and the Inter-American Court of Human Rights. The decision sent a clear message that the Sala IV would be a powerful force in any future constitutional conflicts.

What we may be beginning to see is the attempted exercise of partisan control not through appointment, but through reappointment. This emerging pattern may be a reflection of the extreme salience of the Sala IV. The constitutional chamber is now the final word on a large portion of policy decisions, frequently telling both the executive and the legislature what they can and cannot do in a wide variety of areas. The political significance of constitutional law now encourages elected politicians to challenge the Sala IV in order to score political points. While it is unlikely that an elected politician would attempt to actually dismantle an institution as popular with voters as the Sala IV, any opportunity to influence its decisions becomes extremely important. The Sala IV's own popularity creates an inexorable tension between the desire of individual claimants to push every issue into the realm of constitutional rights and the desire of elected politicians to retain significant policy making authority – even as some elected politicians make use of the Sala IV.

---

[25] Mata, "Congreso saca a magistrado de Sala IV con histórico voto"; Mata, "Fernando Cruz Castro: 'Yo No Tengo Que Pedir Perdón Ni Dar Explicaciones.'"

In other words, highly successful liberal judicial regimes may make elected politicians long for partisan regimes, especially when one was in place in living memory.

THE JUDICIAL CAREER AND THE GROWTH OF A SOCIETALLY AUTONOMOUS JUDICIARY

Speaking generally, one magistrate argued that politicians generally respect the autonomy of the judiciary, although she did share some concerns:

> . . . It depends on what we call independence. If we talk in the sense that they call or pressure, we have to say that yes, [politicians] respect it. In thirty years of my judicial career, I have never received a call or an insinuation, or an unexpected visit, but if we talk in terms of their public appearances, speaking through the press, then, yes, we have to say it's not quite one hundred percent.[26] (CR2009–19)

She went on to indicate that she had heard rumors of judges receiving threats, but had never known of a case personally.[27]

Ordinary judges are appointed and promoted by a judicial council that reviews their education, publications, and other factors through an objective (points-based) system. Judges are disciplined through this council as well. Appointment of judges below the level of the Supreme Court is controlled by the Supreme Court, although they delegate this authority to the judicial council. The *poder judicial* (judicial power or judiciary) oversees the *Ministerio Público* (the prosecutors), the public defenders, and the judicial investigation unit (forensics), in addition to the courts themselves. The constitution guarantees that 6 percent of the national budget will automatically go to the judiciary; those interviewed indicated that this guarantee has not recently been violated by the legislature. Also, the disciplinary process for judges is wholly situated in the judiciary. Magistrates are judged first by their fellow magistrates, who determine whether or not to refer the case to the National Assembly; no case has ever been referred.

Costa Rican judges enjoy considerable security of tenure once hired. The judicial career is bureaucratic in nature, with advancement based on merit.

---

[26] Original: . . . depende en como llamamos la independencia. Si hablamos en sentido de que llamen o presionen, ya tendremos decir que sí la respetan [los políticos]. En treinta años de carrera judicial, nunca he recibido ni una llamada ni una insinuación ni una visita inesperada, pero si decimos en el sentido en que la restan en sus apariciones públicas y hablamos a través de la prensa pues tengo que decir que no es tan cien por ciento.

[27] Many interviewees reported on rumors, although personal experience with threats was only rarely mentioned.

Judges have the possibility of advancing from a juzgado bench to the Supreme Court over the course of a career. Of thirty-four judges who filled out a detailed questionnaire in 2010, all indicated some level of advancement through their career path. None indicated that they had been transferred to another court for negative reasons, but rather because of better location, promotion, or at their own request. Most had participated in legal courses and conferences, including thirteen who had been given the opportunity to participate in these activities outside of Costa Rica. Some judges will leave the career to work as private attorneys, but there is little official pressure or structural limits to force them to do so.

Nor does the disciplinary process appear to substantially infringe on the autonomy of judges. Eighteen of the thirty-four respondents to the 2010 questionnaire had gone through a disciplinary process, half of whom were disciplined in some fashion. Citizens have the ability to lodge complaints with the judicial branch against a judge. Naturally, some of these are frivolous or spiteful. When a judge is accused, the judicial branch itself handles the investigation and resolution of the complaint through its Judicial Inspection Office. The inspection office clarifies on its webpage, citing the judiciary's organic law, that any complaint that asserts that a legal doctrine was either misinterpreted or misapplied will be automatically dismissed. Doctrinal concerns are a matter for the appeals process, not the disciplinary process. This office handles complaints against all judicial employees and not just judges; the only exceptions are the supreme court magistrates.

Judges also enjoy the support of the Costa Rican Association of Judges (Asociación Costarricense de la Judicatura, ACOJUD). ACOJUD was formed in 1993 with the mission of strengthening the independence of judges. A large part of their work has focused on the implementation of the 1994 Judicial Career Law (*Ley de la Carrera Judicial*) and on democratizing the internal governing structure of the judicial branch. ACOJUD also serves to help foster solidarity among judges. In addition to their work within Costa Rica, ACOJUD has been very active in promoting connections between Costa Rican judges and judges in the region and around the world, including routinely participating in international associations and meetings. Based on anecdotal observation in 2010, there appears to be a very collegial relationship between ACOJUD's president and several magistrates of the Supreme Court.[28]

Costa Rican judges and lawyers cited an interesting concern about the societal autonomy of Costa Rican judges: the influence of perceived declining standards of legal education was singled out by one source (CR2009–12) in 2009. He asserted that many of the newer law schools opening in Costa Rica are

---

[28] "Historia | ACOJUD.org."

TABLE 3.1 *Important Factors in the Appointment of Judges in Costa Rica*

Factors	Important or Very Important	Not Important
Experience as a litigating attorney	38.7	32.3
Family prestige	19.4	58.1
Friends within the judiciary or the Supreme Court	9.7	74.2
Friends within the government	9.7	74.2
Affiliation with a political party	6.5	74.2
Previous employment in the judiciary	41.9	6.5
Excellent academic record	90.3	0

Source: Author's 2010 survey (Responses in percentages of total).

producing weaker graduates, many of whom entered the judiciary as interim judges in the early 2000s and then stayed in those positions for many years. He indicated that there had been some "anomalous actions" by these interim judges, especially from those coming from the newer private law schools. While these assertions imply that these interim judges are more corruptible (or, perhaps, less careful) than ordinary judges, the exact proportion of complaints against interim versus permanent judges is not known. Anecdotally, there have been a number of very experienced permanent judges who have been removed from their positions for misconduct and then petitioned for reappointment. Similar differences in preparation and education exist between judges in less desirable parts in the country and judges in San José. Nonetheless, responses of judges to the survey conducted in 2010 suggest that an excellent academic record is the most important factor in the appointment of Costa Rican judge, as can be seen in Table 3.1.

Another concern regarding these interim judges is that they did not enjoy the same career protections as the permanent judges. Interim judges only continue in their jobs if they are reappointed or converted into permanent judges by the president of the Supreme Court. During the early 2000s, when interim judges numbered in the hundreds, the autonomy of trial-level judges from the judicial hierarchy was significantly compromised. By the late 2000s, the number of interim judges had dropped considerably as many more permanent judgeships were filled (CR2009–12).

Judicial autonomy may also be negatively influenced by corruption within politics and within society. One interviewed attorney (CR2009–09) was especially concerned with official corruption, which had negatively affected a number of her clients as well as her husband's business. Although she indicated that the problem of corruption is of course difficult to measure, it clearly had its origins at least as far back as the years immediately following the civil war, when a beloved president enriched himself handsomely. She suggested that it was not uncommon for officials to ask for a bribe when considering a permit or a governmental contract. As a consequence, many businesses would "ask forgiveness instead of asking permission" and simply avoid the permitting system altogether for as long as possible. In response to the question of whether this resulted in many legal actions against officials, she replied, "No. There are officials with a lot of money."[29] The infrequency of lawsuits was for her largely a result of the difficulty in proving that such corruption had occurred.

This same lawyer also related a story of another lawyer in her firm who had been approached by a judge to pay a monthly "fee" in order to guarantee the success of his cases in that judge's courtroom. Again, as long as no witnesses saw such requests occur or they were not videotaped, then it was extraordinarily difficult to prove that such corruption occurred. Nonetheless, she was hopeful that the high-profile cases against two ex-presidents (discussed below) would help to change the culture of corruption or at least shine additional light on it. Although most of the individuals interviewed expressed doubt that judicial corruption was common, one supreme court magistrate (CR2009–19) did voice her concern that the judiciary does not have sufficient measures to detect corruption. Specifically, she cited the lack of a mechanism for confidential complaints or for an investigation to be launched if there was reason to be suspicious. One judge (CR2009–13) echoed that concern, indicating that, while the levels of corruption were not so large as to be alarming, that was no excuse for not establishing appropriate control mechanisms. Recall from Chapter 1 that Costa Ricans perceive a very high level of corruption in their society despite international perceptions such as Transparency International rankings suggesting a less troubling amount of corruption than in most of the world. While this is not the place to analyze the difference between corruption in reality and the public's perception thereof, it bears noting that there may be a mismatch between the two.

A CONTESTED TRANSITION AWAY FROM A PARTISAN JUDICIAL REGIME (1994–2015)

Costa Rica's decision to create the Sala IV came at a time when there was a substantial push in the region and around the world to constitutionalize political conflicts. Furthermore, an active Supreme Court was becoming an expected component of a liberal democracy with checks and balances.

---

[29] Original: No. Hay funcionarios con mucha plata.

Although Costa Rica did not undergo a transition to democracy in the 1980s, the structural adjustment programs accepted in the 1980s instituted massive economic change that also had to be reflected in the legal system. It is not clear that President Arias and his PLN intended to create a body that would provide what O'Donnell would later call "horizontal accountability" by reining in the government itself, but that is what has happened. Indeed, it appears that the constitutional amendment in 1989 that created the Sala IV was an attempt at layering a new feature on top of an old institution. Nonetheless, the reality has been that the Sala IV and its members have in fact converted the Supreme Court into a more active and more forceful body, which has been buoyed by the creation of positive feedback as citizens have become engaged with constitutional claims. Whether or not Costa Rica's elected, partisan politicians intended this outcome, they have at times resisted it and they have also at times taken advantage of it. This section traces several high profile conflicts since 1989 that illustrate the transition in Costa Rica from a partisan to a liberal judicial regime.

The *Banco Anglo Costarricense* Case

Possibly the longest-lasting legal controversy in the economic arena involves the failure of the state-run Banco Anglo Costarricense (Anglo-Costa Rican Bank, BAC) in late 1994. Prior to its failure, the BAC had been managed by a government-appointed board of directors and was heavily regulated in terms of the debt burden it could acquire and the investments it could make. Nonetheless, in the early 1990s, the BAC acquired an investment firm, through which it engaged in a number of illegal investment activities, including taking on some of the sovereign debt of Venezuela. These illegal actions were able to continue in part because of the failure of the legislature to engage in adequate oversight of the board of directors. By the time the bank's director began to publicize the very serious liquidity problems the bank was developing, it was too late to solve them. The BAC shut down on September 14, 1994. The Costa Rican government absorbed the debts of the bank, opened a legislative investigation, changed some of the banking laws, and initiated a large number of criminal prosecutions.[30]

A 2010 study of the failure of the BAC described the closure of the bank as "nearly impossible" under the 1953 banking law that governed the BAC before its failure; the author goes on the say that it is difficult to believe that the bank

---

[30] Trejos Salas, "Informe del Presidente de la Comisión Legislativa encargada de estudiar las irregularidades que condujeron al cierre del Banco Anglo Costarricense."

would have failed had it not engaged in illegal activities.[31] The idea that the failure of a bank is nearly impossible is revealing about both the statism of the social democratic system that had existed in Costa Rica before the rise of neo-liberalism and the reliance placed on those state institutions by workers, citizens, and investors. One consequence of the post-1994 banking reforms, however, has been that the banking sector has been substantially penetrated by foreign banks, creating a significant amount of support for foreign investors. Another consequence has been a proliferation of corruption investigations and even convictions, most of which have not actually been related to the BAC scandal. A number of people have been fined or imprisoned as a result of the scandal, including the former head of the bank and five members of the board of directors.[32]

The BAC case shook Costa Rica dramatically. Even in 2009 and 2010, nearly every interview subject identified the BAC case as among the most significant cases of the previous fifteen years. At the extreme, one Costa Rican scholar identified the scandal in 1995 as a moral crisis, citing numerous government officials calling for a need to restore Costa Rican morality regarding this issue. He suggested that the fall from moral grace could be attributed to the adoption of neo-liberalism, especially as the government called to absorb the BAC's debts and pay for them from Structural Adjustment Plan funds.[33]

Its legal ramifications were still being dealt with as late as 2013, when the courts continued to adjudicate the outstanding debts that the government had absorbed. In one of those cases, a failed banana plantation, overrun by squatters, had been auctioned off to pay its debt at pennies to the dollar and the government was still pursuing the rest of the debt with the corporation that had originally incurred the debt.[34] The continuing struggles over the repayment of these bad debts have created an ongoing burden of uncertainty for investors. However, the process has occurred in an orderly and seemingly fair manner, primarily in the ordinary courts, following standard legal procedures.

The involvement of the constitutional chamber in trade and economic policy is relatively new. One 2007 study of privatization in Costa Rica mentions only one instance in which a court proceeding delayed or influenced an aspect of Costa Rica's economic reform in the 1980s. In that specific case, workers of

---

[31] Oviedo Quesadao, "Principales efectos causados a un grupo de ex funcionarios del Banco Anglo Costarricense: (15 años despues del cierre)."

[32] "Nacion.com, San José, Costa Rica [Sucesos]."

[33] Raventos, "Construcciones y especulacciones en trno al 'descalacro financiero' del Banco Anglo Costarricense."

[34] Gomez, "Banana Industry Is the Principal Debtor of the Former Anglo Bank | Costa Rica News."

the Instituto Costarricense de Electricidad (ICE) won important concessions in a 1988 court arbitration that created a labor relations board within the ICE and provided guarantees of salary increases.[35] Beginning in 2007, however, the Supreme Court, and especially the constitutional chamber, have ruled several times on free trade agreements. The biggest of these agreements is the Central American Free Trade Agreement between the United States, Central America, and the Dominican Republic (CAFTA-DR), which was a major campaign issue in the 2006 presidential elections. Subsequently, the opposition parties petitioned the Sala IV to rule on the constitutionality of CATFA-DR. In a 5–2 decision, the magistrates ruled for its constitutionality.[36] Since that time, they have ruled several more times on various aspects of the implementation of the agreement.[37] Thus, the Sala IV and the judiciary have largely allowed the rise of neoliberalism and the decline of Costa Rica's social democracy even in the face of substantial political and social controversy.

Reelection in the Sala IV

Costa Rican democracy is frequently regarded as a Latin American success story, especially when compared with the other countries of Central America. As discussed at the beginning of this chapter, the roots of Costa Rica's democratic success inspire some amount of myth-making among Costa Ricans. Part of that success must be attributed to the development and maintenance of a liberal judicial regime. In 2000 and 2003, the Sala IV had to consider for itself the question of presidential reelection. While the constitution had prohibited immediate reelection since 1949, it had been amended in 1969 to ban reelection entirely. The 2000 challenge was rejected by a divided court. The majority focused its analysis on the question presented by the claimants: whether the Legislative Assembly's failure to adhere to a twenty-day period in their amendment procedure invalidated the 1969 constitutional amendment that prohibited reelection. The majority ruled that this relatively technical failing did not invalidate the amendment, noting that most amendments to the constitution could be overturned for this reason, creating significant legal and constitutional uncertainty. They then declined to reach the fundamental question about the validity of presidential reelection, deferring to the legislature as the body empowered to amend the constitution.[38]

---

[35] Chamberlain, *Privatization in Costa Rica: A Multi-Dimensional Analysis*, 88–89.
[36] Villalobos, "Sala IV Resuelve Que El TLC Es Constitucional."
[37] E.g., Mata, "Sala Constitucional Frena Último Proyecto Del TLC."
[38] Casos de Edgardo Picado Araya y Jorge Méndez Zamora (Sala Constitucional – Corte Suprema de Justicia de Costa Rica 2000).

The dissenters in 2000 penned three opinions alongside one separate opinion by Magistrado Piza Escalante that concurred in part and dissented in part. The dissents disputed the severity of the Assembly's error and the competency of the Sala to consider the constitutionality of a constitutional amendment. Magistrados Solano and Vargas especially emphasized the competency of the Sala to consider this kind of case, while Magistrada Calzada wrote separately but briefly to argue that the Assembly's error was not merely technical. The rights affected by the ban on reelection, she wrote, went to the heart of the fundamental order of the constitution, such that they could not be reformed through a partial reform or amendment process in the National Assembly. Rather, fundamental questions such as these could only be reformed through a general constitutional reform process, which must take place in a specially convened constitutional assembly, as laid out in Article 196 of the 1949 constitution and previously affirmed by the Sala IV in 1993. Magistrado Piza's separate opinion took a rather different approach, agreeing with Magistrada Calzada that the Sala IV indeed has the power to rule on constitutional revision processes on more than technical, procedural grounds, but then disagreeing with her that the rights at stake in this case touched on the fundamental constitutional order such that a general constitutional reform process would be necessary.[39]

The 2003 challenge to the same 1969 constitutional reform fared better. In a wide-ranging opinion by Magistrada Calzada, the Sala IV ruled that the National Assembly had used the wrong amendment procedure in 1969, thus invalidating the amendment. As she had argued in dissent in 2000, she again argued that the amendment affected the fundamental rights of potential candidates for reelection (i.e., to run for office) as well as the freedom of voters (i.e., to choose from a complete field of candidates) and thus it should be considered a general and not a partial reform of the constitution, requiring a constituent assembly. Joining her in the 2003 majority were the prior dissenters, Magistrados Vargas and Solano, along with the recently-appointed Magistrados Jinesta and Armijo. Of these, Varagas, Solano, and Jinesta wrote separately in concurrence, with Solano specifically detailing precedents to support the competency of the court to hear this case as well as the fundamental nature of the right in question. With the retirements of Magistrados Piza and Sancho, the two remaining members of the majority, Magistrados Mora and Arguedas, now found themselves in dissent. After condemning the second airing of the reelection issue, their dissenting opinion quotes extensively from the 2000 majority opinion.[40]

---

[39] Ibid.
[40] Caso de Edgardo Picado Araya y otros (Sala Constitucional - Corte Suprema de Justicia de Costa Rica 2003).

The direct consequence of this decision was that the still-popular former president and Nobel laureate Oscar Arias Sánchez ran successfully for reelection in 2006. As in the other Latin American countries that have established reelection, especially through the judiciary, the impact on democracy and the rights of ordinary citizens is highly debatable. The right of citizens to vote for the leader of their choice without limitations on the field of candidates seems to logically cohere to the idea of democracy. When the leader seeking reelection is one that dominates the political landscape, including, at least in appearance, the judiciary, one has to question the democratic legitimacy of the decision to allow reelection, as seen in the cases of Ríos Montt in Guatemala and Daniel Ortega in Nicaragua. However, there is no real indication that the Sala IV in 2003 was politically dominated, leaving only the general concerns about democratic legitimacy that are raised whenever a constitutional adjudicator invalidates a section of the constitution that it is adjudicating. The democratic conundrum is all the more troubling given that the Sala IV based their decision in part on the fundamental rights embedded in the American Convention on Human Rights (*Pacto de San Jose*), which was signed at the end of 1969 and not ratified by Costa Rica until 1970 – after the constitutional amendment in question.[41] In her majority opinion, Magistrada Calzada seems to have been responding to these very concerns with her lengthy discourses on presidential reelection in Costa Rican history, the nature of fundamental rights and the rule of law, and the basic rigidity of the 1949 constitution. Thus, while the reelection decision does not necessarily endanger democratic legitimacy in Costa Rica, it is viewed as creating a dent in the legitimacy of the Sala IV.[42]

High Profile Corruption

Costa Rica confronts a problem of official corruption somewhat less widespread than that in many of her neighbors, but nonetheless troubling. The Anglo-Costa Rican Bank scandal discussed above exemplifies the havoc that high-level corruption can wreak on a small country. Since that scandal, there have been a number of high-profile investigations, not least of which are the two involving ex-presidents, Rafael Ángel Calderon Fournier (1990–1994) and Miguel Ángel Rodríguez (1998–2002). Calderon was accused of

---

[41] Barker, *Constitutional Adjudication*; Organization of American States, ":: Multilateral Treaties > Department of International Law > OAS::"; Walker and Schorpp, "Judicial Politics of Presidential Reelection."

[42] Mata, "Congreso saca a magistrado de Sala IV con histórico voto."

accepting kickbacks for using his political influence to pressure his partisans in the National Assembly to award contracts relating to the Costa Rican public health system (the *Caja*) in 2001, although an investigation did not begin until 2004. Calderon maintained his innocence to the point of attempting to run for a new term as president for the February 2010 elections; he abandoned his candidacy when he was convicted in 2009 and sentenced to five years in prison. The criminal chamber of the Supreme Court confirmed Calderon's conviction in 2011, but reduced his sentence to three years and released him on parole, effective immediately. Several other individuals associated with the Caja also had their sentences reduced. As is typical of high level corruption cases, the original conviction was trumpeted in the foreign press, but the appeal was reported primarily locally. As a consequence, Costa Rica attains a reputation as a basically transparent and accountable legal system, while the actual malefactors see very little jail time.

During the same period, ex-president Rodriguez was also under investigation for "instigating corruption" in the partial privatization of the telecommunication services (ICE). Rodriguez also maintained his innocence, although he did so in a manner that brought more attention and even spectacle to the investigation and trial. The investigation was initiated while Rodriguez was serving a term as President of the Organization of American States, a position that he resigned in 2004 to return to Costa Rica to face the charges, in what he called "a battle for the rule of law," the subtitle of his 2006 memoir about the case.[43] Rodriguez fought the charges vigorously, including bringing both a habeas corpus petition and an amparo to the Sala IV. He was ultimately sentenced to five years in prison in April 2011, but remained defiant. Rodriguez challenged especially the use of testimony against him from a former ICE director who had already been charged with corruption himself. A number of other involved persons were convicted, including sentences of fifteen years or more. In December 2012, an appeals court agreed with Rodriguez regarding the validity of that testimony and reversed his conviction. Again, the original conviction received considerably more international press than did the exoneration.

While these investigations revealed the heights that corruption could reach even in democratic, governable Costa Rica, they also gave some people considerable cause to hope that the government finally might be making a real commitment to control corruption. Several lawyers indicated in 2010 that these cases were among the most important cases in Costa Rica's judicial history and that they were positive developments, although there were some differences

---

[43] Rodriguez, *Di la cara: Una batalla por el estado de derecho.*

about the perceived guilt or innocence of the defendants. Other positive signs have emerged as well: the judiciary's main public webpage as of this writing has begun to announce a confidential telephone number through which citizens can register complaints about corruption by judicial employees, including judges.

Environmental Activism in the Courts

Costa Rican NGOs typically do not get involved in the courts, but environmental NGOs are the exception. Environmentalist NGOs do initiate lawsuits, including amparos before the Sala IV to protect the environment. These cases include, notably, a 2009 case challenging the approval of the La Crucitas open-pit gold mine along the San Juan river that forms the border with Nicaragua. In an unusual move, the 2009 hearings for this case, which included considerable technical details, were open to the public.[44] The hearing also attracted public demonstrations in the plaza across from the Supreme Court. In April 2010, the constitutional chamber ruled in favor of the mining operation. However, the mining concession was shut down by the government alongside a legislative ban on open-pit mining, a move that was upheld by the administrative chamber (Sala I) of the Supreme Court in November 2011. The Canadian mining company that had won the mining concession threatened to sue in April 2013 over the loss of its concession, citing $92 million already invested and $1 billion in estimated lost profits.[45] In January 2015, a former minister of energy and the environment, Roberto Dobles Mora, was sentenced to three years for conflict of interest in regards to his certification of the mine as being in the public interest in 2008.[46] This case is significant both for its unusually complex legal history and for it involving mineral extraction, one of the most controversial industries in the region.

It makes sense that environmentalist NGOs would be the exception to the trend of low NGO involvement in the courts. Environmental harms are usually collective harms, the protection of which entails collective action problems in getting individuals to take on the associated costs. Potential doctrinal and procedural problems would also be involved with an individualized, case-by-case approach. A case involving a single individual would necessarily

---

[44] Many cases are resolved entirely in writing, without the opportunity for an oral hearing that could be attended by the public.

[45] "Canadian Gold Company Threatens Costa Rica with $1bn Lawsuit | MINING.com"; "Court Shuts down Crucitas Gold Mine Citing Environmental Harm | AIDA."

[46] Arguedas C. and Miranda, "Exministro Roberto Dobles condenado por firmar decreto minero ilegal"; Láscarez S., "Proyecto Crucitas tuvo un viacrucis de 10 años."

focus on the harm (economic or otherwise) to that individual from the possible environmental damage. An environmentalist NGO, by contrast, can bring a case based on the collective harms to the organization's membership as a whole – or even to the nation as a whole – and is more likely to have the financial and human resources to undertake the research necessary to prove those actual or potential harms.

In environmental cases, then, the easy accessibility of the constitutional process for individual litigants does not provide a sufficient mechanism to protect the interests at stake. Where collective interests are at stake, the rise of legally activist NGOs is thus functional. Furthermore, deeply-rooted ideologies as well as the economic interests of the eco-tourism industry provide support for these NGOs. Why, then, are other potentially collective interests not able to overcome collective action problems in forming a collectivist force? One answer lies in the large state that became a defining element of Costa Rican society in the second half of the twentieth century; the state set out to protect individuals in a variety of ways and so individuals turned to the state when they needed protection. Another possible answer lies in the typically individualistic nature of most legal proceedings, in which there is typically a single victim and a single perpetrator.

These conflicts highlight the extent to which the liberal judicial regime of Costa Rica has risen in political prominence. The judiciary became the moral force in dismantling the failings of the government and the private sector in the BAC case. Despite the slow pace of resolving that controversy, the legitimacy of the judiciary may have improved as a result. Similarly, the prosecutions of the ex-presidents from corruption may have also helped boost the stature of the judiciary. Where the constitutional chamber itself resolved a significant conflict, the judiciary's legitimacy may have actually taken a hit, as in the approval of the CAFTA-DR trade agreement or the approval of presidential reelection. The more recent *La Crucitas* mine controversy has certainly cast a shadow on the various presidential administrations that were involved in promoting the development over more than a decade, but it is less clear how it affects public opinion concerning the judiciary in general or the Supreme Court in particular. The imprisonment of an appointed politician over the mining controversy certainly implies that the Supreme Court was correct in shutting down the mine. If we look at these controversies collectively, a pattern emerges: increasingly forceful ordinary courts are viewed differently by politicians than is the hyperactive constitutional chamber. Elected politicians object to the loss of their policy making (and perhaps corrupt) prerogatives less when controversies are framed as criminal or procedural than they do when the controversies are framed as constitutional. Although the liberal constitutional regime appears to be ascendant, there remain politicians who oppose it.

CONTEMPORARY INFLUENCES IN A DECAYING PARTISAN ENVIRONMENT

Although Costa Rica enjoys a clearly liberal judicial regime in which conflicts are typically handled through legal and constitutional processes and judges are not submitted to widespread threats of violence or enticements to corruption, a variety of influences may nonetheless affect judicial decision-making. Recall that some kinds of influences may be compatible with a liberal judicial regime – and, at manageable levels, may be desirable. Political independence and societal autonomy can go too far, at least in theory harming judicial accountability; this concern drives much of the criticism of "judicial activism" and "politicization" of the courts around the world. This concern leads some to argue for the need to focus on judicial accountability, although accountability measures such as hierarchical control, press monitoring, and other influences may make some judges feel that their societal autonomy or political independence is being infringed.

Hierarchical Control

The issue of hierarchical control is one that makes many trial-level judges chafe. Several judges filed an amparo in 2010 with the constitutional chamber, complaining against a higher-level court that had invalidated their rulings.[47] The constitutional chamber ruled against the amparo. In a politically-charged legal climate such as Costa Rica, it appears that even jurisdictional disputes become constitutional controversies. Even if the constitutional magistrates may be trying to resist this trend, it is clear that the demand for constitutional adjudication is growing and that the legal space occupied by the constitution is likely to keep expanding.

One magistrate dismissed these concerns about hierarchical control, saying:

> Here we have a culture very rooted in the principle of a judge's independence, which is constitutionally guaranteed, yes? And what's more, the judges have their own organization that will back up any act of independence. In fact, the president of the supreme court says that I cannot say if a judge is good or bad. Meanwhile, the disciplinary system does not apply when the decision belongs to the judge [for example, regarding a piece of evidence in a case].

---

[47] Recurso de Amparo, on file with the author.

Except the complaint is received if it's something very obvious. But the rule is that the secretary respects it [the judge's decision].[48] (CR2009–19)

She went on to argue that the judicial career itself is the main way that the judicial hierarchy protects judges, because their jobs are not subject to the whims of changes in political parties through elections. As discussed above, Costa Rican judges do have a significant number of legal and institutional protections. These protections are especially profound when compared with the precarious position of many other Central American judges.

The issue of hierarchical control, as with many of the issues concerning judicial autonomy in Costa Rica, raises questions of how much autonomy is desirable in a liberal judicial regime. Certainly a minimal level is required: lower-court judges should not have all of their decisions mandated by their superiors. However, the rule of law is also not served by having lower-court judges rule arbitrarily without legal discipline. The normal route for ensuring this legal discipline is the appellate process, where some fraction of departures from the law are reversed by a higher court, in an essentially "police patrol" type of oversight. The judicial disciplinary process represents a more "fire alarm" type of oversight, which is important if not over-used.[49] When the disciplinary process begins to be used to harass judges, as it is in Guatemala (see Chapter 5), the infringement on judicial autonomy becomes problematic. Hierarchical control is heightened further when the disciplinary process is carried out by the highest court, as it is in both Guatemala and Costa Rica. Such an arrangement may allow for too much influence by a handful of supreme court magistrates, leading many to prefer the use of an independent judicial council. Such differences, in this author's view, represent reasonable variation within the liberal judicial regime type; individual polities will have to determine for themselves how much power they want to vest in the Supreme Court.

In addition to hierarchical control is the issue of the proper scope of internal independence or autonomy. One magistrate argued strongly against the extension of judicial autonomy into procedural or administrative questions:

---

[48] Original: Aquí tenemos una cultura muy arraigada del principio de la independencia del juez, que tiene garantía constitucional, ¿verdad? Y además los jueces tiene su propio agrupación que respaldaría cualquier acto de la independencia. De hecho, el presidente de la corte suprema . . . dice, yo no puedo decir si cualquier juez está bien o está mal. Tanto que el régimen disciplinario no se aplica cuando es una decisión del juez [por ejemplo, sobre una prueba en un juicio]. Salvo hay recepción si es algo evidente . . . pero la regla es el secretario se respeta.

[49] McCubbins and Schwartz, "Congressional Oversight Overlooked: Police Patrols versus Fire Alarms."

It appears to me that judicial independence has to do exclusively with the concrete case. I believe that judicial independence is the judge in the moment
of making a decision about an issue that has been submitted for his consideration. Then, that is where the judicial independence exists. I believe that
judicial independence should not extend to administrative management,
neither should it extend to procedures, neither should it extend to the introduction of new technologies. That is, judges should not have the possibility
of rejecting innovation.

   Possibly we could be in better conditions in respect to the user, resolving
[cases] more rapidly and in greater quantity if we had this situation clearer
and didn't obtain this shield that judicial independence, judicial autonomy,
the liberty of the judge also implies the liberty to do what he pleases in
procedures.[50] (CR2009–10)

This statement reflects a perception of ordinary trial-level or appellate judges
as being somewhat lazy, taking on the mantel of judicial independence only
to avoid modernization and "innovation" that might require them to change
their work habits. This statement thus implicates all of the tensions that exist
between the different levels of the judicial hierarchy. For the lower-court
judges that brought an amparo in 2010 in rejection of certain acts of appellate
oversight, this tension is no doubt viewed as a very negative conflict. That
does not necessarily mean that such tension is necessarily negative for the
institution as a whole, nor for democracy more generally. The different levels
of a judiciary are intended to check each other by viewing cases through
somewhat different lenses, with trial courts investigating facts in detail and
appellate courts focusing instead on the uniform, correct application of the
law to what are generally taken (at that stage) to be established facts. Judges in
different parts of the judiciary necessarily, as a function of their positions, have
different interests that can be in tension. Just as the media in the United States
complains about a defendant "getting off on a technicality," Costa Ricans may
chafe at the reality that their judiciary experiences internal conflicts in order

---

[50] Original: Me parece que la independencia judicial sí tiene que ser exclusivamente sobre el
    case concreto... Creo que la independencia judicial es el juez en el momento en que ya
    va a tomar la decisión del asunto que le sometieron a consideración de él. Entonces, allí es
    donde existe la independencia judicial. Creo que la independencia judicial no se debería
    extender a las gestiones administrativas, no se debería extender tampoco al proceso, no se
    debería extender tampoco a la introducción de nuevas tecnologías. Es decir los jueces no
    deberían tener la posibilidad de rechazar la innovación...
       Posiblemente, nosotros podríamos estar en mejores condiciones respeto al usuario,
    resolviendo más rápido y en más cantidad si nosotros tuviéramos más claro esta situación
    y no obtuviera ese escudo de que la independencia judicial, que la autonomía judicial, que la
    libertad del juez también implica libertad de hacerlo a que a la gana en el proceso.

to get at correct justice. It is important to understand, though, that a uniform judiciary without such tensions is a hallmark of a homogenized government control judicial regime rather than a liberal system.

Media Influence on the Courts

Another issue that concerned many within the Costa Rican judiciary is the notion of the "*juicio mediatico*" or the case that is tried in the press. More than one magistrate expressed the concern that the Costa Rican press is quick to try and convict suspects in the court of public opinion. When judges then decide to free these suspects because of lack of evidence, the press howls and many people grumble. Supreme Court Magistrate Annabelle de León expressed the following concern:

> I do believe that Costa Rica has passed the original concept of independence, because it is almost impossible that a politician would impose on a judge what he could do, or that a magistrate or a superior judge would do that. But I do believe that we need to pay attention to judgment by law, media judgment, or judgment by an irresponsible press. I do believe that the press has an important role to play in the education of the citizens, but they also play at public condemnation and monitoring, so we must do this so that it does not affect the independence of the judge.[51]

However, not everyone agrees with her assessment. The press plays an important role in a democratic society. Part of that role includes monitoring the justice system and social problems such as crime. Supreme Court Magistrate José Guillermo Ruiz disagreed strongly with his colleagues about the potential for the press to damage judicial independence:

> I believe that the press is important. The press is powerful. And the press has an influence that needs to be made positive. We have to understand, for example, here the beginning was when they began publicizing the whole criminal problem. Then some magistrates said that we have to have a different consideration regarding what really happened and what the press publicized. I did not agree. I thought what the press published was real. The criminal

---

[51] Original: Yo sí creo que Costa Rica tiene superado el origen del concepto de independencia, porque es casi imposible que un político [imponer] a un juez que haga o un magistrado o que un juez superior lo haga, pero sí creo que tiene que prestar atención al juicio por la ley, al juicio mediatico, al juicio por la prensa irresponsable... entonces sí creo que en estos momentos la prensa juega un papel muy importante de la formación de la ciudadanía. Pero también juega para un condena pública a una observatoria... entonces hacemos para no afecta esta independencia del juez.

phenomenon grew, got bigger, and got powerful, it is big . . . I believe that we have to listen to what the press says.[52]

From my observation, the media in Costa Rica certainly do sensationalize crime, but not much more than the media in most countries. As Magistrado Ruiz suggests, there are many good reasons to allow and even encourage the press to actively report on crime, including questioning the decisions and actions of the police and the judicial branch. If the forensic office cannot reliably produce viable evidence in criminal cases, for example, that problem needs to be brought to light and remedied. However, Magistrada de León also makes a good point, as did several judges, that it is a problem when a defendant is tried in the press long before the courts have a chance to resolve the case. The primary consequence of this problem, though, is that the reputation of the judiciary, or at least the relevant judge or judges, is harmed. Because Costa Rica does not use public juries as are known in the United States, the risk of actual contamination of a trial is quite low. The damage to the defendant's reputation, should he be innocent of the charges, may itself prove to be an additional problem.

The Costa Rican judiciary, as well as many of the lawyers who work with it, express significant concerns over the reputation of the judicial system and public perceptions of the constitutional regime. In fact, Costa Rica enjoys public support for its judiciary at fairly high levels compared with other countries and with other institutions in Costa Rica, as demonstrated in figure 3.2. Interestingly, and of some concern to the authors of one 2009 survey, many Costa Ricans indicate that they do not believe that the law should be followed all of the time and that fear of getting caught is one of the primary motivations for compliance.[53] How low levels of latent support for the law affects the judiciary is not immediately clear. Hand-wringing over the willingness of Latin Americans to disregard the law has persisted since reliable surveys have been available. It is logical that this disregard for the law would allow people to accept the presence of or even participate in various forms of corruption. It is more of a leap, however, to generalize that to all sectors of the government and the population.

---

[52] Original: Yo creo que la prensa es muy importante. La prensa es poderosa. Y la prensa tiene una influencia que necesaria se tiene que ser positivizado. Nosotros tenemos que entender, por ejemplo, aquí al principio cuando se empezó a publicitar todo el problema criminal. Entonces algunos magistrados decían que habían que tener una consideración diferente a respeto a lo que realmente sucedía y lo que publicaba la prensa. No estaba de acuerdo. Yo creía que lo que publicaba la prensa era real. Sí el fenómeno criminal se incrementó, se potenció, es grande . . . Creo que lo que dice la prensa tiene que ser escuchado por nosotros.

[53] Cordero et al., *Cultura de la constitución en Costa Rica.*

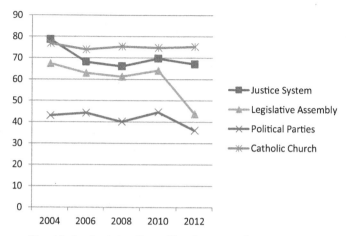

FIGURE 3.2 Trust in Institutions, Costa Rica (2004–2012).
Source: The AmericasBarometer by the Latin American Public Opinion Project
(LAPOP), www.LapopSurveys.org.

The Impact of Criminal Influence on the Judiciary

One pending question in Costa Rica is the effect that rising organized crime
will have. When asked, nearly every judge and magistrate expressed concern
about it and fear of what is to come if the problem gets worse. Magistrate Ruiz
recalled that the problem is not entirely new:

> When I was a criminal judge in Guanacaste [near the Nicaraguan border],
> until 1997. It fell to me to preside over arguments and trials of Colombian
> narcotraffickers. In two opportunities, we did receive threats, but they were
> not effective – some telephone call that says "be careful"... And they have
> to put a policeman at the entrance to the house and nothing else happens.
> There is more worry now... it's that some prosecutors received threats and
> the judicial branch's response really was not good, was not effective.[54]

One lawyer, while disclaiming personal knowledge of intimidation, did suggest that there are entry points for petty corruption such as losing a case file
or a crucial piece of evidence in a narcotrafficking case. He observed, "The

---

[54] Original: Cuando yo era juez penal en la zona de Guanacaste, hasta 1997, me tocó a mí
presidir debates, juicios en donde veían narcotraficantes de Colombia – porque en esa época,
eran Colombianos; ahora son Mexicanos. En dos oportunidades sí recibimos amenazas pero
nunca fueron efectivas – alguna llamada por teléfono que dice "cuídense"... Y que le poner
una policía en la entrada de la casa y nada más. Hay más preocupación ahora... es de unos
fiscales recibieron amenazas y realmente la respuesta del poder judicial no ha sido bueno, no
ha sido eficaz tampoco.

problem is also that the system is designed in a very innocent manner, very much for another era,"[55] continuing to detail a number of proposed and incipient reforms intended to aid in the prosecution of organized crime. These measures include creating a magnetic tracking system for judicial case files. Bunck and Fowler further identify witness protection as an important new innovation, although they also report that it has been underfunded.[56] They go on to report on procedural problems that hamper efforts to investigate and prosecute organized crime, including long-term questions about the admissibility of evidence gained from wiretapping and a prohibition on illegal activity by police officers, which inhibits sting operations. Bunck and Fowler's analysis suggests that the "innocence" of the Costa Rican system extends well beyond prosecution to include limited inspection and "*amigoismo*," a way of operating through networks of friends who share high levels of interpersonal trust. The consequences of this cultural "innocence" include ample avenues for drugs to pass through the country undetected. However, the drug trade in Costa Rica has also remained relatively peaceful, compared with El Salvador, Guatemala, or Honduras.

Indeed, the Costa Rican judiciary has largely been able to operate without significant, widespread attacks by organized crime and drug trafficking. Costa Rican attorneys interviewed in 2009 generally scoffed at questions relating to the idea of intimidation of judges. Judges in San Jose similarly dismissed such concerns. One lawyer suggested that to attack judges would be stupid on the part of criminals because a new judge could always be assigned to the case, seemingly *ad infinitum*. However, some concern was expressed regarding the prosecutors, who are the targets of threats and are far more likely to request personal protection than are judges. Furthermore, the situation of witnesses who are threatened, refuse to testify, or are killed, poses a much more serious problem for efforts to control organized crime. Nonetheless, the overall picture is that of a judiciary operating largely isolated from threats from organized criminals. While there are almost certainly some judges or other justice sector officials who succumb to corruption in the form of bribes, this phenomenon appears to be far from the norm in the Costa Rican judiciary.

However, judges outside of San José are more vulnerable. One judge in Puerto Limón, where the drug trade is a more prevalent problem,[57] reported

[55] Original: También el problema es que el sistema está diseñada de manera muy inocente, muy para otra épica.

[56] Bunck and Fowler, *Bribes, Bullets, and Intimidation*: Drug Trafficking and the Law in Central America.

[57] The drug violence in Limón is somewhat legendary. One lawyer told a story of criminal defendants "burning down" the tribunals of Limón. Independent confirmation of this story could not be found as of this writing.

that she had been kidnapped on one occasion along with several other people. On that occasion, the kidnapper stole the gun from the guard at the entrance to the court and held it to her head. However, she was able to escape when a gunfight broke out several hundred meters from the courthouse. She also indicated that she had been further threatened. When she called the judicial security service in San José, they never provided her with any security and never called her back. She indicated that she felt that her job was dangerous and that the judiciary was not doing enough to protect her. Her experience highlights the problem with uneven distribution of judicial security and judicial autonomy. Judges in San José may in fact be well-protected with extensive security at the entrances to their office buildings and access to police bodyguards when threatened, but this judge's experience suggests that such measures may not be available in all parts of the country. Somewhat more impressionistically, the security at the Limón tribunal was significantly less than that at the main tribunals in San José, despite the proportionally greater number of drug and gang related cases in Limón.

Nonetheless, she also indicated that she had never received any pressure from a politician, never a phone call from a politician nor from an administrative superior to tell her how to rule on a specific case. She did relate a story from some twenty years prior in which a magistrate of the Supreme Court had called a court functionary to interject about a case. However, she also indicated that she knew this story primarily from news accounts at the time and could not vouch for its accuracy. She went on to indicate that she felt that judges are not always well-respected in Costa Rica because, as the face of the judiciary, they are subject to significant criticisms. However, she also indicated that judges in violent Limón are well-respected; they are known to the public and are frequently greeted with terms of respect as they walk through the streets. Thus, although she had been targeted for violence and did not always feel respected, it did not appear that she felt that her autonomy as a judge was at risk, in part because of the support she received from her local community, including the local police.

Non-Governmental Organizations Nearly Absent from the Courts

Costa Rican magistrates generally felt that NGOs are a helpful presence and may contribute to a better administration of justice. One magistrate highlighted the ability of NGOs to funnel public concerns before the Supreme Court (as well as other governmental powers). However, there are in fact very few Costa Rican NGOs that orient themselves toward the justice system per se. Wilson has highlighted the fact that the extensive "rights revolution" in Costa Rica since 1989 has happened largely without the assistance of a legal support network, which has previously been identified by Epp as an essential contributor to successful rights-claiming.[58] The lack of an extensive legally-oriented NGO network in Costa Rica may reflect the lack of a need for one: as was described above, it is quite easy for an individual to submit a claim for rights protection to the court. An individual claim before the constitutional chamber is the easiest kind of action to file – famously available to all comers twenty-four hours a day, 365 days a year, with no need for a lawyer. Magistrates and employees of the Supreme Court were generally proud of this accessibility, in some instances comparing themselves favorably to the rest of Central America, where tremendous procedural hurdles often impede ordinary litigants (CR2009–08).

The respect with which most judges and magistrates view NGOs may be the result of their very absence. Without highly contentious politics between the courts and the NGOs, judges and magistrates are less likely to develop resentments toward and concerns about NGOs. Not one of the judges or magistrates with whom I spoke indicated that they had dealt with a NGO in a legal process. Similarly, all indicated the absence of NGOs that try to work with the justice system, either to represent individuals or to try to strengthen the justice system. Instead, some judges and magistrates had worked with NGOs through conferences and planning committees around issues such as accessibility of the courts to disadvantaged groups such as the physically handicapped or members of Costa Rica's indigenous communities. The experience of one judge is typical:

> Well, here we have never received any NGOs. I have had contact with NGOs because I have participated a lot in conferences, workshops, and the like on feminism, on protections of the rights of women and the like, [there were] some NGOs then . . . but that for me was as an individual and was when I lived in San José . . . I am here since 10 years ago, with nothing. I don't know if here [in my region] any NGOs operate in reality. I imagine that I would know and that I would find out about NGOs here, but I have never seen them intervene in anything, neither in issues of domestic violence, violence against women, nothing, really.[59] (CR2009–18)

---

[58] Wilson, "Changing Dynamics: The Political Impact of Costa Rica's Constitutional Court"; Wilson, "Claiming Constitutional Rights through a Constitutional Court: The Example of Gays in Costa Rica"; Epp, *The Rights Revolution*.

[59] Original: Bueno aquí nosotros nunca hemos recibido a ninguna ONG. Yo he tenido contacto con ONGS porque he participado mucho en conferencias, en talleres y demás de feminismo, de protección a los derechos de las mujeres y demás, entonces algunas ONGS . . . pero eso yo en forma particular y cuando vivía en San José . . . ya desde hace 10 años que estoy aquí con ninguna, yo no sé si aquí [en mi región] opera alguna ONG en realidad, imagínese que

This judge's experience reveals both the divorce between NGOs and the judiciary and the separation between the capitol and the countryside. Although there are certainly active NGOs in Costa Rica, especially around environmental issues, as discussed above, they tend not to interact with the courts – even when they may routinely engage with elected politicians. One routinely sees one or another association protesting in front of the congress, but it is less common for a protest to form in front of the Supreme Court just a few blocks away (and with a more welcoming plaza). That NGOs typically do not engage with the courts in Costa Rica is puzzling when one considers that the Sala IV is indeed one of the most active and activist courts in the region and perhaps the world and is composed of magistrates who voice sympathies with many of the political causes of interest to many of the NGOs.

I suggest two related explanations: the professional distance of the magistrates from political activity and the easy accessibility of constitutional rights-claiming. While magistrates may engage with NGOs openly, it is typically to improve the overall professional functioning of the judiciary, as with the example of the accessibility improvements. In general, the magistrates are relatively removed from the rest of society: their offices are on the upper levels of the supreme court building, accessible only past a security guard, and they enjoy the privilege of having drivers. Although they are appointed with the support of politicians and some have held partisan positions in the past, they generally try to avoid at least the appearance of partisanship or political preferences; this stance provides a shading effect over the court. Of course, as one lawyer (CR2009–02) indicated, Costa Rica is a small country and there are always contacts between lawyers and judges, especially in rural areas, although there are strict rules against discussing cases in such social interactions. Similarly, magistrates are members of the social and political elite in Costa Rica and they surely have social interactions as well. The other side of this professional distance is that there is no need to mediate between most constitutional litigants and the constitutional magistrates; all that a claimant needs to do is make a claim in writing – any writing will do – and deliver it to the court. The wheels of justice are set in motion quite easily and at very little cost to the individual. One is hard-pressed to identify an attorney even in San José who works in amparo practice. What incentive is there then to create NGOs that would engage with the judiciary in particular?

The very different experiences of the judge quoted above between when she lived in San José as a young woman and the decade since she moved to

ni siquiera sé y que yo sepa aquí con nosotros ONGS nunca he visto intervenir en nada, ni siquiera en los asuntos de violencia doméstica, violencia contra la mujer, nada realmente.

her current post in a more rural area reveal some of the weaknesses created by the lack of a legal support system for litigants. Not all legal rights go to the Sala IV, as much as it may at times appear that they do. For the women who appear in her courtroom as victims of domestic violence or other crimes, there are not local NGOs that might protect them or help to guide them through the legal process against their abusers, including possibly a divorce proceeding, a criminal proceeding, as well as some other kinds of civil proceedings governing affected property rights. Similarly, there are few organizations for victims of crime (or their families) in general and they are also concentrated in San José and not in the zones along the Atlantic Coast or the Panamanian border where drug trafficking crime is at the most severe. Such organizations can help to equalize the situations of disadvantaged victims. Costa Rica does offer a variety of public services to victims (as well as defendants), but the success of the state has perhaps too thoroughly discouraged NGOs.

CONCLUSIONS

The statistics regarding the consistently large number of actions brought to Costa Rica's constitutional chamber reveal both a population that is active in voicing their rights and a court that is frequently responsive to those rights. Indeed, the Supreme Court directs a number of activities from its offices that are intended to raise the profile of the court and the rights it protects. Many schools bring field trips to tour the Supreme Court, whose main lobby is open and welcoming to the public. Tales of the Supreme Court's accessibility circulate widely among lawyers; one judicial official (CR2009–08) working in the constitutional chamber reported that someone is available twenty-four hours per day, 365 days a year to receive complaints, primarily amparos, from citizens. Citizens do reportedly appear at the Supreme Court even on Christmas Day when they have a legal crisis. However, the large number of cases also corresponds to survey data indicating that many Costa Ricans don't feel that most of their compatriots obey the law and the constitution.[60]

It appears, thus, that Costa Ricans are actually quite aware of their rights and are willing to go to court to have them protected – and that they often are successful in finding that protection. Anecdotally, lawyers primarily tell stories of amparos involving the poorest and most vulnerable citizens being brought under the sheltering wing of the constitutional chamber. The nature of the amparo process in Costa Rica makes such stories possible; a child can write a letter to the court to inquire as to why he was taken from his mother by state

[60] Cordero et al., *Cultura de la constitución en Costa Rica.*

authorities and they can act on it without need for the child to hire a lawyer who would write his complaint in the proper format. Similarly, sweeping changes to government policy have been brought as well, such as the order that the social security system provide medicine to HIV/AIDS patients.[61] While the constitutional chamber might be perceived as the protector of the poor and vulnerable (an image they themselves try to cultivate), it is nonetheless also at times the protector of the rich and powerful. They are the court that essentially handed Oscar Arias a second presidency and that refused to close the open-pit La Crucitas mine, citing constitutionally guaranteed individual rights in both cases. The creation of the constitutional chamber created a major new political and social opportunity – and it has been widely taken advantage of.

Costa Rica has been presented here as an example of a liberal judicial regime, a category that it represents quite well. In general, the independence of judges is widely respected by elected and unelected politicians. From an official perspective, mechanisms are in place to protect the autonomy of judges from societal actors as well. There are official accountability measures that are highly bureaucratic and thus do not usually target judges unfairly – even though individual judges may chafe at these controls. While security is provided to judges at their request, there is some evidence that such protection is quite weak in the more distant and sometimes more dangerous zones outside of San Jose. The drug trade and organized crime are certainly present, but have been controlled to a much more significant degree that in most of Costa Rica's neighbors. What's more, the Costa Rican judiciary has influenced many of the most significant issues of recent years, including economic governance, human rights, presidential reelection, and corruption.

Cost Rica provides an excellent example of a judiciary that has perpetuated its power through specific strategies to create a popular base of support and legitimation through masterfully controlling framing and generating positive feedback. In the terms used in Chapter 2, the Sala IV, while perhaps intended as a layered institution that could be controlled through power reproduction, instead converted itself into a central player in national politics. The centrality of the Sala IV and the constitutional currency in Costa Rica appears to be, at least in part, an unintended consequence of the 1989 constitutional reform, made possible largely by the decline of the traditional political parties. It is difficult to imagine that even a reformed party system could significantly reign in the powerful Sala IV because of their reservoir of popular support and because of the difficulty of removing magistrates. A complete replacement

---

[61] Wilson, "Claiming Constitutional Rights through a Constitutional Court: The Example of Gays in Costa Rica."

of the Sala IV would require sustained effort over eight years – a period that would overlap at least two iterations of the Legislative Assembly, a body whose members cannot be reelected. Thus, while a message was sent in 2012, the threat that it contained was necessarily limited.

Costa Rica, as a liberal judicial regime, resembles from a legal standpoint the most developed judicial systems in the world. This is not to say that all liberal judicial regimes act and look the same. There is a considerable amount of variation within this regime type; many decisions need to be made by polities through democratic processes. A liberal system may belong to the common law tradition or the civil law tradition, may subscribe to a system of diffuse or centralized judicial review, and so on. Even the exact permutations of independence and autonomy experienced in these countries may vary. Contrast the extreme independence found in life tenure for federal judges in the United States with the eight-year renewable terms found in Costa Rica. Even with the need for a supermajority to deny renewal, a constitutional magistrate was rejected (if ineffectively) in 2012 largely for political reasons. However, one could also contrast the bureaucratic judicial career path in Costa Rica for lower court judges with the judicial elections found in many U.S. states, where a generally competent state court judge could be replaced at election time because of an unpopular decision, even if it was the legally correct decision. Judges, including constitutional adjudicators, must be aware of popular opinion and political winds in every system; liberal judicial regimes persist as long as those influences are minimized.

Liberal judicial regimes provide a number of benefits to a state. They appear to help economic development, human rights, and the functioning of democracy and constitutionalism. At the most fundamental level, however, a liberal judicial regime allows a state to function as a state and especially a democratic state. A transparent, independent, autonomous judiciary can enforce the laws and give them life beyond the moment of enactment. It is especially important in a democracy that this function be carried out impartially, without influence from politicians or interference from the rich, powerful, or criminal. A liberal judicial regime is buffeted by its independence and autonomy to be able to do just that, but also should be able to be held to account in a routinized manner. Costa Rica exemplifies the best of these conditions.

A highly self-aware liberal judicial regime such as Costa Rica's does not come without costs. The ease with which citizens can have their rights protected by the constitutional chamber also creates avenues for citizens to interfere with governmental or economic development plans, for better and worse. The multi-layered, specialized judicial hierarchy may also cause inefficiencies when claimants may have to go (or choose to go) to multiple different parts of the judiciary to find the resolution they desire. As the case of the La Crucitas mine demonstrates, this ability to litigate essentially the same issues in front of multiple courts – even multiple chambers of the Supreme Court – allows for an extreme form of forum-shopping and may produce contradictory decisions and legal confusion. Judges in Costa Rica are so empowered that some chafe at the hierarchical control imposed by the appellate system and may resist efforts to modernize judicial processes. This empowerment no doubt creates headaches within the judiciary, but is unlikely to cause grave harm outside of it. There are costs to any legal or institutional arrangement; the costs associated with Costa Rica's liberal judicial regime must be weighed against the benefits.

4

Government Control Regimes in Central America versus the Rule of Law

The government control judicial regime type is defined by the lack of both judicial independence and judicial autonomy. Government control regimes have a natural affinity with authoritarian political regimes, but there can be a great deal of variation in how one or another judicial regime operates. There may be some level of formal independence while informal practice, such as calling a judge to tell her how to rule ("telephone justice"), guarantees a tightly-controlled judiciary. There also may be some amount of individual liberty for judges than can be used up to a point beyond which a judge finds herself suddenly yearning for the greener pastures of retirement. This second variation is common in authoritarian governments who want to maintain a veneer of constitutionalism or even democracy and has been seen notably in Pakistan and Egypt in the late twentieth and early twenty-first centuries. Another possibility lies in maintaining an apparently independent judiciary that is trained in such a way that it would not consider resisting the authoritarian government either because judges believe in a passive role for the judiciary or actually support the political regime. Pinochet's Chile seems to fit this latter category, as described by Hilbink.[1] The four authoritarian countries considered here also present considerable variation, but all represent government control regimes during the 1980s.

This chapter examines the government control regimes of the 1980s in Guatemala, Honduras, El Salvador, and Nicaragua through the transitions to democracy and the reductions in military prerogatives that occurred in the 1990s. While all four of these countries experienced government control judicial regimes, the differences between them helped to set the patterns that would affect the democratic periods that followed. In all of these countries, international donors helped to push justice sector reform programs that were

---

[1] Hilbink, *Judges Beyond Politics in Democracy and Dictatorship*.

intended to deepen democracy and build the rule of law. The varied forms of acceptance of, resistance to, and cooptation of these reforms drove the development of the judicial regimes that followed. Notably, the pact-making by the major parties in Honduras and Nicaragua led to partisan judicial regimes in those countries. The resistance to purging the justice sector in Guatemala left weak institutions that could not effectively combat growing criminality and that often contributed to that criminality themselves, producing a clandestine control judicial regime there. In El Salvador, judicial reforms met with some early successes, but the influence of the two major parties soon became dominant and the result was a partisan judicial regime, albeit one that overlapped with elements of clandestine control as well. This chapter highlights the development of the "currencies" of conflict resolution that would come to drive judicial politics in these countries by the late 1990s as they transition from official violence to partisan loyalty and unofficial violence.

HISTORICAL OVERVIEW

In the 1970s and 1980s, Guatemala, Honduras, El Salvador, and Nicaragua all suffered under authoritarian, usually military-dominated, regimes. These regimes included a great deal of repression, including in most cases torture, imprisonment, forced disappearance, and extra-judicial killing. At the extreme, there were full-scale massacres of entire villages. Even ordinary citizens found their civil rights violated, including their right to free association and assembly, free speech, free press, and to vote. While there were significant differences in ideology between the military regimes of Honduras, El Salvador, and Guatemala, and the 1980s Sandinista regime in Nicaragua, there are many similarities in how all four governments handled issues of human rights and the rule of law. I classify all four countries in the 1970s and 1980s as "Government Control" judicial regimes because all at various times attempted to maintain functioning courts that could enforce the law without actually limiting the actions the governments could take. However, these courts had neither strong judicial political independence nor judicial societal autonomy and the currency that ultimately decided major conflicts was official violence.

Guatemala's military regimes were the most deadly in Central America, with 200,000 killed or "disappeared." The civil war, which began in 1960, was a product of the Cold War. The basic conflict at the core of the civil war was between peasants, guerillas, and communists on the one hand and elites, the military, and capitalists on the other. As happened in many Cold War conflicts, suspected "subversives" were subjected to extreme violations of their human rights, even when no evidence could be produced to prove that they were a danger to the state. The most brutal period of repression happened between 1979 and 1983, when over half of the deaths and disappearances took place. This period also included a number of measures to try to control the indigenous peasants and force them to support the government: many rural men were forced to join armed Self-Defense Patrols under the supervision of the military, some were forcibly conscripted into the military itself, whole villages were made to move to far-flung parts of the country where they could be better controlled, and an unknown number of massacres took place in the highlands. Some one million Guatemalans were displaced in this period as well.[2]

In Guatemala the process of democratization and the process of peace-building are inextricably linked. Indeed, many Guatemalans will cite the end of the war as being 1985 (the date of the democratic constitution), while others will date democratization from the adoption of the peace accords in 1996. The transition to democracy under General Mejia Victores in 1983–1985 was primarily formal. The military retained most of its prerogatives and the counterinsurgency campaign continued. Jonas and Walker argued that the transition to democracy was allowable only because the brutality of the period 1979–1983 was so successful in reducing the power of the guerillas.[3] Nonetheless, the change to a deeply consolidated democracy is a slow process. Since the peace accords, indigenous citizens of Guatemala have become increasingly assertive of their identities and their rights. Nonetheless, electoral violence continues in the rural areas, corruption is endemic, and citizen security is quite weak. As official violence ceased to control political life, unofficial violence became increasingly dominant.

El Salvador had no significant history of democratic governance prior to the 1980s, being ruled instead by a series of military dictators and military-civilian juntas. A coup in 1979, executed largely in response to increasing leftist militant violence, signaled the beginning of a new kind of regime. Beginning in 1982 and strengthened by a new constitution in 1983, elected civilian presidents would head the government alongside a military that had no real checks on its power. Death squads were in routine use against suspected supporters of the Farabundo Martí National Liberation Front (FMLN). In addition, the use of torture was widespread. Elections, while having some consequence,

---

[2] Comisión para el Esclarecimiento Histórico (Guatemala), *Guatemala, Memoria Del Silencio: Informe*; Proyecto Interdiocesano de Recuperación de la Memoria Histórica (Guatemala), *Guatemala, Nunca Más: Informe.*

[3] Jonas, Susanne and Walker, "Guatemala: Intervention, Repression, Revolt, and Negotiated Transition."

had minimal "range"[4] in that only certain parties – notably those on the right – were allowed to participate and elections were marred by fraud. These democratic elements of the regime were strengthened with the opening of elections to participation by the Christian Democratic Party. At least 75,000 were killed during the thirteen-year conflict and a much larger number were displaced.[5] As in Guatemala and Honduras, the United States trained and financed a repressive military apparatus.[6]

The coexistence of a repressive military and a democratically elected president again makes it difficult to pinpoint the moment of transition to democracy. The peace accords, signed in 1992, allowed for the incorporation of the FMLN into the democratic system for the first time in the elections of 1994. Unfortunately, death squad activity continued in the months leading up to the election and turnout was consequently depressed. Nonetheless, in the 1997 election, the FMLN and its conservative rival ARENA polled roughly equally. The FMLN has grown in strength as a party, first winning the presidency in 2009. They have scaled back the military and reduced its prerogatives considerably, although the defense ministry has remained in military hands. However, they are, like Guatemala and Honduras, plagued by gangs, narcotraffickers, and other violent organized criminality. The have responded with *mano dura* strategies that have brought the military back into internal security and raised concerns about violations of human rights. With the decline of official violence, ARENA began to bargain with the FMLN, producing partisan controls that coexist with the currency of unofficial violence.

Honduras experienced outright military government in the 1970s, including the populist regime of General Oswaldo López Arellano (1972–1975) that included a land reform, which proved to be a successful means of coopting peasant support. The following two conservative military presidents monopolized power but nonetheless allowed for some civil rights. Honduras then transitioned to a hybrid regime with the election of civilian president Roberto Suazo Córdova (1982–1986). The democratic gains of the early 1980s were paired with reversals on human rights as the military continued to dominate society from behind the scenes. Inspired by anti-communism, influenced by authoritarian Argentina, and lavishly funded by the United States, the Honduran military embarked on a "dirty war" in the early 1980s that included torture, assassination, and forced disappearance. Although Honduras had only

---

[4] Booth, "Costa Rica: Buffeted Democracy."
[5] Comision del la verdad para El Salvador, "From Madness to Hope: The 12-Year War in El Salvador."
[6] Bird, Shawn L. and Williams, "El Salvador: Revolt and Negotiated Transition"; Brockett, *Political Movements and Violence in Central America*; Popkin, *Peace without Justice*.

minimal local communist guerilla movements, the military broadly targeted student groups, labor unions, and suspicious peasant organizations. At the same time, Honduran soil was being used with the blessing of the Honduran military as a staging ground for the Contra rebels fighting the Sandinista government in Nicaragua.[7]

Democracy, in the formal electoral sense, was secured in the early 1980s, with the caveat that electoral politics remained primarily an elite game between the long-standing National and Liberal parties with little room for alternative voices. However, Honduras until 1994 could be best classified as what O'Donnell calls a "democradura": a regime with the outward appearance of a democracy but with real power held by the military.[8] In the early 1990s, however, a variety of factors combined to encourage presidents Rafael Callejas (1990–1994) and Carlos Reina (1994–1998) to substantially reduce the power and prerogative of the armed forces. With the departure of the Sandinista regime from Nicaragua in 1990, the United States lost interest in propping up the Honduran military with tens of millions of dollars every year. Scandals broke out when, first, the military tried to cover up an alleged rape and murder by an officer and then refused to surrender to civil authorities members of the armed forces who had been called to answer charges of human rights abuses committed during the 1990s. By the end of the 1990s, the intelligence service had been moved from military to civilian control, press-gang recruitment had been banned by constitutional amendment, and the military had shrunk to around 6,000 members with the creation of the National Civil Police. By 2000, Honduras was no longer a hybrid regime.[9] Official violence, while never as dominating in Honduras, gave way to control over the judiciary by the two major parties.[10]

In Nicaragua, the brutal regime of the dictator Anastasio Somoza fell in a revolution in 1979. A broad coalition initially supported the revolution, including Violeta Chamorro, who would go on to lead the opposition to victory in 1990. By 1982, however, the Sandinista Front for National Liberation (FSLN or Sandinistas) consolidated their power and removed former allies from important positions. At the same time, the United States funded and armed an opposition

---

[7] Ruhl, "Honduras: Militarism and Democratization in Troubled Waters"; Schulz and Schulz, *The United States, Honduras, and the Crisis in Central America.*

[8] O'Donnell and Schmitter, *Transitions from Authoritarian Rule: Tentative Conclusions about Uncertain Democracies.*

[9] Chapter 6 will discuss the authoritarian backsliding that occurred in 2009 and since, with a coup against President Manuel Zelaya and subsequent repression.

[10] Ruhl, "Honduras: Militarism and Democratization in Troubled Waters"; Schulz and Schulz, *The United States, Honduras, and the Crisis in Central America.*

(Contra) army in Honduras that fought against the Sandinista army throughout the decade. The Sandinista regime produced great advances in popular democracy and mobilization, but used the Contra war as a justification for widespread civil rights abuses. Although they adopted an expansive constitution in 1987, they continued to violate it, especially in the areas of freedom of assembly and freedom of the press. More significant repression was aimed at those suspected of sabotage or espionage for the Contras and the United States. In general, the democratic rhetoric of the Sandinista government fell prey to the *caudillo* (strong-man) tradition so dominant in Nicaragua.[11]

The moment of democratic transition in Nicaragua is controversial. While many international observers declared the 1984 election the freest in Nicaragua's history, the boycott by many opposition parties led the United States to condemn it. The new Congress then spent two years writing the 1987 constitution still in force. Finally, under pressure from the United States, the Sandinistas agreed to move up the 1990 election by several months and the unified opposition won, creating an obvious, if not complete, transitional moment. Chamorro began a massive retreat from the social policies of the Sandinistas, including reversing the land reform program. Chamorro governed in part with the benefit of a pact between herself and outgoing FSLN president Daniel Ortega, which made it easier to re-incorporate the contras and reduce the military but also laid the foundation for the corrupt power-sharing pacts between Ortega and Liberal president and party leader Arnoldo Alemán (1997–2002) that is very important to the events discussed in Chapter 6.[12] Again, partisan control came to dominate as official violence waned.

Central America in the 1980s thus presents a theoretically useful range of repressive regimes. At one extreme, Guatemala until 1985 was an extreme-rightist military dictatorship that imposed the highest death toll in the region in connection with the Guatemalan civil war. Nicaragua emerged from a personalist dictatorship to an extreme-leftist revolutionary regime in 1979. Honduras and El Salvador both spent most of the decade as hybrid regimes or *democraduras*. Guatemala after 1985 should also be counted as a hybrid regime. Despite their differences, these regimes all used dependent judiciaries to enforce the laws against citizens without actually subjecting government actors to the same duties and penalties. Corruption was also common: while

---

[11] Schwartz, *A Strange Silence: The Emergence of Democracy in Nicaragua*; Walker, "Nicaragua: Transition Through Revolution."

[12] Close, *Nicaragua: The Chamorro Years*; Close and Deonandan, *Undoing Democracy: The Politics of Electoral Caudillismo*; Walker and Wade, *Nicaragua: Living in the Shadow of the Eagle*.

the courts would not give ordinary citizens satisfaction against the government, they would heed the cries of those with the money or influence to attract the judge's attention.

GOVERNMENT CONTROL INSTITUTIONS

Chapter 2 defined a government control regime as one in which neither judicial political independence nor judicial societal autonomy are present in a meaningful way. This characterization does not mean that the judicial power does not exist or is not exercised, but rather that the judiciary does not meaningfully oppose itself to the government, nor to any other significant power bloc, whether official or unofficial. An authoritarian regime may choose to use its judiciary not just to silence opposition, but also to label that opposition as criminal. A judiciary that enforces the laws against the general public – and, perhaps even at times against low-level government actors – may be functional for an authoritarian regime.[13] For most modern authoritarian regimes, it becomes necessary to somehow manage the judiciary through institutional and extra-institutional controls. Some of the dysfunctions of political independence and societal autonomy present in judicial politics during the authoritarian war years have persistent legacies in the post-cold war era due to the tendency to layer reforms over top of existing dysfunctional judicial systems. A preferable reform that would have replaced personnel and institutions was generally not politically feasible, however. Additionally, these government control regimes relied heavily on the currency of official violence with impunity for official abuses as well as many unofficial crimes alongside a total lack of horizontal accountability.

During this period, the appointment methods did not produce independent judiciaries. In Nicaragua, Honduras, and El Salvador, the constitutions called for the appointment of supreme court magistrates by the Congress and of inferior court judges by the Supreme Court itself. In practice, in Honduras and Nicaragua, presidents dominated the legislatures and were able to appoint judges of their own choosing. One of El Salvador's early judicial reforms was the creation of a judicial council, but the council was entirely dominated by the Supreme Court, making the reform something of a shell game. Following the adoption of the 1985 constitution, the Guatemalan Supreme Court was appointed by the Congress with five of the nine magistrates coming from a list produced by a nominating committee, while the Constitutional Court was nominated through an unusual system still in place that gave each of five

---

[13] Ginsburg and Moustafa, *Rule by Law: The Politics of Courts in Authoritarian Regimes.*

powerful bodies – the President, the Congress, the Supreme Court, the bar association, and the San Carlos University – the right to appoint one titular and one substitute magistrate. The Guatemalan Constitutional Court, unsurprisingly, then became the exception to the rule of politically dependent courts in the region as democracy emerged.

In Honduras under the hybrid regime, the ordinary courts had little independence. Trial judges were appointed by the Supreme Court, which was in turn appointed by the Congress with the often overwhelming influence of the military. A human rights report described the situation as follows in 1984: "The lack of life tenure and the political nature of the appointments process have had a profound and debilitating effect on the independence of the Honduran judiciary. The courts have been largely ineffectual as a check on the other branches of government, particularly in cases where the armed forces are accused of violating human rights."[14] Clearly, the institutional rules in Honduras, as in the other countries, made independent judging unlikely, if not impossible.

Guatemala's military governments engaged in an ingenious form of restricting the societal autonomy of judges by using hierarchical supervision to ensure that lower-court judges ruled "correctly," thus obscuring what were really infringements on political independence. One retired judge (G2009–12) recalled that, when she was at the beginning of her career in the early 1980s, she was a trial court judge. Every month, her supervising judge (an appellate magistrate) would come to review all of her cases. If there was a problem with any of them, the magistrate would tell her how to correct them. This kind of control makes it very easy to ensure that lower-court judges have very little opportunity to go against the military leadership and decide to, for instance, release political prisoners on a habeas corpus petition or pursue a human rights case against a government official. In this way, the judiciary could appear to be independent and impartial. Once the right people were appointed at the top of the judicial hierarchy, the lower judges would be taken care of by an apparently independent institution. Meanwhile, because judges and magistrates throughout the hierarchy were all applying the law in the same way, the system appeared to be impartial.

Corruption, present in all four of these countries, represents a significant intrusion on judicial autonomy. Margaret Popkin reported witnessing several different interactions between lawyers and judges, including military judges, in San Salvador that resulted in the release of prisoners with no actual legal

---

[14] Schulz and Schulz, *The United States, Honduras, and the Crisis in Central America*, 18.

argument being invoked.[15] Corruption was a less successful strategy for political prisoners in Guatemala, where most were tortured and executed long before a judge could get involved; the experience of American nun Dianna Ortiz suggests that a prisoner could be released if the American embassy became sufficiently concerned early enough.[16] Corruption permeated these systems and, while it may not have freed many prisoners outside of El Salvador, it affected the entire justice system in all of these countries. Where some litigants are able to use connections or money to buy "justice," there is no real rule of law. Judges are made less autonomous to the extent that their salaries are sufficiently low and their vulnerability to threats sufficiently high that they are unable to resist this kind of pressure.

It should be noted that judges were not alone in being susceptible to corruption; police corruption and even military corruption were also common. In fact, there is some evidence that the organized criminality that has so severely affected the region has its origins in smuggling rings created by the military, especially military border guards. The black market was notorious in Nicaragua during this period. Furthermore, corruption neither began nor ended in the 1980s in Central America. Nicaraguan dictator Anastasio Somoza and his cronies are believed to have stolen at least $500 million before being deposed and exiled in the 1979 Sandinista revolution, including a substantial portion of the international aid sent to the country after the devastating 1972 earthquake. Not surprisingly, FSLN leaders then took their turn at the "piñata" before leaving power in 1990s, "privatizing" into their own hands a large number of state assets and concerns.[17] It remains a serious problem in all four countries.

Finally, as Pereira rightly points out, it is easy for a regime to allow for a relatively independent judiciary if it moves all politically sensitive cases outside of the courts.[18] There are several ways to do this. Some regimes simply suspend all or part of the constitution, effectively eliminating any constitutional rights-based cases, which Guatemalan dictator General Efraín Ríos Montt did upon taking power in a coup in 1982. Another tactic is to remove any cases involving the military, subversives, or other sensitive cases from the ordinary cases. Some or all cases involving the military or subversives were routinely tried by military courts in El Salvador, Honduras and Guatemala, leaving ordinary judges no

[15] Popkin et al., *Justice Delayed: The Slow Pace of Judicial Reform in El Salvador.*
[16] Ortiz and Davis, *The Blindfold's Eyes: My Journey from Torture to Truth.*
[17] Canales Ewest, "A 20 años de La Piñata."
[18] Pereira, "Of Judges and Generals: Security Courts under Authoritarian Regimes in Argentina, Brazil, and Chile"; Pereira, *Political (In)justice.*

right or ability to intervene.[19] Nicaragua established revolutionary courts where ordinary citizens without legal training but with revolutionary credentials ruled on a wide variety of cases involving "counter-revolutionary" activities. This arrangement was partly the result of necessity after most of Somoza's loyal judges fled the country or were stripped of their positions following the revolution. These untrained judges, however, were also more easily malleable in terms of their societal autonomy. Not only could they be easily denounced and replaced, an infringement on their political independence, but they did not have any independent ideological basis for resisting the regime or cleaving to some constitutional ideal because they had not been trained in what those ideals were.

The limitations placed on the judiciary by these incursions on independence and autonomy were not always functional for the regime. While it was immediately desirable to prevent the judiciary from limiting the repressive capability of the state, the failure of the legal system to respond to grievances also contributed to the opposition, including the armed opposition, to these regimes. Brockett argues that a wide variety of grievances helped to drive contentious behavior, and indicates that many peasants who participated in contentious politics stated that a "sense of injustice" or a "search for justice" were primary motivating factors.[20] Brockett's argument highlights a phenomenon that must have been highly frustrating to these regimes: protests continued and sometimes increased in the face of repressive measures.[21] This suggests that regime durability may be associated with allowing at least some independence for the judiciary, as Moustafa argues was done in Egypt.[22]

Significantly, few activists in this period attempted legal strategies to find justice under the military regimes of the 1980s. During the Laugerud presidency in the 1970s in Guatemala, the university students association (AEU) attempted to bring a case to the Supreme Court to discover the fate of some comrades following a mass disappearance and one labor judge ruled that one labor strike was legal and valid.[23] In general, however, most activists appeared to agree with Verner that the Central American courts – like courts throughout the region – were creatures of the repressive executives, making avoiding

---

[19] This situation was made worse in El Salvador, where the police were officially a part of the military. (Popkin 1994)
[20] One need only think of the Rodney King riots in Los Angeles or the Mothers of the Plaza de Mayo in Argentina to see the anger born of frustration when justice is not provided.
[21] Brockett, *Political Movements and Violence in Central America*.
[22] Moustafa, "Law versus the State: The Judicialization of Politics in Egypt."
[23] Brockett, *Political Movements and Violence in Central America*, 104.

the courts entirely rational.[24] Perhaps this aversion was cultural as well: there was at that time in Central America no tradition of an activist judiciary; Even Costa Rica's famously activist constitutional chamber was not formed until 1989. International incentives to go to court (i.e., to "exhaust domestic remedies") were minimal: the Inter-American Court of Human Rights was only founded in 1979 and did not become a significant player in Central America until it decided the *Velásquez Rodriguez* case involving Honduras in 1988.

In the 1980s, as these military regimes increasingly became hybrid regimes, a variety of human rights legal organizations emerged. Popular organizations were not new to the region; many had maintained a significant presence through all but the most violent periods. However, organizations that used the language of human rights – and thus the language of international law – came about later. Some, like Guatemala's Human Rights Legal Action Center (CALDH) began their work in the United States; CALDH moved to Guatemala in 1989. Others began as local projects, often supported by the Catholic Church. Bishop Juan Gerardi founded the Archibishop's Office on Human Rights (ODHA) in Guatemala in the late 1980s. The Nicaraguan Center for Human Rights (CENIDH), an independent non-religious organization, was founded in 1990, three months after the election of Violeta Chamorro. The organization now known as the Human Rights Commission of El Salvador (CDHES) was founded in 1978 by a group of professionals, students, and workers, with the backing of Archbishop Oscar Romero. The Honduran Center for Investigation and Promotion of Human Rights (CIPRODEH) was founded in 1989; earlier human rights organization such as the Committee of Families of the Detained and Disappeared in Honduras (COFADEH) operated from the early 1980s, but did not receive formal organizational status until the 1990s. All of these organizations worked throughout the protracted democratic transitions to push their governments to respect human rights and legality through concurrent strategies of increasing public awareness and pursuing justice through legal cases. Their legal strategies were often frustrated – and frequently still are, especially as their goals become more ambitious.

CONFLICTS AND AUTHORITARIAN CURRENCIES

Government Control judicial regimes are typified by the use of the authoritarian currency of violence to resolve legal conflicts. In some countries – notably, Guatemala and El Salvador – violence was rarely submitted to the legal process. Indeed, with the suspension of the constitution in 1982 and the

---

[24] Verner, "The Independence of Supreme Courts in Latin America: A Review of the Literature."

extreme level of violence, there were no major human rights related legal cases in Guatemala until after the passage of the new constitution in 1985 and they remained rare for many years after that.[25] In these civil war environments, state violence was at times clandestine and carried out by unofficial or quasi-official actors such as paramilitaries. Political opponents were targeted for torture, disappearance, or killing through extra-judicial and frequently secret processes, but the results were often quite public: in both countries, tortured corpses were often disposed of in public places to send a message. Where the justice sector is bypassed in this way, it is almost meaningless to discuss their independence or autonomy except inasmuch as they are unable or unwilling to hold the government to account for those actions. Honduras and Nicaragua relied more on the threat of official violence through state institutions than on clandestine operations, although both were willing to exercise brutality when it was deemed necessary.

While it is useful for authoritarian regimes to maintain an operating judiciary as a cover for that brutality, they have two primary moments in which they can greatly infringe on the basic independence of the judiciary. When they first come to power, they may purge judges from the old regime, as Guatemala did in 1954 and Nicaragua did in 1979. After that, they have the ability to control judges throughout the life of the regime by controlling appointment and removal. Judges under these regimes, especially in the higher courts, were appointed by the authoritarian government, often through a Justice Minister. Furthermore, they had short tenures so that it was easy to replace them at the whim of the government. Guatemala, Nicaragua, and Honduras still have very short judicial tenures as a legacy of these periods. Short tenures without reappointment encourage corruption as the judge or magistrate needs to look to the outside to find her next job (or to graft to finance her retirement), while short tenures with reappointment maximize government control because judges and magistrates must constantly be trying to please the sitting government[26] to ensure reappointment.

The FSLN in Nicaragua during the 1980s took advantage of a number of means of controlling its judiciary. Immediately following the revolution, they purged the judiciary of any Somocista judges that had not already fled the country. They created a number of specialized tribunals. Even with the

---

[25] Stanley, "Business as Usual? Justice and Policing Reform in Postwar Guatemala," 114.

[26] Alternatively, as Helmke has argued, in a highly unstable regime, judges are constantly trying to predict the next change and please whomever the next rulers will be. Helmke, "Checks and Balances By Other Means: Strategic Defection and Argentina's Supreme Court in the 1990s"; Helmke, "The Logic of Strategic Defection: Court-Executive Relations in Argentina Under Dictatorship and Democracy."

adoption of a democratic constitution in 1987, which explicitly guaranteed judicial independence, infringements continued. The appointment method in practice gave President Ortega the ability to appoint whomever he chose to the judiciary. While officially the National Assembly made the final decision, they typically acted as a rubber stamp to Ortega's choices. Once appointed to the bench, there were not judicial career protections. Judges may have been particularly easily manipulated because of their inadequate training. In the years following the revolution, many professionals, including lawyers, left the country. Consequently, a large number of people without legal training were appointed to District and Local Courts. To be appointed in this way, a person had to be "knowledgeable of the law," which could be accomplished through a training course offered by the judiciary. Consequently, Solis and Wilson report that at the end of the Sandinista era, only 40 percent of District Judges and 5 percent of local judges held law degrees.[27] These judges had no institutional protections for independent actions from the FSLN and likely would have been expected to be loyal to their patrons. These ideological tests for judges presage the partisan loyalties that would be required in the 2000s.

The Supreme Court was somewhat more difficult to dominate because all had independent legal training and the FSLN had chosen to appoint three opposition members to the court. When the Supreme Court acted against the wishes of the FSLN, however, they were simply ignored, as in the land reform case of "La Verona." After this property had been taken and redistributed, the Special Agrarian Tribunal reversed the expropriation. Soon after, the executive seized the land again and the original landowner filed an amparo with the Supreme Court. The Supreme Court ruled in favor of the landowner and ordered the land be returned. Jaime Wheelock, the Agrarian Minister and a key figure in the revolution, then went before the court to announce his ministry's refusal to comply with the amparo. In response, the three opposition magistrates resigned in protest, signing an open letter explaining the situation. Rather than accept the protest, the FSLN asked that the other magistrates step down as well, replacing them all with FSLN loyalists.[28] While similar purges have not happened since, there has remained an identification of Nicaraguan judges with either of the two major political parties throughout the democratic period.

There were direct attacks on the Honduran Supreme Court as well. Leading into the 1985 elections, many were concerned that President Roberto Suazo Córdova (1982–1986) would try to extend his tenure to an unconstitutional

---

[27] Solis and Wilson, *Political Transition and the Administration of Justice in Nicaragua*, 56.
[28] Ibid., 18; Close, *Nicaragua*.

second term. The Congress accused four of the supreme court magistrates, whom Suazo had directly appointed contrary to the constitution, of violating electoral laws to support the president. The Congress then dismissed those magistrates and appointed four new ones in their place. Suazo promptly retaliated by ordering the arrest of the four new magistrates and ordering troops to surround the supreme court building. The constitutional crisis, which also included a power struggle between the president and the Congress over new electoral reforms intended to limit Suazo's influence, soon drew popular attention. Popular organizations called for a reform of the entire Supreme Court as well as the release of the one magistrate who had successfully been arrested. The ultimate result was to bring the crisis to a head and force the parties into negotiations that would produce a significant electoral reform to remove some of the power from the political party leaders.[29]

Even after this crisis, there would continue to be problems with the appointment of supreme court magistrates. In practice, this appointment process has developed into a highly political and highly partisan one. Following the 1985 election, there was a "pactito" (little pact) between the winner, President José Azcona del Hoyo of the Liberal Party and the actual recipient of the most votes, leader of the National Party Rafael Callejas. Among other things, this pact gave the National Party members of Congress the "control of the Supreme Court and half of the other judicial appointments."[30] Pact-making has been held up as a benefit to democratization because of its ability to bring about peaceful compromise in the Southern Cone of South America, but Honduras – and Nicaragua – may demonstrate for us the problems inherent in relying on pacts that are semi-democratic and semi-constitutional at best. In both countries, these friendly arrangements between political elites have allowed for incursions on democracy, as with the use of the Honduran Supreme Court to legitimize a coup in 2009 or the ongoing politicization of the Nicaraguan courts. Both will be discussed in Chapter 6.

The consequence of this lack of political independence was especially pronounced for victims of human rights violations in Honduras. For example, the Inter-American Court ruled against Honduras in 1988 for its failure to effectively investigate and prosecute a case of forced disappearance; the next year the court ordered the government of Honduras to pay compensation to the surviving family.[31] While the *Velásquez Rodriguez* case was a watershed

---

[29] Schulz and Schulz, *The United States, Honduras, and the Crisis in Central America*, 122–28.
[30] Ibid., 132.
[31] Velasquez Rodriguez Case, No. 4 Inter-Am.Ct.H.R. (Ser. C) (Inter-American Court of Human Rights 1988).

that has been lauded by activists and inspired many future complaints to the IAC, international legal processes are poor substitutes for functioning domestic oversight. Using this case as an example, the victim was "disappeared" in 1981, but the complaint filed with the Inter-American Human Rights Commission that same year did nothing to halt the forced disappearance of at least 100 other Hondurans by 1984.[32]

Pressure might also be placed on the courts to resolve high-profile cases that had attracted unwelcome attention from the international community. The murders of six Jesuits, their cook, and her daughter in El Salvador in 1989 attracted just such pressure from the United States. Indeed, Juhn suggests that the Salvadoran armed forces' "error" in killing the Jesuits, and the subsequent reaction by the United States, eventually made peace negotiations possible.[33] In response, the Salvadorans tried nine defendants, convicting only one colonel and his lieutenant but not the confessed triggerman. This trial was plagued by military obstructionism, but was hailed by many as a breakthrough because members of the military were actually convicted of human rights abuses. The International Commission of Jurists characterized the trial as a "breach of impunity," while also suggesting that the jury's reasoning closely traced the military's.[34] Such laudatory reactions are perhaps overly optimistic. As with many similar cases in the region, lower-level officers may be convicted but the "intellectual authors" may never face trial. In fact, frequently, these governments resist reopening the trial to try the people who ordered the abuses on the grounds that the case has already been concluded. Furthermore, the two defendants who were convicted were freed after two years under an amnesty law.[35] An additional problem with such trials is that they only affect the tiny fraction of the cases of human rights abuses that secure the sustained interest of powerful international actors.

If authoritarian government control regimes are defined by their reliance on the currency of state violence, whether official or clandestine, then we can look for shifts in the currencies employed as the political environment changes. In

---

[32] This figure is noted by the IACHR itself in the *Velasquez Rodriguez* opinion.

[33] Juhn, *Negotiating Peace in El Salvador: Civil-Military Relations and the Conspiracy to End the War*, 69.

[34] Observer for Latin America of the International Commission of Jurists, *A Breach of Impunity: The Trial for the Murder of Jesuits in El Salvador*.

[35] Notably, the tide may be turning on this case in Spanish courts. In early 2016, a United States federal court agreed to extradite Colonel Inocente Orlando Montano, considered one of the "intellectual authors" of the UCA murders, under Spanish law. Lakhani, "Spanish Trial of Soldiers Who Killed Priests Raises Hopes of Ending Impunity in El Salvador"; Washington Office on Latin America, "Historic Breakthrough in the Case of Jesuits Murdered in El Salvador in 1989."

the 1980s and 1990s, the region underwent a massive transition away from this reliance on naked violence as it embraced the idea of democracy. The strategies employed during this transition and the changing currencies employed to resolve several significant conflicts led these countries to develop in somewhat different directions.

JUDICIAL REGIMES AND CURRENCIES IN TRANSITION

The Central American military regimes came to an end at the same time that the global expansion of judicial power was beginning. It has only been since the 1980s that a great deal of attention has been paid to building up a strong judicial sector as an aspect of democratization and really only since the 1990s that the developing world's judiciaries have been expected to hold their executives and legislatures accountable.[36] With the democratization processes of the 1980s, a wave of international donors came in to the region with advice and funds for, among other things, judicial reforms.[37] Simultaneously, international norms regarding the judiciary were changing. Judges at all levels began to be expected to be politically independent in order to promote economic development and foreign investment; some degree of judicial review became common as well. While neither of these changes were a cure for the ill of human rights abuses or overgrown military prerogatives, they created new political opportunities within the already-significant changes of the democratization and peace processes.

Hybrid authoritarian regimes may wish to have a formally politically independent judiciary in which certain protections for judges can be found in the laws or the constitution; these regimes nonetheless may maintain considerable control over judges.[38] This control may inhabit the "grey zone" between political independence and societal autonomy as political actors and criminal actors increasingly overlap. Guatemala, Honduras, and El Salvador all became hybrid regimes in the early-mid 1980s, a period in which international attention was beginning to turn to the need for an independent judiciary as a tool for building the rule of law, which would in turn produce better economic and political outcomes. Consequently, the new constitutions adopted in this period did include formal guarantees of judicial independence. However, the reality was that judges and magistrates were often easy to manipulate through

[36] O'Donnell, "Horizontal Accountability: The Legal Institutionalization of Mistrust"; O'Donnell, "Horizontal Accountability in New Democracies."
[37] Carothers, *Promoting the Rule of Law Abroad*; Carothers, "The Rule of Law Revival."
[38] Ginsburg and Moustafa, *Rule by Law*.

informal measures. Notably, Honduras and El Salvador allowed for considerable partisan involvement in the appointment of judges and magistrates, a tradition that continues in those countries.[39] In Guatemala, corruption was more common, as discussed below.

In the 1980s, few judges were assertive enough to attract threats of violence, but these threats did emerge as they became more politically independent through the democratization processes. Threats became a special problem in Guatemala, Honduras, and El Salvador as judges took on the task of trying to bring members of the military and the government to account for their participation in human rights crimes during the authoritarian periods. When military officers stood accused in the assassinations of Guatemalan anthropologist Myrna Mack, killed in 1990, and human rights activist Bishop Juan Gerardi, killed in 1998, judges received so many death threats that more than twenty judges left the Gerardi case rather than risk their lives. A similar problem existed in El Salvador: The first judge assigned to investigate and try the murder of Archbishop Oscar Romero was forced to flee the country after an assassination attempt. The case would never actually go to trial, with an attempt to reopen it in 1987 being denied by the Supreme Court.[40]

For all four countries, democratization was gradual and protracted. Military regimes in the northern three countries voluntarily ceded control to elected civilian presidents between 1982 (El Salvador) and 1985 (Guatemala). This civilian control was somewhat illusory, however, as it did not entail any actual reduction in military prerogatives. Nor did this transition produce substantially better conditions for civil or human rights. In El Salvador and Honduras, repressive violence actually increased after the democratic "transitions." In Guatemala, this political opening was only possible because of the success of the extreme state violence that all but subdued the rebels between 1978 and 1983. Additionally, in all three cases, the left was not included in democratic participation. In El Salvador and Guatemala, the process of democratic consolidation has yet to be completed. In Honduras and Nicaragua, the late 2000s saw significant backsliding in that process, with Honduras experiencing a coup and Nicaragua returning to a hybrid regime, albeit not a military regime.

---

[39] It can be argued that Nicaragua should fall into this category as well. The Sandinista regime that existed under the 1987 constitution had many features of a hybrid regime and the 1987 constitution also included clear guarantees of judicial independence. Like Honduras and El Savlador, Nicaragua too developed a tradition of partisan judging that continued – became stronger, even – into the late 2000s. The distinction is that there was no partisan power-sharing under the 1980s hybrid regime, with the FSLN controlling the entire government and appointing only Sandinista judges and magistrates to the judiciary.

[40] Popkin, *Peace without Justice*, 46.

As was mentioned in the introduction to this chapter, the processes of democratization in Guatemala, El Salvador, and Nicaragua were coincident with the peace processes in those countries. In El Salvador and Guatemala, it was more difficult to obtain a commitment from the military and the government to accept the idea of negotiating with the rebels than it was to obtain from them a commitment to elections. This was in part due to a situation in which the United States would continue to support these governments as anticommunist "democracies" on the basis of elections alone, despite the restrictions on participation in these elections as well as the dominant role played by the military in essential policy areas in both countries. Nicaragua saw a mirror image of this pattern. In Nicaragua, the Contras were so lucratively supported by the United States that they were not interested in pursuing peace negotiations with the government until the Bush administration (1989–1993) began to scale back its support and there was an opposition (pro-Contra) election victory. The war in Nicaragua also had a profound impact on the continuation of the hybrid regime in Honduras. The Honduran military received such significant quantities of military aid in the 1980s in exchange for hosting the Contras in their territory that it encouraged them to actually increase repression. With the withdrawal of those funds upon the winding down of the Contra war, the Honduran military found itself definitively reduced in the 1990s.[41]

The literature on democratic transitions, because of its perhaps too-strong focus on trying to abstract a universal model, has privileged discrete moments of transition, following a punctuated equilibrium model of path-dependent political development.[42] In Central America, if we follow this model, there were two transitions: first from a closed authoritarian regime to a hybrid, semi-open regime, and then from a hybrid regime to an unconsolidated democracy. Only after both of these transitions had occurred could the long process of democratic consolidation take place. The fact that pinpointing moments in these four countries is such a difficult process highlights the problems with this approach. It is preferable to begin from a premise that political situations are always in a process of change stemming from the ongoing power struggles of different groups in society competing to harness state power for their own aims. Each iteration of this struggle changes – to a greater or lesser degree – the balance of power and may even lead to a change in the rules of the

[41] Call, "War Transitions and the New Civilian Security in Latin America," 14.
[42] Przeworski, "The Games of Transition"; Przeworski, "Some Problems in the Study of Transitions to Democracy"; O'Donnell and Schmitter, *Transitions from Authoritarian Rule*; Linz and Stepan, *Problems of Democratic Transition and Consolidation*; Carothers, "The End of the Transition Paradigm."

game. As these cases demonstrate, these changes are neither unidirectional nor teleological.

In the period of the 1990s in Central America, these four countries had to address, in one form or another, a number of complicated issues having to do with the shared history of violence and state repression.

First, they had to be able to negotiate peace. It became clear by the late 1980s that true democratization could not be possible without a lasting peace. In a situation of ongoing civil war and regional warfare, the military had too much claim to dominate politics. In El Salvador and Guatemala, the peace negotiations themselves became an important opportunity to discuss a wide variety of issues related to democracy. As was recognized even by the United States Department of State, a lasting peace would not be possible without somehow rectifying the injustices of the political systems that had reigned throughout the region up to that point.

Second, they had to reduce the size, scope, and influence of the military. The militaries in these countries were bloated from being on a war footing. Militaries needed to be streamlined in keeping with a defensive, democratic role. If nothing else, they presented a significant drain on state resources at a time when international military aid was disappearing and governments were being expected to tighten their belts. If they could not be reined in, they would likely continue to pose a threat to democratic governance.

Third, they had to develop functioning electoral systems. While free elections are not a sufficient condition for a consolidated democracy, they are necessary. All four countries had some history of elections, but many had been unfair in a variety of ways: significant parties or other actors were not allowed to participate, the franchise was limited, or votes were not counted properly, to name a few examples. All four countries were faced with developing a "fourth branch of government" in the form of an independent electoral authority that could manage elections and monitor them for fairness, legality, and accuracy.

Fourth, major justice sector reforms were needed. The police, investigators, prosecutors, and courts of, especially, El Salvador and Guatemala, had been operating under a national security regime. They operated to control dissent rather than to enforce a constitutional order and democratic rule of law. In all four countries, corruption was rampant as well. Justice sector institutions were not trusted, not sought out, and not up to the task of handling the crime that increased dramatically with the arrival of peace in Guatemala, Honduras, and El Salvador.

Fifth, widespread social changes were also called for, although few were ever accomplished. Popular organizations called for improved access to jobs, political participation, and education for peasants and indigenous communities. Labor unions in Guatemala and El Salvador argued for the right to freely organize. Land reform, once a central goal of guerilla movements, was largely left off the table in these negotiations; in Nicaragua, the Chamorro government reversed the land reform to a significant extent. Finally, many people clamored for some kind of accountability for past human rights abuses. Anywhere from hundreds of citizens in Honduras to hundreds of thousands in Guatemala had been murdered by the military and quasi-military regimes. Many more had been displaced, arrested, harassed, or tortured. Many sought (and still seek) to have perpetrators of state terror tried for human rights crimes as a way of closing the door on the past and moving forward with less fear of a recurrence of these events. Others sought to close the door on the past by granting blanket amnesties and opposing truth commissions, believing that the military would never allow the nation to move forward with the possibility of trials of military officers.

In Guatemala, the transition to a hybrid regime took place between 1983, when Óscar Humberto Mejia Victores (1983–1986) removed General Ríos Montt in a coup, and when Vinicio Cerezo was democratically elected. This period included significant openings for political activity, including public demonstrations and participation in the constitution drafting. However, in all areas, much of the left continued to be excluded from participation. Indeed, the military targeted leftists and suspected guerilla sympathizers leading all the way up to and beyond the 1996 peace accords. Political commitment by most of the important Guatemalan actors including, ultimately, the military to the project of electoral democracy was also slow in coming, but appeared to be finally settled with the removal of President Jorge Serrano Elias after he performed an *autogolpe* in 1993. However, even with the rather definitive statement against dictatorship, few were willing to take steps against corruption and human rights violations for some time, especially as anyone who might have taken those steps – members of Congress, the Supreme Court – was implicated in corruption as well.[43]

The peace process would not be resolved until three years later, having stalled out in the face of military intransigence and seeming government disinterest prior to Serrano's coup. While Brockett argues that government disinterest continued and that the peace accords did not gain real speed until President Álvaro Arzú came into office in 1996[44], the importance of the reaction to Serrano's coup should not be dismissed. A return to military dictatorship

---

[43] Chapter 5 discusses the participation of the Constitutional Court in this affair, as well as the impact it had on judicial independence.

[44] Brockett, *Political Movements and Violence in Central America*.

became much less likely following the military's internal decision to support constitutionalism and electoral democracy. Despite the success of the peace process in ending the armed conflict, much remains to be implemented. The military continues to have significant powers and share of the national budget, having been reduced by only 30 percent. While the left, including the revolutionary left, has been brought into electoral politics, peasant and indigenous participation in political life is still quite compromised. The promises of the peace accords to provide extensive rights, services, and guarantees to the indigenous communities remain unfulfilled.[45] Electoral violence, targeting especially peasant leaders, continued to plague the countryside as recently as the 2011 election, with the 2015 election taking place amid a national convulsion of protest against an outgoing president who stepped down to face corruption charges just days before the election.

If democratic transitions can be tied to a moment, there are two in Nicaragua: the revolutionary overthrow of the Somoza dictatorship on July 15, 1979, and the election of Violeta Chamorro at the head of the United Nicaraguan Opposition, on February 25, 1990. During her six years in the presidency, Chamorro did several important things for strengthening the prospects of democracy in Nicaragua. Most importantly, she was able (and willing) to work with both the FSLN and the Contras to put an end to the violent conflict and to pursue a path forward. She retained Humberto Ortega as head of the armed forces, which Walker argues helped to build trust so that the officers were willing to approve of massive budget and personnel cuts. She invited the United Nations in to help mediate the resettlement of the Contras. However, some of her actions were less positive for the democratic rule of law. Of particular concern was her reversal of the land reform, for which she ignored the claims of those to whom the land had been distributed in favor of absentee landholders (many in the United States) without any public debate over the wisdom of the land reform.[46]

Democracy cannot be said to have been consolidated in Nicaragua as of this writing. While Chamorro took some important steps toward democratizing Nicaragua, her successor undid much of that work. Liberal president Arnoldo Alemán (1997–2002) came to the presidency on the momentum of an extensive patronage system he had built as mayor of Managua, the capital and largest city. As president, he engaged in widespread graft, for which he was named one of the world's most corrupt leaders of the late twentieth century in 2004 by Transparency International. Alemán also began the process of

---

[45] Stanley, "Business as Usual? Justice and Policing Reform in Postwar Guatemala," 114.
[46] Walker, "Nicaragua: Transition Through Revolution."

returning the government, including the judiciary, to a spoils system. Alemán's successor Enrique Bolaños (2002–2007) made some prominent moves against corruption – most notably the imprisonment of Alemán – but he was unable to make real progress in the face of the Liberal–Sandinista pact in the Congress. Furthermore, he has been accused of cracking down on NGOs.[47] Problems in the area of the rule of law and judicial independence are especially acute in Nicaragua, with the second presidency of Sandinista leader Daniel Ortega (1979–1990, 2007-) involving extensive manipulation of the courts in order to extend his control over more of Nicaraguan politics. Ortega's control of the courts will be discussed further in Chapter 6.

In Honduras, the judiciary continued to be highly dependent on political parties as the regime became more democratic. Another political controversy struck the Supreme Court leading up to the 1993 elections. In 1992, the president of the Supreme Court, Oswaldo Ramos Soto of the National Party, was removed by the Congress at least in part because he was known to be considering a run for the presidency and could have been a dangerous rival for the president of the Congress, Rodolfo Irías Navas, also of the National Party. Ramos was known to be highly corrupt and highly political. According to Schulz and Sundloff Schulz, he had used court employees as political organizers, including mandatory salary deductions for his political cause.[48] Consequently, Irías organized a panel that investigated Ramos and recommended that his resignation be demanded. Demand it the Congress did, by a vote of 107 to 7. As has so often been the case in Central America – and many other developing countries – political enemies go after each other on the pretense of attacking corruption. While the corruption may have been real, it was by no means limited to Ramos. Irías, we can only imagine, hoped to improve his own presidential hopes, but Ramos was ultimately the Nationalist candidate in 1993 and lost to Liberal candidate Carlos Roberto Reina (1994–1998).[49]

El Salvador transited from a closed, authoritarian regime to a hybrid regime with the relatively fair March 1984 elections. However, the guerilla war and accompanying extensive state violence continued until the signing of a peace accord in 1992. The move to semi-free elections (the FMLN was not permitted to participate) and many subsequent reforms were influenced by thinking within the United States Department of State that creating democracy in El Salvador would help to reduce the attractiveness of armed struggle for

---

[47] Close and Deonandan, *Undoing Democracy*.
[48] Schulz and Schulz, *The United States, Honduras, and the Crisis in Central America*, 295.
[49] Political Database of the Americas, "1993 HONDURAN PRESIDENTIAL ELECTION."

those who had previously been left out of Salvadoran politics. Nonetheless, the United States continued to support the repression of the FMLN through much of the 1980s, balking only when the Salvadoran military and death squads seemed to attack people who were, in the eyes of the United States, outside of the conflict, such as the six UCA Jesuits.

Following the 1992 peace accords, President Alfredo Cristiani (1989–1994) issued a blanket amnesty covering all those implicated by a United Nations truth commission – an amnesty that stood until July 13, 2016. ARENA, the party that had controlled the political sphere during the civil war, continued to dominate politics after the peace. The FMLN eventually became a normalized part of El Salvador's new democracy, winning the presidency for the first time only in 2009. In many regards, El Salvador is a case study of successful transition from civil war, but nonetheless some tensions have continued or arisen anew. The ARENA government pursued neo-liberal economic policies, which exacerbated social and economic inequalities. There has been no transitional justice as a result of the amnesty law. Salvadorans have continued to immigrate in large numbers. Furthermore, the end of widespread political violence opened the door for skyrocketing criminal violence.[50]

If, as Przeworski so elegantly argued, democracy is a "contingent institutional compromise," and thus easily changeable as conditions change, then why are these transitions so important? Central America demonstrates better than many countries the importance of a democratic rule of law. The absence of a democratic rule of law leaves the citizens of this region not necessarily without a democratic voice – the usual concern of committed democrats – but with both less than adequate protections and more than appropriate burdens from the state. These citizens consequently have limited ability to participate in ordinary struggles over politics and social grievances. That this situation is a clear injustice seems obvious but bears noting. When some citizens can influence the government but others can only hope to avoid being punished by it, their citizenship means less. When the police can murder suspected criminals or even just undesirables such as street children with impunity, a whole class of society is denied justice. Democracy without some modicum of justice may be substantially cruel and equally capricious as its authoritarian predecessors; this lack of justice is one of the last remaining vestiges of the militarism that continued during the hybrid regimes of the 1980s and 1990s.

[50] Collins, *Post-Transitional Justice: Human Rights Trials in Chile and El Salvador*; Moodie, *El Salvador in the Aftermath of Peace: Crime, Uncertainty, and the Transition to Democracy*; Call, *Constructing Justice and Security After War*.

The view of politics as contingent institutional compromise and of political change as always possible is optimistic as well as pessimistic. While it is true that events such as those in Honduras in 2009 and Nicaragua since the late 2000s suggest that countries with long-term commitments to non-democratic social and political arrangements will tend to revert back to that norm, the focus on shifting coalitions allows for more hopeful possible outcomes. With the end of the Cold War, many of the international players in the region changed their focus. Many turned their attention – and their financing and expertise – to building democracy and the rule of law. The 1990s were, for many countries in the region, an optimistic era of rule of law promotion. While their motives and techniques varied – and sometimes came into conflict – these international actors helped to shift more power within the region to non-governmental organizations and, in some cases, to the powerless – peasants, victims of crime, and even in some cases the criminals themselves. These reforms were somewhat weakened, however, by the broad package of neoliberal economic reforms adopted concurrently region-wide.

JUDICIAL REFORM'S ATTEMPT TO SHIFT CURRENCIES

Judicial reform programs were an important part of the peace-building and democratization processes in Central America – indeed in all of Latin America and other areas of the developing world. Judicial reform programs generally sought to promote judicial independence, judicial efficiency, and access to justice for all, in order to promote justice, peace, democracy, and economic development. These programs were initiated as early as the 1980s in some countries, but became much more important during the 1990s during the period of democratic consolidation and peace building. Much of the impetus for these programs came from the outside; sponsors included international financial institutions (IFIs) like the World Bank or the Inter-American Bank, multilateral actors such as the Organization of American States or the United Nations Development Program, and a variety of individual countries' aid organizations. In large part because of the number of donor groups with different priorities, the judicial reform project in the region did not cohere as well as it might have.[51]

---

[51] Dakolias, "A Strategy for Judicial Reform: The Experience in Latin America"; Domingo and Sieder, *Rule of Law in Latin America*; Hammergren, *Envisioning Reform*; Hammergren, *The Politics of Justice and Justice Reform in Latin America*; Taylor, *Judging Policy*; Ungar, *Elusive Reform*.

While there was some consensus on the basic goals of judicial reforms, donors prioritized these goals differently from each other with consequences for the program areas funded. The IFIs focused primarily on the effect that a reformed judiciary and a strong rule of law could have on increased economic development and funded programs in rewriting commercial codes, improving judicial efficiency, and ensuring the security of contracts and property rights, which was of particular concern as Nicaragua exited from socialism. The United States Agency for International Development (USAID) focused on democracy-promotion during the 1980s, funding programs to improve the administration of criminal justice in particular.[52] As crime rates spiraled in the 1990s and beyond in Central America, USAID expanded this focus. The United Nations Development Program was often more concerned with democratization and assisted with programs to increase judicial independence. The United Nations missions in El Salvador (ONUSAL) and Guatemala (MINUGUA) were oriented toward peace-building and human rights and thus devoted a significant part of the mission to monitoring the legal system.[53] Finally, some of the European agencies, such as the Swedish International Development Cooperation Agency (SIDA) and Germany's Friedrich Ebert Foundation, were more oriented toward a variety of improvements to protect human rights.[54]

Because so many of these programs had the same sponsors from one country to another throughout the hemisphere, one can find some commonalities between all of these programs. One common feature was the creation of independent judicial councils that would play a significant role in the appointment and discipline of judges as well as overseeing promotion through the judicial career. Many countries also adopted a constitutionally-guaranteed share of the national budget for the judiciary. Many countries increased the tenure of their judges, although a few others reduced tenure from life terms to something shorter.[55] In addition to these changes, which often required constitutional reforms, many civil, criminal, and procedural codes were re-written to foster all of the goals of the reform projects. A variety of judicial trainings were

---

[52] Calleros, *The Unfinished Transition to Democracy in Latin America*, 56.
[53] Popkin, *Peace without Justice*.
[54] Bowen, "International Imposition and Transmission of Democracy and the Rule of Law: Lessons from Central America."
[55] Where, as in Mexico under the PRI or in Argentina through much of recent history, judges are appointed in a fashion that makes them dependent on and loyal to one political party, it may not be desirable to allow that party to appoint judges for a lengthy term. However, the very short terms of Honduras, Guatemala, and Nicaragua make corruption more possible and attractive to office holders.

made available to judges, frequently including the ability to travel to foreign countries including the United States for trainings on the government's (or the donor's) largesse.[56] Efficiency-oriented reforms offered more practical supports such as purchasing computers and case-tracking software for judicial offices and providing trainings to judges and judicial staff.

One potentially problematic aspect of these judicial reform programs involved what to do with the judges who were already on the bench, having been appointed by governments that were semi-democratic at best. Both El Salvador and Guatemala partially purged their judiciaries. A retired Guatemalan judge, who served as a supreme court magistrate immediately following the purge, recalled that the purge was largely the result of perceived corruption revealed by President Serrano's 1993 *autogolpe*. As a part of the constitutional reforms that followed the coup, a new Supreme Court was elected, with a term shortened by one year. The purge in El Salvador was not a response to a single event, but was rather a part of the judicial reform strategy. The Supreme Court at that time enjoyed life tenure and resisted reform efforts that might change their work and political practices. Consequently, a constitutional reform was passed that reduced the length of the term to nine years with appointments staggered after the initial appointments in 1994. In this manner, an obstructionist president of the Supreme Court was removed from office and a new slate of magistrates was able to be named with minimal influence from the military. Nonetheless, the appointment of new magistrates remained highly politicized and partisan.

Police reform frequently accompanied the judicial reforms. The Salvadoran police force had previously been a part of the military. The old police force had to be decommissioned and a new one formed. According to a 1994 report from the Washington Office on Latin America, this transition was accelerated following a "bloody bank heist" in which a member of the old National Police was identified on camera committing the crime.[57] However, the report continues, the government was unwilling to dissolve the "Anti-Delinquency Batallion" and instead absorbed it completely into the new National Civil Police. The vetting process was partially successful, including quotas of 20 percent former members of the National Police, 20 percent former members of the FMLN, and the remaining 60 percent civilians who had not participated on either side of the civil war.[58] In Guatemala, a similar transition was necessary,

---

[56] It should be obvious how readily this can turn into a benefit granted only to those judges who have found favor with the politicians or magistrates in control of the purse strings.

[57] Popkin et al., *Justice Delayed*, 10.

[58] Zamora and Holiday, "The Struggle for Lasting Reform: Vetting Processes in El Salvador," 98.

but again the problem of overlapping projects caused problems. The National Civil Police were developed with the help of Spanish donors and modeled on the Spanish Guardia Civil. However, an anti-narcotics force was developed at the same time with the assistance of the United States and modeled on the Drug Enforcement Administration. Reforms undertaken in Nicaragua in 1993 included the creation of new women's police stations and the adoption of community policing models.[59] In Honduras, the new office of the Human Rights Ombudsman proved instrumental in pushing to reform the security services.[60]

Another common reform, while not strictly judicial in nature, was the creation of new offices of human rights ombudsmen. During the 1980s and 1990s, all four of these countries created an independent office within their governments to monitor and enforce human rights. Nicaragua's ombudsmen's office is the most recently created, having been established in a constitutional reform in 1995 but not actually installed by the National Assembly until 1999.[61] Ombudsmen's offices may be quite extensive and have a variety of subordinate offices that focus on the rights of women, the rights of children, or the environment, among other concerns, as is the case in Guatemala. El Salvador at one time had several different ombudsmen and consolidated them under one office to maximize its power and influence. Ombudsmen receive and investigate complaints, compile annual reports to publicize issues related to human rights, and may, as in El Salvador, have an extensive apparatus to support their investigative functions.[62] Typically, their public documents identify their offices explicitly with transitions to democracy.

In El Salvador, judicial reform was initiated largely due to pressure from the United States in the late 1980s. As mentioned above, the United States hoped to push out communism and guerilla warfare by improving the conditions that were attracting people to those forces. Reform programs began the same year as the assumption of semi-democracy. This program focused on creating "a Commission to Investigate Criminal Acts, a commission to reform Salvadoran legislation (CORELESAL), a judicial protection unit, and judicial administration and training."[63] USAID was heavily involved in these efforts and pledged to work only with democratic governments who desired such

---

[59] Jubb, *Regional Mapping Study of Women's Police Stations in Latin America*; Ungar, *Policing Democracy*: Overcoming Obstacles to Citizen Security in Latin America.

[60] Call, "War Transitions and the New Civilian Security in Latin America," 14.

[61] "Como Nace la PDDH" www.pddh.gob.ni/?page_id=163 accessed March 15, 2017.

[62] "Unidad de Realidad Nacional" www.pddh.gob.sv/menuinfo/manustruct/menuescuela2/manurrmn accessed March 11, 2011.

[63] Popkin, *Peace without Justice*, 58.

programs. Unfortunately for USAID, such desires are difficult to ascribe to an entire government. According to Popkin, there was in fact little indigenous demand within the Salvadoran government for a fairer justice system and the president of the Supreme Court was particularly obstructionist.[64]

Judicial reform took on greater scope and significance when it was coupled to the peace process in El Salvador. A truth commission found numerous violations of human rights, but declined to refer any cases to the judiciary, finding that "El Salvador has no system for the administration of justice which meets the minimum requirements for objectivity and impartiality so that justice can be rendered reliably."[65] With the advent of peace, popular demand for judicial reform grew, including from the business sector who desired the legal stability that an independent judiciary could support.[66] While some consensus existed amongst FMLN supporters, some ARENA supporters, the business sector, and human rights activists that judicial reform was necessary, they had very different priorities for that reform. Human rights activists were primarily focused on criminal procedure, including trying to eliminate extra-judicial confessions and shortening pre-trial detentions, while business leaders were more focused on the need to secure property rights. The massive spike in violent crime that occurred in the 1990s further confused priorities as many people balked at extending human rights protections to criminals and viewed the accomplishments of postwar reforms disappointing.[67] Also, an anti-drug trafficking unit created with the assistance of the United States Drug Enforcement Agency strongly resisted efforts to incorporate it into the new National Civil Police, with its requisite training and screening of officers.[68]

Reforms also attempted to improve the independence of the judiciary and, for a time, succeeded. The most significant changes were within the judicial council, which had been originally created in 1989 after being included in the 1983 constitution, but had been dominated by the ARENA-associated president of the Supreme Court. This National Judiciary Council was given control over the judicial appointment process and was reformed to remove it from the control of the Supreme Court in 1999. Furthermore, a new judicial career law was passed to provide objective criteria for judicial selection. At the same time, attempts were made to purge the judiciary of corrupt judges, although these efforts were only partially successful.[69] Constitutional reforms were passed in

---

[64] Popkin, *Peace without Justice*.   [65] Ibid., 140.   [66] Ibid., 200.
[67] Call, "Democratisation, War and State-Building: Constructing the Rule of Law in El Salvador."
[68] Popkin, *Peace without Justice*, 184–85.
[69] Popkin reports that the Supreme Court declined to consider seriously thirty of forty-eight cases referred by ONUSAL in 1994–95. However, the next President of the Supreme Court was somewhat more aggressive, removing thirty judges and sanctioning others. Unfortunately,

1991 that mandated the appointment of a new Supreme Court under shorter, staggered terms at the expiration of the sitting Court's term in 1994. In Popkin's words, the new court "reflected an unprecedented ideological pluralism, with the majority chosen for their professional merits rather than their identification with a particular political party."[70] Unfortunately, as will be discussed in Chapter 6, this high degree of ideological and partisan independence would not become the norm in future appointment rounds.

Guatemala has been a target of international reformers since the 1980s, but the government only truly committed itself to judicial reform with the signing of the peace accords in 1996.[71] The peace process included a significant role for a United Nations verification mission (Misión Naciones Unidas en Guatemala or MINUGUA) to monitor compliance with the accords. Considering the broad scope of the peace accords MINUGUA could reasonably concern itself with many issues in Guatemalan politics, including rights protections. MINUGUA repeatedly called for justice sector reform, but focused its own attentions on the prosecutor's office.[72] There was less success in other arenas. As Popkin reports,

> As it focused on institution-building, MINUGUA found that expectations for reform were often unrealistic and that Guatemalan institutions had a limited capacity to absorb international assistance. Technical assistance could have only a limited impact on institutions plagued by structural problems such as insufficient resources and skilled staff, and lacking objective standards and effective mechanisms for evaluation and supervision."[73]

As Popkin makes clear, the tremendous resources poured in to Guatemala proved to be no match for the even greater problems of the mid-1990s.

The departure of MINUGUA in 2004 in no way spelled the end of judicial reform in Guatemala. Numerous other actors continued to be active in the country, including the International Financial Institutions, USAID, and several European unilateral donor agencies. An employee of one of these agencies reported to the author in 2004 that the proliferation of these donors created significant problems for the overall project of reform because there was insufficient coordination between these organizations. Nonetheless, some

---

these purges and the media leaks associated with them led many first-instance judges to feel that they and their profession were "under attack." Ibid., 210–14.

[70] Ibid., 202.

[71] Popkin reports that government commitment was so low prior to the peace accords as to lead USAID to pull out of the country altogether in 1991. Ibid., 262.

[72] Ibid., 253.   [73] Ibid., 254.

very significant reforms were made, such as the introduction of oral proceedings in criminal trials[74], as well as some practical improvements in efficiency and technology. Unfortunately, improvements in each institution within the justice system only produced new bottlenecks down the line: More arrests meant more cases for the Ministerio Público, a more productive MP meant more work for the already backlogged and under-staffed courts, and more efficient courts would ultimately mean more convicts sent to the extremely overcrowded prisons.

The disputed character of the Sandinista regime poses problems for tracing judicial reform and rule of law growth in Nicaragua. Major changes were made to the judiciary under the Sandinistas, including purging the judiciary of pre-revolutionary Somocista judges and replacing them with Sandinista partisans, some of whom did not have legal training, as discussed above; the Chamorro government after 1990 populated the judiciary with representatives of the right.[75] Sandinistas, led by supreme court president Alejandro Serrano Caldera, enshrined significant commitments to the rule of law and judicial independence in the 1987 constitution. The constitution writing process included input not only from a variety of civil society actors, but also from a large number of international legal experts.[76] It appears, however, from the "La Verona" case that these guarantees of independence were not enforced.

The 1990s saw greater international involvement in Nicaragua's judiciary. Numerous international donor groups and unilateral governmental organizations participated in judicial reform efforts, including the Inter-American Bank and the World Bank, USAID, the European Union, and the Spanish, Norwegian, and German governments, up to as many as eleven donor groups working with the justice sector as a whole.[77] One interviewee in 2004 lamented that this proliferation of donors allowed the supreme court magistrates, whose approval was needed for any project to be implemented, to use the project funds as clientelist resources. These international efforts may have produced gains in efficiency and even crime prevention in the rural areas[78], they appear to have done little to develop true judicial independence. As Chapter 6 will

---

[74] Hendrix, "Innovation in Criminal Procedure in Latin America: Guatemala's Conversion to the Adversarial System."

[75] Close, *Nicaragua*.

[76] Serrano Caldera, "The Rule of Law in the Nicaraguan Revolution."

[77] Salas, "From Law and Development to the Rule of Law: New and Old Issues in Justice Reform in Latin America."

[78] Quintanilla, "Support for the Administration of Justice in Nicaragua: The Rural Judicial Facilitators Program."

examine in more detail, the 2000s brought deeper political dependency of the judiciary.

Since 1982, the Honduran constitution has promised Hondurans an *estado de derecho* that will provide for human rights, civil rights, and the availability of the legal processes of amparo and habeas corpus to enforce those rights. That document also asserts the independence of the judiciary as a third equal branch of government, although its politicized selection process raises some concerns. According to Custodio, judges in the 1980s were chosen for their political obedience, severely curtailing the possibility of rights-enforcement.[79] Honduras, along with Guatemala and El Salvador, was part of the first round of judicial reform efforts in Latin America, owing to the early presence of donors in these troubled countries in the 1980s. Early efforts in the 1980s focused primarily on capacity building and budgeting with the goals of strengthening an institution considered vital for both democracy promotion and market growth.[80]

The nature of the abuses of judicial integrity in the 1980s and their impact on human rights appear to have laid down established patterns that continued through the 1990s (and, indeed, through the 2000s, as will be discussed in Chapter 6). Because judges were formally independent, politicians did not have the political will to create reforms that would take away the informal political dependence of judges. The dominance of two, long-lived parties in Honduras has contributed to the ossification of those patterns of partisan domination. In addition, because there was no true peace process, neither international nor domestic actors had the opportunity and leverage to push for fundamental justice sector reforms. However, the reductions in the military did remove one source of infringements on judicial autonomy. As such, by the 1990s, Honduras developed into a partisan judicial regime.

CONCLUSION: JUDICIAL LEGACIES OF AUTHORITARIANISM AND REFORM

The institutions that comprised the government control regimes of Guatemala, Honduras, El Salvador, and Nicaragua during their repressive periods, as well as the efforts to reform those institutions during the protracted transitions to democracy, produce significant and troubling legacies for their contemporary judicial regimes. The strategies used and the currencies employed to resolve

---

[79] Custodio, "The Human Rights Crisis in Honduras."
[80] Hammergren, "Twenty-Five Years of Latin American Judicial Reforms: Achievements, Disappointments, and Emerging Issues."

major conflicts during these periods go on to shape the contemporary judicial regimes found in these countries a decade or two later. Where the judiciary was controlled through patronage and partisan cronyism in Nicaragua and Honduras, the practice of pact-making has not necessarily diminished. The practice of agreeing on the distribution of judicial and bureaucratic patronage has led to a highly partisan judiciary in those two countries. While pact-making has been less significant of an influence in El Salvador, there remains a substantial partisan influence on the judges in that country due in large part to the appointment practices. Some of these practices are the result of an extensive reform process that saw initial successes being somewhat overshadowed by traditional political practices.

Meanwhile, crime skyrocketed immediately following the peace processes in Guatemala, El Salvador, and Honduras. Some argue that this is a continuation of the legacies of violence that took place during the war years, but it appears to have more to do with inadequate processes of demilitarization and decommissioning. The rise of drug-trafficking gangs on the isthmus can be traced directly to the lack of oversight of military and security forces during the 1980s. The Washington Office on Latin America has traced the origins of several specific gangs to the activities of then-active military in transporting contraband in Guatemala.[81] Members of the Honduran military and the Contra army operating in Honduras became heavily involved in the drug trade, to the extent that the Contras had become almost self-sustaining financially and were able to resist for a short time attempts by the United States to close them down.[82] The most famous kidnapping ring in El Salvador was run by the military during the 1980s.[83] The arrival of peace would bring no respite, either: with the reduction in military forces and the reintegration of Contras and other guerillas, a glut of weapons flooded the black market in the region, bolstering the activities of criminal organizations across the isthmus.

Another long-term legacy of authoritarian rule has been the prevalence of corruption in all four countries. While many factors contribute to the enduring popularity of corruption around the globe, government control judicial regimes create a particular set of incentives for citizens to engage in it when dealing with the courts. Because there were not open legal avenues to reliably seek to exonerate and free the innocent (nor the guilty), corruption was often the only option for those facing the organized violence of the state. For those

---

[81] Peacock and Beltrán, "Hidden Powers in Post-Conflict Guatemala: Illegal Armed Groups and the Forces Behind Them"; Brands, *Crime, Violence, and the Crisis in Guatemala.*

[82] Schulz and Schulz, *The United States, Honduras, and the Crisis in Central America.*

[83] Williams and Walter, *Militarization and Demilitarization in El Salvador's Transition to Democracy,* 135.

with the right friends, whether in the embassy or the military, and enough money or other power, it might be possible to escape state violence by means of a private conversation and exchange. In contemporary Central America, the organized violence of the state remains escapable for many through similar connections, private conversations, and exchanges. The difficulty in escape now is largely a result of inefficiencies and delays rather than a deliberate military or government policy of extrajudicial detention, but the effect of leaving many innocent, powerless people in prison without a trial for lengthy periods is not that different.

Not all legacies of this period are negative, however. In Guatemala and El Salvador, the judiciary was largely not asked to legitimate state violence as they were largely ignored by the authoritarian governments. It appears to be easier for a judiciary that has been "left out" of authoritarian government to establish itself as a politically independent institution in a democratic transition. While imperfections remain, Guatemala's judiciary since 1993 has been relatively independent. Problems with political independence in El Salvador have been more stubborn, however. The strong partisan backing of the judiciary in Nicaragua and Honduras through the repressive period, through the transitions, and into the contemporary period has created a situation in which politically loyal judges enjoy enough patronage to be protected in general from incursions on their day-to-day autonomy.

The reform processes introduced in this chapter had as their intention the creation of liberal judicial regimes in all of these countries. They succeeded in a number of areas, especially where technical improvements were needed. Ultimately, however, these reform efforts have failed to achieve the kinds of judicial institutions and behaviors that reformers sought. Reforms have fallen short not necessarily because of a lack of expertise, nor a lack of local knowledge, nor a lack of coordination of resources or programs, but because of a political problem. Even where politicians expressed their (perhaps even sincere) support for judicial reforms and the rule of law, elites both political and otherwise lacked the will to adopt constitutionalist strategies when major politico-legal conflicts arose. In some cases, they changed the strategies they adopted and the currencies they employed, but they often shifted to legalist or partisan-political currencies or to the use of unofficial and non-governmental violence. The currencies employed to resolve these conflicts helped to guarantee the success or failure of the general reform project.

5

Clandestine Control in Guatemala

We are living in a very difficult period now, because... Corruption is one thing and intimidation is another. Because corruption is not necessarily intimidation, right? Intimidation is a form of obliging a judge to not apply the law. And that affects a lot in all levels because then the judge out of fear doesn't do what the law says... There is no prompt and complete justice. This is a grave harm in this country at this time.[1]

– (G2009–02)

After the resumption of civilian democratic rule in 1985, Guatemala experienced a shift from a government control judicial regime to a clandestine control judicial regime. Institutional changes were made to enhance judicial independence from partisan influence, including by changing the actors who participate in the process of appointing magistrates. However, few changes were made that could adequately respond to the rising power of the so-called "hidden powers" that would come, by the 2000s, to wield considerable influence over all levels of the judiciary, as well as the police and prosecution services. In fact, some of the efforts to enhance independence may have contributed to the decline in judicial autonomy as societal actors have engaged in perverse formalism to punish judges and each other. Guatemalan judges work under a situation of substantial threat, primarily from organized crime. After more than four decades in which incursions on justice could be routinely blamed on the armed forces, it appears that, by the late 2000s, the military had

---

[1] Original: Estamos viviendo una etapa muy difícil en la actualidad porque... una cosa es la corrupción y la otra es la intimidación. Por la corrupción no necesariamente es intimidación, ¿verdad? La intimidación es una forma de obligar a los jueces a que no aplican la ley. Y eso sí afecta muchísimo en todo nivel porque entonces el juez por temor no hace lo que la ley le dice... No hay una justicia pronta y cumplida. Eso es un grave daño en este país en este momento.

largely stepped back from interfering with the justice system. Unfortunately for Guatemalans, organized crime surged forward as the military pulled back.

Guatemala's movement from a government control regime to an impunity regime was far from inevitable. Had the civilian police and prosecution services been made stronger upon the return to democracy in 1985, had miscreants in the military not been allowed to operate openly, and had corruption been more closely controlled within the justice sector from the beginning of democracy, Guatemala might have moved to a liberal judicial regime. The deterioration of the Guatemalan state after 1985 allowed for the development of an impunity regime. Institutional design choices that provided multiple entry points for corruption and allowed societal actors to use the law selectively in a sort of perverse formalism compounded these problems. However, events in 2015 gave some indication that efforts to overcome this clandestine control may be gaining traction. Widespread street protests in response to a corruption investigation led to the resignation of the president. The "Guatemalan Spring" and the changes that produced it, including numerous investigations by a resident international commission that also worked to strengthen domestic institutions produced a watershed moment in Guatemala, but it remains too soon to know whether those changes will prove lasting or fundamental. Concerns about the impact of criminal and other pressures on judicial societal autonomy remain.

JUSTICE IN A CONTESTED "NONTRANSITION": 1986–2002

The fifteen years following the reintroduction of democratic rule in Guatemala witnessed a struggle between efforts to promote the rule of law, constitutionalism, and human rights on the one hand and efforts to preserve old privileges on the other. Guatemala's 1986 transition to democracy has been termed an "electoralist nontransition" as the military continued to dominate politics in the context of a bloody civil war despite the adoption of electoral politics.[2] The new constitution, however, reiterated a commitment to judicial independence and created a constitutional court that could provide a check on the actions of the government. Furthering these changes, Guatemala became host to a variety of efforts to improve the functioning and independence of the judiciary. At the same time, sometimes halting moves were made to diminish the role of the armed forces in Guatemalan politics. The judicial response to the 1993 *autogolpe* by President Serrano ushered in a series of reforms to the judiciary and jump started the then-faltering peace process. Other high-profile

---

[2] Linz and Stepan, *Problems of Democratic Transition and Consolidation.*

legal battles would follow concerning the murders of human rights activists by members of the military. The 1996 peace accords allowed the pro-democratic legal moves to happen and initiated the gradual and partial removal of the military from the political scene. Unfortunately, the postwar era's diminished repressive capacity has coincided with the rise of organized crime, leading to the large amounts of violence and insecurity seen in the 2000s.

The manner in which these conflicts were contested and resolved helped to create parallel tracks, with the democratic rule of law on one track and clandestine control on the other. In this period, it was possible to enforce a democratic rule of law only in a few, well-supported cases, while other significant conflicts would be resolved through corruption, presenting a façade of a democratic rule of law, but in reality resisting that transition. These conflicts established standard operating procedures for politico-legal conflicts in Guatemala. These conflicts helped to solidify the uses of certain "currencies" of power, pitting the constitutional currency against the currency of unofficial violence.

The "Serranazo" and the Cloaking of Military Power

During the first ten years of democracy (prior to the 1996 peace accords), there was negotiation between civilian state powers and the military over the proper role of the military and the desirability of democracy.[3] In the early 1990s, with the civil war stalemated in the highlands and increasing international pressure for a peaceful resolution, there were several officers' mutinies. In the face of a hostile, fractious Congress and a declining ability to govern, President Jorge Serrano Elias (1991–1993) initiated an *autogolpe*, seeking to reconstitute all of the state powers, including the judiciary and the Constitutional Court, with his supporters. Ultimately resolved through the joint efforts of the civil society, the military, and the Constitutional Court, the *Serranazo*, as the incident is known, represents an important milestone in the development of Guatemala's weak democracy. Although this event cemented civilian government in Guatemala, it was only possible for the Constitutional Court to play the role of democratic watchdog because the military ultimately decided to side with democracy. Many Guatemalan lawyers listed this case as among the most important cases handled by the Guatemalan courts in the previous twenty years. In a 2010 interview with the author, Constitutional Court President Roberto Molina Barreto went so far as to call it "a classic example of what this court does," i.e., protecting the constitutional order. The resolution of the *Serranazo* could

---

[3] Schirmer, *The Guatemalan Military Project: A Violence Called Democracy.*

have been a critical juncture that put Guatemala on the path to a stronger democracy and stronger rule of law based on constitutionalism, but forces of unofficial violence resisted and maintained a parallel track for conflict resolution.

In 1993, Guatemala was still a very weak democracy. The writing of the 1985 constitution was done under military guidance and against the backdrop of an ongoing civil war. The election of Serrano produced a peaceful alternation in power, but it was between two right-wing parties; a left-wing president would not be elected until 2007. Rather than indicating a strong democracy, the alternation in power from one party to another in Guatemala is a symptom of the weakness of the political parties. Few political parties have lasted more than one electoral cycle and broad-based coalitions with vague ideologies have been the norm. Additionally, infringements on civil liberties, including the use of forced disappearance and torture, continued in 1993, albeit at lower levels than the 1979–1983 height of the civil war.

President Serrano was elected in 1991 with 68.1 percent of valid votes in the second round. As has become typical in Guatemala's feckless party system, he was elected under the banner of a "movement" and had short coattails. Only 18 of 116 deputies in the legislature belonged to his movement. Consequently, compromise and coalition building were vital to his presidency from the beginning. The need to create coalitions allowed for the expansion of corruption within the Congress. Corruption also permeated other sections of the government, most notably the Supreme Court. Serrano was also unable to get complete support for the peace process to end the three-decades-old civil war and talks had floundered. By 1993, Serrano found that disagreements with the Congress had become intractable. A substantial cleavage was developing between the president and the other political elites. Looking to follow the model of Peruvian president Alberto Fujimori's successful *autogolpe* in Peru the previous year, Serrano suspended the constitution on May 25, 1993, and dismissed both the legislature and the two high courts.[4]

One retired judge recalled the events of the Serranazo as a time in which many good people did not feel they could say no:

> Serrano dismantled the Supreme Court and then put in his own magistrates and, sadly, among them were many good people who did not have the character to say no. I had a colleague in the court who it came to [to be

---

[4] Edelberto Torres-Rivas, "Guatemala: Democratic Governability," in *Constructing Democratic Governance: Latin America and the Caribbean in the 1990s, Part IV: Latin America and the Caribbean*, ed. Jorge I. Dominguez, and Abraham F. Lowenthal (Baltimore, MD: The Johns Hopkins University Press, 1996).

put on the court]. He said, "I can't. I suffer from an ulcer." And they didn't manage to make him accept.[5] (G2009–07)

In this recollection, this retired judge hinted at the intricate difficulties that would come as Guatemala tried to recover from the coup and to purge its judiciary and legislature: Much of the political class was implicated in the coup and the corruption that preceded it. Where could a reformer begin?

As Suzanne Jonas notes, "from the first moment, public opposition to the coup was clear" as several cabinet ministers refused to resign and continued their posts in "open constitutional defiance."[6] Rachel McCleary describes the quick response of the organized civil society to oppose the coup. She argues that this response was only possible because of long-term cooperation and trust-building within the economic sector. In her book, she traces a flurry of meetings and contacts among the Coordinating Committee of Agricultural, Commercial, Industrial, and Financial Associations (CACIF) and politicians during the brief period of the coup.[7] Edelberto Torres Rivas argues that the response to the "Serranazo" coup was arguably the first time that the business interests unequivocally rejected non-democratic solutions to the country's political problems, as well as being almost certainly the first time that civil society had been so unified. Torres Rivas also points out that the military's role in moving to support civil society and constitutionality and backing away from support of the *autogolpe* was similarly ground-breaking.[8]

McCleary's account gives primacy to the actions of the organized business sector, minimizing the significance of the actions of the Constitutional Court and other actors. However, on the first day of the coup, the Constitutional Court magistrates met in secret at a downtown law firm with members of the College of Lawyers and Notaries (Colegio de Abogados y Notarios de Guatemala) after the Court had been locked out of their offices and told to dissolve themselves. They issued a *sentencia* condemning the coup and declaring it unconstitutional. However, they were unable to have it published in the official government newspaper, which would have given it official authority. As negotiations developed between the military and civil society interests, military leaders made clear that they would not act against the president unless there was a clear statement that their actions would be constitutional. On

---

5 Original: La Corte suprema de Justicia Serrano desmanteló y después puso sus propios magistrados y, lamentablemente, entre ellos había muy buena gente que no tuvieron el carácter de decir no. Yo tuve un compañero en la corte al que lo llevaron [para puso a él en la corte]. Él se ha dicho "yo no puedo. Sufro de úlcera." Y no lograron que [él] aceptar.

6 Jonas, "Electoral Problems and the Democratic Project in Guatemala," 35.

7 McCleary, *Dictating Democracy: Guatemala and the End of Violent Revolution.*

8 Torres-Rivas, "Guatemala: Democratic Governability," 57.

May 31st, the Constitutional Court issued a second decision, which was published in the official newspaper, reiterating its previous invalidation of Serrano's *autogolpe* and ordering agents of the state to take necessary measures to end the crisis. The Court thus simultaneously legitimated military action against the president and removed any legal barriers (i.e., the possibility of future trials) that might have prevented the military from acting. On June 1st, the military announced that it would comply with the Constitutional Court's order. Serrano resigned as president and was permitted to fly with his family into exile. One judge, reflecting on the Serranazo in 2009, lamented that an effort to extradite Serrano to stand trial had not been successful (G2009–13).

The Constitutional Court was left as the only option to remove Serrano in 1993 because of the corruption of the Congress. Civil society leaders initially approached the Congress to try to engineer an end to the crisis and were frustrated. Because the Congress had acquiesced to the suspension of the constitution and to their own dismissal, it was not clear that they had any authority to act until the constitution was restored. They might have been able to overcome that problem, however, if not for the concerns of many deputies that they not be subjected to prosecution or purges due to their own corrupt acts. The civil society coalition pushed for the Congress to submit letters of resignation *en masse* to provide for an investigation and purge of corrupt deputies. Not enough deputies were willing to do this and the plan fell apart. Even after the Constitutional Court acted and the military removed Serrano, civil society leaders called for the Congress to purge itself, as the constitution did not allow for an external purge. As the crisis receded and normalcy returned, the deputies felt more secure in their positions and refused to submit to any purge, although there was a purge of the Supreme Court and the judicial branch.[9]

As then-Constitutional Court President Eduardo Epaminondas González Dubón memorialized the events, he reported that he was driven by the Constitutional Court's "essential function," which was the "defense of the constitutional order."[10] Given the personal risk involved in opposing the *autogolpe*,[11]

---

9 McCleary, *Dictating Democracy.*
10 *Ley de Amparo*, art. 149 reads: *"Función esencial de la Corte de Constitucionalidad: La Corte de Constitucionalidad es un Tribunal permanente de jurisdicción privativa cuya función es la defensa del orden constitucional; actúa como Tribunal colegiado con independencia de los demás organismos del Estado y ejerce funciones específicas que le asigna la Constitución y esta ley."* (Essential Function of the Constitutional Court: The Constitutional Court is a permanent tribunal with exclusive jurisdiction whose function is the defense of the constitutional order; it acts as a collegiate tribunal with independence from the other State organs and exercises specific functions assigned to it by the Constitution and by this law [the *Ley de Amparo*].)
11 In 1993, Guatemala was still at war with the guerrillas, although the actual fighting was largely at a stalemate. There were factions within the military who were anxious to resume aggressive

the magistrates could have been expected to obey the decree and leave their posts, as the Supreme Court did. It seems likely that the *sentencia* issued on May 25th was the product of strong personal conviction among the magistrates, as supported by the civil society elites. Their later two decisions were clearly designed to fulfill the needs of the civil society organizations, however sincerely the magistrates may have believed in them. The Constitutional Court's opinion of its actions was so strong that it published all of the documents related to its involvement in this affair in a small volume, in the interest of future generations knowing "how much has been necessary to maintain the rule of law in Guatemala"[12]

A retired judge, interviewed in 2009, recalled the important role of the Constitutional Court in bringing the coup to a clean end. She praised the Constitutional Court for avoiding the need for future coups or a rupture in the state, drawing explicit parallels to the events unfolding in 2009 in Honduras related to the coup against Honduran President Manuel Zelaya:

> This court [the one installed by Serrano] delayed very little because then came the coup and then came the total reform of the coup against Serrano... Nobody played a preponderant role like the Constitutional Court. They went to the commanders, they saw... In this country, what happened in Honduras [in 2009] didn't happen because the Constitutional Court assumed this role... that's without the need for a coup against the state or a rupture of the state.[13] (G2009–07)

The decision of the military to side with the civil society coalition and the Constitutional Court against the president marks an important turning point: Guatemala would not return to official violence as a way of government. However, this development did not succeed in ending the reliance on unofficial violence. On the contrary, unofficial violence quickly reasserted itself in the assassination of the president of the Constitutional Court less than a year later. In the years following the Serranazo, unofficial violence would continue to grow, eclipsing official violence. This violence, including the assassination of

tactics against the guerillas, and who had attempted coups and mutinies in recent years. Furthermore, constitutional democracy was only several years old and it had not yet been a decade since the period of the greatest levels of repression and human rights violations.

[12] In the original: "...*para que las futuras generaciones tengan una fuente en la cual puedan enterarse de un acontecimiento de los tantos que han sido necesarios para mantener el Estado de Derecho en Guatemala.*".

[13] Original: Esta corte [la corte instalado por Serrano] tardó muy poco porque vino el golpe y vino la reforma en todo el golpe a Serrano... Nadie tuvo un papel preponderante como la corte de constitucionalidad. Ellos fueron a los comandantes, ellos de vera... en este país, no pasó lo que pasó en Honduras [en 2009] fijo que la corte de constitucionalidad asumió [este papel]... da que es sin la necesidad de golpe de estado o rompido del estado.

the Constitutional Court president should be understood as a part of the tug of war between forces of violence and forces of the rule of law. Certainly, this assassination signaled the success of the power of violence, but the peace process and constitutional reforms would prove to dramatically reduce the official violence that was permitted prior to Serrano's coup.

In the aftermath of Serrano's coup, significant constitutional reforms were passed including a shortening of the terms of the supreme court magistrates who had been in office during the coup and changing the method of electing magistrates. As one retired magistrate recalled in 2009:

> I was a Supreme Court magistrate between 1994 and 1997. We arrived as the Supreme Court after a constitutional reform. What that did was change the way that magistrates were chosen. Really, the magistrates had to be replaced. And it had been politicized: the Congress had the power to choose. There was an element of corruption between the Congress and the Supreme Court. And that was a way to justify the coup by the president then, Jorge Serrano Elías, that took down the Congress and the Supreme Court. Thus, there was a need to purge the Court and the Congress. The people understood the causes of the coup, everybody knew there was corruption, it's similar to what's happening now in Honduras. We wanted to use the right method of purging. For that, a popular referendum to shorten the terms of the Supreme Court. And after that, they changed the form of selection.[14] (G2009–12)

The primary change to the election process for Supreme Court magistrates was the creation of the selection committees. The goal was to remove power over the Supreme Court from the hands of a corrupt Congress that had refused to submit to the purge of its members. The solution was the creation of two selection committees for the appellate courts and the Supreme Court. This retired magistrate suggested, as did another retired judge, that the selection committees worked quite well in 1994 to reduce the amount of corruption in the selection of magistrates. However, as will be discussed further below, the

---

[14] Original: Yo era magistrada de corte suprema de justicia entre 1994 y 1999. Llegamos a la corte suprema después de una reforma constitucional. Y que se hizo para cambiar la forma en que se eligen los magistrados. Al que realmente los magistrados habían tenido que ser reemplazados. Y entonces había politizada: El Congreso tenía [el poder] de elegir.... Había un elemento de corrupción entre el congreso y la corte suprema de justicia. Y ese era un vía para justificar un golpe de estado [por] el presidente entonces, Jorge Serrano Elías, que desavió la corte y desavió el congreso.... Así la necesidad de que había una depuración de la corte y del congreso. Las personas comprendían las causas del golpe, todo sabíamos que había corrupción, es similar que hoy es pasando en Honduras. Deseamos que usaran un camino correcto de depurar. De eso, una consulta popular a la gente vota para cortar los periodos de la corte suprema. Y después de eso, cambiaron la forma de elección.

selection committees had themselves become contested sites of corruption by 2009.

Another consequence of the 1993 *autogolpe* was the resumption of the peace process, which ultimately concluded with a comprehensive set of accords signed by all parties on December 29, 1996. Ramiro de León Carpio, the former human rights ombudsman who was appointed to serve the rest of Serrano's term, helped to usher the peace process to a successful conclusion – despite the murder in July 1993 of his cousin who was participating in the peace negotiations. The accords included details about reducing the size and role of the military, increasing the role of civil society in national life, and protecting the rights of indigenous Guatemalans, among other things. The end of the thirty-six year long civil war also helped open the door to international reformers, including a United Nations verification mission, MINUGUA. The goal of these reformers and observers was to ensure that Guatemala transitioned to being a democratic state in which all could participate and all would be governed by the rule of law. The reality was more difficult: efforts to build up policing did not keep pace with the drawdown military power, unregulated weapons flooded the country, and criminal violence grew exponentially.

Battles Over the Past: Transitional (In)Justice and Human Rights Trials

In 1996, an amnesty law was passed that eliminated the possibility of transitional justice in the form of trials or widespread purges beyond what had been attempted following the Serranazo. Transitional justice has been an important goal for many in transitions to democracy, especially following civil wars.[15] However, Guatemala was one of many countries wherein high profile "transitional trials" were not possible at the time because those in control of the repressive violence prior to the transition largely remained in power and sought to protect themselves. Even without an official process for transitional justice trials, the drive to bring human rights violators to justice has been strong among at least some sectors of Guatemalan civil society. The trials for the murders of anthropologist Myrna Mack and Monsignor Juan Gerardi, starkly revealed the rival systems of governmentality[16] and the forces behind them. That members of the military were ultimately convicted of both murders suggests that the Guatemalan state was becoming less willing

[15] Sikkink, *The Justice Cascade*; Lutz and Sikkink, "The Justice Cascade: The Evolution and Impact of Foreign Human Rights Trials in Latin America"; Olsen, Payne, and Reiter, *Transitional Justice in Balance.*

[16] Rose, O'Malley, and Valverde, "Governmentality."

to tolerate official or quasi-official violence. These verdicts carry great significance in Guatemala even though many suspect that the "intellectual authors" who planned these murders remain free; nearly every Guatemala lawyer and judge interviewed in 2009 mentioned them among their top five most significant trials.

Myrna Mack was a Guatemalan anthropologist who studied marginalized communities among Guatemala's indigenous Mayan population. Through her work, she had been critical of the Guatemalan government and military for their treatment of the Mayans. On September 11, 1990, she was assassinated by a military death squad. Her sister Helen Mack, who would found the Myrna Mack Foundation and remains a prominent voice in Guatemalan civil society, filed a complaint to the Inter-American Human Rights Commission. For over five years, Helen Mack tried to push the case through the resistant Guatemalan courts before the Commission would accept that it would not be possible to "exhaust domestic remedies" in this case, as the American Convention of Human Rights requires. In 2000, the Guatemalan government admitted "institutional responsibility" for the murder. The government ultimately paid compensation to the Mack family in 2004.

However, the process before the Commission took place entirely outside of the Guatemalan judicial system, largely as a result of delays and intransigence within Guatemala. A parallel process occurred within Guatemala, where one member of the military was convicted of the murder in 1994 and the complaints against three others remained open under orders of the Supreme Court. In 1995, those three cases were referred to a military tribunal for further proceedings. According to the Myrna Mack Foundation, those cases remain open. Notably, the intellectual authors who planned and ordered her murder have not been sanctioned. Despite the government's acknowledgement before the Commission that the government itself ordered the murder, no individual has been convicted of giving that order. It is also noteworthy that the most productive period in this case on the domestic side coincided with the period immediately following President Serrano's coup, when the newly-elected Supreme Court was at its least corrupt. In sum, the Myrna Mack case was significant for the Guatemalan government's admission of guilt, which suggests that the government was moving in the direction of at least voicing support for the rule of law. Nonetheless, the case is also significant for revealing the seeming permanence of impunity for human rights violations within the Guatemalan legal system.

The second major murder trial that shook Guatemala in the 1990s involved the 1998 murder of the Catholic priest who had been active in fighting for the rights of the indigenous majority in Guatemala and had founded the

Archbishop's Office on Human Rights (*Oficina del arzaobispado para los derechos humanos*, ODHA), Monsignor Juan Gerardi. Gerardi was murdered in his garage two days after presenting the report of the Recovery of Historical Memory Project, the first truth commission report in Guatemala's history. Ultimately, Gerardi's murderers would be tried in domestic, civilian courts. Gerardi's former organization, ODHA, would make itself an accessory prosecutor in the case, helping to push the investigation and prosecution forward. The institution of the accessory prosecutor (*querellante adhesivo*, or the QA) has become an important tool for Guatemalan NGOs, as it allows an interested party, once certified, to act as an accessory prosecutor. Once certified, the interested party gains the right to view all evidence collected by the prosecutor's office and to conduct their own investigations in the case, including making motions before the court to compel discovery.

Nery Rodenas, a staff attorney at ODHA interviewed by the author in 2004, indicated that the prosecutors from the Ministerio Público with whom they worked on these cases were generally dedicated and worked within their abilities to further the cases, but were often hampered by lack of resources, lack of training, and external pressure to not prosecute. ODHA's lawyers were insulated from official pressures and could often dedicate more resources to the Gerardi case than could the MP alone. Notably, ODHA was able to draw on the support of international organizations who could provide experts in forensics, something that has continued to be important as more cases have been prosecuted in the 2000s involving the mass murders of the war years. Although a large number of judges were threatened off the case before it could be resolved, three members of the military were convicted of the murder in 2001 and sentenced to thirty years; another priest was sentenced to twenty years as an accomplice. On appeal, two of the officers' sentences were reduced by ten years; the third officer had been killed in prison in the interim. Although some have argued that the trial was a politicized show trial and that Gerardi's death was really the result of a gay tryst gone wrong,[17] the verdict remains important as one of the emblematic trials in post-war Guatemala.

Both of these cases also reveal the power of the institution of the QA. By taking on the role of the QA, NGO lawyers and activists put themselves in a position of needing to increase their capacity for investigation and legal maneuvering. Very often, this strengthening was done by reaching out to other

---

[17] This theory is most famously put forward in the book *¿Quién mató al Obispo?* and was echoed by one of the lawyers interviewed for this research in 2009. It is notable that the Guatemalan government has explained away human rights violations against Catholic clergy through accusation of homosexual trysts more than once.

NGOs, both local and international, which could help handle investigative tasks and share effective legal techniques. It is also worth mentioning that these coalitions of organizations, especially those including international organizations, can also help to provide security that is desperately needed when an organization investigates an assassination by members of the military. Becoming a QA gives an interested party a tremendous amount of influence over the course of a prosecution, especially in cases where the government's prosecutors may not be able or willing to investigate and prosecute adequately. The QA role has been used by a number of human rights NGOs since the 1990s and has contributed to the development of their legal capabilities. Additionally, the QA activity of NGOs has aided the state prosecutors as well. The interactions between the state prosecutors and NGOs have been relatively cooperative, but NGOs acting as QA have significantly more freedom to make progress in these investigations than NGOs that are not QAs. The Myrna Mack Foundation and ODHA remain very powerful and active NGOs in Guatemala.

THE CREATIVITY OF PERSISTENT CORRUPTION: 2003–2014

Attempts by international and domestic reformers to create in Guatemala a strong liberal judicial regime within a liberal polity have been frustrated by the decay of the state. The enforcement of the currency of constitutional law, which is integral to a liberal judicial regime is only possible with a strong state that effectively penetrates most reaches of social and territorial space. As with most state endeavors, the constitutional project is greatly aided by a state that is not just strong but also legitimate. Guatemala has witnessed extensive rule of law reform efforts with little success. This long-term failure can be attributed largely to state weakness. Crime is rampant and allows the least democratic elements of society to penetrate the state. This criminal colonization of the state apparatus depresses the legitimacy of the government, the constitution, and even the peace accords. One result of these phenomena is a government that can effectively employ neither constitutional law nor political legislation, the respective defining currencies of liberal and partisan regimes. Consequently, the judiciary becomes implicated in the web of unofficial violence, in effect trapped by it.

Fundamentally, the state itself shrunk when the military was cut back because a strong civilian state had not yet been created. Making matters worse, some of the very military officers who were decommissioned were the actual leaders of smuggling rings. The Washington Office on Latin America has detailed the connections between certain former military officers and the gangs,[18] although little evidence exists of connection between the current military high command and the drug gangs. Indeed, it appears that the military command is making efforts to regain control of Guatemalan territory by attacking the *narcos*. However, that does not mean that individual members of the armed forces may not be involved in organized crime. Anecdotally, there are whispers of private citizens providing information to the military in exchange for promises of protection, while others refuse to do so out of fear that someone within the military will reveal the informant's identity to the *narcos*.

Guatemala's difficult economic situation has also contributed to the rise of organized crime of all kinds. In the absence of economic and social opportunities in most of the country, poor migrants have poured into the capital, making Guatemala City the largest city in Central America and the Caribbean. The consequence of this widespread dislocation has been the creation of sprawling, marginal communities in Guatemala City where workers travel long periods to get to their jobs and their children are left largely unattended either by their parents or by an unevenly distributed education system. One informant suggested that these children comprise the majority of gang members as teenagers and young adults. Most of these gangs are not involved in drug trafficking, but rather in robbery, kidnapping, and extortion rings. The problem of robbery has become particularly acute on the intra-city buses; in 2009, *Prensa Libre* reported that one route was attacked an average of seven times a day. In response, there have been many strikes by bus drivers, some bus companies have hired armed guards, and the city has begun to provide a service of secured buses that carry no cash and pick up passengers only at designated stops guarded by the police.

By 2012, societal actors posed a more significant threat to citizens than the government. Amnesty International reported that Guatemalans, especially human rights activists, are still at risk of being threatened or tortured – but that the culprit is more likely to be the drug-trafficking gangs.[19] Human Rights Watch reported, "Guatemala's weak and corrupt law enforcement institutions have proved incapable of containing the powerful organized crime groups and criminal gangs that contribute to one of the highest violent crime rates in the Americas. Illegal armed groups are believed to be responsible for ongoing threats and targeted attacks against civil society actors and justice officials."[20]

[18] Peacock and Beltrán, "Hidden Powers in Post-Conflict Guatemala: Illegal Armed Groups and the Forces Behind Them."
[19] Amnesty International, "Annual Report 2012: Guatemala."
[20] Human Rights Watch, "World Report 2012: Guatemala."

Even if Guatemala's politicians were angels, the state apparatus remains too weak to combat the violence of street gangs and drug traffickers. As one lawyer interviewed in 2009 opined:

> What we see not as accentuated is the theme of corruption, but the theme of intimidation is very accentuated. Where judges can receive complaints against them for doing something so that they would stop or things that really are part of their legal duties, but how it affects them, when the opposing party presents complaints against the judges . . . It is a form of intimidating the system of justice. Who does these kinds of things? They are people very powerful in Guatemala. It's people who are involved in very delicate cases, or cases of corruption, or cases involving a lot of money, or in organized crime. They are involved in that type of thing. And then when a judge comes . . . well, by one manner or another, they intimidate him or they involve him in an act of corruption. And when they don't manage [to corrupt him], here comes the intimidation. That is very hard.[21] (G2009–02)

A push and pull between violence and the rule of law continues, only the primary threat to the rule of law in Guatemala is now unofficial violence.

The Persistence of Power: A General Runs for President

Ten years after President Serrano's coup, a constitutional crisis erupted between the Supreme Court and the Constitutional Court over the presidential candidacy of General Ríos Montt. The lines between official and unofficial violence blurred in the attempt by General Efrain Ríos Montt to become president in 2003. Ríos Montt had previously attempted to run for president, but his candidacy was rejected under Article 186 of the 1985 Guatemalan constitution, which bans anyone who has taken power through a coup from becoming president. Ríos Montt had taken power in a coup in 1981 and had overseen some of the bloodiest abuses of the civil war. He nonetheless enjoyed a lengthy civilian political career following democratization in 1986, primarily representing the right-wing Guatemalan Republican Front (*Frente*

---

[21] Original: Lo que nosotros miramos no es tan acentuado la tema de corrupción, pero sí es muy acentuado la tema de la intimidación. En donde los jueces por hacer algo reciben denuncias en contra él para que los hubren o cosas que realmente sí es parte de su atribución legal pero como afectan, cuando le contra parte presente denuncias en contra los jueces . . . es una forma de intimidar a la sistema de justicia. ¿Quién hace eso tipo de cosas? Sí es gente muy poderosa en Guatemala. Es gente que están en casos muy delicados, o en casos de corrupción, en casos de cantidad muy multa de plata, o en crimen organizado. Están involucrados en esto tipo de cosas. Entonces cuando venga un juez . . . pues, de una u otra forma o lo intimidan o lo acuden en acto de corrupción. Y cuando no [logran corromperlo], vienen la intimidación. Eso es bien duro.

Repúblicano Guatemalteco, FRG) in the Congress. He had attempted to run for president in 1990 and 1995, being rebuffed by the Constitutional Court both times. When the FRG nominated him again in 2003 and the Supreme Electoral Tribunal (Tribunal Supremo Electoral, TSE) rejected his candidacy on the same grounds as before, he filed an *amparo* challenging the TSE's order. A trial court rejected the amparo, as did the Supreme Court. However, he appealed his case to the constitutional court, arguing successfully that enforcing this provision against him would constitute an illegal *ex post facto* law. Subsequently, the Supreme Court ordered the TSE not to enforce the Constitutional Court's order, arguing that it was an unenforceable unconstitutional order. A very public constitutional crisis then came to a head.

The *"jueves negro"* ("Black Thursday") riots occurred on July 24, 2003, when the FRG bused thousands of *campesinos* into the capital to form angry mobs surrounding the Supreme Court, the Constitutional Court, and the offices of several government agencies viewed as enemies of Ríos Montt, including the human rights ombudsman. One journalist died in the violence. A number of government and NGO employees were rescued from rooftops in dramatic fashion by the human rights ombudsman's helicopter. In the following days, the newspaper *Prensa Libre* published photographs of members of Ríos Montt's family and party appearing to direct the mobs from short distances away. The Constitutional Court, speaking through a slate of magistrates that was stacked with FRG supporters, ordered the TSE to inscribe Ríos Montt as a candidate and forbade any other court from issuing further decisions on the matter. The spectacle helped usher Ríos Montt into his candidacy, but appeared to alienate him from voters; he ultimately lost in third place.

One lawyer working for an NGO recalled these events in 2009 as emblematic of the kinds of corruption that has been possible in Guatemala:

> Let's remember the theme of when the nomination of Ríos Montt conceived the role of the Guatemalan constitution, notwithstanding what Article 186 establishes and he was inscribed as a candidate. He requested some four magistrates of the Constitutional Court, by giving information openly illegally and with a high level of public knowledge at all levels. But, that's just one important experience in one intense moment, then the practice is common. There are judges that will be corrupt for money, for narcotraffickers, for politicians, for military members, and thus the possibility of justice is very slow, very difficult.[22] (G2009–04)

---

[22] Original: Recordemos el tema de cuando la selección de Ríos Montt concibió rol de la constitución política de la república de Guatemala y no obstante lo que establece al artículo 186 de la constitución y fue inscrito como candidato. Que ya solicitó unos cuatro magistrados

If a presidential candidate can muster ostensibly unofficial violence to bully his way on to the ballot, there are significant problems with the rule of law, indeed. The use of former civil defense patrolmen ("ex-PACs" in Guatemalan parlance) as the primary force in the riots also brings together unofficial violence under political control with at least the appearance of corruption. President Alfonso Portillo (2000–2004), a member of Ríos Montt's political party, promised the ex-PACs in 2003 that they would receive long-delayed compensation for their unpaid, largely compelled military service during the early 1980s, in what was charged to be attempted vote buying and thuggery. The 2003 controversy thus revealed and cemented the ability of unofficial violence as a means of achieving political ends, even if the success of such violence is questionable.

In addition to demonstrating the rise of unofficial violence as a way of settling political disputes, the controversy over Ríos Montt's candidacy and the related events included a significant component of seemingly corrupt action by the Constitutional Court. According to Juan Hernandez Pico[23], the panel of magistrates that ruled on the candidacy case in the Constitutional Court was the result of a highly unusual chain of events, including the sudden, unexpected illness of one magistrate and the abrupt dismissal of the court official in charge of doing the random draw of magistrates. Such machinations suggest the exploitation of every possible institutional channel for corruption. It is worth noting that the option of a military coup was not pursued. Just as after the Serranazo, Guatemala would not return to military rule. Even a former dictator who was willing to unleash a riot against the courts appeared to seek the constitutional imprimatur that only an amparo success could provide.

The anger in response to the riots among Guatemalans was palpable at the time and can be seen in the extensive reporting in the national press of the photographic evidence of the apparent direction of the riot by political operatives on cell phones mentioned above. The press reaction may have been especially oppositional because of the death of a journalist, whose funeral the following day was also splashed across newspaper front pages. Indeed, pictures suggest that more Guatemalans turned out to see the funeral procession pass through the streets than participated in the riots themselves. There were several consequences of the public reaction to the riots: Ríos Montt was discredited at the very moment he became a candidate, efforts were made to try him

---

de la corte de constitucionalidad, por dar datos abiertamente ilegales y con un grado de conocimiento público a todo nivel. Pero, es aparte un solamente vivencia importante en momento intenso la practica entonces es común. Hay jueces que se ya corromper por dinero, por los narco traficantes, por los políticos, por los militares, y entonces la posibilidad de justicia es muy lenta, muy difícil.

[23] "La Revelación Parcial de Los Poderes Ocultos."

in connection with the riots that ultimately led to his being tried in 2013 for genocide, and an international commission was proposed to try to reign in what Guatemalans call "the hidden powers".

The hidden powers permeate Guatemalan politics and Guatemalan society. One report, published by the Washington Office on Latin America, alleged that many of these gangs have their origins in rings of current and former military officers who were involved in smuggling and other illicit activities during the war years.[24] These "hidden powers" were "partially revealed," in the words of one Guatemalan scholar, by the inscription of General Ríos Montt as a candidate for president in 2003.[25] Brands reports further that several gang networks were represented in high positions of the administration of Alfonso Portillo and that in 2008, President Álvaro Colom (2008–2012) fired two top advisors because they had planted surveillance devices in the presidential offices.[26] It bears mentioning that most of the damning evidence points to former members of the military rather than current soldiers or officers. Indeed, if Schirmer is correct about the military having adopted a new semi-democratic and professionalized ideology, it stands to reason that the military high command would be committed to fighting the chaos produced by the gangs.[27] The now-common street patrols by military agents under police command are in keeping with such an ideology.

A Tale of Two Commissions

The public outrage stemming from the events of July 2003 also helped provide the necessary pressure to create a United Nations commission to help investigate and prosecute these "hidden powers." The peace accords had imagined a significant and sustained effort by the Guatemalan government to root out illegal security forces and clandestine groups,[28] but successive governments proved either unwilling or unable to eliminate these groups. One lawyer recalled these roots of the international commission in 2009 in the following manner:

> Because the origins of CICIG are in the peace accords, namely that the CIACs, this clandestine armed groups and all that, made it to the peace accords and the state of Guatemala as one of the commitments under the

[24] Peacock and Beltrán, "Hidden Powers in Post-Conflict Guatemala: Illegal Armed Groups and the Forces Behind Them."
[25] Hernandez Pico, "La Revelación Parcial de Los Poderes Ocultos."
[26] Brands, *Crime, Violence, and the Crisis in Guatemala.*
[27] Schirmer, *The Guatemalan Military Project.*
[28] This commitment is spelled out in the Global Human Rights Agreement, signed on March 29, 1994, commitment IV, numeral 1.

accords undertook to prevent those kinds of groups from exercising any sort of intimidation and or violence against human rights activists. This is very plainly said there, but it turns out the state of Guatemala hasn't done much of anything to deal with that enough. (G2009–08)

This lawyer's recollection, however, overlooked some of the difficult route in Guatemala to establish the International Commission Against Impunity in Guatemala (*Comisión Internacional Contra la Impunidad en Guatemala*, CICIG).

Discussion to create an international commission, then known as the Investigative Commission of Illegal Bodies and Clandestine Security Operations in Guatemala (*Comisión de Investigación de Cuerpos Ilegales y Aparatos Clandestinos de Seguridad*, CICIACS), had begun prior to the jueves negro riots. A United Nations team of experts had been visiting Guatemala to investigate that very issue when the riots occurred. Nonetheless, the efforts to create the CICIACS progressed slowly while international human rights organizations petitioned the Secretary General of the United Nations to support such a commission. The agreement was finally formalized on January 7, 2004, one week before FRG president Alfonso Portillo left office, but met resistance in the Congress. Subsequently, the new president asked the Constitutional Court to weigh in on the issue with a "Consultative Opinion." On August 5, 2004, the Constitutional Court declared provisions of the CICIACS agreement incompatible with the Guatemalan constitution on the grounds that they improperly authorized the CICIACS to carry out functions designated by the constitution to be carried out by specific state entities such as the judiciary and the prosecutor's office.[29]

The Comisión Internacional Contra la Impunidad en Guatemala (CICIG) ultimately would not be formed until 2007. The mandate of the CICIG includes the following:

First, CICIG shall investigate the existence of illicit security forces and clandestine security organizations that commit crimes that affect the fundamental human rights of the citizens of Guatemala, and identify the illegal group structures (including links between State officials and organized crime), activities, modes of operation and sources of financing.[30]

It is unique within the United Nations system and it was hoped that its work would help to strengthen the national institutions of criminal justice. It has

---

[29] Expediente no. 1250–2004.
[30] (http://cicig.org/index.php?page=mandate, October 30, 2010).

also contributed to various legal reforms. The CICIG is, in essence, a brokerage institution that seeks to make connections between state actors and
entities (with the support of the NGO sector) in order to promote reforms
and strengthen those state entities. A consequence of this liminal status of the
CICIG – and of its origins in the defeated CICIACS project – is that some
confusion persists about its actual purpose. As one lawyer tried to explain it:

> Well, um, I think that CICIG is doing several different things. They have
> through these sort of how could we call that actually? It's such a sui generis
> kind of institution that it's a sort of interface with the prosecutor's office, but
> it belongs to the prosecutor's office . . . (G2009–08)

The CICIG is primarily an investigative unit that advises Guatemalan legal and
political actors on how to proceed in high-profile cases, using the Guatemalan
status of *querellante adhesivo*. The most celebrated early case that the CICIG
worked on was the investigation stemming from the death of attorney Rodrigo
Rosenberg in 2009. Rosenberg had represented a client whose assassination,
which also killed the client's daughter, had not been investigated to his satisfaction. In early 2009, shortly after recording a video warning that the president
wanted to kill him, Rosenberg was killed by hit men while bicycling before
work. The outcry about the Rosenberg case was so great that the CICIG was
asked to take over the investigation; it also led to the reform of the process of
selecting magistrates (see below). In the end, the CICIG's investigation traced
the phone calls setting up the hit to Rosenberg's own apartment, leading them
to the conclusion that Rosenberg, depressed over the death of his client's
daughter, with whom he had been conducting a secret affair, had ordered the
hit against himself.[31] An article in *The New Yorker* several months after the
resolution of the case suggests that the stress of the case caused CICIG head
Carlos Castrasena to resign and return to his home in Spain.[32]

In addition to the Rosenberg case, they have also worked on a variety of
cases where linkages between government actors and the "parallel state" were
suspected. In a 2013 update, they reported that they had been involved with
fifty high-impact cases that were at that time "under investigation or before the
courts," from which twenty sentences (most involving multiple convictions)
had been secured, including the cases of Rosenberg and his client, but also

---

[31] It may not be possible for any outside observers to know if this conclusion is typical of the
bizarre excuses that Guatemalan governments have given for political killings in the past or
if Rosenberg was a genuinely disturbed man. At the least, it is suspicious. Nonetheless, the
then-head of the CICIG, Carlos Castresana, had a very good reputation within pro-human
rights circles.

[32] Grann, "A Murder Foretold: Unravelling the Ultimate Political Conspiracy."

including police officers, prison guards, and a mayor.[33] Less successful was the trial of former president Alfonso Portillo[34] for embezzlement charges; after being found not guilty, he was extradited to the United States in 2012 to stand trial for money laundering charges.[35]

More important than the individual cases that the CICIG has investigated or assisted in prosecuting is the work that they have done to strengthen Guatemala's domestic justice sector institutions. The commission's earliest and still most prominent partner has been the Ministerio Público, which created a specialized unit, now known as the Special Anti-Impunity Prosecutors Bureau (Fiscalía Especial contra la Impunidad, FECI), to work with the CICIG in September 2008. The relationship with the MP was aided by the appointment of Claudia Paz y Paz as Attorney General in 2010; the CICIG's annual reports also report favorably on its relationship with her successor, former Supreme Court Magistrate Thelma Aldana, in place since 2014. The relationship with the National Civil Police (Policía Nacional Civil, PNC) was difficult in the early years of the CICIG's operation because of objections by some in the PNC to CICIG efforts to investigate and prosecute rings of corrupt officers, as related in the CICIG's third annual report in 2010; joint investigations eventually helped to build trust and personnel changes at the head of the PNC and related government offices brought greater cooperation. By 2015, the eighth annual report detailed training programs for young police officers to learn and work alongside national and international functionaries. The judiciary has had one of the most antagonistic relationships with the CICIG.

Judges have not always been supportive of the reforms pushed by the CICIG. In April 2010, a decree was passed by the Congress allowing the prosecutor's office to investigate judges for obstruction of justice. Some judges viewed these changes as threatening. One judge shared the following perception of these legal reforms:

> This year there was Decree 17–2010. That decree was pushed by . . . the whole world knows, right? By the CICIG . . . This decree is terrible. It is criminalizing the judge for the act of not resolving [a case] in conformity with the Ministerio Público (prosecutor's office). That cannot be! The Ministerio Público

---

[33] "Convictions in proceedings supported by CICIG" http://www.cicig.org/uploads/documents/2013/SENT-20131018-01-EN.pdf March 24, 2015.

[34] In an additional example of the densely networked nature of the Guatemalan elite, Portillo is also Ríos Montt's son-in-law.

[35] Portillo pled guilty in the United States in 2014 and served a one year sentence before being released in 2015 and returning to Guatemala. He then tried to run for the Congress in the 2015 elections, but was rejected by the electoral tribunal on the grounds that he lacked the requisite honorableness to be approved.

is an institution that helps the judicial system but cannot be them . . . If not, there would be no reason for the existence of a judge.[36] (G2010–01)

This judge was not alone in her concerns. According the newspaper *Siglo XXI*, the Myrna Mack Foundation petitioned the president to veto the decree, arguing that it was an unconstitutional infringement on the independence of judges. The Association of Judges and Magistrates joined the Myrna Mack Foundation in this objection and the president ultimately vetoed it in June. Nonetheless, in November 2012, the CICIG submitted a report to the Attorney General, detailing irregularities in orders and decisions of eighteen "impunity judges," as the report provocatively termed them. The names of all eighteen judges were also listed on the CICIG's website.[37] In 2013, the Supreme Court agreed to open investigations of ten of these judges. As of the CICIG's eighth annual report in September 2015, four judges and one appellate magistrate had been indicted, with only three having been captured at that time.

The CICIG has also helped to create programs for witness protection, assets forfeiture, and police wire-tapping as well as justice sector reform more broadly. Another substantial aspect of the CICIG's mission has been the training of Guatemalan justice sector officials, especially in prosecution and related fields. They have also promoted greater career protections and prospects for prosecutors and a new judicial career law. Although some of those interviewed in 2009 were highly skeptical of what the relatively small staff of the CICIG could accomplish, the commission has contributed to potentially very powerful changes in Guatemala. Much of the skepticism centered on the idea that Guatemala should be able to fix its own problem without what one lawyer called a "nanny" (G2009–08); another suggested that the CICIG would be like not allowing kids to learn on their own (G2009–05/06).[38] Some of this skepticism came from the lengthy delay between the initiation of the commission and the eventual results, which were still limited in 2009 (G2009–13).

If contemporary Guatemala is a battleground between competing ideas of governmentality, one of which favors the rule of law and the other of which

---

[36] Original: Este año fue un decreto 17–2010. Ese decreto fue impulsado por . . . todo el mundo sabe, ¿verdad? Por la CICIG . . . Este decreto es terrible. Está criminalizando al juez por el hecho de no resolver conforme con el Ministerio Público. ¡Eso no puede ser! El Ministerio Público es una institución que coayude el sistema judicial pero no pueden ser ellos . . . si no, no tendría objeto de ser la existencia de un juez.

[37] Press Release 093: Impunity Judges Report Submitted. November 29, 2012. http://www.cicig .org/index.php?mact=News,cntnt01,detail,0&cntnt01articleid=307&cntnt01returnid=105 March 24, 2015.

[38] It is worth noting, however, that the NGO lawyers and activists interviewed in the same period were quite supportive of the CICIG.

favors impunity and violence, the CICIG has begun to tip the scales in favor of the former. By 2014, the CICIG, in conjunction with the strengthened prosecutor's office, had dismantled at least some of the "hidden powers" in Guatemala and homicide rates had declined since their peak in 2008–2009. Indeed, the CICIG reported in 2013 that impunity for "crimes against life" had declined from 95 percent in 2009 to 72 percent in 2012. The future of impunity or the rule of law in Guatemala will depend less on the number of "hidden powers" left operating after the CICIG leaves and more on the strength of the national institutions that will continue to operate in Guatemala. Corruption and violence are unlikely to ever be eradicated, but their impacts can be minimized by strong institutions. Unfortunately, the design of many of Guatemala's justice sector reforms has left open multiple entry points for corruption without sufficient oversight capacity.

Perpetuating Clandestine Control: Entry Points for Corruption Frustrate Reform Efforts

Guatemalans are acutely aware that there exist problems with their justice sector and have pursued numerous avenues for reform. Nonetheless, corrupt and criminal actors have been able to penetrate state institutions almost without exception. Potentially watershed moments such as the aftermath of President Serrano's coup have been lost when reform efforts are met with both immediate, overt resistance and long-term, often subtle disregard. The selection process for Supreme Court and Courts of Appeals magistrates is an excellent example of these dynamics. Although the process was reformed in 1994 (and a new Supreme Court appointed), successive selection rounds have been heavily colonized by corrupt and criminal actors. The very reforms that were intended to diminish the power of corrupt politicians at the same time created multiple entry points for a wider field of corrupt actors. The problems with the selection processes are another example of a problem with a "layering" reform process that proceeds without any significant successful purges of corrupt officials.

The selection process for trial judges did change with the Judicial Career Law in 1994, which assigned judicial appointments to the Supreme Court. In Guatemala, as in most civil law countries, ordinary trial-level judges are appointed through bureaucratic processes. Upon graduating from law school, aspiring judges enroll in the judicial training school, after which approximately half are given positions as judges. Survey respondents in 2010 indicated that the most significant factors in receiving a judicial appointment were having an excellent academic record, previous employment in

TABLE 5.1 *Important Factors in the Appointment of Judges in Guatemala*

Factors	Important or Very Important	Not Important
Experience as a litigating attorney	53.3	13.3
Family prestige	35.6	35.6
Friends within the judiciary or the Supreme Court	8.9	75.6
Friends within the government	15.6	71.1
Friends within the armed forces	8.9	84.4
Affiliation with a political party	15.6	77.8
Previous employment in the judiciary	62.2	26.7
Excellent academic record	88.9	4.4

Source: Author's 2010 survey (Responses in percentages of total).

the judiciary,[39] and previous experience as a litigating attorney. (See Table 5.1.) Within the judicial system, there is relatively little opportunity for promotion other than lateral transfers to more desirable courts, but trial-level judges are generally secure in their tenure. It is not uncommon for ambitious judges to continue their education to the doctoral level: Of the 43 judges who filled out questionnaires in 2010, 80 percent indicated that they hold a Master's degree of higher. In addition, 95 percent indicated that they participate in either "some" or "many" professional trainings annually. Just over half of respondents also indicated that they had been able to attend training or other professional courses outside of Guatemala.

However, truly ambitious judges cannot expect to be automatically promoted to the appellate level. Some judges will move from the judiciary into private law practice. One judge interviewed in 2009, who had submitted her application to the nominating committee for the Courts of Appeals that year, expressed her frustration that the assessment formulas used by the committees awarded more points for experience as a litigating attorney than they did for an exclusively judicial career. One retired magistrate, who had served at all levels of the judicial hierarchy during her career, suggested that it was no longer possible to have a judicial career like hers because the appointment system created by the 1985 constitution cut off opportunities for advancement: "I had the good luck to have my judicial career. Now there is a judicial career, but

---

[39] Impressionistically, many judicial clerks and other judicial employees are working their way through law school by working in one of the courts. Some of these individuals expressed considerable interest in the surveys and interviews being conducted while the author was in their court's office suite.

there can be no judicial career if every five years the court changes and every five years the judge can change."[40]

Appointments of magistrates to the appellate courts, the Supreme Court, and the constitutional court are highly politicized, although they now involve many more actors than just the Congress or the executive. In the 2004 and 2009 processes, there was increasing attention paid by civil society activists to developing a profile of an ideal candidate for the magistracy. These profiles included objective factors such as a high level of education and a lengthy period of service in the judiciary. For some organizations, such as the Myrna Mack Foundation, there was also something of a political test: they sought to have the commissions reject judges who were viewed to have colluded with the military or police in frustrating human rights claims, especially in the trial for the murder of Myrna Mack herself. In pushing this political test, the human rights organizations were disappointed with the nomination of one judge who had been involved in the Myrna Mack case and who was viewed as having ruled in favor of the military. However, many of the more general recommendations were taken into consideration by the commissions and were included in the rating formula.

In 2009, significant changes were made to the selection process. These changes were largely the result of years of work by the NGO coalition Foro Guatemala, although the timing of the reform had to do with the controversy over the Rosenberg case. One activist indicated that the law to reform the process had been allowed to lie dormant before having its third and final reading. However, once the murder of Rosenberg happened, the new law was passed in fifteen days. (G2009–18) These reforms were done in response to the widespread belief that the members of state institutions generally, including the judiciary, were not independent and were often corrupt. The most significant change was to create a proportional representation system of choosing members of the bar association to sit on the nomination committees. As well, an objective rating system was to be devised by each committee to choose its judicial nominees.

As described in the new law, the *comisiones de postulación*, or nomination committees, are composed of nine representatives of the bar association, the nine law school deans, and nine representatives of the Supreme Court or the Court of Appeals. There are separate committees for the Court of Appeals and the Supreme Court; nine Supreme Court magistrates serve on the committee

---

[40] Original: Tuve la suerte de tener mi carrera judicial . . . Ahora hay carrera judicial, pero no puede ser carrera judicial si cada cinco años se está cambiando la Corte y cada cinco años se pueden cambiar juez.

to select the Court of Appeals nominees and nine Court of Appeals magistrates sit on the committee to select the Supreme Court nominees. Once the committees have chosen their nominees, the Congress then selects half of them to serve as magistrates; those not chosen serve as substitute magistrates. In this fashion, the significant actors within the legal community are involved in the process of choosing the magistrates. The president is not involved in the selection process. The president is also unlikely to hold significant influence through his party, which does not typically hold a majority of the Congress due to the proliferation of parties in Guatemala's feckless party system.

On the face of it, this system should significantly reduce corruption and intimidation in the process of selecting magistrates, which was the intention of the reform. Because there are several different groups represented, someone wishing to corrupt the process would have to influence at least fourteen individuals. However, because bargaining between different factions on the selection committees was widespread, it was not difficult for just a few corrupt individuals to ensure the nomination of a number of magistrates who they hoped would be in the pocket of corrupt or criminal interests. Indeed, the fractured nature of the nomination committee may have actually created more entry points for corruption rather than fewer. The influence of corruption and organized crime are pervasive in Guatemala and rather easily found their way into the nomination process through the bar association's representatives, according to one source. (See below)

In addition to the new procedures, there were significant efforts by civil society organizations to ensure the transparency of the process. Foro Guatemala and a related organization, Movimiento Pro Justicia, endeavored to monitor the nomination process, including having volunteers present in all the meetings to report any improprieties, publishing reports by these volunteers on a website every evening, and undertaking a publicity campaign in conjunction with several international donors to raise public interest in the outcome of the nomination process. These organizations also supplied their compiled records of complaints against attorneys and judges to the committees. Similarly, the Myrna Mack Foundation acquired from the Supreme Court a list of all attorneys who had been fined for abusing the *amparo* process and who had not paid their fines and supplied that list to the committees, arguing that frequent abusers of the constitutional process should not be allowed to serve as magistrates.

The introduction of proportional representation in the election of representatives of the bar association encouraged the entry of a variety of different slates of candidates, including a reform slate that was pledged to eliminate corruption in the judiciary and from the selection process. As part of this pledge, this slate of candidates published on the internet the source of every contribution they received and how they spent their funds. While they publicly requested other slates to do likewise, that did not happen. Slates of candidates spent lavishly in the efforts to woo votes from members of the bar, including parties in luxury hotels to introduce the candidates to the legal community. Rumors of corruption in the voting process proliferated; lawyers may have been pressured by their superiors in their firms or even paid off.

One lawyer, who indicated that he had voted for the reform slate, lambasted the influence of corruption and criminality in the process:

> Then there's what we call the dark side are people linked to Mr. Roberto Lopez Villatoro, *el rey del tenis*, he's the biggest smuggler of tennis shoes into Guatemala, ex-husband of Zury Ríos the daughter of General Ríos. This guy has made a hobby out of controlling courts so there's a group that's clearly linked to him. There's another group that's always linked to the Government which puts a lot of pressure on the attorneys that work in all government institutions; the Attorney General, the Solicitor General and all the Ministries. (G2009–03)

In addition, one slate was associated with well-known defenders of drug traffickers. The government slate won the most votes in the election, with the "Tennis Shoe King's" slate of candidates coming in second and the reform slate coming in third.

The election of the bar association's representatives on the nominating commissions distilled many of the problems of Guatemala's weak democracy into a much smaller scale. There was concern about corruption in the campaigns and candidates supported by both the government and organized crime. In addition, there was some controversy over the application of the new proportional representation type of voting. An amparo was filed with the Supreme Court and then appealed to the Constitutional Court alleging that the votes had been counted incorrectly and demanding that the seats be reapportioned. A competing amparo was then filed to demand that the count be approved so that the selection committees could convene and proceed with their work. Ultimately, the petitions were dismissed and the committees began their work only slightly delayed. Another concern involved the qualifications of the lawyers voting. One lawyer expressed the concern that some of the law schools are turning out unqualified lawyers through accelerated programs. He pointed to rumors that the San Carlos University was selling the title. As a result of this, 500 attorneys had been sworn in immediately prior to the election of representatives to the selection commissions, compared to a usual rate of 100 every few months. In a proportional representation election with only 5500 attorneys voting, 500 votes could create a significant shift in the outcome.

The significance of corruption within the selection committees goes beyond the Courts of Appeals and the Supreme Court because of the role of the Supreme Court in filling one of the five seats on the Constitutional Court. As one attorney described, corrupt and criminal organizations quickly caught on to this:

[The selection committee process] worked very well for the first term because the several political groups and the private interest groups and the narcos and several other factions and groups interested in manipulating justice hadn't yet understood how the system was going to work and they didn't have any time to prepare. But from the second process on, they've become more and more specialized and the amount of resources that they invest in achieving their goal and purposes are just enormous . . . It's amazing. You wonder why? But of course, you know, there's a lot at stake because in addition to the power that Court of Appeals judges and Supreme Court justices on their own, it turns out that the Supreme Court appoints one justice and one alternate justice to the Constitutional Tribunal, where questions such as "Could [First Lady] Mrs. Colom run for president?" will be determined. So if you have a majority in the Supreme Court appointing a justice and an alternate justice, the president has the power and authority to appoint another two and the Congress another two, so they already have a majority in the constitutional tribunal. So all those very important political questions are ultimately decided there and therefore there are huge interests at stake. (G2009–08)

As the above quote dissects, Guatemala has a rather unusual way of selecting magistrates for its constitutional court, one more in keeping with a political body than a judicial one. The constitutional court is composed of five titular magistrates and five substitute magistrates. Each of five institutions representing the legal and political communities chooses one titular and one substitute magistrate. Three of these institutions represent the legal community: the bar association, the dean of the San Carlos University, and the Supreme Court. In addition, the president and the congress each have the power to name magistrates. In this way, the two most important political institutions have representatives on the Constitutional Court as well. Although the same institutions are represented as in the selection of non-constitutional magistrates, there is a significant difference in the process: In the case of constitutional magistrates, there is no nomination committee. Each relevant institution names its titular and supplementary magistrates on its own, with no official mechanism for outside influence or oversight. Consequently, the constitutional magistrates more closely resemble representatives of the naming institutions and are often described in the media based on who appointed them.

There is perhaps more room for corruption in this process than there is in the nomination of non-constitutional magistrates. One activist cited rumors about the election for the magistrates from the San Carlos University. The university had been a major source of activism during the civil war and, as a result, its students had suffered severe repression. It is surprising, then, that the San Carlos magistrate would support one of the worst perpetrators of that repression (General Ríos Montt) by allowing him to be inscribed as a presidential candidate in 2003. Given that the university allows students to vote for its magistrates, one might expect to see left-wing or at least pro-human rights magistrates come from that institution. However, according to rumors, students are routinely paid to vote for particular candidates. Again, the diffusion of the selection process allows for multiple entry points for corruption.

Constitutional Court president Roberto Molina Barreto objected strongly to this characterization of the appointment process in 2010. He insisted that the magistrates do not represent the powers who appoint them. In his case, he was appointed by President Óscar Berger (2004–2008) but said he had cut all of his ties to the president upon joining the court. He also indicated that he had resigned his membership in his political party. However, he also indicated that the 2003 Ríos Montt controversy, in which constitutional magistrates appeared to be following the orders of the appointers, had greatly harmed the prestige of the constitutional court. Although the current magistrates were, in his view, generally respected, the Court is still not as prestigious as it once was, particularly as much as it was following the *Serranazo*. Nonetheless, the perception persists that the constitutional magistrates maintain some association with the body that appointed them.

An additional problem that affects the autonomy of magistrates in the Constitutional Court (as well as the Courts of Appeals and the Supreme Court of Justice) is the short tenure that they are guaranteed. While trial-level judges have career positions from which they cannot be fired without cause, magistrates are in their positions for only five years and the historical practice is against reappointment. The consequence of this is that most magistrates have to look for another position at the end of their term as magistrate. Some appellate magistrates are able to become Supreme Court magistrates, but there are not sufficient positions on the Supreme Court to accommodate the number of appellate magistrates. Few Supreme Court or Constitutional Court magistrates wish to move down the hierarchy by joining the Courts of Appeals. This short tenure creates a situation in which powerful political and societal actors have the ability to enter into symbiotic relationships with magistrates.

A politician may gain influence with a magistrate by promising to find him a position within the executive upon the expiration of his term. Similarly, a wealthy private individual may curry favor with a magistrate by arranging a lucrative future job in a powerful law firm. This kind of influence is likely to be largely hidden from view, but may represent a significant limitation on the autonomy of magistrates. Importantly, such influence, even when it involves politicians, may not actually limit the inter-branch independence of the judiciary as an institution. Nonetheless, it significantly diminishes the likelihood of the courts contributing to the construction of a democratic rule of law.

Genocide Comes Before the Courts

The past bedevils Guatemala. For decades, no one was held to account for human rights violations, especially those conducted during the war years. The cases discussed above concerning the murders of Myrna Mack and Monsignor Juan Gerardi remained, until very recently, exceptional. An amnesty law governing the war years was passed in 1986, governing solely the years in which Ríos Montt and his immediate successor were president. Although that decree is no longer in effect, having been invalidated by the 1996 National Reconciliation Law, it continues to cast a shadow over attempts to seek justice for atrocities committed during those years. An additional impediment to prosecutions has been the long-time presence of General Ríos Montt in civilian electoral politics. Efforts to bring charges against him related to the *jueves negro* riots were ultimately abandoned when he returned to the Congress and regained official immunity from prosecution. Nonetheless, NGO activists and, more recently, prosecutors and the CICIG, have pursued genocide charges against Ríos Montt and members of his military high command. Two prominent cases, one directly against Ríos Montt and a broader one concerning the Dos Erres massacre, represent the culmination of these efforts.

In 1999, following the model of the attempted prosecution in Spain of Chile's former president Pinochet, the Rigoberta Menchú Foundation, a Guatemalan NGO, filed a complaint in Spain against Ríos Montt and his high command. The charges of terrorism, genocide, and systematic torture fell under Spain's universal jurisdiction law, which allows prosecutions for some human rights violations committed outside of Spain even without the involvement of Spanish citizens. Following a negative ruling on jurisdiction in 2001 by the trial court in Spain, the Spanish Supreme Court ultimately ruled in favor of jurisdiction in 2005. Attempts by the Spanish prosecutor to depose witnesses in Guatemala in 2006 were frustrated when amparo filings could not be resolved with sufficient speed. Ultimately, arrest warrants were issued by the

Spanish court in November 2006 and the government of Guatemala was asked to extradite the defendants to Spain. After first approving of the extradition, the Guatemalan Constitutional Court ruled against the extradition request in December 2007, on the grounds that universal jurisdiction was not valid under Guatemalan constitutional law.

One NGO attorney expressed his frustration with the situation in 2009, lamenting:

> In late 2007, the Constitutional Court released a ruling in favor of the military, invoking the fact that it could not pin down the concept of universal jurisdiction. For example, they could not be made to be judges in a Spanish court. Then they should thus be judged in a national court. But what national court? Just in the Dos Erres case, for example, there exist more than thirty amparos that have delayed this case in lamentable fashion.[41] (G2009–04)

As this lawyer indicated, few in Guatemala believed that any Guatemalan court could successfully pursue a genocide prosecution domestically. The Mack and Gerardi cases had been plagued with threats against judges and prosecutors, with some judges abandoning their judicial careers altogether rather than be subjected to the dangers of presiding over these prosecutions. Surely, a prosecution of a former military dictator that went to the core of the violence of the war years would be much more difficult. Although many witnesses had testified before the Spanish courts in this case, increasing the international pressure on Guatemala to cooperate, real progress toward convictions had been frustrated in Spain. As a result, Guatemalan courts became the only possible venue for justice for the genocide in Guatemala.

In January 2012, the Guatemalan Attorney General Claudia Paz y Paz indicted Ríos Montt on charges of genocide. The Guatemalan prosecutorial strategy was similar to the strategy in the Spanish courts, even using some of the same expert witnesses. He ultimately stood trial in March and April 2013; his conviction for genocide was the first by a national domestic court against a former head of state. However, his April 2013 conviction was invalidated by the Constitutional Court three days later on procedural grounds. A retrial began in February 2016 and then was restarted again in May 2016 following the severing of Ríos Montt's trial from that of his former spy chief. That verdict,

---

[41] Original: En las finales de 2007, la Corte de Constitucionalidad emitió una resolución en favor de los militares, invocando el hecho de que no podía preciso concepto de jurisdicción universal. Por ejemplo, no podían hacer juzgados por un corte Española. Entonces por esto, hacer juzgados en una corte nacional... ¿pero en cual corte nacional? Solamente en el caso de Dos Erres, por ejemplo, existen más que treinta amparos que han retrasado este caso en forma lamentable.

when it comes, is likely to be appealed; like Pinochet, the now elderly Ríos Montt, who reportedly suffers from dementia, may die before he can finally be sentenced. Although many still want to see a final verdict and for Ríos Montt to be sentenced, one victory has already been achieved: much of the country now must acknowledge that a genocidal campaign was waged against Guatemala's indigenous Maya population.

A second case deals with just one massacre, at Dos Erres in the Péten province in northeastern Guatemala. As a part of "Operation Ashes," Ríos Montt's government ordered the razing of villages suspected of providing aid the rebel guerrilla forces. The 1982 Dos Erres massacre, conducted in retaliation for an attack on an army convoy earlier in the year, resulted in the death of an estimated 350 villagers, among them infants and children, and included the rape and mutilation of the village's women and girls. An Argentine forensic anthropology team investigated the village site in 1994 and 1995, resulting in the ability to identify at least some of the dead. The Guatemalan NGO Families of the Detained and Disappeared (FAMDEGUA) filed a complaint against military personnel in 1994, but the Ministerio Público did not pursue the case at that time as a result of death threats against prosecutors. Recall that this complaint was filed before the peace process had been completed and while the 1986 amnesty law was still in effect.

Subsequently, surviving family members brought a complaint to the Inter-American Commission on Human Rights, before which the Guatemalan government admitted responsibility in 2000. Pursuant to a subsequent settlement, the Guatemalan government agreed to pay reparations and to prosecute the case. However, following years of delays and threats against judges, the Guatemalan Constitutional Court agreed in 2004 with the defendants' assertion that they were protected by amnesty provisions within the 1996 Law of National Reconciliation. The Commission then referred a new complaint to the Inter-American Court of Human Rights in 2008, which ruled in 2009 that the government of Guatemala had violated the complainants' rights under the American Convention on Human Rights. Specifically noted were the rights to a fair trial and to judicial protection. In 2010, Guatemala began the process of implementing the Inter-American Court's ruling by re-opening the criminal prosecution against the alleged perpetrators of the massacre; arrest warrants were issued for seventeen former members of the military.

That trial occurred in 2011 and included testimony from other former members of the same military unit. These witnesses were able to do so as a part of the new programs for witness protection that had been promoted by the CICIG before being passed into Guatemalan law. It was also one of the most prominent trials to take place in the High Risk Courts (*Tribunales de Mayor*

Riesgo), which were established in 2009 and give those judges additional security and resources to allow them to focus on risky prosecution such as those against narcotraffickers. In August 2011, four defendants were convicted in the massacre and sentenced to over 6,000 years each for involvement in over 200 murders and other human rights violations; an additional defendant was similarly convicted and sentenced in 2012. An additional former member of the Guatemalan military accused of participating in the Dos Erres massacre was sentenced to ten years in the United States for concealing his past on immigration paperwork; it is not known whether he will be extradited to Guatemala to face trial there.[42]

These two prosecutions represent a significant break in the impunity that has reigned in Guatemala for decades. These successes were only possible through significant and sustained commitment by well-known Guatemalan NGOs working in concert with international actors. Indeed, it was necessary even in 2009 to bring complaints to the Inter-American system before the Guatemalan courts would act. Even then, the conviction of Ríos Montt was overturned by the Constitutional Court on what many view as flimsy grounds. It is possible that future prosecutions will be easier because of the creation of the High Risk Courts, because of the training of specialized prosecutors, and because of the example set by these two prosecutions. Some of these advances are directly a result of the CICIG, but much of the impulse and effort came from domestic actors in Guatemala. The CICIG – along with other international actors – has been a powerful force for the rule of law, but it would have accomplished little without the actions of Guatemalans. Nonetheless, the rule of law is far from won in Guatemala. Although impunity is often caricatured with the face of General Ríos Montt in Guatemala, even his eventual departure from the political scene will not eliminate impunity. There remain many intricate networks of crime and corruption in Guatemala that will resist the rule of law as long as they can.

PERVERSE FORMALISM, OVERLAPPING JURISDICTION, AND POLITICAL INDEPENDENCE

Various reforms to Guatemala's judicial system, beginning with the 1985 Constitution, have attempted to respond to concerns that the judiciary is not sufficiently independent. However, in their efforts to craft a judicial system that would be largely independent from the executive and the military,

---

[42] Canada, where he lived for many years, also seeks his extradition to stand trial for war crimes in Canadian courts.

Guatemalan reformers have created substantial overlaps of power and influence that in practice create multiple entry points for corruption. In effect, the overlapping jurisdictions of the Supreme Court and the Constitutional Court create multiple veto points; the corruption of several magistrates in either institution can have devastating effects for the rule of law. While it is indeed true that the executive appears to have less influence over the judiciary in the past two decades, the judiciary remains far from autonomous from society. The contemporary Guatemalan judiciary is instead influenced primarily by criminal actors and secondarily by political ones, although networks of influence that overlap governmental and societal actors persist.

Guatemala's legal institutions take a somewhat unusual form that may seem especially foreign to North American readers. Appendix B highlights some of the most important of these distinctions: the civil (code) law system, the twin high courts, and the more limited nature of access to the courts to make constitutional claims. Although this chapter describes a clandestine control judicial regime in which the formal rules are often ignored, these institutional arrangements are nonetheless important for fully understanding the Guatemalan system. Guatemala's clandestine control regime is not anarchic; these rules provide both a structure and a cover for the kinds of corruption and criminality that are likely to succeed. If a judge or magistrate broke the rules in an obvious way, it would likely end her career as a judge. Inducements to corruption of that level would have to be sufficiently extreme that a judge would be willing to give up her job and perhaps, ultimately, her right to live freely in her own country. Because the overlapping complexity of legal institutions creates multiple entry points for corruption, most corruption follows the line of the formal rules while it simultaneously undermines them.

One attorney working for a human rights NGO suggested that we cannot understand the current state of the judiciary without understanding how it was during the war years:

> To understand the lack of independence of the judges, you have to understand the historical context of this country. From a condition in which, for example, a judge not only is a supreme entity, almost invisible to public opinion, where her conducts will be very autonomous, very independent, but very subject of course to the powers that could be political, military, or economic . . . Thus we talk about certain political links that the Supreme Court magistrates have that I know, with GANA, with UNE, with the FRG, for example. And that greatly limits the possibility that these people, political people like Efraín Ríos Montt or many others could be tried.[43] (G2009–04)

---

[43] Original: Para entender la falta de independencia de los jueces, hay que entender el contexto histórico de este país. De una condición la cual por ejemplo un juez no solamente es un ente

This attorney's discussion suggests an important theme: where the judiciary in the war years was subject to the control of the national powers but respected and above societal influence, the judiciary today is linked to various powerful actors, including political parties. Historical developments in Guatemala thus created two important shifts in judicial politics: first, direct executive control was removed and, second, more diffuse and clandestine control took its place.

Guatemala's institutional arrangements must be understood within the context of the civil (code) law system. The logic of the civil law system is that judges are mere appliers of the law and should not engage in interpretation. Traditionally, prior cases had no precedential power when considering future cases, making civil law high courts substantially weaker than common law high courts such as in the United States and Canada. During the war years, the Guatemalan courts subscribed to a vision of their judicial role that was in keeping with the most traditional image of the civil law judge: passive and unwilling to challenge the sitting government. Beginning with the introduction of the 1985 constitution, some aspects of the civil law system in Guatemala have been eroded. First, the introduction of constitutional review clearly implies a different vision of the magistrate's role. Second, oral trials (albeit without juries) have been adopted in the criminal context since 1994, creating a need for a more powerful and active trial court judge.[44] Finally, the appointment processes for magistrates have become highly contested, although in a broader sense of the term "political" than merely partisan, as described by one attorney:

> As a matter of fact, the creation of this system of nominating committees, *comisiones de postulacion*, was a reaction on behalf of those in the 1985 constitutional convention to the widely shared belief that the judiciary is not independent. So several of them thought, how can we make the judiciary more independent from the political process? How do we go about isolating the judiciary far enough from the partisan political processes that have kept it more or less dependent on a number of private and or political and or public interests, that's special interests rather than the public interest. That's how they came up with this nominating committees idea. (G2009–08)

supremo, casi invisible a la opinión pública, donde sus actuaciones, serán muy autónomas, muy independientes, pero muy sujetos por supuesto a los poderes que sea político, militar o económico... Así hablar de ciertas vinculaciones políticas que tienen los magistrados de la corte suprema de justicia que sé yo, con la GANA, con la Une, con la FRG, por ejemplo. Y que mucho que le limitan en la posibilidad de que estas personas, personas políticas como Efraín Ríos Montt o muchas de los personas puedan será enjuiciadas.

44 Hendrix, "Innovation in Criminal Procedure in Latin America: Guatemala's Conversion to the Adversarial System."

The nominating processes that began with the 1985 constitution included a substantial representative aspect. Rather than having the President or the Congress appoint the constitutional magistrates, the 1985 constitution created a system in which the five major legal powers[45] would each name one titular and one substitute constitutional magistrate. Following the 1993 *autogolpe* by President Serrano (see below), reforms were made to the judicial career and the processes of appointing appellate court and supreme court magistrates. That process remains in use today. These reforms have dramatically reduced the influence of the political branches of government, but the majority of those interviewed in 2009 (during one round of appointments) expressed concern about the role of corruption in the selection committees, as was discussed above.

An additional problem identified by this attorney is the length of judicial tenures:

Unfortunately, in my opinion, they left out an element that is even more important, which is the length of time that judges and justices and everyone is appointed. Because, although, for the first time in 1993 or 1994, depending on what date you look at, when the constitution was amended, the first time reference was made to the career in the judiciary, *la carrera judicial*, again, trying to create yet more independence, or less dependence. The funny thing is that if you look at the statutes of the *carrera judicial*, it's written as if the five year limits did not exist, but that is just absurd because they are in the constitution. So what has happened is that over this couple of decades since our present constitution was approved, the special interests of several different kinds have clearly understood that it has become more costly and more complex, but that you can still manipulate the process so that judges and justices of your party or whatever kind of interest that might be involved will be nominated and elected. Suppose this would happen with a few individuals every five years, it would still be a problem, but when it happens concerning everyone in the Supreme Court and everyone in the Court of appeals, then you have a huge problem because everyone is at stake and the impact in terms of in which direction the system will lean, in favor of whom, is huge. Because everyone is there for renewal and or removal. So, if you are an incumbent, you basically have two choices: Either, I do not do anything and do not try to get close to what seems to be the potential winner . . . and just cross my fingers and hope that I will somehow be nominated and then elected by sheer chance or I try to be part of the whole thing. And of course, most everyone

---

[45] These include: the President, the Congress, the Supreme Court, the bar association (Colegio de Abogados y Notarios), and the law school of the national university (Universidad San Carlos, USAC)

does exactly that, except those that have made it to the Supreme Court and for any reason because they have a law firm to go to or they just want to retire and are sick and tired of the whole thing or simply have no expectation that they will be supported to go back to the court of appeals or whatever.

So, therefore the two elements that I think are particularly negative are the five-year term and everyone at the same time. (G2009–08)

As this attorney suggests, the brief judicial tenures cause a significant number of problems. Most dramatically, all magistrates must very quickly begin to look to their next position, which they will need to have established within five years. In essence, this law makes potential lame ducks of all of the magistrates. They have incentives to engage in corruption in order to secure their own futures. Moreover, they have few incentives to eschew corruption because of the minimal ability to hold them accountable for it. Losing their position is essentially meaningless when the term would likely expire before an investigation could be completed; any serious investigation could likely be put off in the many ways that all investigations can be obstructed in Guatemala. The appointment of all of the new magistrates at the same time magnifies the potential for corruption in these processes. This kind of mass selection process invites bargaining among interested actors over who will and will not be selected. As discussed above, there is considerable evidence for just such bargaining.

One retired magistrate lamented the deterioration of the justice sector through these malignant appointment practices, evoking the idea of the judiciary as a "Cinderella":

The judiciary is always seen in Guatemala as the "Cinderella" of the state because it's like that. Nobody gives it the most importance . . . The people don't understand that the judiciary has an importance equal to the other state organs . . . That when they are elected by the [Congressional] Deputies, the Deputies do not have in consideration what a judge should be, what a magistrate should be, and the damage that is done to society by naming and electing people that don't respond. But what interests them more than anything in that moment is to "pay the bill." It is terrible. I cannot generalize, but it's really making it so we have scandals. Because the Justice system has deteriorated in general, the police, the prosecutors . . . [46] (G2009–07)

---

[46] Original: El organismo judicial siempre se ve en Guatemala la cenicienta del estado porque es así. Nadie le dada mayor importancia . . . . La gente no entiende que el organismo judicial tiene una importancia igual a los otros organismos del estado. . . . Que cuando son electos por los diputados, los diputados no tienen en cuenta lo que deben ser un juez, lo que debe ser un magistrado y el daño que se hace a la sociedad nombrar y eligiendo gente que no hay responder. Pero lo que les interesa nada más es que en el momento es cobro la factura. Es

There is thus a sense in which the judiciary has in fact declined since the resumption of democracy and the end of the civil war. Again, this "deterioration" is not due to heavy-handed imposition by the president, the military, or even the political parties directly. The actors that have come to play a role in damaging the rule of law in Guatemala are quite varied – essentially any interested party with sufficient power or money can try to corrupt a judge.

Corruption in Guatemala is never naked, however. As stated above, the formal institutional rules of the Guatemalan system provide structure and cover for corruption. A particular type of abuse comes through the abuse of constitutional review, especially in the action known as an amparo. Amparos seek to protect a specific person from a specific unconstitutional action by a government actor. The constitution and amparo law lay out specific rules for which courts should hear amparos depending on the particular government actor in question. Notably, judicial decisions, including all of those that take place throughout the trial and not just the ultimate resolution, can be challenged through an amparo claim by the aggrieved party. One lawyer described the problem with amparos thus:

> Here more in the constitutional theme is when the judges don't apply the law correctly. When they don't correctly apply the law, our regulation does permit us to turn to the avenue that we call the amparo or the inconstitutionality, to denounce that something has happened that doesn't apply the law correctly . . . And the negative effect that those have is that those claims delay the process. . . All lawyers turn to this avenue, the courts are very saturated with work . . . It is one of the things that is most criticized about the Amparo Law . . . there are no areas in which the amparo does not apply. In all of the areas, you can lay on an amparo. It opens up the possibility a lot then that lawyers will make use – use and abuse – of the form of the amparo. For that, to lay on an amparo, the principal trial must stop. You can stop it one, two, three years. There are complaints that are pending three years and everything is stopped. Then, when there are four, five amparos, that does a lot of damage to the justice system, because in the system, justice is not prompt.[47] (G2009–02)

---

terrible. No puedo generalizar, pero realmente estando que estamos en escándalos. Porque sí ha deteriorado el Sistema de justicia en general, la policía, el ministerio publico . . .

[47] Original: Aquí más en el tema constitucional es cuando los jueces no aplican correctamente la ley. Ya no aplican correctamente la ley, nuestra regulación sí permite que nos acudamos a la vía lo que llamamos el amparo o la inconstitucionalidad, denunciar que algo ha pasado que no aplica la ley correctamente . . . Y el efecto negativo que tiene esos que los expedientes [se demoran] mucho el tramite . . . todos abogados acudimos esa vía, las cortes son muy saturados con trabajo . . . Es uno de las cosas por lo cual se critica señala mucha la ley de amparo . . . no hay ámbitos en que no se aplica al amparo. En todos los ámbitos, puede imponer al amparo. Hace muy abierta la posibilidad entonces sí hay abogados que hacen uso - uso y abuso – de la

This complex structure of having two high courts with sometimes overlapping jurisdictions in the area of amparos allows for a particularly legalistic kind of manipulation of the legal process. Any amparo heard first by the Supreme Court may be appealed to the Constitutional Court, allowing litigants to do an amount of forum-shopping. If a litigant is dissatisfied with a resolution of the Supreme Court (or the appellate court), he can appeal the amparo to the Constitutional Court. Similarly, a persistent litigant can appeal the outcome of the trial to the appellate courts, then seek cassation review from the Supreme Court and then attempt to win an amparo claim in the Constitutional Court challenging the resolution of the cassation process. Litigants are thus able to call on the Constitutional Court to change decisions from the Supreme Court, even though the Constitutional Court is officially outside of the ordinary judicial hierarchy. Adding corruption to the considerable discretion of the Constitutional Court in these matters produces a toxic situation for the rule of law: the Supreme Court may feel free to rule corruptly knowing that it cannot officially be monitored or sanctioned by the Constitutional Court, while the Constitutional Court can act selectively against the Supreme Court knowing that it will also likely never be sanctioned. Even without any corrupt rulings, this overlapping jurisdiction fosters the indefinite delays and perverse formalism that are so desirable to those with a lot to lose in court.

The action of amparo has also come to fill the function of hierarchical supervision, albeit also in a perverse fashion. The action of amparo provides a judicial response to a concrete unconstitutional action by a government official in a specific case. In recent practice, it has become the primary means for litigants to complain of inappropriate or even merely disagreeable decisions by lower court judges. Such cases are heard by the Supreme Court, but can be appealed to the Constitutional Court. As a consequence, the caseload of the Constitutional Court is dominated by these types of claims.[48] According to a representative of the Myrna Mack Foundation, hundreds of lawyers were delinquent in paying fines for filing frivolous amparos in 2009, some having been fined ten times or more. In July 2010, the Constitutional Court announced that it would use precedential jurisprudence to reject most of these appeals.

The phenomenon of overlapping jurisdiction and the ease of corruption that it produces should be understood as the result of an excess of independence.

figura del amparo. Para eso, al imponer el amparo, el juicio principal se detiene. Se detiene un expediente uno, dos, tres años. Hay expedientes que se tienen tres años pendientes y todo está detenido. Entonces, cuando hay cuatro, cinco amparos, eso da mucho daño al sistema de justicia, porque en el sistema, la justicia no es pronta.

[48] In 2015, 2,567 amparo appeals were filed in the Constitutional Court, out of 3,909 total cases.

Neither the Supreme Court nor Constitutional Court magistrates can be officially sanctioned by another court. The Supreme Court sits at the pinnacle of a self-regulating judiciary while the Constitutional Court sits outside of that hierarchy altogether and can only be sanctioned under extraordinary circumstances. Independent of the issues related to the appointment processes discussed above, the mere existence of more than one high court creates multiple entry points for corruption and criminality. A corrupt individual has multiple courts to try to buy and will generally only need to buy one. Moreover, because of the inequalities within Guatemalan society, those who lose to corrupt individuals in court will rarely have the resources to go through the multifaceted appeals processes themselves. Furthermore, the practice of the courts of only publishing very brief and highly formal explications of their decisions enhances the ease of corruption. Without the need to substantially justify their decisions, the magistrates may very easily camouflage corruption as strict adherence to code law.

Elements of perverse formalism exist at all levels of the judiciary. One attorney highlights an additional problem that underlays the problems with formalism and delay: lower-level judicial functionaries can easily "lose" files or neglect to notify an attorney of a step in the process:

> I would say that one terrible cost for us lawyers to deal with the judiciary system that is not independent is that we don't only have to study the case and to deal with the case, but we waste a lot of time in paying attention to how the case is evolving within the court. We have to be very careful in what is happening and keep our eyes on the case in the court, without confidence. We don't feel confident in how the cases are being handled. So we waste twice the time necessary because we have to be there almost watching how the file moves from one desk to another. And that's tense and that's time wasted for law firms, I would say. (G2009–05/06)

In short, despite extensive formal protections for the laws and the rights of citizens and litigants, entry points for corruption permeate the judicial processes at all levels. Because the justice system is so permeable, the multiple layers of protections found through the action of amparo are likely to retard justice rather than promote it.

The problem with the justice system can be summarized as one in which laws and processes that seem sound on paper become warped in practice by the easy availability of corruption. As one retired magistrate summarized the situation:

> In theory, everything should function, the laws are not bad in Guatemala, these institutions are not poorly thought out, but you can always find a way to

evade the law. There's a phrase here, "made the law, made the trick" and it certainly does apply . . . There are people who are ingenious at finding a way around it.[49] (G2009–12)

That people are "ingenious" in finding ways around the law owes a great deal to the tremendous incentives within Guatemala to do so. While she discussed loopholes here, the problem is more than simple creative legal interpretation. The problem is that tremendous quantities of money from criminal activities flood Guatemalan society and many are willing to bribe, threaten, or kill justice sector officials to hold onto it.

INTIMIDATION, PRESSURE, AND INFRINGEMENTS ON AUTONOMY FROM ALL SIDES

Influences on the courts by criminal actors necessarily loom large, as do efforts to control those criminal actors. While these criminal constraints go to the heart of a clandestine control regime, there are a number of other forms of pressure that affect judges and magistrates such as hierarchical controls, legal activism and NGOs, and negative attention from watchdog groups and the media.

Hierarchical Control

In 2010, I asked forty-three Guatemalan judges in a questionnaire about several different kinds of possible infringements on their independence that they may have experienced, including involuntary transfers and disciplinary proceedings. Of course, there may be times when involuntary transfers and disciplinary proceedings are appropriate, but they may also be used as a means of punishing judges. Twenty-three Guatemalan respondents indicated that they had been transferred, most for promotions or rotations. Only one indicated that this transfer was made because of pressure from political parties, while another indicated that a transfer had been made for the judge's security. These two incidents should of course be a matter of significant concern, but they represent relatively small numbers of the respondents.

Twenty of the Guatemalan respondents indicated that they had been subjected to disciplinary proceedings, but only one was actually sanctioned. This

---

[49] Original: En teoría, todo debería funcionar, las leyes no son malas en Guatemala, estos instituciones no son malas pensadas, pero siempre encontrar una forma de evadir la ley. Aquí hay una frase, "Hecha la ley, hecha la trampa" y claro que sí se aplica. . . . Hay gente que son muy ingeniosos en encontrar camino para la vía da vuelta.

may lend credence to the suggestion of some Guatemalan judges in interviews that disgruntled litigants routinely file complaints with the judiciary (*Organismo Judicial*) regarding a judge's behavior as a form of harassment. One lawyer indicated that, with some frequency, disciplinary complaints against judges are used as a way of intimidating judges. An anonymous appellate magistrate interviewed in 2010 echoed this concern. Constitutional Court President Molina described a recent example of this phenomenon against the constitutional magistrates: Following the Constitutional Court's intervention in the 2009 selection process for the Supreme Court, which "made uncomfortable" many within organized crime, numerous complaints were filed in the ordinary courts against the constitutional magistrates. The Supreme Court then had to decide whether to send these cases to the Congress to consider action against the constitutional magistrates. Fortunately for Molina and his colleagues, the Supreme Court rejected all of the complaints, following a constitutional provision protecting magistrates who have appropriately carried out their duties in deciding amparos. Nonetheless, Molina described this period as a "crisis." Again, while it is necessary to have methods of disciplining judges, these processes can easily be abused by litigants or judicial superiors.

The Media

Similar concerns were raised about the press. Judges interviewed in 2009 reported being uncomfortable with press coverage of their cases and feeling that this coverage sometimes did constitute a form of pressure that harmed their autonomy. The Guatemalan press is very interested in crime and justice issues and can be sensationalistic in its reporting. One can hardly read the daily newspapers without seeing stories about crime; high-profile charges against current or former government officials routinely make the front page. Indeed, one can hardly walk into the court building in Guatemala City without seeing reporters waiting in the hall outside at least one of the criminal courts. Several private lawyers indicated that they generally tried to avoid press coverage of their cases, although one NGO lawyer reported his organization does sometimes try to make use of press coverage to bring the controversy to public attention and put pressure on the government.

Most judges and magistrates interviewed in 2009 and 2010 indicated that direct pressure from politicians or other powerful people was rare, but that indirect pressure was common. One source of this indirect pressure is public demonstrations outside of the courts, which are then heavily publicized in the media. These demonstrations are fairly common when highly publicized and controversial cases are being decided. Public opprobrium is directed at all of the Guatemalan courts, but the Supreme Court and the Constitutional Court are the most visible and frequent targets. The relative security of the ordinary courts may be a simple matter of geography and architecture: there are public parks and plazas near the two high courts while most trial courts are collected in a sixteen-story tower tucked behind the Supreme Court.

One attorney summarized these concerns nicely in arguing that the press is helpful when it sheds light on issues within the justice system, but not when it takes positions on particular cases:

> I would say that media, the press, instead of taking a position with respect to one case, they should simply help those organizations that watch over cases to inform what is going on instead of taking positions over cases. The problem with media is they have taken a specific position with respect to specific cases and I would say that does not help the independence of the judicial system. That what you have just raised, that is the watch over the system by organizations with the help of press, that would be an immense help. For example, it would be very important to have organizations that help to know all the rulings that come out from the judges. Nobody knows what the judges say and that's something wrong. They might have ruled in a terrible way without legal support and nobody knows that. (G2009–0506)

Sadly, very few independent domestic NGOs exist to simply observe the judiciary. Although it is somewhat the job of the CICIG to watch over the justice system and to publicize (and even prosecute) concerns, there remain limited outlets for neutral observation of the judiciary, including in the press.

Crime

The rise of organized crime has become a major problem for the political system in Guatemala. Colombian drug cartels were long a problem in Guatemala. Since 2005, however, the Mexican drug gang *Los Zetas* has been on the rise. By mid-2009, it was estimated that the Zetas were operative in 75 percent of the country. The Zetas initially worked closely with domestic organized crime known as the "hidden powers," but the increasingly ambitious Zetas began to clash openly with Guatemalan gangs in 2008. The Zetas are also suspected of orchestrating the substantial electoral violence in 2007, although it is believed that the "hidden powers" participated in the bloodbath as well. As Brands argued in 2010, this violence was intended both to "prune" the electoral field of the most troublesome candidates, especially in the rural areas, while also sending a warning to those that were elected not to challenge the gangs. The murder of three Salvadoran PARLACEN (Central American Parliament) members and their driver in 2007, followed by the murder while in custody of the police officers suspected in the killings, highlighted for many Guatemalans the extremity of the situation.[50] The prevalence of crime in Guatemala has produced significant problems for the autonomy of individual judges, especially at the lower levels of the judiciary. Constitutional Court President Molina opined that organized crime wants impunity and tries to "co-opt" all of the institutions of the state from the ordinary courts to the prosecutors and the constitutional court. The clearest form of intimidation is direct threats against judges. Judges who work in high impact criminal cases are given bodyguards, as are Supreme Court and Constitutional Court magistrates as a matter of course, although not all judges or magistrates choose to take advantage of this. One criminal judge reported in 2009 that she felt very secure as a result, although one civil court judge indicated in 2009 that she did not feel well protected by the judiciary. The general climate of violent criminality in Guatemala leads to a vague, general sense of intimidation. For example, when a judge was murdered in Guatemala City in 2009, there was immediate speculation in the press that her murder was related to her work as a judge, although it turned out that she had been murdered by her maid because of a financial dispute. The ease with which a person can be murdered contributes to the power of threats when they do happen. One appellate magistrate who requested anonymity described this "terrorism" as a very grave threat to judicial autonomy.

The questionnaires distributed in 2010 included questions about bribery and threats. Eleven of the Guatemalan judges reported having been offered bribes, in some cases by more than one person. Two were offered bribes by the Executive, one by a member of the legislature, two from parties to the case, one by an attorney, one by a prosecutor, and four by "others." One also indicated that the person offering the bribe was unknown. Thirteen Guatemalan judges indicated that they had been threatened, some again by multiple persons. Not surprisingly, the highest number of threats (four) came from parties to the case or their relatives. One indicated that she had been threatened by a member of the executive branch, while another had been threatened by the media. Two were threatened by litigating attorneys, one by a member of the *Organismo Judicial*, three by "others," and two by persons unknown. Notably, not everyone who reported being bribed reported being threatened, nor vice versa. While the survey did not ask the respondents to indicate how they handled the bribes and threats (nor how the judiciary did), this does give us some indication of how widespread these problems are and from where they originate. It is particularly troubling in Guatemala that there are reports

---

[50] Brands, *Crime, Violence, and the Crisis in Guatemala.*

of threats and bribes from official actors, including prosecutors and members of the executive and legislative branches.

Lawyers are also subject to these threats, which limits the availability of legal representation for people confronting organized criminals or involved in gang-related crimes. Some lawyers shrug off these threats. Two different private lawyers indicated that they had been able to diffuse threats against them by adhering carefully to ethical standards and making it clear that they would not be deterred. A lawyer working for a human rights NGO indicated that his office had internal procedures that they carefully followed, but did not hire bodyguards because the government provided police officers when they requested. However, he indicated that he did not accept police protection because many threats are carried out by corrupt police officers. Another private attorney, who had previously worked in the prosecutor's office, indicated that he feared for his life.

The Influence of Non-Governmental Organizations

While less obviously problematic, Non-Governmental Organizations are another source of indirect pressure on judges and magistrates. Guatemala has a large number of NGOs, many of which enjoy the strong backing of the international community. Many of these organizations take an interest in the resolution of various court cases and some organizations such as the Myrna Mack Foundation, the Human Rights Legal Action Center, the Pro-Justice Movement, and the Archbishop's Office on Human Rights, focus much of their work on the justice system. These organizations routinely make public evaluations of the judiciary (and other parts of the justice system), whether in the form of written reports launched at public events or through statements to the press. Additionally, some of these organizations have been drivers of human rights prosecutions as described above. When asked about the role of NGOs, judges and lawyers generally characterized this role as potentially both beneficial and harmful. While it was generally acknowledged that monitoring of the judiciary is important and can strengthen the judiciary, many were concerned that some NGOs use their position to pursue politicized or self-serving goals.

One attorney gave the following statement, which is typical of the ambivalence surrounding NGOs:

> There's good and bad, you know all types of things. There are probably some that... I would dare to say that Myrna Mack Foundation does more good than bad, not everything they do is good, but they do more than good than bad. I really don't have in mind any other NGOs that are putting into the

judicial process or involved with the judicial branch. AID programs for example have been good, programs developed that they have promoted toward the
formation of justice have been good. As well as some other from other governments to fortify the judicial branch and the Attorney General's office.
Regarding the judicial branch, specifically. Regarding all the other areas, I
think NGOs are probably destructive rather than constructive. For example,
in mining or hydroelectric, they can be manipulative and vehicles of misinfor-
mation. The developers recognize the need to acknowledge, the urgency to
acknowledge the necessities of the communities where the projects are being
developed. They really cannot operate at the same level that the NGOs operate. That makes it very difficult to create business and to carry out business
here. (G2009–03)

As in the quote above, most attorneys who said positive things about NGOs
talked about organizations (some of them in fact international organizations
and donors) that helped to strengthen the judiciary and to push general
reforms. There was a general sense, echoed by more than one attorney, that
if NGOs and international actors did not push for reforms, reforms would
probably never happen.

Another attorney expressed particular misgivings about NGOs that back
particular sides in cases:

I have mixed feeling with respect to the work that some NGOs do. I like
very much those NGOs that work for the preservation of the system, that
put an eye on how things are doing, but the ones that take one position
in one case very specifically at the beginning of the case and that they get
involved with the press and they assume that there is justice only if the case
is ruled according to their position. Those things don't help very much. I
would say that is making groups around specific interests with one case and
their might be groups on one side, there could also be groups forming on
the other side. So it is difficult to have NGOs doing that kind of work and
not putting into jeopardy some kind of independence, basically when they're
working together with the press. If they act with respect to general things,
they're OK. We might see that NGOs could be formed around ideologies,
specific interests, either economic or any other type, but if they take a position
in specific case with their interests, then it is not general justice that is being
discussed, but it is how specific interests are moved through the field and
then the judiciary organism becomes also a field instead of the organism of
the state that resolves, but a field where they're going to fight. (G2009–0506)

Of course, the category of organizations that back one side in a case would
include nearly all of the Guatemalan NGOs working in the area of human
rights. Indeed, the Myrna Mack Foundation praised by lawyer G2009–03

would fall squarely into that description. Furthermore, it is unlikely that any of the major human rights prosecutions would have occurred without pressure from these sorts of NGOs, as was discussed earlier. Nonetheless, it is clear that tension surrounds the role of NGOs in the justice system.

EPILOGUE: THE CICIG AND THE 2015 "GUATEMALAN SPRING"

Guatemala experienced a political convulsion between April and September 2015, beginning with the arrest of high-ranking customs officials and ending with the resignation of President Otto Pérez Molina (2012–2015). These events were sparked by an investigation, known as "*La Linea*," into corruption in the customs system (the SAT). The *La Linea* investigation was initiated by the CICIG following audits of the SAT security service that began at the SAT's request in 2012, but much of the investigation and actual prosecution has been carried out by the specialized domestic prosecutorial unit that has been trained by the CICIG (the FECI). The initial round of arrests on April 16, 2015, sparked a protest movement on social media, using the hashtags #JusticiaYa (Justice Now) and #RenunciaYa (Resign Now). These protests were initially targeted at Vice President Roxana Baldetti, who resigned to face charges on May 8, but quickly came to include rejection of corruption and impunity more generally. By August, large numbers of people were taking to the streets of Guatemala City on a daily basis, calling for the president's resignation. Following a national strike that began on August 27, Pérez Molina resigned on September 3, 2015.

The so-called "Guatemalan Spring" illustrates many issues relating to the CICIG and justice sector reform in Guatemala. First, it reveals how deeply ingrained the illegal networks have been in Guatemalan politics; *La Linea* ultimately implicated the president, vice president, members of the cabinet, and members of the legislature, along with lower-level officials. Second, it demonstrates the tensions inherent in having a corrupt government in a position to host an international commission that seeks to investigate that very government. In April 2015, when the first arrests were made, Baldetti and Pérez Molina both argued to the United Nations that there was no need to renew the CICIG for another two-year mandate. Once the investigative findings became public, that argument became harder to make and Pérez Molina signed an agreement for another two-year term, lasting until September 2017. Third, it reflects the shifting relationships both between the CICIG and domestic institutions as well as within the domestic institutions themselves in that the CICIG was originally invited by the SAT itself to begin an audit that ultimately led to the unraveling of the customs ring. Fourth, it reveals the growing strength of the prosecutor's office, which is prosecuting the case in national courts. It is difficult to imagine such a prosecution a decade prior. Finally, it also reveals a popular awareness and rejection of corruption, impunity, and violence. If the #JusticiaYa movement can maintain any strength and cohesion, it may provide the popular pressure to force political will to fight corruption and impunity even after the end of the CICIG's final mandate.

Three days after President Pérez Molina resigned, regularly-scheduled presidential elections occurred, despite efforts by some to postpone them given the circumstances. A television comedian with no experience in political office, Jimmy Morales, and a former first lady, Sandra Torres, advanced to the second round. In a clear rejection of the political establishment, Morales won with nearly 70 percent of the vote in the second round. Although Morales was an outsider, his party has ties to business interests and military officer who are accused of civil war-era human rights violations. It remains unclear whether he will support transitional justice efforts or continued penetrating measures against corruption. Whether a political neophyte can navigate such a tumultuous situation remains to be seen.

CONCLUSIONS

International donor groups contributed considerable amounts of money, personnel, equipment, and training to the Guatemalan judiciary from the 1980s to the 2000s in order to build the rule of law. What most stymied these efforts has been the failure to control the problem of violent organized crime that grew in the 1990s and 2000s. The growth of organized crime is in large part a failure of the newly democratic and demilitarized government to maintain – or even obtain at the beginning – effective control of the society by the state. The state had the most control of the society during the mid to late 1980s, when the military still exercised considerable control through repression. Even then, state control was far from complete: the guerrillas were still able to maintain their positions in some areas long enough to force a negotiated settlement in the early 1990s. Similarly, few measures were taken at the time of the peace accords in 1996 and after to reintegrate demilitarized soldiers, paramilitaries, and guerrillas into civilian society. Meanwhile, many clandestine networks remained in place that, coupled with easily corrupted border guards, had allowed for the movement of illegal arms and goods throughout the country. At the return of civilian government in 1985, the military maintained reserves of power and did not initially contribute to the growth of strong "power institutions" such as police, courts, and investigation. Initially, the police were poorly trained, underpaid, and inadequately overseen, a perfect combination for the growth of corruption. As the military was cut back and lost some of its power gradually from the late 1990s to the early 2000s, the police force was not adequate to meet the criminality that quickly spiked.

It is the lesson of the Guatemalan case that judicial independence is not enough if there is not also judicial autonomy. Without judicial autonomy, some justice sector users are able to attain beneficial treatment that is unavailable to the ordinary user. Anytime this inequality of legal treatment is widespread, the rule of law is called into question. Where this kind of inequality is married to criminality and a governing regime that has been unable to fully break with a repressive, racist and classist past, the rule of law is turned on its head. Instead of a liberal regime that treats all as equals or even lifts up the poor, an impunity regime treats some better than others, with the poor and powerless made to bear the burden of the laws and the state. When a poor person is killed by a gang, the crime will likely go unpunished. When a rich or powerful person is killed by a poor person, the poor person (or *some* poor person) will be made to pay the price. When a rich person (with or without gang connections) kills anyone, the rich person can expect to be able to exploit the many avenues for corruption and delay to maintain his freedom for many years, if not indefinitely.

The other lesson of the Guatemalan example is that it is extraordinarily difficult to build societal autonomy for a judiciary that has lost it. With the assistance of the CICIG, Guatemalans have begun to gain ground on building the rule of law. Significantly, prosecution rates are rising and crime rates are dropping in the wake of major reforms to policing and prosecution as well as high profile prosecutions of organized crime rings, especially those including public officials in their networks. These measures are fundamental; without them, Guatemala would be unlikely to ever build the rule of law. They are also insufficient; even with them, institutionalizing the rule of law in Guatemala will require considerable political will, sustained effort, and additional reforms. The CICIG has played an important role as a brokerage institution that could work with all of the players in Guatemala's justice system. Once the Commission, with its tremendous international backing, departs, it is not clear whether any other agency or actor will have a similar amount of weight to bear on political debates over the justice system. Whether or not General Ríos Montt is convicted and imprisoned, the generation that oversaw the civil war is passing out of political life; it is quite likely that international interest will wane at the same time. A major test now awaits Guatemala's justice sector.

6

Partisan Systems

El Salvador, Honduras, and Nicaragua are presented in this chapter as examples of the partisan judicial regime type. At the core of this judicial regime type is the control of the judiciary, at least at its apex, by partisan political actors. In other words, partisan judiciaries do not enjoy inter-branch judicial independence. However, they may nonetheless enjoy significant autonomy from societal actors. A partisan judiciary differs from a government control judiciary in three ways. First, the partisan judiciary is typically controlled by democratically elected politicians or their co-partisan political associates rather than authoritarian leaders or their military associates. Second, partisan judiciaries frequently divide the judicial spoils between two or more parties, as is explicitly done by political pact in Honduras and Nicaragua. As a result of this partisan sharing of judicial positions, there is a degree of ideological and partisan diversity within the judiciary, often including in the Supreme Court. There is thus always the possibility that the courts could rule against the government on even sensitive matters, depending on the composition of the court or the judge who hears the case. Nonetheless, the reality in Honduras and Nicaragua, at least, has been that of political and partisan collusion as the dominant mode of operations. The third way in which a partisan judiciary differs from a government control judiciary has to do with the dominant and ultimate "currency" for dispute resolution. Whereas government control judicial regimes are backed by official violence, a partisan judiciary will typically rely on political law over constitutional law. This tendency is certainly more democratic than a government control judiciary, even if it is not always respectful of republican notions of constitutional rights.

The presence of strong and relatively stable political parties is an important factor in creating partisan judicial regimes; a feckless party system could not sustain the long-term relationships and bipartisan agreements necessary for partisan control. El Salvador, Honduras, and Nicaragua all have the requisite stable party systems. Nicaragua and Honduras are both clear examples of partisan judiciaries. El Salvador, however, presents some variation on the theme, in large part because the judicial appointment rules do not allow for the same extent of negotiated appointments. El Salvador's judicial regime also reflects significant aspects of the clandestine control type, and is a useful example of some of the overlaps between official and unofficial influences. The Salvadoran judicial regime appeared in 2015 to be in greater flux than either Nicaragua's or Honduras'. These judiciaries are empowered in some areas; such empowerment can be highly functional for these democratic systems for many of the same reasons Moustafa argues that judicial empowerment can benefit autocrats, including policing the bureaucracy and providing legitimacy to government actions.[1] Importantly, we should understand that a truly partisan judge or magistrate may be very powerful in that she is entrusted, by virtue of her partisan affiliation, to implement and enforce an ideology that she believes in.

NICARAGUA: REVOLUTIONARY LOYALTIES CONTINUE IN PARTISAN FORM

A series of pacts between the FSLN and Liberal Party politicians have dominated modern Nicaraguan democratic politics. Close has argued repeatedly that these pacts have dominated Nicaraguan politics from the time that the FSLN handed power to Violeta Chamorro (1990–1996) and the *Unidad Nacional Opositora* (National Opposition Union, UNO) in 1990 and that they allowed the Sandinistas to continue to enjoy a share of national power even from second place.[2] With the predominance of pact-making in Nicaragua came unwillingness either to conduct a systematic lustration process or to otherwise put a legal *punto final* on the events of the Sandinista years. Instead, the dismissal, retention, and selection of government officials have been driven substantially by partisan political concerns. This tendency is reflected in the choices to hold accountable for corruption and other abuses primarily those official actors who are out of favor with the current government, most notably former president Alemán.[3] Similarly, reform processes have been layered on top of existing formal institutions and informal networks of clientelism, thus failing to provide real change to the nature of the justice system. Nicaragua

---

[1] Moustafa, *The Struggle for Constitutional Power.*
[2] Close, *Nicaragua*; Close and Deonandan, *Undoing Democracy*; Close, "From Guerrillas to Government to Opposition and Back to Government: The Sandinistas since 1979."
[3] Indeed, this logic seems to hold true even in relatively transparent Costa Rica.

has little "horizontal accountability"[4] as a result, especially as against San-dinista president Daniel Ortega (1979–1990, 2007–), who exercises power in an increasingly personalist fashion. The judiciary nonetheless operates fairly effectively with regard to the control of crime and citizen security.

Pacts and the Lack of Accountability in Nicaragua

While the close cooperation between the FSLN and Chamorro established the pattern of pact-making, the 2000 pact between Danieal Ortega and the *Partido Liberal Constitucional's* (Liberal Constitutional Party, PLC) President Arnoldo Alemán (1997–2002) dramatically extended this cooperation. The 2000 pact included important amendments to the constitution, including a change to the electoral threshold for the presidency that would ultimately allow for Daniel Ortega's return to the presidency in 2007. More significant for the judiciary, however, was the agreement to share appointments to a number of important government positions, including many judgeships as well as a variety of bureaucratic posts. As a consequence, the normal appointment process is subverted to partisan preferences. The constitution indicates that the magistrates of the Supreme Court will be chosen as a single slate by the National Assembly from two lists – one produced by the deputies of the National Assembly and one by the president – by a 60 percent super-majority. Even when the Liberals controlled the presidency and the majority of the National Assembly, they did not control the requisite 60 percent and needed the cooperation of the FSLN Deputies to appoint magistrates. The super-majority requirement could be read to ensure that appointees are not odious to either major party, but the practice has been instead for the two parties to divide the spoils by divvying up the list between them. Not surprisingly, Nicaragua's Supreme Court magistrates are closely associated with either the Sandinista camp or the Liberal camp. Significantly, the same appointment process is applied to many other state transparency institutions.[5]

Lower-court judges are named by a judicial council (Consejo Nacional de Administración y Carrera Judicial), which is dominated by the Supreme Court. Magistrates of the Supreme Court and the appellate courts serve a term of five years, but trial-court judges can serve for longer in a more bureaucra-tized career. The constitution still allows that non-lawyers can be named to lower-court judgeships, although they would not be qualified to be appointed subsequently to the higher courts. As with most of the world's constitutions,

---

4 O'Donnell, "Horizontal Accountability: The Legal Institutionalization of Mistrust."
5 "Constitución Política de la República de Nicaragua," sec. 138.

the political independence of judges and magistrates is announced. In addition, the judiciary is guaranteed 4 percent of the national budget. On paper, the constitution appears to provide for the independence of the Nicaraguan judiciary, at least below the Supreme Court. However, because lower-level judges are appointed by a highly politicized Supreme Court, the practice is that of a politically dependent judiciary overall. Judges are known as Liberal or Sandinista judges and they typically act in accordance with the ideologies and desires of the parties with which they are associated. Nicaragua thus presents an interesting example of the paradox of the partisan judiciary in that the judiciary is a relatively strong institution vis-à-vis the citizenry, but dependent on partisan politicians.

"Sticky" Partisan Pacts between Elites

The lack of inter-branch judicial independence in Nicaragua is a clear and intentional result of the pacts of the post-revolutionary period. Magistrates are chosen according to partisan political allegiance and they, in turn, largely control the selection of lower-court judges. This partisanship overlaps with the personal power of Ortega and Alemán, who have dominated the Nicaraguan political scene since the 1980s and 1990s, respectively. The development of this system diminished public opinion of the judiciary in the middle 2000s; however, public opinion rebounded by 2012 such that both the Supreme Court and the justice system as a whole enjoyed majority confidence.[6] The reasons for this rebound are unclear. Perhaps the majority of Nicaraguans simply approved of the recent actions of the courts, however politicized; after all, the Sandinistas extended their majority to a supermajority when Ortega was reelected in 2011. The tensions in this partisan system can be seen in the lengthy saga of the prosecution, conviction, and ultimate release of Arnoldo Alemán and in the Supreme Court decision that allowed for immediate presidential reelection.

As president, Arnoldo Alemán was declared by Transparency International as one of the ten most corrupt national leaders in the world. At the center of this declaration were the charges for which he was ultimately convicted – embezzlement and forgery of 100 million dollars. While still president, his personal fortune was estimated by his opponents at 250 million dollars.[7] An

---

[6] Booth, *Political Culture of Democracy in Nicaragua and in the Americas, 2012: Towards Equality of Opportunity*, 150.

[7] Briones Loasiga, "Calculan en US$250 millones fortuna de Arnoldo Alemán."

investigation was initiated under the presidency of Enrique Bolaños (2002–2007) and Alemán was convicted by a Sandinista judge in December 2003 to twenty years under house arrest. Nonetheless, Alemán and Ortega continued their political relationship, with Alemán largely continuing to direct his loyal followers in the PLC from house arrest – to the detriment of Bolaños and any other erstwhile Liberal party leader.[8] Following a series of legal maneuvers, Alemán succeeded in winning his freedom from the Supreme Court in January 2009. Following his absolution and release, Alemán ran unsuccessfully for a second term as president in the 2011 elections. According to the more *Liberalista*-leaning daily, *La Prensa*, an "Ortegista" judge was continuing to "blackmail" Alemán by threatening his campaign through the possibility of new or renewed charges.[9]

Pact-making appeared to be diminishing in the early years of the presidency of Enrique Bolaños, in particular with his decision to push the prosecution of his predecessor, Alemán. As Close reports, this prosecution took place under a Sandinista judge, who then went on to suggest an indictment of President Bolaños in April 2004.[10] Another pact followed between Bolaños and Ortega in 2005, which amended the constitution to require the super-majorities described above. The 2005 pact also lowered the threshold necessary for a presidential candidate to win outright in the first round of voting, which would prove instrumental in allowing Ortega to win the presidency again in the 2006 election. Ortega undertook a series of political maneuvers in 2005 to accept that pact, then delay it, then join calls for Bolaños' impeachment, and then resume his support for Bolaños and the pact, presumably to demonstrate his distance from the then-imprisoned and at least somewhat discredited Alemán and bolster his efforts to win the presidency in the 2006 election. Ortega ultimately won the 2006 election and returned to the presidency after seventeen years in the opposition in 2007.

As the Alemán case progressed in 2003, it appeared alternately as a heroic stand by President Bolaños against a corrupt member of his own party and as a calculated effort to win the support of the world by attacking a political rival, but Ortega's role in this saga is the most intriguing. Alemán was convicted by a Sandinista judge, whose presence on the bench was in part due to pacting between Ortega and Alemán. However, Alemán was given great latitude as a convict and continued to make arrangements between the PLC

---

[8] Indeed, one such erstwhile Liberal (though not PLC) candidate, Eduardo Montealegre told *La Prensa* March 17, 2013, that Alemán was "the worst thing that has happened to this country."
[9] Cruz, "Justicia de Ortega vuelve con chantajes a Alemán."
[10] Close, "From Guerrillas to Government to Opposition and Back to Government: The Sandinistas since 1979."

and the FSLN during his six years under house arrest. In the end, it was a Sandinista-dominated Supreme Court during Ortega's second presidency that freed Alemán. When the Supreme Court invalidated the prohibition on immediate reelection and cleared the way for Ortega to run again in 2011, many in Nicaragua and around the world decried the two cases as clear tit-for-tat.[11]

A 1995 reform to the 1987 Sandinista constitution had included a prohibition on consecutive re-election; a president had to sit out one interim term before he could be elected president again. Thus, the 2006 election of Daniel Ortega to a second presidency[12] did not run afoul of the constitution, but a subsequent candidacy in 2011 would. Consequently, Ortega and the FSLN brought an amparo challenge to the Constitutional Chamber of the Supreme Court. As described by Walker and Schorpp, Sandinista magistrates were able to hear and vote on the amparo without any involvement of Liberal magistrates because they filled the slots of absent Liberal magistrates with Sandinista substitute (*suplente*) magistrates.[13] This maneuvering of substitute magistrates closely follows the 2003 decision by the Guatemalan Constitutional Court to allow Efrain Ríos Montt to run for president despite a blanket constitutional prohibition on reelection, as discussed in Chapter 5. Walker and Schorpp point out, however, that the reasoning very closely follows the legal reasoning of the 2003 presidential reelection case in Costa Rica.[14] The Nicaraguan decision, however, was grounded in the principle of "unconditional equality" found in Nicaragua's revolutionary constitution.

Some have directed their anger over "*Orteguismo*," the domination of Nicaraguan politics by Alemán and Ortega, corruption, and the general state of legal affairs at one specific magistrate of the Supreme Court, Rafael Solís. Solís has long-standing Sandinista credentials, having fought in the guerrilla war against Somoza in the 1970s and helped to construct the 1987 Sandinista constitution. He was among the first round of magistrates appointed in the wake of the 2000 Alemán–Ortega pact and has been a close legal advisor to Ortega, while voting in favor of Alemán's freedom and Ortega's reelection. Reportedly, Solís also exercises a great deal of personal influence with lower-court judges, in part by acting as their advocate when they need one.[15] Such close ties between politicians and high-level jurists are common in Nicaragua and may be the consequence of the recency of the Sandinista revolution.

---

[11] Silva, "El pacto Ortega-Alemán y la reelección."
[12] Astute observers might note that Ortega technically served two terms in the 1980s, but the constitution was written and adopted following his election to his second term. What's more, he was not actually elected to his first term, but came to power as a part of the revolutionary *junta*, which muddies that question further.
[13] Walker and Schorpp, "Judicial Politics of Presidential Reelection."
[14] Ibid.   [15] Cruz, "El 'padrino' de la justicia."

While there exist dissident political parties such as the *Movemiento Reno-vador Sandinista* (MRS), which retains much of the Sandinista ideology but would like to move beyond the leadership of Ortega himself, the young men who defeated Somoza in 1979 and tried to build a revolutionary state have remained, largely through the agreement of their opponents, in ever-more powerful positions in the government. The Supreme Court is no exception to this trend.

The real impacts of partisanship can be seen in the case of the Punta Teonoste resort, which calls itself "one of the most exclusive boutique Ressorts [sic] in Nicaragua"[16] and was seized by the government in 2012.[17] Nicaragua's land titling and land tenure problems are widespread and date to the confiscations and redistributions of the revolutionary era. The Teonoste resort has come up against a new round of problems, however: according to its owner, the government was still claiming a portion of the property to give to a former guerrilla leader, Éden Pastora, without any alleged flaw in the resort's title. One year after the seizure, *La Prensa* reported that the courts continued to be "paralyzed" regarding the case, while land title records were quietly being updated to reflect the assignment of the property to Pastora.[18] Because it involves such large investments that could easily be seized at a total loss to the investor (i.e., real estate), the tourism sector is especially vulnerable to the legal irregularities of Nicaragua. Notably, this instance involved political favors rather than mere popular lawlessness or deliberate legal obstructionism.[19]

Despite Substantial Partisan Influence, Few Other External Pressures

Hierarchical control appears to provide entry for both the exertion of partisan pressure and the exertion of societal pressure. Lower-court judges are appointed by a Judicial Council following training and an examination process. Once appointed, they are disciplined through the same Judicial Council. Because four magistrates of the Supreme Court head the judicial council, there is significant possibility for the injection of political influence into both of these processes. Disciplinary processes are regulated by the Judicial Career Law and the 2006 *Reglamento de la Carrera Judicial*. Judges are suspended in their functions during an investigation and could be suspended for as long as three months or fired if found guilty of a very grave offense. According to a 2007

---

[16] "Hotel Punta Teonoste."
[17] Vidaurre Arias and Quintero, "Empresarios cierran filas a favor de Punta Teonoste."
[18] Vásquez, "Inscriben despojo a Punta Teonoste."
[19] Indeed, further reporting in January 2014 suggested that it might be some time before the case was even considered by the Granada Appellate Court, much less resolved. The Liberal Nicaraguan daily newspaper *La Prensa* held it up as an example of the general problems with "juridical security" in property in Nicaragua. Vásquez, "Propiedad sigue en problemas."

study by the Due Process of Law Foundation, a large proportion of complaints allege *"retardación de justicia"* (in essence, unjustified delay), the majority of which are found to be without merit. These figures suggest that disciplinary complaints are being used in Nicaragua as they are in Guatemala as a means for litigants and lawyers to retaliate against judges;[20] on the other hand, some Nicaraguans express continued, serious concern about these problems.[21] The magistrates of the Supreme Court, each of whom oversees a given region of the country, can reassign judges to different posts within the country, another way in which judges are sometimes punished for unpopular opinions. The Due Process of Law Foundation's report quotes a judicial employee as saying about this problem, "as long as you don't have the certainty that transfers without consent don't exist, you cannot give yourself the luxury of having principles, because principles don't feed your sons and daughters, they don't see you, they don't go to school."[22,23]

The public media in Nicaragua are extremely partisan. Of the two main daily newspapers, one *(La Prensa)* is closely affiliated with the Liberal Party; indeed President Violeta Chamorro's late husband was the publisher prior to his assassination by the pre-Sandinista Somoza dictatorship in January 1978. The other *(El Nuevo Diario)* is a Sandinista mouth piece, having been founded by revolutionary defectors from *La Prensa* in 1980. Neither appears to report heavily on the courts, although their partisan commitments influence the editorial line when they do. Some of this lack of reporting may be the result of the overall low rates of crime; reporters have fewer sensational stories to exploit. Nicaraguan human rights NGOs do make use of the media to publicize their concerns, including by providing press releases and hosting public conferences and presentations on a wide variety of issues of interest to the NGOs. The media does report on the major cases before the courts, especially the Supreme Court, but tends to do so with greater enthusiasm when a partisan opponent can be vilified in the process. The partisan nature of the Nicaraguan press allows partisan judges and magistrates to disregard much of the press reporting as simple partisan attacks, whether or not genuine problems are reported on.

Crime and corruption pose considerably less danger in Nicaragua than they do in her Northern neighbors. While Latin American and legal sources cite

[20] Fundación para el Debido Proceso Legal, *Controles y Descontroles de la Corrupción Judicial: Evaluación de la corrupción judicial y del los mecanismos para controlarla in Centroámerica y Panamá*, 369.

[21] "Retardación de justicia."

[22] Original: "mientras no tenga la certeza que no existan traslados sin consentimiento, no puede darse el lujo de tener principios, porque de principios sus hijos e hijas no comen, ni se visten, ni van a la escuela."

[23] Fundación para el Debido Proceso Legal, *Controles y Descontroles de la Corrupción Judicial*, 363.

significant concerns about the very high incidence and perceptions of corruption in Nicaragua, recent Americas Barometer survey data actually suggest that Nicaraguans perceive less corruption among public officials than do citizens of the other Central American countries as well as most of the rest of the hemisphere, including the United States. Notably, despite concerns about corruption under the second presidency of Daniel Ortega,[24] "[t]he net change in perceived corruption from 2006 to 2012 on our 100 point scale has been a decline of 21.1 points."[25] Reported incidence of being asked to pay a bribe is also relatively low when compared to the rest of the hemisphere at 11.4 percent, compared with 23.5 percent in Guatemala.[26] Again, the incidence of this kind of victimization has decreased since 2006 by 6.6 percentage points.[27] The statistics, at least, suggest that judicial corruption, while still problematic, is coming under control in Nicaragua.

One possible reason for the reduced levels of corruption, especially within the judiciary, may be the relatively low levels of crime, including drug crime. The Americas Barometer report also indicates that Nicaraguans experience relatively less citizen insecurity than their counterparts in the region. 13.6 percent reported being the victim of a crime in the prior year in 2012, down from 19.2 percent in 2010 and lower than in Guatemala and Honduras, but slightly higher than in El Salvador and significantly higher than in Costa Rica.[28] These victimization figures are mirrored in Nicaragua's relatively low homicide rate compared with her neighbors to the North, as shown in Chapter 1. Not surprisingly, as criminal victimization has declined, Nicaraguans have shown increasing support for a style of policing that respects the law and the constitution rather than a *mano dura* approach.[29] Such data also speaks highly of the use of community-based policing in Nicaragua.[30] Narcotrafficking of course exists in Nicaragua, but its effects are still substantially more controlled than in her neighbors.[31] For example, several judicial functionaries including five judges and three courts of appeals magistrates were fired in 2011 for conspiring to free traffickers, suggesting that, despite the judiciary's problems, it can at times police itself.[32]

NGOs are an active part of the Nicaraguan political scene, but are less court-focused than those in Guatemala. In their May 2009 Alternative Report to the United Nations Committee Against Torture, several Nicaraguan NGOs,

[24] Baca and Navas, "Nicaragua entre países más corruptos del continente."
[25] Booth, *Political Culture of Democracy in Nicaragua and in the Americas*, 2012, 108.
[26] Ibid., 110.   [27] Ibid., 112.   [28] Ibid., 118.   [29] Ibid., 127.
[30] Ungar, *Policing Democracy*.   [31] Bunck and Fowler, *Bribes, Bullets, and Intimidation*.
[32] Organización Mundial Contra la Tortura, "Violaciones de los derechos humanos en Nicaragua: Informe alternativo e informe seguimiento presentado al Comité contra la Tortura de la Naciones Unidas."

working together with the World Organization Against Torture, cited a variety of concerns. These concerns included excessive use of force by police during arrests and investigations as well as poor conditions in prisons. In fact, this report estimated that some 30 percent of police officers have been accused of human rights abuses of some kinds – although it does acknowledge that the accused are investigated through official channels and that approximately 27.9 percent are then sanctioned. They also mention three incidents, all during the last year of the Bolaños administration (2006), in which protesters were arbitrarily arrested, which should be understood as a form of political harassment given that the protesters were released within 1–4 days.[33] Such political harassment of protestors continues as of June 2013, however, when gay rights demonstrators were forcibly turned away from one of the major traffic circles in Managua.[34]

A balanced analysis of the human rights situation in Nicaragua suggests that there continue to be problems, but that the situation is less abusive in Nicaragua than it is in Honduras, El Salvador, or Guatemala. The life of a criminal suspect is less harrowing in Nicaragua than in some of her neighbors. Nicaraguan human rights NGOs take a broad view of human rights, however, and frequently raise concerns about violence against women, intra-family violence, and worker's rights. Notwithstanding these important considerations, state violations of basic human rights to bodily integrity appear to be minimal. Despite the judiciary's general reluctance to hold government officials accountable for abuses, human rights violations in general remain at a much lower level than in Nicaragua's northern neighbors. The United Nations Office of the High Commissioner for Human Rights, for example, cites many problems related to poverty, discrimination, and generally poor institutional functioning, but does not include any reference to severe or widespread violations of bodily integrity.[35] Similarly, Amnesty International in 2013 raised concerns about the abortion ban and the potential for restrictions on freedom of expression that might flow from clashes between the FSLN and their opponents.[36] Human Rights Watch was also primarily focused on the abortion ban.[37] The international community, thus, is not overly preoccupied with the most fundamental human rights involving bodily integrity.

[33] Ibid.
[34] Centro Nicaragüense de Derechos Humanos, "Policía Impide a Diversidad Sexual Celebrar El Día Internacional Del Orgullo Gay."
[35] Office of the High Commissioner for Human Rights, "Nicaragua Homepage."
[36] Amnesty International, "Nicaragua Human Rights."
[37] Human Rights Watch, "Nicaragua."

It is notable however, that the 2012 report of the Nicaraguan Center for Human Rights (Centro Nigaragüense de Derechos Humanos, CENIDH) opens with a discussion of the third inauguration of Daniel Ortega as president, an act that it describes as "unconstitutional, illegal, and illegitimate."[38] For opponents of the FSLN, Ortega's reelection, made possible by the Supreme Court, has been a clear sign of the decline of both democracy and the rule of law in Nicaragua, especially in light of Ortega's increasingly personalist governing style. However one feels about presidential reelection, there have been other reasons to be concerned about how Nicaragua's electoral democracy is being protected by the judiciary, in particular regarding the ballot access and legal personality of smaller political parties. In 2005, the Inter-American Court of Human Rights ordered the Nicaraguan government to recognize a smaller political party representing indigenous Miskito communities and to compensate candidates who were denied a place on the ballot in the 2000 municipal elections.[39] Similar concerns have been raised regarding the denial of ballot access and legal personality to dissident parties such as the MRS and the Partido Conservador (Conservative Party) in the 2008 municipal elections and the 2011 general elections.[40] In all of these cases of electoral regularities, the Nicaraguan courts have not provided adequate recourse for these political aspirants.

Events leading up to the 2016 election, however, suggest a consolidation of personalist and one-party rule in Nicaragua. The FSLN-dominated Supreme Electoral Council disqualified the leadership of most political parties from running for any office in a decision that was subsequently approved by the Supreme Court in June. Subsequently in July, they approved of the expulsion of twenty-eight "independent" opposition Deputies from the National Assembly for not accepting the new leadership of their party. In August, the presidential ballot was finalized, with Ortega as the sole candidate alongside his wife as his vice-presidential candidate. The MRS and other dissident groups called for a boycott of the election.

Political Dependence Doesn't Eliminate Basic Judicial Functioning

One reason for the relatively high functioning of Nicaragua's ordinary courts may be that the lengthy reform process undertaken since 1990 in Nicaragua have finally settled in and borne fruit. Numerous international donor programs

---

[38] Centro Nicaragüense de Derechos Humanos, "Derechos Humanos en Nicaragua 2013," 1.
[39] Campbell, "The Right of Indigenous People to Political Participation and the Case of Yatama v. Nicaragua"; Yatama v. Nicaragua, No. 127 Series C (I/A Court H.R. 2005).
[40] Centro Nicaragüense de Derechos Humanos, "Derechos Humanos en Nicaragua 2013."

and international financial institutions have sought to improve the functioning of Nicaragua's justice system alongside its political system in general. As I
have elaborated elsewhere[41], this process often suffered from confusion, con-
tradictions, and duplication of efforts because of the large number of international actors involved and their sometimes clientelist relationships with various
Supreme Court magistrates. Nonetheless, a number of programs have seen
successes, including a transition from an inquisitorial system to an adversarial
one, the introduction of oral trials, and the adoption of the Judicial Career
Law and its accompanying regulations. Some of these changes are sweeping in
nature and surely have sent judges' heads spinning; ideally efforts to improve
judicial education (including continuing education), such as those sponsored
by the Instituto Interamericano de Derechos Humanos[42] will yet produce a
genuinely well-functioning judiciary.

Courts are rarely the saviors of democracy or the drivers of economic development, but they play an important role in both in addition to their indis-
pensable role in protecting human rights. Nicaragua's Supreme Court has
done little to safeguard individual rights in any of these three areas, but the
lower courts and other quasi-judicial organs are frequently able to fulfill those
functions. Such a pattern is in keeping with a partisan judiciary. A partisan,
dependent judiciary, especially a highly politicized Supreme Court – either
through pressure or through the genuine preferences of the partisan judges
and magistrates – typically protects the interests primarily or even exclusively
of their co-partisan patrons. To the enemies of their patrons, they may be
hostile, but they are likely to be indifferent to ordinary litigants. Aside from
the problems associated with inefficiency and petty judicial corruption, that
indifference approximates protection for many – although not all – ordinary
litigants. Although the primary "currency" of conflict resolution is not the constitution, it is also not clandestine violence. Political law reigns in Nicaragua,
for better and worse. Thus, Nicaragua's partisan judiciary can be autonomous
from society while being politically dependent.

HONDURAS: A PARTISAN JUDICIARY PRODUCES CRIMINAL IMPUNITY AND POLITICAL PARALYSIS

Like Guatemala and El Salvador, Honduras faces a daunting level of violent
criminality. Brutal maras are active in the cities while drug traffickers make

---

[41] Bowen, "International Imposition and Transmission of Democracy and the Rule of Law:
Lessons from Central America."
[42] Instituto Interamericano de Derechos Humanos, *Acceso a la justicia y derechos humanos en
Nicaragua: Módulo autoformativo.*

use of the Caribbean coast as a trans-shipment point. Honduras has adopted a *mano dura* approach to try to control the gangs. The judiciary is weak, corrupt, and subject to influence from both politicians and criminal elements. Unlike Guatemala and El Salvador, Honduras did not experience a clear transition "moment" similar to the internationally-monitored peace processes in her neighbors. The 1982 transition to democracy occurred prior to the resumption of international attention to judicial reform and also in the midst of the Cold War violence that gripped Central America. As such, substantial abuses were allowed to continue through democratization and political will never coalesced in favor of sweeping reform. The same elite, partisan politics that dominated the judiciary since democratization also contributed to the 2009 coup d'etat against President Manuel Zelaya. Although the level of violence and threats against judges, journalists, and activists has diminished since the months immediately following the coup, Honduras continues to see problems with both official and unofficial actors violating human rights.

Pact-Making and the Dependent Judiciary in Honduras

In practice, the appointment process has developed into a highly political and highly partisan one. According to a 2000 reform of the Honduran constitution, the fifteen magistrates of the Supreme Court are chosen at the same time by a two-thirds vote of the Congress as a single slate selected from a group of forty-five nominees. The nominees are forwarded to the Congress by a nominating committee composed of representatives of the Supreme Court, the College of Lawyers and Notaries (the organized bar), the National Human Rights Commission, the Consejo Hondureño de la Empresa Privada (a private industry organization), the law school of the National Autonomous University of Honduras, civil society organizations, and the workers' federations.[43,44] Magistrates serve seven-year terms and can be re-elected. In turn, the Supreme Court is responsible for the selection of appellate magistrates, trial court judges, and justices of the peace, based on the advice of the Judicial Council. The Supreme Court is also charged with directing the judiciary as well as being the court of last resort.

The use of layering reforms rather than true conversion reforms has frustrated reform efforts in Honduras. The judicial council was created in 1980 on the Costa Rican model, but much of its reform promise was limited by

---

[43] The constitution gives no details as to how "civil society organizations" or "workers' federations" are to select one representative per sector, in contrast to the relative specificity of the other organizations represented.

[44] "Constitución Política de Honduras," sec. 311.

executive obstructionism.[45] Consequently, the judicial selection process has not eliminated the influence of Honduras' two long-standing political parties. When a super-majority is needed to select a slate of candidates from a pool, there is ample room for partisan bargaining, especially in the selection of Supreme Court magistrates. The Supreme Court, as a de facto partisan entity, then has strong incentives to select partisan lower-court judges; again, the selection of a slate of candidates from a pool allows the spoils to be shared by the parties. Indeed, in 2003, two-thirds of Honduran judges identified membership in a political party as a paramount qualification for becoming a judge.[46] Judges in Honduras have two different professional associations that are recognized by the Supreme Court, Judges for Democracy (*Asociación de Jueces por la Democracia*) and the Association of Judges and Magistrates of Honduras (*Asociación de Jueces y Magistrados de Honduras*). After the 2009 coup, there was significant conflict between Judges for Democracy members and the governments of Roberto Micheletti (2009–2010) and Porfirio Lobo (2010–2014).

Although the 2009 coup continues to cast a long shadow over discussion of democracy, human rights, and the judiciary in Honduras, the judiciary was politicized long before 2009. Concerns had been raised by domestic and international organizations alike about the politicization of Honduras' judiciary, but the political will was not present to commit to the deep reforms that would have been needed to change the partisan judiciary. The reforms to the appointment process of 2000 were characterized by the Due Process of Law Foundation in 2007 as having "revealed disappointing results."[47] As was reported in 2007, "The social perception continues to be the same as occurred in the past, there is politicization and partisan action on the part of the members of the Supreme Court; at the same time, it is known that the Judicial Career Law is not followed either."[48] A major source of this politicization is the Supreme Court itself; consequently, numerous domestic and

---

[45] Ungar, *Elusive Reform*, 172.

[46] Díaz Rivillas and Linares Lejarraga, "Fortalecimiento de La Independencia Judicial En Centroamérica: Un Balance Tras Veinte Años de Reformas."

[47] In the original: "sus resultados se revelan desalentadores." The report goes on to acknowledge that some observers do believe that these reforms represent a shift away from the politicization of the Honduran judiciary. Fundación para el Debido Proceso Legal, *Controles y Descontroles de la Corrupción Judicial*, 276.

[48] Original: "[L]a percepción social sigue siendo la misma que ocurría en el pasado, hay politización y actuación partidista por parte de los miembros de la Corte Suprema de Justicia; asimismo, es sabido que la Ley de la Carrera Judicial tampoco es aplicada." Herrera Cáceres, *Análisis sobre los principios avances, obstáculos y desafíos que el poder judicial presenta en la lucha contra la corrupción en Honduras*, 21.

international agencies throughout the 2000s urged Honduras to increase the political, administrative, and financial independence of the Supreme Court and the rest of the judiciary.[49] Similarly, in 2008, a "Citizen's Proposal for the Processes of Election of the Supreme Court Magistrates, Attorney General, and Assistant Attorney General" was released, highlighting the lack of involvement of civil society in the process of selecting these officials despite the 2000 constitutional reform, as well as the need to depoliticize the judiciary in order to strengthen the rule of law.[50]

None of these recommendations were heeded. The Honduran government lacked the political will to remove itself from the operations of the judiciary. To some extent, this is due to the fact that the 2000 reform was insufficient to get to the heart of the problem, which is the partisan collusion that drives much of Honduran politics. Although the 2000 reform sought to bring in more voices to the appointment process, it left the final decision to the Congress, which continued to be able to divvy up the judgeships along partisan lines. Again, a judicial reform was adopted with the backing of the international community but without real commitment from the national government. The 2000 constitutional reform failed to change the fundamental rules of the game and left open significant avenues for the continuation of partisan influence over the judiciary. That this reform was layered on top of existing power structures and did not change them made it possible for those power structures to be reproduced under the new rules. One consequence was that the Supreme Court authorized a coup in 2009, which led to continuing partisan purges of judges.

A Partisan Judiciary Approves a Coup

Honduras' Supreme Court of Justice ordered the military to remove President Manuel Zelaya in June 2009 in response to his insistence on holding a referendum that had previously been declared unconstitutional. The removal of Zelaya took place in the context of regional polarization around the "new left" politics represented most prominently by Venezuela's President Hugo Chavez. Although Ajenjo Fresno described the first year of Zelaya's presidency as having "the same political agenda" as the National Party government that had

---

[49] Herrera Cáceres, *Análisis sobre los principios avances, obstáculos y desafíos que el poder judicial presenta en la lucha contra la corrupción en Honduras*; Fundación para el Debido Proceso Legal, *Controles y Descontroles de la Corrupción Judicial.*

[50] Alianza por la Justicia, *Poder Judicial, Ministerio Público y Estado de Derecho: Una Propuesta Ciudadana para los Procesos de Elección de los Magistrados a la Corte Suprema de Justicia, Fiscal General, y Fiscal General Adjunto.*

preceded it,[51] the political situation began to deteriorate in 2008 as Zelaya strengthened ties to Chavez. In March, Zelaya joined Petrocaribe (Chavez's system for selling oil at reduced prices to friendly countries in the Caribbean basin) and then signed on to the Bolivarian Alternative for the Americas (ALBA, a financial alternative to the World Bank and general alliance of "new left" Latin American countries) in July. Also controversial were a 60 percent increase in the minimum wage and statements criticizing the war on drugs. These moves alienated members of the business community and the opposition as well as many within his own party and government, although some of these moves endeared him to labor unions. Zelaya's efforts to change the constitution, allegedly to allow his reelection, led to the defection of a critical mass of the political elite and, ultimately, his removal from office by the Supreme Court.

After several years of discussion, on March 24, 2009, Zelaya scheduled a referendum for June 28, 2009, that would have asked Hondurans if they wanted to have a fourth ballot[52] in the November 2009 elections in which they could vote for or against a Constitutional Convention. Many saw this move as an effort by Zelaya to aggrandize his power in the manner of referenda carried out by other ALBA countries, including Venezuela and Bolivia. In particular, many believed that Zelaya was attempting to change the constitution so that he could be reelected, although Zelaya denied this and a constitutional convention could not have been convened under any circumstances until Zelaya had already left office. However, Honduras' constitution is intentionally difficult to amend and article 374 prohibits the amendment of several important provisions relating to the system of government; a constitutional convention and writing a new constitution was Zelaya's only possibility of making changes. It was the very possibility of making serious changes that panicked the political elite who benefit from the current system. Honduras' 1982 constitution enshrined a difficult compromise between the two major parties and the military that allowed the country to return to electoral democracy after two decades of violent military rule. Zelaya's efforts to change the constitution were thus a substantial break with the accepted rules of the political game in Honduras.

The day after Zelaya announced the referendum, the attorney general informed Zelaya that the referendum would constitute an official abuse of power. On May 27th, the Court of Contencioso Administrativo ruled that the referendum was unconstitutional. Zelaya continued with the plan for the referendum regardless and on June 24th, fired Romeo Orlando Vasquez

[51] Ajenjo Fresno, "Honduras: Nuevo Gobierno Liberal Con La Misma Agenda Política."
[52] The first three are for the president, the Congress, and local government.

Velasquez, head of the armed forces, for refusing to carry out the military's constitutional duty to provide security for elections in the upcoming unconstitutional referendum. On June 25th, the Supreme Court ruled in Vasquez' favor in an amparo ordering his reinstatement. It appears that Zelaya's subsequent refusal to reinstate Vasquez created the final rupture between Zelaya and the rest of the political elite, as the military then defected as well. On June 26th, the Supreme Court issued a secret order commanding the armed forces to stop the referendum and to arrest Zelaya for, among other charges, abuse of authority and treason.[53] Early in the morning of June 28, 2009, soldiers surrounded Zelaya's home, arrested him, took him to the airport, and sent him into exile on board a plane to Costa Rica. Upon arrival in Costa Rica, Zelaya immediately made a public statement that he had been the victim of kidnapping and a *coup d'etat.*

Although the removal of Zelaya had the support of most of the ruling political elite, including many from Zelaya's Liberal Party, it deeply divided the Honduran people. A Gallup poll taken days after the coup reported both a slight plurality opposed to the coup and a plurality who believed that Zelaya's ouster was justified.[54] Many among labor activists and the poor supported Zelaya and took to the streets to demand his return to power. In response, curfews and states of emergency were imposed in major Honduran cities. According to a CID-Gallup poll conducted a few days after the coup, 68 percent of respondents said that most or many were afraid to express their political opinions. In the same poll, 71 percent saw the political situation in Honduras as "not stable at all" and 47 percent agreed that Honduras was headed for a civil war. However, the same share (47 percent) of the population said that Honduras was not heading for a better democracy as had in September 2008, suggesting that the coup might have shaken people up but not actually changed political opinions all that much. In an August 2009 poll carried out by a Honduran polling company, 52 percent of respondents stated their opposition to the coup while only 17.4 percent were in favor of it. In addition, 60.1 percent

---

[53] This summary of events is based on documents released by the Supreme Court of Justice of Honduras, available at http://www.poderjudicial.gob.hn/. Accessed January 3, 2011. Also on file with the author.

[54] The Honduran press initially reported the figure that 41 percent supported the ouster, while 28 percent felt it was not justified and 31 percent were undecided or refused to answer. In a later Voice of America interview, the president of CID-Gallup reported another number, indicating that 41 percent agreed with the coup while 46 percent opposed the coup. http://www1.voanews.com/spanish/news/latin-america/Honduras-pais-dividido-golpe-estado-zelaya-50408857.html. It appears that this confusion resulted from Gallup having asked two different questions: first, whether the ouster was justified by Zelaya's unconstitutional actions and, second, whether the respondent agreed with the actions to remove Zelaya.

responded that Micheletti should step down and 51.6 percent supported Zelaya returning to power. Additionally, respondents blamed a wide variety of actors for promoting and financing the coup, including international capital, the military, and the business sector.[55] However, the efforts by activists in Honduras and many in the international community to have Zelaya reinstated ultimately failed as Porfirio Lobo Sosa of the opposition National Party was elected in November and installed relatively peacefully in January 2010.

Partisan control of the judiciary appears to have contributed significantly to the June 2009 coup against President Manuel Zelaya. The magistrates of the Supreme Court who authorized the military to remove Zelaya had only recently been appointed by Roberto Micheletti as president of the Congress; that they then approved Micheletti's assumption of the presidency is unsurprising. As the coup's denouement dragged on through the installation of the newly-elected President Porfirio Lobo in January 2010, the Supreme Court was the loudest and most insistent defender of the coup, even invalidating a Congressionally-approved power-sharing agreement that would have partially reinstated Zelaya and restored Honduras' international standing. The Supreme Court, or at least the majority faction, also used the coup and its aftermath to aggrandize its power over the rest of the judiciary. In the year following the coup, members of the judiciary who had opposed the ouster found themselves subjected to forced transfers to less desirable posts and disciplinary processes, some of which resulted in the removal of judges and even one magistrate from their positions.[56] Only one of those who petitioned for reinstatement was successful.[57] In October 2015, the Inter-American Court of Human Rights ordered the reinstatement of four judges.[58] Only in May 2016 did the Supreme Court announce that it would comply with that order.

The Supreme Court was conscious from the beginning of the coup of the need to manage world opinion of its participation in the coup. On the day of the coup, Supreme Court president Jorge Alberto Rivera Avilés made a public statement that the military had acted properly under orders of a competent judge, which was reported by *The Daily Telegraph* online that evening. On July 2nd, he sent letters justifying the court's role in the coup to important courts around the world, including the International Court of Justice, the European Court of Human Rights, the Inter-American Court of Human Rights, the

---

[55] COIMER & OP, "Estudio de Opinión Pública: Nivel Nacional."

[56] Amnesty International, "Document - Honduras: Independence of the Judicial System Is Seriously Undermined as the Dismissal of Justice Officials Is Confirmed | Amnesty International."

[57] Human Rights Watch, "World Report 2012: Honduras."

[58] Caso López Lone y otros vs. Honduras (Corte Interamericana de Derechos Humanos 2015).

International Criminal Court, and the International Law of the Sea Tribunal, along with several leading national high courts. The Supreme Court also published documentation relating to the coup, including court orders, evidence submitted against Zelaya, and the letters to international courts, which was prominently displayed on its institutional website. As events unfolded in the summer and into the autumn, the Supreme Court took a harder stance than other parts of the Honduran governing elite. When Micheletti and his supporters agreed to the Pacto de San José, which would have allowed for Zelaya's return, in August, the Supreme Court ruled that Zelaya could not be reinstated as president. When a power-sharing agreement was reached in November, the Supreme Court again recommended to the Congress that they not reinstate Zelaya as long as criminal charges were pending against him. It appears that the court struggled to maintain the legitimacy of its actions in June by refusing to permit any compromise of its position.

Opportunity for Reform Squandered Amidst a Crisis of Violence

Calls to reform the judiciary, in part in response to the crisis of citizen security caused by gangs and organized crime, have focused in part on the need to purge corrupt judges from the judiciary.[59] Doing so would create the possibility of interrupting the reproduction of traditional, partisan power through the judiciary. A system of annual reviews of judges was adopted for the first time in December 2011. Importantly, the 2011 *Ley del Consejo de la Judicatura y la Carrera Judicial* (Law of the Council of the Judiciary and the Judicial Career) reinforced judicial independence by prohibiting political and partisan activities (beyond personal voting), protecting judges against involuntary transfers, and establishing better systems for training and disciplinary review. That this review process was housed within the judicial council and not in the Supreme Court is promising in that it moves the oversight function out of a partisan entity and into a multi-sectorial one. The promise of this reform fell short, however, when, in March 2016, the Supreme Court invalidated the Law and the Judicial Council it created. As a result, all of the Judicial Council's functions returned to the supervision of the President of the Supreme Court.

In December 2012, a conflict arose between President Porfirio Lobo and the Supreme Court. After the Supreme Court invalidated a police reform on the grounds that it violated the due process rights of police officers, the president launched an investigation of the Supreme Court and the Congress subsequently removed the four members of the Supreme Court who had

---

[59] Redacción, "Presidente de la Corte quedaría fuera del Consejo de la Judicatura - LaPrensa.hn."

voted against the law. President Lobo declared that these actions were taken in order to prevent the Supreme Court from performing a coup against him, as they had against Zelaya in 2009. Meanwhile, the ousted magistrates and their supporters declared their removal a "technical coup" that usurped the position and power of the Supreme Court. The United Nations stepped in to denounce the action as a "grave attack on Honduras' democracy." In contrast to the vindication of Magistrado Cruz Castro in Costa Rica, neither the Congress nor the Supreme Court (re-integrated with four new magistrates) provided relief for the ousted magistrates by February 2013,[60] leaving the magistrates with international justice as their only option. The Inter-American Commission on Human Rights released a statement in their support in January 2013.[61]

According to United Nations statistics, Honduras was, as of 2011, the most dangerous country in the world in terms of violent crime. With a homicide rate of 86 per 100,000 inhabitants, extensive penetration by drug-trafficking cartels, and levels of street gang violence that approach anarchy in some areas of Tegucigalpa and San Pedro Sula, the situation for citizen security was dire. As described by Bunck and Fowler, Honduras has never established a rule of law culture and, as a result, law-enforcement institutions are largely without positive effect. Drug-trafficking cartels entered Honduras relatively early because of widespread poverty, sparse population, and a perpetually weak state alongside a variety of factors that created a favorable environment in which they could flourish. Local street gangs produced enough violence to keep the inadequate police force occupied, while a growing domestic market for drugs further encouraged complicity with the cartels and escalated violence.[62] Rampant corruption within the justice sector has also made Honduras a hospitable country for the cartels. The fact that many Honduran officials are immune from prosecution as long as they remain in their positions or until the Congress strips them of that immunity makes control of corruption especially difficult. Widespread impunity for the highly independent armed forces has been taken advantage of by officers engaged in the drug trade.

Judicial corruption lubricates this organized criminality as judges are routinely bribed or threatened to release criminal suspects. Resistance can come at a high price for judges; in the wake of the assassination of judge Olga Laguna in 2010, *El Heraldo* newspaper reported on twenty-two current death threats against judges across the country.[63] Efforts to curb judicial corruption

---

[60] "Honduras: Corte Suprema Rechaza Reponer Exmagistrados."

[61] "In View of Situation in Honduras, IACHR Stresses Importance of Principle of Independence of the Judiciary."

[62] Bunck and Fowler, *Bribes, Bullets, and Intimidation.*

[63] "Amenazas a muerte contra 22 jueces de Honduras."

remain relatively weak, despite numerous international programs intended to strengthen the judiciary. In 2013, the Organization of American States reported that Honduran judicial officials desired specialized anti-corruption tribunals. Complicating all of these matters is the lack of an organic law of the judiciary, which could deal with many inefficient holdovers from the old inquisitorial system such as the requirement that multiple criminal judges work simultaneously on each criminal case. Sadly, the recommendations from the OAS require such broad and penetrating reforms, including extensive new training programs and "[c]onsider[ing] taking the legislative measures necessary to create a legal framework for anticorruption that sets out a comprehensive policy on the topic," as to be comical.[64]

Skepticism aside, the 2015 "Guatemalan Spring" had an echo in Honduras. As early as March 2015, even before the Guatemalan protests began, Honduran citizens were in the streets in major cities to protest a growing scandal regarding the Social Security system, in which embezzlement may have led to the death of multiple patients due to a lack of medicine in public hospitals. President Juan Orlando Hernández (2014–) allegedly received campaign donations from the embezzled funds. These protests sparked significant discussion in Honduras as to how to combat corruption there; by July, a United States diplomat, Thomas Shannon, argued for the creation of CICIG-like institutions in Honduras and El Salvador while on a tour of the region.[65] President Hernandez initially argued that Honduras would be better served by creating its own anti-corruption institutions. By the end of 2015, however, Honduras had entered an agreement with the Organization of American States to create the Support Mechanism to Confront Corruption and Impunity in Honduras (Misión de Apoyo contra la Corrupción y la Impunidad en Honduras, or MACCIH), which was formally launched on February 22, 2016.[66] As of July 2016, the MACCIH was in place and conducting investigations, including one into the Social Security scandal.

A Politicized Judiciary that Harms Judicial Functioning

The problem of impunity for past human rights violations during and immediately following the 2009 coup remains significant. A Truth and Reconciliation Commission was established after the election of President Profirio Lobo in

---

[64] Committee of Experts on the Follow-Up on the Implementation of the Inter-American Convention Against Corruption, "Republic of Honduras: Final Report."
[65] "'Cicig En Honduras Y Salvador Sería Inteligente.'"
[66] "A Glimmer of Hope in Central America."

late 2009. While this commission has identified a number of abuses, the government has been reluctant to actually hold anyone accountable for them. Meanwhile, impunity reigns for a variety of other official and unofficial violations of human rights. Police officers and prison guards routinely use excessive force and engage in arbitrary detention; it is rare for these state actors to be charged with any offenses. Private security guards and gang members are also routinely allowed to continue violating the human rights of the population in general. In response, much of the population has become supportive of the *mano dura* approach that itself tends toward more official violations of the human rights of criminal suspects and prisoners.[67] As a consequence, the state continues to be a violator of human rights, to be reluctant to hold officials accountable for those violations, and to also be unable to protect the human rights of citizens against private actors.

Democracy in Honduras remains fragile in the years following the 2009 coup, as the 2012 ouster of four Supreme Court magistrates reveals. Honduras faces grave problems relating to its economic development, the protection of human rights, and violent criminality, among others. Dramatic changes may be necessary to make progress on any of these fronts, but the calcified political system makes compromise between the two major parties difficult. That the judiciary is enveloped within partisan politics complicates matters further. Even when major initiatives are adopted, the Supreme Court may strike them down for a variety of reasons, some embedded in the constitution and some embedded in partisan fighting. It may be that economic reforms and police reform laws require that the constitution be amended and it may be that such amendment would be desirable. However, one of the consequences of the 2009 coup has been the extreme politicization of the constitution and efforts to amend it such that Lobo – like Zelaya before him – is charged with a coup against the constitution when he tries to pursue major changes. A partisan judiciary in the midst of a country in crisis leads to constitutional paralysis.

EL SALVADOR: STRATEGIC PARTISANSHIP

El Salvador today has a judiciary that is controlled both by political parties and by clandestine forces. El Salvador is nonetheless classified as being primarily partisan in nature because the dominant mode of operation is still to defer to partisan agreements and political law – even as those currencies are actively contested. Political parties in El Salvador are much stronger than in Guatemala in that they persist over many elections with stable leadership that is able to

---

[67] Inter-American Dialogue, "Security and Human Rights in Honduras."

make credible commitments (and credible threats) to other political actors. El Salvador's internationally-supervised peace process included substantial attention to judicial reform, which included the creation of independent judicial council to oversee the judicial career.[68] While this reform and others did initially produce a much more independent judiciary, partisan influence has since resurfaced. Whereas the Supreme Court of the 1990s ruled against the ruling party, recent re-appointment processes have changed that dynamic. Martinez Barahona and Linares Lejarraga have highlighted the political horse-trading involved in the final selection of justices as a major contributor to the politicization of the Salvadoran high court.[69] Additionally, the power of organized crime has increasingly overwhelmed the protections of judicial autonomy that were established by those reforms.

Contradictions of Inter-Branch Independence in El Salvador

El Salvador's partisan system provides a useful contrast to the more purely partisan systems of Honduras and Nicaragua. The differences in, primarily, appointment and reappointment procedures create a substantially different dynamic for judges vis-à-vis elected politicians. The longer judicial terms and staggered appointments do limit partisan pact-making, but the need for reappointment still leaves individual magistrates vulnerable to partisan pressures. Initial growth in judicial independence in the 1990s was reversed through the appointment processes that played out in the National Assembly.[70] The politicization of the appointment process, especially for the Supreme Court, has produced a court that, at least at times, appears to engage in what Helmke has called "strategic defection" by trying to anticipate the changes in the political winds so that they can rule with the winners.[71] Formally, the courts appear to have more independence than Guatemala's, Nicaragua's, or Honduras', given that judges enjoy lengthier tenures (nine years) and the judiciary is more institutionally independent of the executive and legislative branches. Nonetheless, the perception is clearly of a judiciary that is not independent of political influence.

---

[68] Popkin, *Peace without Justice*.
[69] Martinez Barahona and Linares Lejarraga, "Democracy and 'Punitive Populism': Exploring the Supreme Court's Role in El Salvador."
[70] Díaz Rivillas and Linares Lejarraga, "Fortalecimiento de La Independencia Judicial En Centroamérica: Un Balance Tras Veinte Años de Reformas."
[71] Helmke, "Checks and Balances By Other Means: Strategic Defection and Argentina's Supreme Court in the 1990s"; Helmke, "The Logic of Strategic Defection: Court-Executive Relations in Argentina Under Dictatorship and Democracy"; Brinks, "'Faithful Servants of the Regime': The Brazilian Constitutional Court's Role under the 1988 Constitution."

The National Assembly appoints the magistrates of the Supreme Court from a list generated by the judicial council, for a renewable term of nine years. One-third of the magistrates are appointed every three years.[72] There are two important consequences of these staggered terms: first, there will be more continuity of institutional culture within the Supreme Court because all of the members will not be up for renewal at the same time and, second, partisan bargaining regarding the composition of the Supreme Court will be somewhat muted and more iterative. Where the entire court turns over at the same time, as in Honduras, Nicaragua, and Guatemala, the stakes are much higher for any given appointment period because the bargain struck at that time can typically not be modified for another five (or seven in Honduras) years. By contrast, in El Salvador, the legislature will likely have two chances to influence the composition of the court during its term in office. Additionally, with fewer magistrates being appointed at one time, direct horse-trading is more difficult and legislators are more likely to have to find individual compromise candidates. The rules of the appointment process should give the Salvadoran Supreme Court more inter-branch independence than in Nicaragua or Honduras, but the need for reappointment still creates the impulse to curry favor with the legislators that will be deciding on reappointment. El Salvador is thus a case in point for the argument that only lifetime appointments truly protect judicial independence.[73]

The Supreme Court then has the power to appoint the magistrates of the appellate courts, the judges of the trial courts, and the justices of the peace, from candidate pools selected by the judicial council.[74] Although the original judicial council (*Consejo Nacional de la Judicatura*, CNJ) was dominated by magistrates of the Supreme Court, the 1999 reforms changed the membership to exclude supreme court magistrates in favor of representation from the appellate courts, the ministerio público, the public University of El Salvador, the private law schools, and the legal profession.[75] These changes create a nominating power that is similar to the ones in Guatemala (see Chapter 5) and similarly opens up multiple avenues for corruption beyond simple partisan influence. Nonetheless, this change was seen as a necessary outgrowth of the 1992 Peace Accord and its concern with reforming a judiciary whose head had been implicated in civil war abuses. The CNJ is appointed by the legislature with a two-thirds vote. Although the judicial council's

[72] "Constitución de la Republica de El Salvador," sec. 186.
[73] Melton and Ginsburg, "Does De Jure Judicial Independence Really Matter?," 195.
[74] "Constitución de la Republica de El Salvador," sec. 182.
[75] Consejo Nacional de la Judicatura, "Reseña Histórica."

independence is declared in the constitution, its election process suggests that it may nevertheless be a conduit for partisan influence. The power to discipline and remove lower-court judges lies with the Supreme Court, not the CNJ.

While not a direct attack on the independence of the judiciary *per se*, 2011's Decree 743 was an attempt to limit the power of the Constitutional Chamber of the Supreme Court. Decree 743, which initially passed the Congress as a reform to the law governing the judiciary, would have required the constitutional chamber to rule unanimously. The constitutional chamber declared Decree 743 unconstitutional because the constitution requires a four-fifths super-majority in the chamber; Decree 743 thus contradicted the clear rule in the constitution. The Congress subsequently revoked the decree, but not before creating an institutional crisis in El Salvador and uproar among international defenders of judicial independence.[76] Decision rules often seem like technical matters that might escape the attention of the public, but a requirement of unanimity would have opened up the possibility for a variety of forms of corruption of the constitutional chamber. Because it would only take one magistrate to maintain the constitutionality of a law, the Congress or president would need to have only one loyal partisan in in the constitutional chamber – an easy bar to cross given that partisan influence is already present in the Salvadoran judiciary. Similarly, corrupt officials or powerful unofficial interests such as gangs, drug traffickers, or wealthy elites would be able to buy at least some kinds of legal and constitutional approval more easily.

Impunity and Compromised Judicial Societal Autonomy

Impunity remains a problem in El Salvador. The Salvadoran government continues to violate the human rights of its citizens, albeit typically in isolated events, generally refuses to hold either politicians or military officers accountable for past violations of human rights, and also fails to enforce the human rights and human dignity of citizens against private actors. Like Honduras, El Salvador has very powerful maras or street gangs. With corruption rampant in the judiciary and among groups such as prison guards, the maras are frequently able to operate with impunity. Significant anti-mara legislation was passed in the early 2000s following a *mano dura* approach. As many as 84 percent of those arrested in anti-*mara* sweeps in the early 2000s, however, were permanently

---

[76] See, e.g. CEJIL, "CEJIL Urge Al Presidente Funes a Sancionar La Derogación Del Decreto 743."

acquitted.[77] Such a datum indicates both overreaching by security forces and an inability to convict suspects; the two phenomena are intertwined. It does not appear that these extreme legal measures have done much to curb the violence and they may have increased the incentives to engage in corruption to avoid conviction in the criminal courts.[78] Only 3 percent of criminal cases that make it to the courts result in sentences.[79] The March 2012 mara truce that produced some respite from violence in El Salvador[80] is in part a reaction to that impunity – only the maras can control the maras.

By 2015, it increasingly appeared that the maras of El Salvador were seeking to exert political pressure. In July 2015, the gangs made a targeted attack on the bus system, killing six transportation workers and burning two buses. Some 1,000 buses stopped running, primarily in and around San Salvador, until the police began assigning armed officers to ride each bus later that week.[81] Speculation suggested numerous explanations: that the gangs were angry at being denied access to the outside world from prison, that they were trying to provoke new dialogue with the government, and even that they were conspiring with the opposition ARENA party to discredit FMLN President Sánchez. The bus strike happened in the context of a massive spike in violence: July 2015 marked the first month to see violent deaths at rates equal to the civil war years. Nonetheless, Sánchez and his government remained committed to criminal prosecution of gang members as the gang members entered into a new truce in April 2016.[82]

While it is difficult to find detailed, comparable data on attacks on judicial autonomy in El Salvador, there are some indicators. The World Bank embarked on a project from 2004 to 2010 to create new judicial centers to modernize the Salvadoran judiciary, improve access to justice, and increase the accountability of the institution.[83] The results of these efforts remain mixed, with one high-profile drug trafficker (as of 2013 cooperating in a high profile prosecution) claiming to have bribed two judges and a prosecutor to secure his own release in 2011.[84] Such anecdotal reports are bolstered by a 2012 report that 80 percent of Salvadoran judges had some kind of complaint pending

---

[77] Martinez Barahona and Linares Lejarraga, "Democracy and 'Punitive Populism': Exploring the Supreme Court's Role in El Salvador," 59.
[78] Frühling, "Maras and Youth Gangs, Community and Police in Central America."
[79] Moodie, *El Salvador in the Aftermath of Peace.*
[80] "El Salvador's Gangs: The Year of Living Less Dangerously."
[81] Lohmuller, "Gang-Enforced Bus Strike Increases Pressure on El Salvador Govt."
[82] Partlow and Maslin, "El Salvador's Gangs Call a Cease-Fire, but Many Doubt It Will Hold."
[83] The World Bank, "News & Broadcast - Improving and Modernizing El Salvador's Judicial System."
[84] Cawley, "Key Witness in El Salvador Case Says He Bribed Judges."

against them, with some dating as far back as 1995 without being investigated or resolved.[85] The Judicial Council created a "Transparency Portal" as a part of its web page,[86] but their primary mission is in judicial selection, training, and promotion, not discipline.[87] *La Prensa Grafica* reported that the individual in charge of discipline was replaced in the wake of the 2012 reporting.[88] Nonetheless, it seems clear that Salvadoran judges are subject to significant threats to their autonomy, while their superiors at the Supreme Court are similarly subject to inter-branch attacks on their independence.

In the 2013 Global Corruption Barometer, Transparency International reported that 81 percent of Salvadorans viewed their judiciary as corrupt or highly corrupt. Of the twelve public institutions rated, only the police (87 percent) and political parties (85 percent) rated worse.[89] Unfortunately, Transparency International included no other Central American countries in the 2013 Global Corruption Barometer, making direct comparisons difficult. Judicial corruption, especially as it relates to criminal prosecution, is central to the Central American Regional Security Initiative sponsored by the United States Department of State and the United States Agency for International Development (USAID).[90] These issues and their solutions are intertwined; a major recipient of USAID funds related to this initiative is FUNDE, the Transparency International affiliate in El Salvador.[91] Although the Salvadoran legislature decided against seeking the formation of an international commission such as the Guatemalan CICIG or the MACCIH in Honduras, they nonetheless have a number of cooperation programs with the United Nations Office on Drugs and Crime, including a special anti-corruption project approved in March 2016.

The human rights situation in El Salvador today poses similar problems as Guatemala's in its complexity. The number of actors has increased, their interests have diversified, and the connections between them have become more obscure. Salvadorans live in a very violent society, as reported in Chapter 1. The capitol, San Salvador, is routinely ranked among the world's most dangerous cities. As put by the United States Department of State, "The principal human rights problems were widespread corruption, particularly in the

[85] Knott, "El Salvador Investigating 80% of Country's Judges"; Ávalos, "CSJ Acumula 1,085 de Denuncias Contra Jueces."
[86] Consejo Nacional de la Judicatura, "Portal de Transparencia: INICIO."
[87] Consejo Nacional de la Judicatura, "Quienes Somos."
[88] Ávalos, "CSJ Acumula 1,085 de Denuncias Contra Jueces."
[89] Transparency International, "El Salvador"; Morán, "Salvadoreños Perciben Más Corrupción."
[90] U.S. Department of State, "Central America Regional Security Initiative Fact Sheets."
[91] FUNDE, "SolucionES."

judicial system; weaknesses in the judiciary and the security forces that led to a high level of impunity; and violence and discrimination against women."[92] They go on to cite isolated unlawful killings as well as poor conditions in prisons and pre-trial detention. They also recognize that these problems are made considerably worse by the impunity enjoyed by those within the security forces that do violate human rights. The problem of official impunity is considerably deepened by the takeover of eleven prisons by the military.[93]

Movement in the El Mozote massacre investigation may suggest that the Salvadoran judiciary and government was willing to look beyond the 1993 amnesty law in some cases even before invalidating it in July 2016. In October 2012, the Inter-American Court of Human Rights declared that the amnesty law could not shield those members of the military involved in the 1981 massacre, in which more than 1,000 were killed. The government of El Salvador was ordered to investigate the massacre and to pay reparations to the families of the victims.[94] The exhumation and investigation process is likely to be slow and lengthy. It is being carried out with international assistance from, among other places, Guatemala and Argentina. However, it has also proved to be contentious; in April 2015, some victims' families successfully halted the exhumations through a court order because of concerns that families were not sufficiently involved in the process and that the investigators may not be showing sufficient care for the remains.[95] Like the Dos Erres massacre case in Guatemala, the El Mozote investigation will raise significant questions in El Salvador about the amnesty law and how it should be handled. The leftist FMLN retained the presidency in 2014 and have supported the investigation thus far; whether a future government will block a possible future trial remains to be seen.

Muted Partisanship Elevates Political Strategy over Justice

Unlike the other partisan regimes of Honduras and Nicaragua, El Salvador has not experienced significant democratic backsliding in recent years. On the contrary, a left-wing party (the FMLN) that had begun as an insurgent movement before transitioning to a democratically-oriented political party won the presidency for the first time in 2009. El Salvador's recent elections

---

[92] Bureau of Democracy, Human Rights, and Labor, United States Department of State, "Country Reports on Human Rights Practices for 2011: El Salvador."

[93] Amnesty International, "Annual Report 2012: El Salvador."

[94] Case of the Massacres of El Mozote and nearby places v. El Salvador, No. 252 Series C (Inter-American Court of Human Rights 2012).

[95] Morán, "Suspenden Exhumaciones Relacionadas a El Mozote."

have been largely unmarred by violence and widespread irregularities and the 2009 presidential election saw voter turnout of nearly 62 percent, down only slightly from the 2004 presidential election, which saw turnout at just over 66 percent.[96] From an electoral perspective, then, El Salvador's democracy is fairly robust, compared with her neighbors. This electoral handover of power to a former combatant group suggests substantial commitment on all sides in El Salvador to the democratic system, although it has not created the sea change that may have been promised in the campaign. As the 2011 conflict over Decree 743 demonstrates, partisan control over the judiciary remains a threat but may be overcome by sufficient public and international outcry. Among the partisan systems studied here, El Salvador retains a far stronger democracy.

The Salvadoran judiciary continues to be perceived as corrupt and highly partisan despite formal institutional rules that should give judges and magistrates expanded independence. On the one hand, the partisanship is driven largely by the need for magistrates to seek reappointment directly from the legislature. With the legislature dominated by two ideological parties, magistrates will strategically play in the waning years of their terms to the preferences of the majority party. This dynamic differs from the pattern seen in Nicaragua and Honduras because there is less direct bargaining between collusive parties. Salvadoran magistrates and judges need to be sensitive to partisan concerns, but may not necessarily be true believers in one or the other party's ideology. On the other hand, widespread corruption is made possible by poor institutional oversight and poor judicial operation. With litigants trapped in a slow and sometimes draconian process, the temptation of bribery is very high. At the same time, rampant violent crime, combined with often clumsy and overreaching policing, has made threats against judges viable. Although I have classified El Salvador as a primarily partisan system, it should be understood to also have significant elements of a clandestine control system as well.

CONCLUSION: STRONG DEPENDENCE?

These three partisan judicial regimes reveal an interesting paradox regarding dependent judiciaries. Contrary to the usual image of a politically dependent judiciary as one that is dominated by the rest of the government, in which judges may find themselves living in fear for their careers or even their lives, partisan judges may in fact be quite strong. Given that partisan judges generally subscribe sincerely to the ideologies of the parties that appoint them, they

---

[96] International IDEA, "Voter Turnout Data for El Salvador (Parliamentary, Presidential)."

may in fact be strong champions of those ideologies. Dependent judiciaries should be viewed as having at least some degree of strength that derives from their partisan natures. Specifically, a highly socially autonomous but deeply partisan judiciary such as Nicaragua's is better able to control crime and certain kinds of impunity than a more independent but less societally autonomous judiciary, such as in Guatemala (see Chapter 5). Whether or not they are able to contradict elected or unelected officials, however, will vary with how balanced the two parties are. Honduras' partisan judiciary, on the other hand, remains unable or unwilling to control crime while at the same time being unwilling to challenge powerful elites. In El Salvador, the combination of parties that are more ideologically polarized and a staggered (re)appointment system has created a different strategic environment for magistrates, who must attempt to predict the future legislative majority as they near the end of their tenures.

Judicial dependence in partisan judiciaries is primarily made possible – and persistent – because of the presence of a small number (typically two) of long-standing political parties whose elites can bargain with each other effectively. Because they are longstanding and their top elite transitions slowly, they can make credible commitments, or at least they can judge each other's credibility over iterated negotiations. In Honduras, the two main political parties continue to be the parties that have dominated Honduran politics since well before the political violence of the 1970s and 1980s; they collude quite easily. One might expect one legacy of Nicaragua's ideological Contra War to be political polarization, but the Sandinistas and Liberals have been led essentially by the same two men for two decades. The personal relationship between Alemán and Ortega has allowed for substantial collusion, especially as the two parties have softened their ideologies. Again, El Salvador differs from the other two partisan systems because the two parties are less inclined to bargain over judicial appointments. However, they have less need to do so because of the staggered terms in the Supreme Court. The primary enforcement of partisan dependence in El Salvador, then, is the reappointment process every nine years.

These strengths of partisan regimes are significant, but also should not be read too broadly. The specific patterns of political (in)dependence and societal autonomy drive the ability of the judiciary to control crime, promote economic development, and enforce a democratic rule of law. Nicaragua, while seeing little criminal impunity, nonetheless has what should be considered at best a weakly democratic rule of law because of impunity for Sandinista politicians and declining commitment to democracy within the FSLN more broadly. The Honduran judiciary has had a poor record of controlling either crime or political malfeasance; the 2009 coup crisis was in large part extended by the Supreme Court itself. El Salvador's justice system has been ineffective against violent crime, although they are now tolerating the initiation of investigations in the El Mozote massacre case. Despite their potential strengths in some areas, partisan judiciaries are quite weak in areas of horizontal accountability and other mechanisms for enforcing democracy. One conclusion to be drawn from these cases, then, is that the strong political parties often seen as beneficial to democracy may in fact be detrimental to the rule of law, especially if the parties do not share an ideological commitment to a liberal state.

Conclusion

Judicial Regimes and the Democratic Rule of Law

In this concluding chapter, I return to the ideas with which I opened the book: the democratic rule of law and the relationship between the judiciary and democracy. Much has changed in the past several decades; it is now impossible to imagine a strong democracy without a well-functioning judiciary. Even weak democracies such as can be found in four of the five countries studied in this book want at least the appearance of a strong judiciary. The norm that democracies require the rule of law is sufficiently strong as to provide ammunition for pro-democracy and pro-human rights activists in domestic and international milieus. Few political elites in the world have the strength to openly challenge the norm of an independent judiciary, although many are willing to undermine it through sometimes surreptitious actions. This book is grounded in the divergent experiences of countries in which at least part of the political elite actively seeks a stronger rule of law as a part of a more robust democracy – a goal that has proved elusive. The reasons for the difficulty in securing the rule of law vary considerably from one country to another, but I argue that they can be seen in the patterns of juridical and political conflict resolution that have been pursued by competing elements of these societies.

Scholars of comparative judicial politics have been looking in the wrong places. They need to turn their attention to judicial autonomy from societal actors in order to understand and promote the democratic rule of law. Democracy flourishes best when citizens are empowered and independent, autonomous, and empowered judiciaries are an important aspect of building a robust participatory democracy. Despite sometimes massive problems with poverty, criminality, violence, and corruption in Central America, many citizens remain committed to the democratic idea. While living with the fear of violence can be disempowering, many Central Americans both within the judiciary and outside of it do empower themselves to monitor their governments, to bring cases to the courts, and to demand justice. These actions reveal one important distinction between official and unofficial violence: official violence may be called upon to arrest unofficial violence, and it sometimes does. In the civil war years, citizens had no real protections. Today, as imperfect as they may be, official protections do exist. Citizens do demand justice of their governments. Lawyers do pursue dangerous cases. Judges do rule according to the law. Criminals are punished, including the most powerful and the most dangerous. None of these mechanisms can be considered complete, but the last three decades have seen very real changes. Further improvement will require governments and reformers to focus on deeper and perhaps more difficult forms of empowerment that include autonomy from powerful societal actors.

WHAT KIND OF JUDICIARY IS NECESSARY FOR THE DEMOCRATIC RULE OF LAW?

Creating a typology of judicial regimes suggests a question: what kind of judiciary is necessary for democracy? The literature on judicial politics as well as on judicial reform has tended to view what I have called a liberal judicial regime as the ideal for promoting democracy and the rule of law. This inclination flows naturally from the emphasis on inter-branch relations and political independence as it is the liberal judicial regime that favors constitutionalism. The dominant currency for resolving legal-political conflicts in liberal judicial regimes in constitutional law, typically funneled through a constitutional court exercising judicial review. Certainly constitutionalism in liberal judicial regimes is good for the democratic rule of law, but that insight is neither new nor sufficient. In this section, I wish to turn to the question of whether a liberal judicial regime is necessary, as well as what some of the strengths of the other judicial regime types might be. The emphasis on political independence may have blinded us not just to the dangers of a lack of societal autonomy, but also to the at least partial benefits that may flow from weak political independence in some circumstances.

In Chapters 1 and 2, I defined the democratic rule of law as a system in which power is exercised through democratically enacted formal laws applicable to all equally and is checked by formal accountability institutions. Additionally, power should respect those political rights that are necessary for democratic participation and provide for relevant social rights to be enjoyed equitably. The countries of Central America are excellent case studies of partial exercise of the democratic rule of law. Indeed, as the preceding chapters have demonstrated, Central America has been the location of dramatic battles over the democratic rule of law. These battles have ranged from attempts to rein in corruption to trials of human rights violators to conflicts over economic development strategies. Powerful actors in both society and the official political realm have demonstrated their awareness of the significance of these battles and the relatively new battleground of the courtroom. Politicians, criminals, and activists care so acutely about who is named to the courts precisely because of the salience of these judicial battles.

A democratic rule of law is protected best by a judiciary that is willing to put fundamental human rights and human dignity above simple legislative pronouncements. This statement should not be misunderstood to mean that democratically-enacted laws should carry little or no weight; rather, that the global consensus on human rights circumscribes the acceptable range of democratic decision- making. An empowered judiciary is critical for the policing of democratic excess, but this policing is and should remain controversial. There is room for variation in democratic judicial regimes and political compromises regarding judicial power should be expected to evolve. Thus, there is a persistent tension in constitutionalism, allowing policy and institutions to evolve while maintaining a core set of commitments, primarily to rights. The age of rights in which governments now find themselves does imply constraints on state power, but those constraints are not absolute and can shift over time. The Central American democracies studied in this book find themselves especially constrained by the assertiveness of the Inter-American system and the sometimes complementary and sometimes contradictory influence of the United States. Politicians sometimes chafe at these external powers and may seek to resist them, but they may also comply depending on how they suit the particular political needs of the moment.

International pressure may help to promote constitutionalism, judicial review, and a liberal judicial regime. However, decades of judicial reform have attempted to do just that with minimal success. It appears that international influence is most successful when it is relatively intense, sustained, and focused on a fairly small issue. However, by the 2000s, it was clear to students of the reform process that a major reason for the weakness of judicial reform outcomes was the tendency to pursue reforms on a piecemeal basis, going after the easier reforms first and hoping that initial success would pave the way for greater buy-in to more fundamental reforms later.[1] Perhaps, then, efforts to promote an idealized liberal judicial regime are misguided and it is better to begin where these states are now. If we begin with a clear examination of the strengths and weaknesses of different judicial regimes, we can find the

---

[1] Ungar, *Elusive Reform*; Prillaman, *The Judiciary and Democratic Delay in Latin America.*

patterns within each that could be reinforced to strengthen the democratic rule of law, as well as the elements that may be more harmful to democracy and should consequently be opposed. The failure to recognize the differences between partisan and clandestine control judicial regimes has contributed to the limitations of reform. Government control regimes appear to be compatible only with authoritarianism, but conflating clandestine control and partisan judicial regimes as equally illiberal masks the true diversity of non-liberal judicial regimes.

A partisan regime may indeed be compatible with a robust democracy, as long as certain basic commitments to rights protections are in place. The United Kingdom, with its parliamentary form of government and lack of genuine constitutional review, could easily be classified as a partisan control judicial regime, but that should not give us cause to question the functioning of its democratic rule of law. The logic of parliamentary supremacy is slowly being replaced in many parliamentary systems by the logic of constitutionalism. The empowerment of judiciaries in parliamentary systems – especially those with their roots in Westminster such as New Zealand, Australia, and Canada – comes largely at the expense of the parliament. However, the power ceded by the parliament is primarily the power to violate new bills of rights. The basic contours of policy making remain solidly under parliamentary oversight. It may be that, in the advanced democracies, few examples of partisan judicial systems remain as constitutionalism has been widely embraced and the European states have endorsed the supra-national constitutionalism embodied in the European Union. Nonetheless, one would not argue that France prior to the empowerment of the Constitutional Council was not democratic or did not have the rule of law; rather, France shifted from a primarily partisan judicial regime to a substantially liberal one. Costa Rica's path was similar.

The developing world, however, has many examples of partisan judicial regimes, many of which coexist with weakly democratic political regimes. The global consensus around constitutionalism requires most fledgling democracies to adopt the institutions that would seem to lead to a liberal judicial regime such as formal recognition of judicial independence and the empowerment of a constitutional court.[2] Like the Central American countries studied here that followed similar prescriptions, many weakly democratic politicians quickly found that it is relatively easy to appoint loyal followers to the constitutional court or to otherwise ensure the partisan loyalty of the supposed protectors

---

[2] For present purposes, I am not concerned with the distinction between specialized constitutional courts and courts of more general jurisdiction that have the power of constitutional review.

of the constitution. Sometimes the justices seek to take up the cause of con-stitutionalism even against government opposition – and sometimes they are eliminated from the political scene, as has happened in Egypt and Pakistan. International judicial organizations have sought to enhance the independence of judges, including judges whose assertiveness is not welcomed by national politicians. I would expect to see continuing and even increasing conflict between judges and partisan politicians in the developing world as judges' role-orientations are increasingly shaped by international norms that conflict with partisan desires. One could also argue that many authoritarian or hybrid political regimes coexist with essentially partisan judicial regimes, but that question is beyond the scope of this study.

How then may partisan judiciaries help or hurt democracy? Partisan judi-ciaries can reinforce the democratic enforcement of the laws, including across successive governments, which could help to build respect for the law as well as institutionalizing democratic politics. A well-institutionalized democratic partisan judiciary may be relatively easy to reform into a liberal judiciary, as happened in Costa Rica in 1989. Even where such an outcome is unlikely, partisan judges may enjoy some strength in at least some areas of their work. Judges who enjoy what I have called "strong dependence" may be able to significantly influence society in regards to law-abidingness, even enforcing at least some aspects of equality and rights protection and creating elements of the democratic rule of law. This partisan rule of law is likely to be limited in that loyal partisans are likely to be treated better by the courts than non-partisans and the rights of groups out of favor with the government are not likely to be fully respected. That such a partisan rule of law is partial does not mean that it should be discounted; a partial rule of law still protects many even as it declines to protect all.

Clandestine control regimes are unlikely to ever be compatible with a robust democracy, however, because they are so destructive of the state apparatus and governmental legitimacy. While Guatemala is a democracy, its government continues to have low levels of legitimacy and numerous indicators suggest that the quality of its democracy continues to be relatively low. A few coun-tries among the advanced democracies have struggled with the influence of organized crime over their justice sectors, including some parts of the United States and Italy. In neither of these cases has organized crime penetrated the judiciary over the entire national territory, yet the fight against crimi-nal influence has still required extensive governmental resources. Developing countries rarely have that level of resources available. Colombia has also strug-gled with drug cartels as well as armed insurgency groups; maintaining some degree of societal autonomy required intensive security interventions on behalf of judges. Even so, the result is a mixture of clandestine control and liberal elements.

While clandestine control judicial regimes may not be compatible with a robust democracy, they nonetheless contain elements that can contribute to strengthening the democratic rule of law. There may be a general sense within the judiciary of the need to treat litigants as equals before the law such that succumbing to bribery or threats is generally seen as a perversion of justice rather than a norm. There may be some gains in rights protections, especially against lower-level governmental offenders. Progress toward prosecutions for high level government violations in either the recent or distant past may be possible. The presence of at least moderate political independence implies that many in the government support an empowered judiciary and would thus endorse reforms that would expand independence, modernize judicial training, and improve security, among other measures. Unfortunately, the high levels of crime that typically accompany a clandestine control judicial regime so stress the budget and other resources of the justice system that it may prove extremely difficult to realize the promise that can be found within clandestine control judicial regimes. However, those same high levels of crime may provide the needed impetus for a government to commit the necessary resources and political will. The CICIG in Guatemala has been a massive undertaking and it is not yet clear that it has reached the heart of the problem. Sadly, it may be relatively easy to slide into clandestine control from any of the other judicial regimes.

LESSONS FROM THE JUDICIAL REGIME APPROACH

Applying the judicial regime approach in Central America is revealing. By distinguishing between political independence and societal autonomy, we can better understand the different but sometimes overlapping influences on the judiciary in these countries. By shining a light on societal autonomy as distinct from political independence, the judicial regime approach reveals a significant oversight in most of the literature on "judicial independence" and judicial politics. Identifying this additional set of influences on the judiciary leads us to reframe the major questions that frame the literature.

Why Do Politicians and Societal Actors Not Build Independent Institutions?

The evolution of the particular patterns of the different judicial regimes presented here may shed some light on how the rule of law can be developed or devalued under the collective weight of certain factors. First, and perhaps most evident, is the nature of the party system. A stable and competitive two-party system will tend to produce a partisan system, as is the case in Nicaragua, Honduras, and, to a lesser extent, El Salvador. This finding is somewhat different from the "political insurance" thesis suggested by Ramseyer, Finkel, and others that a competitive party system will produce an empowered or even activist judiciary because partisans expect to become the opposition in the future and wish their enactments to be protected by an independent judiciary and not swept aside from future incumbents. Honduras and Nicaragua teach us that a competitive two-party system will not necessarily produce a politically independent judiciary when the two parties have cooperative leaders. These two party systems should perhaps be understood as operating primarily through collusion rather than competition, even while elections continue to produce alternations in power. This collusion produces a highly partisan judiciary, but one that does not demonstrate the volatility that one might expect to accompany electoral alternation.

After democracy was re-introduced and reinvigorated in the 1990s, the four non-liberal judiciaries diverged considerably. El Salvador, Honduras, and Nicaragua developed partisan control judicial regimes as the two major parties in each country struck bargains to share judicial appointments along with a variety of other appointments. In Nicaragua, this tendency developed into explicit pacts between the Liberals and the Sandinistas and the recent facilitation by the judiciary of Sandinista President Ortega's backsliding toward nondemocratic rule. In Honduras, the partisan judiciary in 2009 gave its approval to a military coup against President Zelaya and subsequently blocked all efforts to reinstate Zelaya. The Honduran judiciary, while hostile to Zelaya, has generally been reluctant to police the elected branches. El Salvador presents a muted version of partisan control. Salvadoran judges do appear to seek the approval of the legislature when reappointment time comes and Salvadoran legislators do appear to engage in partisan bargaining around appointments, but Supreme Court magistrates are only appointed or reappointed one-third at a time and ordinary judges are thus more insulated from partisan pressures. Guatemala's feckless political party system has been unable to solidify any kind of long-term control of the judiciary. Coalitions shift quickly as parties rise and fall, often on the fortunes of particular presidential candidates, rendering long-term cooperation difficult. Instead, many elected politicians engage in corruption themselves; they may try to influence judges in particular cases, but usually through corrupt means rather than institutional ones.

This research also indicates that institutional rules do operate as significant shapers of the judicial environment, even in relatively unstable systems. Length of judicial tenure is found to be a significant contributor to both political independence and societal autonomy, confirming previous research. Where, as in Costa Rica, judicial tenures are relatively long and stable, judges and magistrates have developed a great deal of political independence and societal autonomy. Where judicial tenures are relatively short, as in Guatemala, Honduras, and Nicaragua, judges and magistrates are likely to be dependent on *someone*, but other factors such as party dynamics and levels of organized criminality will determine on whom they are likely to depend. The strong political parties of Nicaragua and Honduras are able to both protect and exert influence over judges. In Guatemala, by contrast, judges and especially high court magistrates faced with five-year tenures are also seeking professional protection, but by and large they must find it outside of political parties. Instead, they often find it in elite law firms, which may or may not have ties to corruption or criminal activities.

Similarly, a practice against reappointment will tend to produce a less autonomous judiciary whose members must look beyond the bench for the remainder of their careers, whereas a practice for reappointment may produce a more partisan judiciary when coupled with short tenures. The timing of appointments also has a significant impact on the nature of the judiciary as a whole. When all of the members of the high court are appointed at once, partisan horse-trading is encouraged. When they have lengthy tenures and are replaced either on staggered cycles or upon death or retirement, there can be less horse trading, that horse trading is less likely to dominate the court as a whole, and the weight of past governments will be felt longer. Honduras, Nicaragua, and Guatemala all have short judicial tenures and replace all of the magistrates at the same time. In all three countries, we see a rush to put loyal friends on the high courts or at least to try to insure one's influence over the courts. El Salvador, with its somewhat longer term (nine years) and system of reappointing only one-third of the Supreme Court at one time, sees a much more muted version of this kind of political negotiation of influences. Costa Rica is the only one of the countries studied that has entirely staggered terms in that supreme court magistrates are appointed and considered for reappointment individually. The consequence of this approach has been the high political salience of these opportunities to influence the Supreme Court and especially the powerful constitutional chamber. However, any political bargaining to be done must involve other, legislative compromises; more often, there is difficulty in identifying and appointing suitable compromise candidates as no one party has recently been able to attain the supermajority needed to appoint a candidate agreeable only to it.

A somewhat dismaying finding of this research concerns the impact of different methods of appointment of judges and magistrates. These countries have all adopted a bureaucratized career path for trial-level judges, who are chosen according to examination and relatively transparent criteria at the entry level. In Costa Rica, bureaucratic mechanisms continue to drive the judicial career throughout the several levels of lower courts, while in the other countries studied herein, advancement depends on non-bureaucratic mechanisms. Judicial appointments that are overseen by the partisan supreme courts of Honduras, El Salvador, and Nicaragua allow for the injection of partisan influence on the selection even of ordinary trial court judges, despite the presence of nominally independent judicial councils. In Guatemala, given the relative political independence of the Supreme Court, there is less political influence on the selection of early-career judges. However, as discussed in Chapter 5, the judiciary's internal disciplinary system has been a site of considerable abuse and corruption, where honest judges are more likely to be targeted by dishonest lawyers than are corrupt judges to be so much as named. In short, the judiciary as a whole may follow the politicization of the Supreme Court.

The processes by which judges are able to advance through the judicial hierarchy compound the external controls over the judiciary, be they partisan or criminal. In Nicaragua, the higher courts are appointed in practice according to the operation of a partisan pact in the Congress. Honduras appoints its magistrates according to a politicized process in the Congress as well. In El Salvador, a judicial council has significantly more influence, allowing magistrates to be somewhat less politicized, although the final decision and decisions regarding renewal still rest with the legislature. Guatemala has gone the furthest to remove the influence of electoral concerns from the appointment process for its appellate courts, using a system of councils that include representatives chosen or elected from several different sectors of legal society. While this system has minimized direct partisan or electoral influence, such influence is likely to have been weak given the weak and feckless nature of most Guatemalan political parties. However, this system failed to close the appointment process to corrupt influence from the powerful, wealthy, or criminal. Avenues of entry for corrupt influences likely exist in any system, but those avenues will vary from one to another.

Finally, the choices of individuals both with and without official power also influence the nature of the judiciary in these countries. At one extreme, we see Costa Ricans at every level of society seeking the aid of the courts and submitting to their jurisdiction when required. At the other extreme, we see Guatemalans with the ability to do so avoiding the courts whenever possible, through threats and bribery when necessary. Rodrigo Rosenberg could have brought a complaint to the prosecutor's office or even to the CICIG, but instead he orchestrated an elaborate piece of political theater that included his own suicide by proxy. In similarly high crime environments in Honduras and El Salvador, many people avoid the courts in a similar fashion as in Guatemala, but high-ranking political actors also make use of the courts to validate political actions. Honduran President Zelaya could have been removed without the Supreme Court's involvement, but Michelleti and his supporters chose instead to seek the validation that could come with an order from the Supreme Court.

How Does an Empowered Judiciary Not Institutionalize the Rule of Law?

Democracy preservation and strengthening is an area in which judicial independence has generally been given the utmost priority. The government control regimes of the authoritarian or semi-democratic periods of the 1980s in Guatemala, Honduras, El Salvador, and Nicaragua were typified by judiciaries that rarely if ever challenged non-democratic policies and actions. In none of these countries were the judiciaries reliable protectors of individual rights, be they human rights or economic rights. Individuals were able to be protected, released, or otherwise vindicated through corruption, but only rarely by ordinary means. Those ordinary means were constructed to reinforce the power of the government, not to check it. Only in Guatemala did the Constitutional Court reinforce the transition to democracy, but even their opposition to the 1993 *autogolpe* by President Serrano was buffeted by the military. Moreover, it was only the Constitutional Court that took this stand; the Supreme Court and the ordinary courts remained silent. Other courts were actively obstructionist, as in El Salvador, or opportunistic, as in Nicaragua. Nicaragua's Supreme Court championed the 1987 constitution it helped author, but its commitment to constitutionalism coincided very closely with its commitment to the Sandinistas.

Certainly, partisan or otherwise political incursions on judicial prerogatives can be a major impediment to democratic consolidation, especially the development of constitutionalism. El Salvador's magistrates have increasingly needed to worry about such political incursions, and even Costa Rica saw a magistrate nearly sacked seemingly for ideological reasons. However, clandestine control can be just as dangerous for democracy, with various forms of threat against the Constitutional Court of Guatemala over the years. The inability to enforce democratically enacted laws should also be seen as damaging democracy. However, clear partisan control presents an interesting challenge. It is true that the partisan supreme courts of Nicaragua and Honduras have allowed authoritarian backsliding, it would be perhaps more accurate to say that those courts actively supported and facilitated that backsliding. The judges and magistrates are not weak and cowed, but rather enthusiastically empowered supporters of their partisan causes. Partisan judiciaries can be understood as not being independent, but they should not be assumed to be weak as a consequence.

Guatemala has seen an explosion of criminal violence since the end of its civil war in 1996. This violence overwhelms state capacity in a variety of ways, most prominently in the way it combines with corruption to bring police, military officers, businessmen, and judicial personnel into criminal networks. This criminal penetration is so extensive that Guatemala has since 2007 been host to an international commission designed to aid in investigating the cases too sensitive or difficult for the ordinary prosecutors. Judges routinely reported in 2009–2010 that they feared for Guatemala's democracy, that another war might be possible, and that they felt threatened for doing their jobs. Some also chafed, however, at the restrictions being placed on their working conditions by this international commission and the fight against corruption more generally. Notwithstanding the limitations on their societal autonomy, Guatemalan judges enjoy relatively high levels of inter-branch independence. Inter-branch independence without societal autonomy can still be cancerous to the rule of law.

Finally, Costa Rica has developed a fairly robust liberal judicial regime in which the judiciary as an institution is generally granted political independence by the other branches of government and individual judges are generally respected and left to do their jobs unmolested by societal actors. However, some lawyers did report some instances of judicial corruption. Judges interviewed and surveyed in the capitol reported a very different set of concerns from their northern neighbors: politicians do not call them, thugs do not threaten them, but at times the media questions them. This is not to say that the situation is perfect. One judge in Puerto Limón did report being threatened with substantial violence and not being satisfied with the judicial protection service. At the Supreme Court, magistrates enjoy longer tenures and greater respect than their counterparts in the region, but they are also not immune to attacks from politicians and the popular media. It seems, however, that a fundamentally independent and autonomous judiciary is an important part of the Costa Rican ideal of democracy.

Moving from democratic persistence to human rights protections, the judicial regime has a strong impact on what kind of human rights violations are likely to be punished. Costa Rica's liberal system has seen a robust "rights revolution" that offers to protect the human rights and constitutional rights of anyone in the country. The partisan regimes, on the other hand, tend to protect primarily their partisan friends – who are also forgiven for their transgressions against the rights of others. We can see this in the repression of civil society and political parties opposed to Sandinista rule in Nicaragua. The high levels of criminality in Honduras and El Salvador have been highly politicized in a way that the poor are often constructed as criminal enemies of the state; the state does not extend its protections to their rights as a general rule and there are no consequences for the loyal partisan judges for these failures. In Guatemala, the state fails to extend its protection to most citizens, although this failure results more from the personal insecurity of judges than from their partisan professional security. Personal insecurity of judges is also a factor in Honduras and El Salvador, but it is usually overshadowed by partisan logics.

Discussions of human rights in Central America are never far from discussions of justice for human rights violations during the war years. Guatemala has seen considerable activity around bringing human rights violators to justice, including the possibility that a former military dictator might be finally convicted for the massacres he ordered. General Ríos Montt continues to be a highly polarizing figure in Guatemala, however, and a retrial has been stalled as of this writing. El Salvador's peace accords did not mandate an amnesty, but the one that was passed in their wake remained in place until mid-2016, rendering any transitional justice efforts impossible. Honduras has not seen trials for high level human rights violations perpetrated during the 1980s nor following the 2009 coup. The partisan nature of the judiciary has been reinforced since 2009 with purges of some pro-Zelaya judges, significantly reducing the likelihood that any such trials would occur in the near future. Although the lack of societal autonomy and the accompanying environment of threat increase the danger to judges who consider cases against high level human rights violators, it appears that those trials are more likely to happen in a clandestine control regime than in a partisan regime.

In Costa Rica and Nicaragua, the issue of high level corruption has been more prominent than the issue of high level human rights violations. While human rights violations continue to happen in both countries, they are more frequently carried out by lower level officials and do not typically appear to be ordered by high level government officials. Indeed, there is evidence in both countries that processes are in place to monitor and sanction those low-level violations. Both countries have also seen presidents tried and convicted for corruption. In both countries, ex-presidents have been convicted for corruption but have been successfully released on appeal. In Costa Rica, the appeals appear to have been done according to the law, but in Nicaragua there appears to have been a quid pro quo involved in the release of ex-president Alemán from prison in 2009, the same year that the Nicaraguan Supreme Court approved of presidential reelection. In both judiciaries, it was possible for ex-presidents convicted of corruption to be released before finishing their sentences, but the price was different. The price in Nicaragua's partisan system was the retrenchment in power of President Daniel Ortega and his FSLN with Alemán's Liberal Party becoming a relatively docile opposition. In Costa Rica, the price is less clear; corruption scandals have continued to plague Costa Rican administrations, but international opinion of Costa Rica's ability to control corruption remains high. It may be that partisan judiciaries can combat official corruption, but they are likely to do so only when the accused is of the opposing party as the judge and also out of favor with the current president. Without those two factors, corruption is likely to go unpunished. Corruption scandals and trials follow a similar pattern in Costa Rica, with the accused typically being out of favor with the current president, although the party of the judge is not relevant. It appears that, regarding the punishment of official corruption, even liberal regimes can come up lacking.

PATH DEPENDENCE AND POWER REPRODUCTION THROUGH REFORM PROGRAMS

With so much attention paid to these judiciaries by international reformers, why have reforms been so unsuccessful? There has been considerable international consensus since the end of the 1980s that strong judiciaries are necessary for democracy, economic development, and human rights enforcement, but insufficient subtlety as to what it means for a judiciary to be "strong." With the exception of Costa Rica, Central American judiciaries entered the 1990s in a position of institutional weakness, which ultimately contributed to state weakness. As repressive military apparatuses were diminished, civilian police forces, often newly-created or reformed, were slow to catch up. Reformers and activists in the 1990s, reeling from years of government repression and under the influence of neo-liberal political thinking, often looked to contain the repressive institutions of the state. Institutional strengthening reforms often took the form of technical innovations and trainings rather than capacity building. Overall, reforms were too focused on limiting government power, with the ultimate result that governments were not able to confront rising crime in the region. Furthermore, reforms were, with few exceptions, layered on top of existing institutions, leaving many pre-reform incumbents in power. Because of the need to have incumbents buy into the reform programs, incumbents within the judiciary often helped to design the very reforms they would then evade, creating an environment in which incumbent power could easily be reproduced.

One Guatemalan attorney speculated as to the reasons for this official reluctance:

Again, I can understand how political leaders don't really want to change the rules, because at the end of the day, how are politicians and congressmen, politicians of all sorts and kinds made accountable. Where is it at the end of the day that anyone is made accountable? In the courts of law. You took this money, you didn't spend it well, you didn't do what you had to do, whatever. That's where you become accountable at the end of the day. And they've understood that it's probably not a bad idea to have a very weak judiciary and more or less submissive . . . that's probably not a bad environment to be a politician. (G2009–08)

Layering Reforms and the Problem of Power Reproduction

A significant source of the weakness of reform programs in Central America has been the tendency to rely on incremental reforms that are "layered" on top of existing institutions. A reform is considered layered when the pre-existing institution is able to persist with its fundamental structure and personnel intact. Political realities often make layering the only viable strategy for reform, especially in the short term. Central America did see exceptional moments when deeper reform may have been possible, such as in the peace processes of the early 1990s, especially in Guatemala and El Salvador. However, in those moments, a tremendous amount of political capital was expended on reforming the police and the military in order to reduce human rights revolutions and put the national governments of those two countries into a peaceful mode of operations. Police reforms did meet with some successes in both countries and were certainly pressing concerns. Nonetheless, little political capital remained to be expended on the seemingly less abusive judiciaries. In Honduras and Nicaragua, it is not clear that the political will ever existed to create a non-partisan judiciary. Only in Costa Rica do we see a judicial reform that goes substantially beyond layering. The creation of the constitutional chamber introduced a largely new institution, to which new members would be appointed who were not already members of the Supreme Court. Costa Rica's reform strategy, then, allowed for the growth of new institutional norms and power relationships, even if that was not the intent of the reform.

The major problem with layering reforms is that incumbents are typically left in place. The rules may be changed and sometimes responsibilities and roles may change, but the individuals operating the reformed judiciary are typically the same people who filled those positions previously. Some incumbents may immerse themselves in their new roles, taking trainings seriously and generally embracing the reform program. Others, however, may see the reform process as an opportunity to aggrandize their power and enrich themselves personally. A major element of these reform programs has been to pour additional resources into judiciaries to improve institutional functioning. For reasons of ensuring judicial independence, the judiciary itself – often primarily the magistrates of the Supreme Court – typically controlled and distributed those funds, allowing a small number of incumbents to reward and punish others within the institution. Similarly, an increasing number of training opportunities were made available, including international meetings and seminars. The ability to take advantage of these subsidized travel opportunities has not been uniformly distributed. This uneven distribution of educational opportunities also affects future advancement opportunities for these judges as they progress through their careers.

Power reproduction suggests more than just aggrandizement. It also suggests that incumbents are able to ensure that future openings will be filled by people with the same political or institutional inclinations as they have. Reforms that have increased the judiciary's control over its own personnel decisions can actually promote this aspect of power reproduction. The more bureaucratized judicial career should be some protection from this kind of influence, but when the Supreme Court – or a judicial council dominated by the Supreme Court – is in control of appointments, promotions, and discipline, then the members of the Supreme Court will be able to make the judiciary over in their own image. Processes of appointment to appellate courts and the Supreme Court may also provide this opportunity, as in Guatemala where one-third of each nominating commission is composed of members of either the appellate courts or the Supreme Court. Appointment, promotion, and disciplinary mechanisms can reproduce the power of incumbent members of the judiciary – especially those at the top – and thus help to reinforce judicial regimes.

Path dependent arguments often assume that institutions are strong and that they indeed constrain behavior, but the reform experiences of Central American countries suggest that powerful incumbents can and will frustrate institutions through their resistance to having to give up their power. In Chapter 2, I argued that path dependence should be understood primarily through models of gradual accrual of choices rather through models of critical junctures. One of the lessons of these reform experiences is that apparent critical junctures may produce only partial changes before incumbents subvert those changes and reestablish old patterns. A prominent choice may be made at the moment of choosing a reform, but a long series of less prominent choices follow. Some incumbents choose to participate in the reform enthusiastically while others choose to resist and still others participate with an eye toward subverting the reform. Institutional change only becomes institutionalized when the incumbents who support the reforms are able to outweigh the incumbents who resist or subvert it. In other words, institutional change becomes real only when the dominant incumbents – and users – become habituated to the new way of doing things.

As I argued in Chapter 2, institutional changes need to be understood not just as cyclical and evolutionary, but also as conflictual. These accruing choices to accept or resist reforms are made in the context of conflicts between opposing forces. In Guatemala, the dominant conflicts have come to be between people fighting for constitutionalism and the rule of law on the one hand and what they call the "hidden powers" – those fighting to gain and maintain power and wealth through illegal and quasi-legal means – on the other. In the partisan systems, these conflicts have been primarily partisan. In Nicaragua and El Salvador, the stakes were raised by the incorporation of former combatants into the party system, such that former enemies on the battlefield now battle each other through political and legal institutions. Costa Rica historically saw many partisan battles waged in its judiciary, but during the period of study, the dominant form of conflict has been between citizens and the state. The dynamics of these battles, including the ability of one side or another to gain an upper hand will shape the direction and likelihood of success of institutional reforms.

Clientelism and Layering Reforms in Central America

Many attribute the problems of corruption and partisanship within the judiciaries of the developing world to a political culture that fosters clientelism. On the contrary, I argue that clientelism is a response to institutional weakness rather than being its primary cause, although that clientelism does then provide incentives to resist institutional strengthening that could challenge the power and wealth of political and institutional patrons. Weak institutions that fail to provide an appropriate career path for incumbents and also fail to provide appropriate outcomes for those who seek their services invite job-seekers and service-seekers alike to pursue solutions based in clientelism and corruption. Career paths must be strengthened so that job seekers do not need to rely on clientelist or partisan connections to get ahead. Institutions must be made stronger and more efficient so that citizens do not need to resort to corruption to open businesses, obtain social services, or come to legal resolutions. An important part of institutional strengthening must be lustration; as long as powerful patrons remain in office, they will continue to engage in rent-seeking clientelism and corruption as long as they can, ultimately undermining reforms. It is not enough to write new rules if friends still help friends find their way around them.

Worse, some reforms were done in a way that actually enhanced clientelist practices. The Nicaraguan Supreme Court was able to exert considerable control over the reform process there because of the need for any reform to have the clear support of at least one magistrate. As such, the magistrates were able to greatly enhance their prestige and power through their control over the distribution of resources that came through the reform programs. Furthermore, the magistrates were able to shape the practical effect of the reforms through their control of the process. Any reform that allows an incumbent to have control over others' careers and access to needed professional resources is likely to enhance the ability of that incumbent to engage in clientelist practices. A magistrate who can offer professional resources, aid in promotions, and invitations to international trainings to loyal subordinates – and deny them to disloyal subordinates – has the ability to be a patron. Breaking this clientelist pattern requires that we break the link between loyalty and advancement, something that can be done through career reforms and either genuinely egalitarian or genuinely competitive application processes.

The most drastic approach to trying to interrupt power reproduction in the context of criminal penetration of the state is Guatemala's International Commission Against Impunity (CICIG). The goals of the CICIG – to end impunity and also to strengthen Guatemala's own institutions – rely on a strategy of identifying, investigating, and prosecuting corruption and criminality in the government. Some high-profile politicians have been accused and some of those have found their way to prison. An investigation by the CICIG led to a massive popular movement demanding the resignation of the vice president and then, once the vice president resigned, the president himself. The resignation of a president may have less long-term impact than the institutional changes that the CICIG has been aiding. The CICIG has been able to operate with relative independence precisely because it is a new institution – and one that works alongside, not for, the Guatemalan government. It has also helped to forge new work groups within the Guatemalan justice sector, creating some degree of insulation for those who would investigate and prosecute corruption and organized crime. However, its mandate is also regularly subject to renewal by the Guatemalan government and it is not yet clear what legacy the CICIG will leave behind when its mandate is finally terminated.

While the CICIG has seen some successes and El Salvador and Honduras have taken steps toward similar international commissions in their own countries to help deal with their own organized crime and democratic struggles, the CICIG has significant flaws as a model for justice sector reform. Because it is an international commission, it requires the invitation of the government, something that is less likely to occur in a country with a partisan judicial regime. Even in Guatemala, the original version of the commission was invalidated by the Constitutional Court. It is also an extremely expensive undertaking and likely would require substantial international donation for operating costs. An international commission to prosecute domestic crimes raises questions about national sovereignty that would reduce the chances of politicians within the government, who may or may not be implicated in the criminality and corruption that would be investigated, would support the agreements necessary to allow such a commission to be created. Finally, the CICIG is designed around a clandestine control judicial regime wherein the judiciary already had relative independence from political parties. Translating the model to judicial regimes that have significant partisan control would require a number of modifications; it is possible that partisans within the judiciary would stymie many prosecutions because of the partisan ties of those under investigation.

Tailoring Future Reforms

The judicial regime approach can be a helpful guide when considering reform strategies for the future. It is tempting to point to one judicial regime type as the most functional or democratic and ask "how do we get there from here?" This impulse should be resisted. Judicial regimes do change, sometimes dramatically and suddenly, but more often gradually and subtly. Years of internationally-backed judicial reforms projects in the region have failed to produce dramatic change in these countries. The change produced was perhaps most dramatic in El Salvador, but the Salvadoran judiciary has nonetheless trended toward remaining an entrenched partisan judicial regime. Reform programs are unlikely to produce a wholesale shift in judicial regime, short of a total change in political regime as accompanied the collapse of communism in Eastern Europe.[3] Rather, judicial reformers should focus on identifying the various avenues of entry for corruption in specific judiciaries and work with governments and their judiciaries to determine the best ways to reform those.

Where inter-branch judicial independence is compromised, reformers need to focus on creating intermediating institutions between the elected branches of government and the judiciary. Intermediating institutions may be especially

---

[3] Even in Eastern Europe, extensive reform programs did not produce uniformly politically independent and societally autonomous judiciaries. One wonders whether potential reforms in the face of the likely retreat of communism in Cuba following the end of Castro rule will produce a radically different judiciary than exists there currently.

needed to distance elected politicians from the judicial appointment process. A judicial council or other nominating commission may help to reduce partisan influence in the selection of judges. Although the final selection of judges or magistrates may still be made by the legislature, the deputies would typically only be given the power to choose from a list selected by the judicial council. The judicial council may have representatives of the elected branches of government, but more often represents the judiciary and, in somewhat varied fashion, the legal society. The bar association may have representation as may law schools. Other aspects of civil society are sometimes present as well. While these intermediating institutions can be a helpful means of reducing political influence over the selection process, reformers should nonetheless be cautious about the potential for societal actors – especially criminal actors – to gain influence via this mechanism, as has happened in Guatemala.

In addition, reappointment and removal proceedings should be clarified and should ideally be difficult; if inter-branch review is considered appropriate, as it often is for constitutional magistrates, super-majorities should be required. The near-removal of Magistrate Cruz Castro in Costa Rica in 2012 indicates that political preferences may still force judges out, but the super-majority requirement that is present there raises the bar to removal, limiting such events to only those times when a large political coalition exists against a judge or when genuine misconduct has occurred. It is because of the political influence inherent in reappointment proceedings that some have argued for considering life tenure alone to be a sufficient guarantee of judicial political independence. Thus, lengthening judicial terms, especially for constitutional court or supreme court magistrates is also an important reform; ideally, renewals or new appointments should be staggered to minimize disruptions and to maximize the need to find judicial candidates who are either truly independent or are able to win cross-partisan support. Costa Rica and, to a lesser extent, El Salvador demonstrate the benefits of such staggered, lengthy terms, while the short and uniform terms in Honduras and Nicaragua allow for pure partisan horse-trading to the detriment of inter-branch independence.[4] Constitutional minimums for judicial budgets are also important; budgetary attacks were not seen in any of the countries under study.

Societal penetration of the judiciary requires a substantially different set of reforms, many of which are related to judicial protection and otherwise limiting bribery and threats. Case-tracking software and cashless judicial offices may help minimize bribe-taking and petty corruption, but meaningful

---

[4] Guatemala also has short and uniform terms, but the horse-trading is of an entirely different nature.

disciplinary procedures will be necessary as well. Even in Costa Rica, there are stories of judges asking for bribes such that judicial discipline will always be a real necessity. In Guatemala, the bribes may come unbidden and with an implicit or explicit attached threat. The judge is expected to accept the money that has been deposited into her account and do as she is told or face the consequences. More extensive banking and financial reform may also be necessary to minimize the ability of criminal actors to access accounts or for bribe recipients to launder these funds. It may be appropriate to simply monitor the accounts of judges and magistrates or to require routine reporting of gifts and other irregular transactions. Such reforms would go beyond the realm of simple judicial reforms, implicating the financial sector and investigative and prosecutorial offices.

Where judges are subject to threats, judiciaries need to have substantial programs of judicial protection, with armed guards available to judges and their families. While all of the countries studied offer some amount of judicial protection, it tends to be inconsistent at best. Recall that even in relatively pacific Costa Rica, one judge on the Caribbean Coast had been kidnapped at gunpoint and still had not seen a substantial increase in her judicial security detail. The situation is worse in Guatemala, where many may not trust their official security forces, given the history of corrupt agents participating in assassination attacks. Unfortunately, in the high crime countries of Guatemala, Honduras, and El Salvador, it is likely necessary to make available to judges security that will protect them in their homes and vehicles as well as their courtrooms. Often, the courtrooms have been secured to a significant degree, but most judges are then unprotected once they leave their workplaces.

Unfortunately, few of these reforms and programs have been carried out in a consistent or widespread fashion, perhaps because of the focus on inter-branch independence that dominates most of the discourse within both the scholarly and the international donor communities. The focus on inter-branch independence leads to a focus on a single model of a good judiciary and thus a less flexible set of reforms. The notion that one type of judicial regime is the best model for all countries is pernicious and even dangerous. It is easy to point to Costa Rica as a model of a highly functional and democratic judiciary, but such an observation proves neither that the Costa Rican model can be translated to other contexts, nor that it is somehow without its own concerns. Judiciaries do not exist in the abstract. It would be preferable to step back and ask whether the judiciary promotes a democratic rule of law – a concept that can comfortably carry considerable variation from one setting to another – and how the interplay with the rest of government and society either enhances or detracts from that goal. El Salvador has shown us that sweeping judicial reform will regress when the rest of the government does not substantially reform itself. Guatemala has demonstrated the ultimate weakness of political and judicial will in the face of widespread criminality. A close look at Costa Rica reveals that her seemingly strong safeguards may buckle in moments when societal attention and political support weaken. Securing the democratic rule of law, then, is necessarily related to the context in which it operates.

THE ACHILLES HEEL OF DEMOCRACY REVISITED

Calling the judiciary "the Achilles Heel of democracy" is a provocatively damning indictment of judicial power. In much of Central America, judicial power is a significant point of vulnerability for the region's fledgling democracies. The preceding chapters have detailed a number of weaknesses and failing on the part of the region's judiciaries. However, it may also be possible for the judiciary to fortify the democratic rule of law. A strong judiciary can provide a peaceful, institutional means of conflict resolution, both at the intra-governmental level and at the grassroots level. The judiciary can also reinforce representation by ensuring that the laws as enacted are carried out properly – and also that none are unduly excluded from the ability to participate in policy making. Most fundamentally, a strong judiciary can make rights real by holding government officials at all levels accountable for violating citizens' rights and also by ensuring that citizens have recourse against private incursions on rights and dignity. The judiciaries that do enforce rights best do so with attention to the equality of citizens. In these manners, the judiciary need not be the Achilles Heel of democracy, but can in fact be a force for deepening democratic practices, norms, and rights.

Judicial power needs to be understood as a route for empowerment of citizens and not only as a route for determining and distributing power within the government. As Arjomand has pointed out in a study of constitutionalism in the Middle East:

> Judicial power needs to be evaluated not just in relation to other branches of government, but also in relation to the citizens on whose behalf it is exercised. What needs emphasis is that empowerment is not a zero-sum game, and judicial review also results in the political empowerment of the citizens.[5]

As Arjomand suggests, an empowered judiciary empowers citizens as well. Costa Rica's powerful constitutional chamber clearly shows this; it has become

[5] Arjomand, "Law, Political Reconstruction and Constitutional Politics," 27.

almost legendary there that any citizen can find relief at the Sala IV. A weak judiciary weakens citizenship as well. When the judiciary is under partisan control, it values citizenship on a partisan basis. A judiciary captured by societal elements, especially criminal elements, devalues citizenship for most citizens. If democracy means more than the enforcement of majority will, then judicial review and judicial empowerment are necessary.

The tendency to view judicial review as diminishing the power of the people rather than empowering the people stems from the flawed assumption that legislation closely reflects the will of the people and that the "will of the people" is something that can be understood in a unitary way. Legislatures and presidents, while elected, do not perfectly translate the will of the people into legislation; there are many possible sources of distortion of popular will. However, even a perfect translation of the will of the people can be a problem when the laws passed target particular groups in society, usually the powerless, poor, and ethnic out-groups. These groups may comprise a significant part of society and even be the majority; "the people" need to be disaggregated in our understandings of democracy just as does the elite. When a court protects the rights of the poor or powerless groups in society against the tyranny of the majority (or the influential minority), it nonetheless protects democracy. This protection cannot occur without judicial independence, but it is also unlikely to occur without sufficient judicial autonomy from powerful groups within society.

The judicial regime approach applied in this book is a valuable tool for disaggregating the various powers of and influences on judiciaries. Foregrounding judicial societal autonomy sheds important light on the functions, strengths, and weaknesses of judiciaries. This judicial regime approach reveals more dimensions of judicial power and politics than do previous approaches to judicial politics. It also does so in a holistic way, requiring that we understand the judiciary both at the top (the high courts) and the bottom (the trial courts), taking seriously the pressures that flow from above and below. This approach takes seriously the location of the judiciary within a democratic system, especially in weakly democratic systems where traditional approaches have often obscured some of the challenges inhibiting judicial power. Nonetheless, this approach does not idealize or demonize any one judicial regime type; instead, I have argued for understanding the various challenges in each and using the idea of judicial regimes as a guide for crafting reform programs. Although this book has focused on Central America, the judicial regime approach should be applied to and tested against other weak democracies.

Too often, the autonomy of judges from societal actors has been either ignored entirely or conflated with judicial political independence. This tendency has obscured the reality of both judicial vulnerabilities and judicial powers. In weak states where political power is significantly contested by political and societal actors alike, it is especially important to understand the different challenges posed by these two sectors. There may be other pressures from other sources of power; future research on judicial politics either within or outside of Central America should take seriously this possibility. An additional avenue for fruitful exploration involves the connections between the judiciary and other parts of the justice system. This book has only been able to hint at issues facing the police, the prosecutors, and the prisons, but these institutions are intimately connected with the democratic rule of law. Like the judiciary, these institutions may too be subject to both political and societal pressures. Future research on the justice system writ large would benefit from taking account of the issue of societal autonomy.

Methodology and Sample

The research for this book was conducted in two primary parts. The first component includes a series of interviews with judges and lawyers in Guatemala and Costa Rica in 2009 and 2010. The second component included a detailed survey questionnaire distributed to judges in Guatemala and Costa Rica in 2010. Additionally, the chapter on Guatemala draws in a more limited fashion on field research conducted in 2002, 2003, and 2004, totaling approximately six months. That research functions primarily as background, but figured prominently in the discussion of the 2003 electoral controversy, which occurred while the author was in Guatemala. Several interviews from this period of research are cited in Chapter 5; they are not also included in the table of interviews because of the difficulty in keeping them confidential. Additionally, I conducted three months of field research in Nicaragua in 2004 that serves as background for the section on Nicaragua in Chapter 6. Interviews conducted in Nicaragua in this period are not directly quoted or cited; thus, I have not included them in the table of interviews. The sections on El Salvador and Honduras are based entirely on secondary research.

In 2009 and 2010, I conducted fifty interviews with lawyers and judges in Costa Rica and Guatemala. I began by interviewing attorneys contacted through their law firms and expanded the sample through recommendations of these attorneys to judges. Several lawyers were also contacted directly as a result of their having written columns in local newspapers. There are some limitations of this strategy; the primary one is that it biases the sample toward attorneys working for larger law firms. Nonetheless, several solo practitioners were also able to be interviewed through referrals from initial contacts. A benefit of this approach is that it allowed me to penetrate the often socially-closed and professionally cautious legal profession by beginning with more prominent attorneys and then relying on their introductions. This approach also gave me access to two retired supreme court magistrates in Guatemala who were invaluable in providing insight into the period surrounding the 1993 *autogolpe* by President Serrano. Additionally, in Costa Rica, three political party representatives were interviewed during the protracted process of naming a new constitutional magistrate in 2009; in those cases, I went to the National Assembly building and visited their offices. Table A.1 provides basic characteristics about those interviewed. I promised all of my interlocutors confidentiality; as such, I have provided only limited information about them.

The survey conducted in 2010 focused primarily on judges at the trial level and appellate magistrates, but not supreme court or constitutional court magistrates (who were interviewed when possible). This questionnaire was based on Elena Martinez Barahona's survey of high courts magistrates and is intended to complement that study.[1] All survey respondents were assured anonymity, with respondents directed to not record their names or to answer any questions with which they were not comfortable. In Guatemala, surveys were delivered to the judge or the judge's secretary in a manila envelope and picked up several days later from the secretary without the judge's name. Numbers were attached to the surveys later. In Costa Rica, where surveys were distributed and collected via email on the advice of the president of the judges' association, the files were downloaded, scrubbed of identifiers, and saved with a numerical identifier, after which the email was deleted. The de-identified surveys were then coded by a research assistant. This survey was conducted In Guatemala City, Guatemala, in August 2010, and in San José, Costa Rica in September 2010. Forty-six judges returned the questionnaire in Guatemala; thirty-four were returned in Costa Rica.

In both countries, the sample included judges from different levels of the judicial hierarchy. In Guatemala, 91 percent came from the trial-level courts, include several justices of the peace in addition to a large number of first-instance judges. There were also a small number of appellate magistrates, but no Guatemalan supreme court magistrates participated in this survey. In terms of area of specialization, 60 percent of the respondents worked in the area of criminal law, with almost all of the remainder working in civil law. Some respondents indicated more than one area, with over one tenth indicating that they worked in other areas, such as labor courts or family courts.

The Costa Rican respondents were also primarily from the first-instance courts, with another third coming from the appellate level. Some respondents indicated more than one level. As in Guatemala, many judges also gave multiple answers regarding their area of specialization. Roughly a third each

---

[1] Martinez Barahona, *Seeking the Political Role of the Third Government Branch: A Comparative Approach to High Courts in Central America*.

TABLE A.1 *Interviews, 2009–2010*

GUATEMALA

Identifier	Description	Method	Record	Length
G2009–01	Private attorney	Telephone	concurrent notes	0:20
G2009–02	Private attorney	in person	audio recording & concurrent notes	0:49
G2009–03	Private attorney	in person	audio recording & concurrent notes	0:49
G2009–04	NGO attorney	in person	audio recording & concurrent notes	0:35
G2009–05	Private attorney	in person w/06	audio recording & concurrent notes	1:01
G2009–06	Private attorney	in person w/05	audio recording & concurrent notes	1:01
G2009–07	Former CSJ Magistrate	in person	audio recording & concurrent notes	0:55
G2009–08	Private attorney & newspaper columnist	in person	audio recording & concurrent notes	1:01
G2009–09	Private attorney	in person	audio recording & concurrent notes	1:01
G2009–10	Researcher	in person	audio recording & concurrent notes	0:52
G2009–11	Law school Dean	in person	audio recording & concurrent notes	0:31
G2009–12	Former CSJ Magistrate	in person	audio recording & concurrent notes	0:54
G2009–13	Judge	in person	audio recording & concurrent notes	0:39
G2009–14	Private attorney	in person	audio recording & concurrent notes	0:45
G2009–15	Law professor	in person	audio recording & concurrent notes	0:59
G2009–16	Judge	in person	audio recording & concurrent notes	0:26
G2009–17	Private attorney	in person	concurrent notes	1:00
G2009–18	NGO activist	in person	audio recording & concurrent notes	1:49
G2009–19	Judge	in person	concurrent notes	1:00
G2009–20	NGO researcher	in person	audio recording & concurrent notes	0:45
G2009–21	Analyst, aid organization	in person	audio recording & concurrent notes	1:00
G2009–22	Administrator, OJ	in person	audio recording & concurrent notes	0:38

(continued)

GUATEMALA Identifier	Description	Method	Record	Length
G2010–01	Appellate magistrate	in person	audio recording & concurrent notes	0:35
G2010–02	CC President	In person	concurrent notes	0:30
G2010–03	CC Magistrate	in person	concurrent notes	0:30

COSTA RICA Identifier	Description	Method	Record	Length
CR2009–01	Researcher	in person	audio recording & concurrent notes	2:00
CR2009–02	Private lawyer	in person	audio recording & concurrent notes	0:41
CR2009–03	Private lawyer	in person	audio recording & concurrent notes	0:52
CR2009–04	Private lawyer	in person w/05	audio recording & concurrent notes	1:02
CR2009–05	Private lawyer	in person w/04	audio recording & concurrent notes	1:02
CR2009–06	Private lawyer	in person	audio recording & concurrent notes	0:26
CR2009–07	Private lawyer	in person	audio recording & concurrent notes	0:30
CR2009–08	Court employee	in person	audio recording & concurrent notes	2:00
CR2009–09	Private lawyer	in person	audio recording & concurrent notes	1:00
CR2009–10	CSJ Magistrate	in person	audio recording & concurrent notes	0:47
CR2009–11	Private lawyer	in person	audio recording & concurrent notes	0:29
CR2009–12	Judge	in person	audio recording & concurrent notes	1:30
CR2009–13	Judge	in person	audio recording & concurrent notes	0:47
CR2009–14	PLN official	in person	concurrent notes	0:20
CR2009–15	PAC official	in person	concurrent notes	0:20
CR2009–16	ML official	in person	concurrent notes	0:20
CR2009–17	CSJ Magistrate	in person	audio recording & concurrent notes	0:40
CR2009–18	Judge	in person	audio recording & concurrent notes	0:28

TABLE A.1 (continued)

COSTA RICA Identifier	Description	Method	Record	Length
CR2009–19	CSJ Magistrate	in person	audio recording & concurrent notes	0:27
CR2009–20	Judge	in person	audio recording & concurrent notes	0:31
CR2010–01	CSJ Magistrate	in person	audio recording & concurrent notes	0:45
CR2010–02	CSJ Magistrate	in person	audio recording & concurrent notes	0:36
CR2010–03	CSJ Magistrate	in person	audio recording & concurrent notes	0:22
CR2010–04	CSJ Magistrate	in person	audio recording & concurrent notes	0:35
CR2010–05	CSJ Magistrate	in person	audio recording & concurrent notes	0:39

answered that they work in criminal, civil, and other areas of the law. Smaller numbers indicated that they worked in administrative and constitutional law.

Judges in both countries are often highly educated, although Guatemalan respondents indicated more participation in advanced courses and trainings than did their Costa Rican counterparts. One notable difference between the two countries was that the Costa Rican judges came from a broader range of universities than did Guatemalans. Thirty-seven of the forty-three Guatemalan respondents indicated that they were graduates of the public Universidad San Carlos, while the public Universidad de Costa Rica produced only just over half of the Costa Rican respondents. Judges in both countries have participated in advanced trainings and courses in high numbers. Nearly two-thirds of Costa Rican judges have Master's degrees, with another nearly 10 percent having doctoral degrees.[2] Between one-quarter and one-fifth reported participating in individual courses. Some 80 percent of Guatemalan respondents indicated that they hold Master's degrees or higher, with a quarter indicating that they hold doctoral degrees. More than half also indicated that they had participated in individual courses. Figures A.1 and A.2 present the data on postgraduate education. When asked about annual participation in professional trainings, seven-tenths of Costa Rican respondents indicated that they attend some or many trainings every year. Nearly all Guatemalan respondents indicated that

---

[2] Note that the basic law degree in these countries is a bachelor's degree.

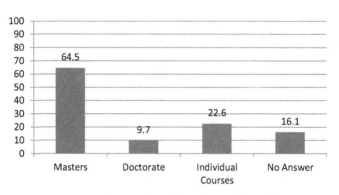

Postgraduate Experience, Costa Rica

they attend these trainings, with nearly half saying that they attend "many." Figures A.3 and A.4 provide the data on trainings.

The first question on the survey asked judges to rate their perception of the state of democracy in their countries. As the graph below illustrates, the difference between the two countries is striking. 96.8 percent of Costa Rican respondents felt that Costa Rican democracy is either stable or very stable, while the picture for Guatemala is almost a mirror image. 46.7 percent of Guatemalan respondents rated their democracy as unstable, with another 28.9 percent calling it not very stable. Only 22.2 percent felt that Guatemalan democracy is stable or very stable. Figure A.5 compares the responses to this question from the two countries. The differences in preferred regime are much smaller, however, indicating that judges in both countries generally prefer democracy under all circumstances. Only 3.2 percent of Costa Rican judges

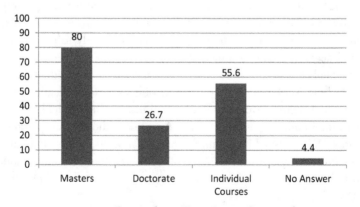

FIGURE A.2 Postgraduate Experience, Guatemala

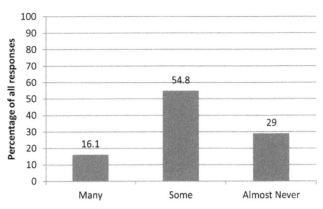

FIGURE A.3 Annual Participation in Professional Trainings, Costa Rica

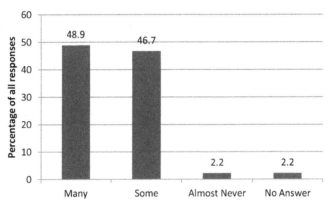

FIGURE A.4 Annual Participation in Professional Trainings, Guatemala

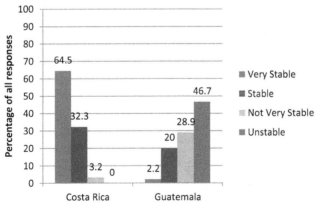

FIGURE A.5 State of Democracy

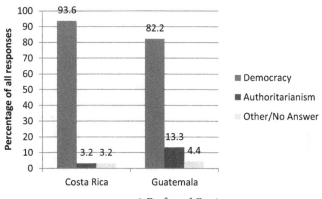

FIGURE A.6 Preferred Regime

and 13.3 percent of their Guatemalan counterparts felt that authoritarianism could be preferable in times of crisis. While it may be disheartening to see any support for authoritarianism among state functionaries, it is perhaps not surprising that some Guatemalans would feel this way in light of the weakness of democracy there and the tremendous crises of the economy and violent crime that face that country. These responses are presented in Figure A.6.

Judges were also asked to rate the functioning of the several justice sector institutions. This data is arrayed in Figure A.7. Not surprisingly, Costa Rican judges' views are more positive than those of Guatemalan judges.

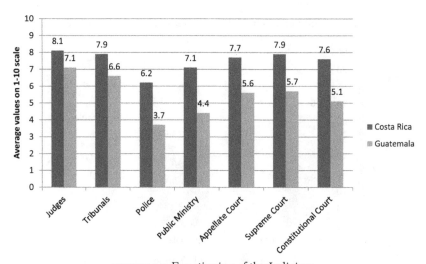

FIGURE A.7 Functioning of the Judiciary

TABLE A.2 *Political Views of Self and Government*
(Averages for Each Country)

	Costa Rica	Guatemala
Personal Ideology	6.1	5.9
Government Position	7.9	5.2

A final note on the participants in the survey relates to their ideologies. Respondents were asked to indicate their own position on a simple left-right scale of 1–10. They were also asked to indicate the position (in their view) of the government. In general, the two scores in each country were quite close to each other, indicating that these judges view their ideologies as being fairly closely aligned with the government's, as can be seen in Table A.2. Overall, the Costa Rican judges placed themselves and their governments further to the right of the Guatemalan scores. Guatemalan scores averaged in a very moderate position, while Costa Rican scores were somewhat right of center. Costa Rican judges viewed their own ideologies as somewhat to the left of their government (the Arias government, at the time the survey was done), putting them in a more moderate position, while Guatemalans aligned themselves more closely but slightly to the right of their government (the Colom government at the time the survey was done). Caution should be taken when comparing these figures between countries or at anything other than an aggregate level because of the highly subjective nature of this particular question, but it appears that judges in both countries view themselves as relatively moderate in ideological terms and not radically divergent from their governments.

Technical Aspects of the Costa Rican Judiciary

Costa Rica's judiciary is organized in a manner that enhances its political independence and attempts to secure the societal autonomy of its judges and magistrates. Nearly all aspects of the justice system are under the supervision and budget of the judiciary, including the prosecutorial and forensic investigation services; most policing (including the Fuerza Pública and the intelligence service) is independent of the judiciary. The constitution guarantees that the judiciary receives a minimum of six percent of the national budget. While the National Assembly complies with this requirement as a matter of course, some within the judiciary complain that it is nonetheless insufficient given the increasing duties, primarily in areas related to investigation, that the Assembly has assigned to the judiciary. In practice, politicians do not tamper with this system of hierarchical control of the judiciary. Judges must complete their training at the judicial school that is a part of the judicial power and their careers from hiring to promotion to discipline are handled by various offices under the supervision of the president of the Supreme Court. While this provides the possibility for a politicized or otherwise dependent supreme court president to wield substantial power in an undesirable fashion, the protections for the independence of supreme court magistrates, who elect their own president, provide a significant shield against that potential problem.

The Costa Rican judiciary is organized into a hierarchy of *juzgados* (trial courts), *tribunales* (appellate panels), and the four *salas* of the Supreme Court. The judiciary has adopted oral proceedings for trials, a principal which was being given "special emphasis" in judicial school training materials as of 2009.[1] The courts at all levels of the judiciary are separated by subject matter. To take

---

[1] Sánchez Fallas, *La tramitación de los procesos penales*, 18.

just the criminal area, the *Anuario Judicial 2010* reports that there were 189,595 cases resolved in 2010, approximately 83 percent of the cases that entered those courts. Of cases resolved, 74.2 percent were dismissed and another 13.2 percent resulted in acquittals. 38,958 cases were still pending at the end of the year, an increase from the beginning of the year, suggesting that most cases are being resolved within a year, but still giving the judicial planning office (*oficina de planificación*) some concern about delays in resolving cases.[2]

Following a trial, a convicted criminal will go to a second-instance hearing in a higher *juzgado* and will be sentenced by a third *juzgado*. Only after those three procedures will most defendants have the opportunity to appeal their cases to an appellate tribunal. In criminal cases, an additional level of review is available: the criminal cassation tribunal. All other (non-criminal) litigants would follow a somewhat less elaborate path through the judiciary, going from a *juzgado* to a tribunal and then, possibly, to a supreme court *sala*. With so many layers of the judicial hierarchy, especially in the criminal area, there are ample opportunities for petty corruption to arise. However, there are also several layers of control which should limit the effects of that corruption. These multiple layers also allow for potentially abusive delays by criminal defendants who might be able to use creative lawyering to exhaust all of their possible remedies and appeals in the hopes of either obtaining the desired acquittal or, at least, delaying the inevitable. Of course, the ability to access creative and persistent lawyers depends substantially on the defendant's ability to pay them.

The Supreme Court is divided into four chambers (*salas*), for administrative law, civil law, criminal law, and constitutional law. Each *sala* has five members, with the exception of the constitutional *sala* with seven, including a chamber president chosen by the members of the chamber from amongst themselves. The Salas are administratively distinct and do not hear cases as a full court, although they are all under the same supreme court president and collectively are assigned the duty of administering the judiciary as a whole. This division of the court can lead to some confusion in the non-Costa Rican press about whether they are one court or several. They are constitutionally one court, but they often function as four separate courts; however, none has authority over the others. Each has its unique jurisdiction and a litigant cannot appeal from one Sala to another. This arrangement does not mean that creative lawyers never try to bring the same underlying facts to more than one *sala*, successively. The case of the La Crucitas mine, discussed in Chapter 3, is one such example

---

[2] Sección de Estadística and Departamento de Planificación, "Anuario Judicial 2010."

of this kind of creative lawyering. The typical case, however, would go to just one of the salas, having passed through the hierarchy of tribunals appropriate to the case. The constitutional chamber is the only one of the four that exercises original jurisdiction within its subject matter as a matter of course; in that sense, it is the only one of the supreme court's salas that is not actually an appellate tribunal.

Technical Aspects of the Guatemalan Judiciary

As one of the five independent state powers,[1] Guatemala's judiciary enjoys formal independence within the constitutional structure. An important part of this independence is the guarantee of three percent of the national budget for the judiciary every year. This automatic funding limits the need for representatives of the judiciary to go begging to the legislature every year while also making it more difficult for the legislature to punish the judiciary for defying the wishes of the legislators. Many judges interviewed, however, felt that the budget was nonetheless inadequate for their institutional needs.[2] The judiciary is granted further independence in that the Supreme Court selects lower-court judges and maintains the discipline of the judicial branch without input from the Congress. As part of its position at the top of the judicial hierarchy, the Supreme Court supervises the legal profession and hears all ordinary and extraordinary appeals, as well as *amparo* complaints against lower government officials. Constitutional conflicts, however, are reserved to the Constitutional Court.[3]

In addition to the Supreme Court, Guatemala has a constitutional court, the existence of which creates the opportunity for additional judicial delay as litigants exploit the overlaps between the two high courts. The Constitutional Court is a specialized tribunal and, as such, does not share in the ordinary jurisdiction or responsibilities of the Supreme Court. Its jurisdiction is limited to extraordinary writs that directly or indirectly affect the constitutional order,

---

[1] The independent state powers are the Judicial Power (headed by the Supreme Court), the Executive Power (headed by the President), the Legislative Power (headed by the Congress), the Electoral Power (headed by the Supreme Electoral Tribunal), and the *Procuraduría* of Human Rights (headed by the Human Rights Ombudsman).

[2] Indeed, Guatemala's guaranteed share is half of its analog in Costa Rica.

[3] "Constitución Política reformada por Acuerdo Legislativo No. 18–93 del 17 de Noviembre de 1993 [Guatemala]," secs. 203–222.

as well as appeals of amparos. On paper, the Constitutional Court does not have jurisdiction over ordinary appeals or cassations.[4] In practice, however, the amparo appeal is often used to try to smuggle non-constitutional issues before the Constitutional Court, or at least to delay the resolution of the underlying case while the Constitutional Court considers the matter. While there have been occasional struggles over authority between the Constitutional Court and the Supreme Court, the Constitutional Court officially has the final word on all constitutional questions. The Constitutional Court is composed of five magistrates and five supplementary magistrates, with a rotating presidency. For each case, a panel of judges is drawn at random by the Secretary of the Court.[5]

While Constitutional Court magistrates are afforded a wide degree of independence once named to the court, they are selected in a manner that assures that they will reflect the dominant political forces within the country. One magistrate and one substitute magistrate each will be chosen every five years by the President, the Congress, the Supreme Court, the College of Attorneys and Notaries (*Colegio de Abogados and Notorios*),[6] and the San Carlos University.[7] In this manner, the dominant political attitudes are likely to be represented on the court. In cases of judicial misconduct, the President has the authority to remove a magistrate before the end of the five-year term.[8] While there is little concrete evidence, various political commentators consistently raise

---

[4] The action of cassation is a final review of a criminal case, which typically concerns only the procedures followed in the trial.

[5] As was discussed in Chapter 5, this random draw can also be penetrated by corruption. Such corrupt influence appeared to contribute to the decision to allow General Ríos Montt to run for president in 2003.

[6] The College of Attorneys and Notaries is a self-regulating professional association similar to the American Bar Association.

[7] San Carlos University, founded in colonial times by the Jesuit order, is the only public university in Guatemala. Its budget and autonomy are constitutionally protected. During the civil war, the university was a major site of protest and student activism, which attracted massive retaliation from the military.

[8] This process is instituted by Art. 269 of the *Constitución Política de la República de Guatemala*. Compare this to the process for supreme court magistrates outlined in Art. 215: the Congress elects by a two-thirds vote all of the Magistrates to five-year terms, drawing from a list of candidates selected by a commission including the rectors of the nation's universities, the deans of the faculties of law and of political and social science, representatives of the Courts of Appeal, and representatives of the College of Lawyers and Notaries. In addition, Art. 217 requires that, in addition to the basic requirement to be a judge, supreme court magistrates must have served at least one year on an appellate court or a "court of equal dignity." The selection process for supreme court magistrates appears designed to produce a cadre of highly qualified and professional magistrates, while the selection process for Constitutional Court magistrates appears to be designed to empower political representatives in the legal realm.

the charge that the magistrates can be bought or that they serve particular masters.[9]

The Constitutional Court hears four types of actions brought by ordinary citizens, in addition to two different mechanisms for abstract review of legislation.[10] With the 1985 constitution, a substantial portion of amparo cases were placed within the jurisdiction of the newly created Constitutional Court, along with all cases of the new constitutional challenge (*acción de inconstitucionalidad*). The actions of amparo and personal exhibition (habeas corpus) had existed under the old legal system, and were generally handled by the Supreme Court. During the war years, these actions were not typically used successfully against the military governments.

The constitutional challenge was created in the 1985 constitution that re-established civilian, democratic rule. The general constitutional challenge is in the exclusive original jurisdiction of the Constitutional Court and access to it is limited.[11] The general constitutional challenge may be brought against any law or regulation (or provisions thereof) on either substantive or procedural grounds, regardless of the date of passage of the law; the Court may suspend all or part of the impugned law.[12] Parties to pending cases may also file a "concrete case" constitutional challenge, which requests review of the applicability of the law in the particular facts of the concrete case in progress.[13] It appears, however, that the average constitutional challenge consumes more of the Court's time and resources than the average amparo, in that a larger panel of magistrates sits on constitutional challenges and the decisions are typically longer and treat

9 "Constitución Política reformada por Acuerdo Legislativo No. 18–93 del 17 de Noviembre de 1993 [Guatemala]," secs. 268–272.

10 These actions are established in the 1985 constitution, and are regulated by the Law of Amparo, Personal Exhibition, and Constitutionality (*Ley de Amparo, Exhibición Personal y de Constitucionalidad*, hereinafter, Amparo Law), which was one of the fundamental laws promulgated by the National Constituent Assembly in the process of establishing the new constitution prior to the seating of the Congress in 1986. This is found in Decreto no. 1–86 of the National Constituent Assembly, as reformed by Acuerdo no. 4–89 of the Constitutional Court, which instituted various complementary regulations.

11 The general constitutional challenge may only be brought by the governing council of the national lawyer's association through its president, by the Public Ministry (prosecutors) through the Procurador General de la Nación, by the Human Rights Ombudsman, or by any citizen with the assistance of three attorneys. (Art. 133–34)

12 (Art. 133, 140) While most challenges are brought very quickly following the promulgation of the law (frequently as a continuation of debates and controversy that accompanied the debates on the law), one case brought in 1997 challenged the validity of the 1859 treaty with Britain setting the boundaries of British Honduras (now Belize). While the case was not successful on the merits, the Court did not dismiss the complaint. *Expediente* 1129–96, gazeta 45.

13 These cases are filed and heard in the court then handling the case in most instances, but then may be appealed subsequently to the Constitutional Court. (Art. 116–32)

the matter in more depth. The Constitutional Court also performs abstract, pre-promulgation review when it is asked to do so by one of the other state organs, or when the legislation in question modifies any of the constitutional laws.[14] These cases form only a small part of the Court's caseload.

While one might imagine that the constitutional challenges would be the more controversial aspects of the Court's caseload, the seemingly minor action of amparo proves to be far more significant. The action of amparo provides a "subsidiary and extraordinary" (i.e., adjunct to other types of review) form of review of government actions that harm or threaten to harm the rights guaranteed by the constitution. The law specifically provides that all issues are reviewable by amparo and that it applies only to government actions, which in practice include a broad range of semi-governmental organizations.[15] The Constitutional Court has exclusive original jurisdiction over those amparos filed against the Supreme Court, the Congress, and the President and Vice President of the Republic.[16] Other cases, depending on the offending entity, may be brought before the Supreme Court, the Courts of Appeals, or the first instance courts (excluding justices of the peace); all appeals of amparos are heard by the Constitutional Court.[17] Amparos may be filed by any person (or juridical person) whose rights are directly affected by the impugned action, or by the Public Ministry (whose responsibilities include, *inter alia*, criminal investigation and prosecution) or the Human Rights Ombudsman.[18] The parties, the Public Ministry, and the Human Rights Ombudsman, are all authorized to appeal an amparo decision.[19]

---

[14] Constitutional laws are given special status in the legal hierarchy, and are all identified in the constitution (though many were written after the constitution). They may be amended more easily than the Constitution, but less easily than ordinary laws. They include a wide variety of organic and fundamental laws, although the two that have involved the most of the Court's time have been the Electoral Law and the Amparo Law. They also include the Organic Law of the San Carlos University (Art. 82), the Civil Service Law (Art. 108), the Public Order and States of Exception Law (Art. 139), the Responsibilities Law governing cabinet members (Art. 201), the Civil Service in the Judicial Branch Law (Art. 210), the Organic Law of the Budget (Art. 238), a constitutive law of the military (Art. 250), The Municipal Service Law (Art. 262), and the Amparo Law (Art. 276).

[15] (Ley de Amparo, Art 8–9)   [16] (Art. 11)

[17] (Art. 12–14, 60)   [18] (Art. 10, 25)   [19] (Art. 63)

Technical Aspects of the Nicaraguan Judiciary

The Nicaraguan constitution establishes that the judiciary implements justice as delegated by the people.[1] As in most constitutions, the independence of the judiciary and their fidelity to only the constitution and the laws is announced, but it is also tied to the principle of equality, among others.[2] In practice, a great deal of power is concentrated in the Supreme Court of Justice and the president thereof. The Supreme Court includes sixteen magistrates, all of whom are appointed as a slate by a vote of sixty percent of the National Assembly every five years.[3] The Supreme Court is further subdivided into four chambers for constitutional law, civil law, criminal law, and administrative law, with each *sala* electing its own president. Each *sala* has six members, including its president, and magistrates sit on more than one *sala*. Additionally, the constitution creates a judicial council that governs the judicial career below the level of the Supreme Court as well as judicial discipline, management of forensic medicine and public defenders, and budgetary matters for the judicial power, among other competencies. The judicial council is headed by the Supreme Court president and its other members include three magistrates of the Supreme Court who do not sit on any of the *salas* but who do participate when the court convenes as a whole.[4] In this fashion, the judicial council is a creature of the Supreme Court and thus appointed essentially by the National Assembly. The judicial power is guaranteed 4 percent of the national budget.[5] Military courts are limited to considering only cases directly related to military matters and their decisions can be appealed to the full body of the Supreme Court, who also appoint the members of those tribunals.[6]

---

[1] *Constitución Política de la República de Nicaragua*, Art. 158.   [2] Art. 166.   [3] Art. 163.
[4] The judicial council is governed by article 165 of the Nicaraguan constitution as well as by the second chapter of the Judicial Career Law (*Ley de Carrera Judicial*).
[5] *Constitción*, Art. 159.   [6] Art. 164.

Nicaragua's lower courts are organized according to specialization into the areas of criminal law, civil law, family law, and labor law, with an additional trial-level court for cases involving adolescents. Many criminal defendants can choose between being tried before a jury or before a "technical judge" (*juez técnico*), although more serious crimes such as narcotrafficking cases and sexual crimes cannot be tried before a jury. Jury verdicts cannot be appealed and do not involve the publication of reasoning, whereas technical judges must publish their findings of fact and their reasoning so that an appeal might be possible. Non-jury trials may occur in a local criminal court (*juzgados locales de lo penal*) if it is a relatively minor crime or in a district criminal court (*judgados distritos de lo penal*) if it is a more serious crime. Decisions of the local courts can be appealed to the district courts, while decisions of the district courts are appealed to the appellate tribunals (*tribunales de apelaciones*). Only limited kinds of local court conflicts are allowed to be appealed to the appellate tribunals. Appellate tribunals also hear many kinds of amparos as well as challenges to the admissibility of evidence. The criminal chamber of the Supreme Court then hears cassation challenges. A settled verdict and sentence would then be implemented and overseen by an executing court (*juzgados distritos penales de ejecución sentencia*).[7]

---

[7] *Ley Orgánica del Poder Judicial de la República de Nicaragua*, Ley N° 260 del 7 julio 1998, La Gaceta N° 137 del 23 julio 1998

Technical Aspects of the Honduran Judiciary

The Supreme Court of Justice is composed of fifteen magistrates, who serve for seven years and can be reelected. These magistrates are named as a slate by two-thirds of the National Congress from a list containing at least three times the number of candidates as there are seats, which is to have been compiled by a nominating body (*Junta Nominadora*). The nominating body includes seven members: a representative of the supreme court, a representative of the bar association, the human rights ombudsman, a representative of private business (through the Consejo Hondureño de la Empresa Privada), a representative of the law professors, a representative of the civil society, and a representative of the worker's confederations (*las Confederaciones de Trabajadores*).[1] The Supreme Court president is elected by two-thirds of the magistrates, but must be approved by the National Congress, reserving some influence over the judiciary for the National Congress.[2] The Supreme Court operates in four chambers (*salas*) for civil law, criminal law, constitutional law, and labor and administrative law, although the constitution addresses only the constitutional chamber.[3] The constitutional chamber has jurisdiction to hear habeas corpus petitions, amparos, and constitutional challenges, as well as to resolve conflicts between powers of the state.[4] The constitutional chamber has five members, while the other three chambers have only three members each. The judiciary is guaranteed no less than 3 percent of the national budget.[5]

Administration of the judicial career has been in flux in Honduras since 2011. Prior to 2011, the judicial career law (*Ley de la Carrera Judicial*) was in force. According to that law, there was a council of the judicial career,

---

[1] *Constitución Política de la República de Honduras de 1982*, Actualizada hasta el Decreto 36 del 4 de Mayo de 2005, Art. 311.
[2] Art. 315.   [3] Art. 316.
[4] Ibid. This provision explicitly includes resolution of conflicts affecting the Electoral Tribunal.
[5] Art. 318.

which served the supreme court president in his administration of the judicial career. However, the new judicial council authorized in 2011 removed control of the judicial career from the supreme court president, along with budgetary control. However, as discussed in Chapter 6, the constitutional chamber of the Supreme Court invalidated the law that created that new judicial council in March 2016, returning control over those matters to the Supreme Court itself.

Criminal cases in Honduras have a somewhat clearer path than do those in Nicaragua or El Salvador. Justices of the Peace (*Juzgados de Paz*) provide justice in smaller communities in Honduras, in which they must reside. They are not required to be attorneys.[6] Justices of the peace adjudicate small crimes.[7] Trial judges (*Juzgados de Letras*) are required to be attorneys and try both minor and serious crimes, also hearing appeals of cases from Justices of the Peace.[8] The Appellate Courts (*Cortes de Apelaciones*) hear appeals of cases from the trial judges, as well as any complaints regarding the conduct of those trial judges.[9] The criminal chamber of the Supreme Court then hears cassation claims. Finally, an execution court (*juzgado de ejecución*) will implement the sentence or punishment.

[6] *Ley de Organización y Atribuciones de los Tribunales*, Decreto no. 76, Art. 18.
[7] Ibid., Art. 26.   [8] Ibid., Art. 40.   [9] Ibid., Art. 55.

Technical Aspects of the Salvadoran Judiciary

El Salvador's judiciary is organized in a manner that concentrates power in the Supreme Court and especially in the President of the Supreme Court. The judiciary is guaranteed a 6 percent share of the national budget.[1] Supreme court magistrates are appointed for nine-year terms in thirds every three years by a two-thirds majority of the Legislative Assembly, from a list of candidates proposed by the judicial council. The Supreme Court is broken into four chambers (*salas*). The constitutional chamber has five magistrates and their president is also the President of the Supreme Court. The administrative chamber has four magistrates, while the criminal and civil chambers have three members each. The constitutional chamber has exclusive jurisdiction over constitutional challenges to laws, amparos, habeas corpus petitions, and conflicts between the executive and the legislative branches.[2] The other chambers have final appellate jurisdiction in their respective competencies. The courts of second instance in the capital also have original jurisdiction over complaints brought against the State within their competence; these can then be appealed to the relevant chamber of the Supreme Court.[3] The judiciary as a whole and the judges who comprise it are guaranteed their independence, including a statement that the law should guarantee to judges protections such that they can operate without influences; the same article to ensure a "just remuneration" so that they can live an "adequate" life befitting their responsibilities.[4]

The judicial career is specified in the constitution as well: all judges below the Supreme Court are named by the Supreme Court from candidates

[1] Constitución de la República de El Salvador, 1983, as amended 2003, art. 172.
[2] Art. 183   [3] Art. 184   [4] Art. 186.

proposed by the judicial council.⁵ All judges, magistrates, and justices of the peace are to be secure in their positions unless removed for cause.⁶ The duties and structure of the judicial council are laid out primarily in the 1999 Law of the National Council of the Judiciary.⁷ The judicial council includes seven members: three representatives of the organized bar; one law professor from the University of El Salvador; one law professor from the private law schools; one lawyer representing the Prosecutor's Office (Ministerio Público); and one member elected by the second-instance magistrates, the first-instance judges, and the justices of the peace.⁸ While the judicial council is thus a body that represents all of the legal community except for the Supreme Court, its recommendations for judicial appointments are made to the Supreme Court for their final approval. The results of performance reviews are similarly forwarded to the Supreme Court for action after being produced by the judicial council.⁹ The judicial council has considerably more independence, however, in operating the judicial training school.¹⁰ The hand of the Supreme Court can be seen over the judicial council even in its governing law, parts of which were invalidated by the constitutional chamber in 1999, including the provision that would have drawn the judicial council's budget out of the judiciary's share of the national budget.

Similar to Costa Rica's system, El Salvador's criminal court structure sends those accused of more significant crime through a number of courts. Minor crimes may be tried in a Justice of the Peace Court (*Juzgado de Paz*) and all crimes will have their preliminary hearing there, but more serious criminal cases will typically be forwarded to an Instruction Judge (*Juez de Instrucción*) for an investigative phase and then will go before a Jury Tribunal (*Tribunal del Jurado*). All crimes will be sent to a Sentencing Tribunal (*Tribunal de Sentencia*), although the most serious crimes will also have their public trial before the Sentencing Tribunal. As in Guatemala, it is possible for a private or accessory prosecutor (*querrellante adhesivo*) to participate in a criminal proceeding in El Salvador. All cases can then be appealed to a Second-Instance Chamber with criminal competency (*Cámara de Instancia Segunda*). Certain kinds of appeals, including cassation claims, can then be brought to the

---

⁵ Art. 182, sec. 9. The Supreme Court also has the power to name other justice sector officials, including the Forensic Medicine department.

⁶ Art. 186.

⁷ *Ley del Consejo Nacional de la Judicatura*, Decreto no. 536.

⁸ *Ley del Consejo Nacional de la Judicatura*, art. 9.

⁹ *Ley del Consejo Nacional de la Judicatura*, art. 22(h).

¹⁰ *Ley del Consejo Nacional de la Judicatura*, art. 22(e).

Criminal Chamber (*Sala de lo Penal*) of the Supreme Court, and cassations can subsequently be appealed to the full Supreme Court.[11] Finally, there are also separate Execution Courts (*Juzgados de Vigilancia Penitenciaria y de Ejecución de la Pena*) that oversee the application of the sentence or punishment.

[11] *Codigo Procesal Penal*, Decreto no. 733.

Works Cited

"A Glimmer of Hope in Central America." *Wilson Center*, February 24, 2016. www .wilsoncenter.org/article/glimmer-hope-central-america.

Ajenjo Fresno, Natalia. "Honduras: Nuevo Gobierno Liberal Con La Misma Agenda Política." *Revista Ciencia Política* 27, no. Esp. (2007): 165–81.

Alianza por la Justicia. *Poder Judicial, Ministerio Público y Estado de Derecho: Una Propuesta Ciudadana para los Procesos de Elección de los Magistrados a la Corte Suprema de Justicia, Fiscal General, y Fiscal General Adjunto*. Tegucigalpa, Honduras: FOPRIDEH, 2008.

"Amenazas a muerte contra 22 jueces de Honduras." *El Heraldo*. April 5, 2010, sec. Sucesos. http://archivo.elheraldo.hn/content/view/full/384769.

Amnesty International. "Annual Report 2012: El Salvador." Accessed December 29, 2012. www.amnesty.org/en/region/el-salvador/report-2012.

"Annual Report 2012: Guatemala." Accessed December 29, 2012. www.amnesty.org/ en/region/guatemala/report-2012.

"Document – Honduras: Independence of the Judicial System Is Seriously Undermined as the Dismissal of Justice Officials Is Confirmed | Amnesty International," June 2, 2010. www.amnesty.org/en/documents/amr37/010/2010/en/.

"Nicaragua Human Rights." Accessed July 12, 2013. www.amnestyusa.org/our-work/ countries/americas/nicaragua.

Ansolabehere, Karina. "More Power, More Rights?: The Supreme Court and Society in Mexico." In *Cultures of Legality: Judicialization and Political Activism in Latin America*, edited by Javier A. Couso, Alexandra Huneeus, and Rachel Sieder, 78–111. Cambridge Studies in Law and Society. New York, NY: Cambridge University Press, 2010.

Arguedas C., Carlos, and Hulda Miranda. "Exministro Roberto Dobles condenado por firmar decreto minero ilegal." *La Nación*. de enero de 2015, sec. Sucesos. www.nacion.com/sucesos/juicios/Exministro-condenado-firmar-decreto-ilegal_0_1466453376.html.

Arjomand, Said Amir. "Law, Political Reconstruction and Constitutional Politics." *International Sociology* 18, no. 1 (2003): 7–32.

Ávalos, Jessica. "CSJ Acumula 1,085 de Denuncias Contra Jueces." *La Prensa Grafica*. August 31, 2012. www.laprensagrafica.com/el-salvador/judicial/280431-csj-acumula-1085-denuncias-contra-jueces.

Baar, Carl. "Judicial Activism in Canada." In *Judicial Activism in Comparative Perspective*, edited by Kenneth M. Holland, 53–69. New York, NY: St. Martin's Press, 1991.

Baca, Lucydalia, and Lucia Navas. "Nicaragua entre países más corruptos del continente." *La Prensa*. October 27, 2010, sec. Política.

Barker, Robert S. *Constitutional Adjudication: The Costa Rican Experience*. Lake Mary, FL: Vandeplas Publishing, 2008.

Barros, Robert. "Courts Out of Context: Authoritarian Sources of Judicial Failure in Chile (1973–1990) and Argentina (1976–1983)." In *Rule by Law: The Politics of Courts in Authoritarian Regimes*, edited by Tom Ginsburg and Tamir Moustafa, 156–79. Cambridge, UK: Cambridge University Press, 2008.

Baum, Lawrence. *Judges and Their Audiences: A Perspective on Judicial Behavior.* Princeton, NJ: Princeton University Press, 2006.

Bickel, Alexander M. *The Least Dangerous Branch: The Supreme Court at the Bar of Politics*. Indianapolis: Bobbs-Merril, 1962.

Bird, Shawn L., and Philip J. Williams. "El Salvador: Revolt and Negotiated Transition." In *Repression, Resistance, and Democratic Transition in Central America*, edited by Walker, Thomas W. and Ariel G. Armony, 25–46. Wilmington, DE: SR Books, 2000.

Booth, John A. "Costa Rica: Buffeted Democracy." In *Repression, Resistance, and Democratic Transition in Central America*, edited by Walker, Thomas W. and Ariel G. Armony, 89–110. Wilmington, DE: SR Books, 2000.

Costa Rica: Quest for Democracy. Boulder, CO: Westiew Press, 1998.

Political Culture of Democracy in Nicaragua and in the Americas, 2012: Towards Equality of Opportunity. Managua, Nicaragua: U.S. Agency for International Development, 2013. www.vanderbilt.edu/lapop/ab2012.php#Nicaragua.

Bottorff, Andrea. "JURIST – Paper Chase: Spain High Court Acquits Judge Garzon in Abuse of Power Case." Accessed May 6, 2012. http://jurist.org/paperchase/2012/02/spain-high-court-acquits-judge-garzon-in-abuse-of-power-case.php.

Bowen, Rachel E. "International Imposition and Transmission of Democracy and the Rule of Law: Lessons from Central America." In *Globalazing Justice: Critical Perspectives on Transnational Law and the Cross-Border Migration of Legal Norms*, edited by Donald W. Jackson, Michael C. Tolley, and Mary L. Volcansek, 161–78. Albany, NY: State University of New York Press, 2010.

Brands, Hal. *Crime, Violence, and the Crisis in Guatemala: A Case Study in the Erosion of the State*. Carlisle, PA: U.S. Army War College, 2010.

Brinks, Daniel M. "'Faithful Servants of the Regime': The Brazilian Constitutional Court's Role under the 1988 Constitution." In *Courts in Latin America*, edited by Gretchen Helmke and Julio Ríos Figueroa, 128–53. Cambridge, UK: Cambridge University Press, 2011.

The Judicial Response to Police Killings in Latin America: Inequality and the Rule of Law. Cambridge, UK: Cambridge University Press, 2008.

Brinks, Daniel M., and Varun Gauri. "A New Policy Landscape: Legalizing Social and Economic Rights in the Developing World." In *Courting Social Justice: Judicial Enforcement of Social and Economic Rights in the Developing World*, edited by Varun Gauri and Daniel M. Brinks, 303–52. New York, NY: Cambridge University Press, 2008.

Briones Loasiga, William. "Calculan en US$250 millones fortuna de Arnoldo Alemán." *La Prensa*. May 14, 2001, sec. Politica. www.laprensa.com.ni/2001/05/14/politica/ 800926-calculan-en-us250-millones-fortuna-de-arnoldo-alemn.

Brockett, Charles D. *Political Movements and Violence in Central America*. Cambridge Studies in Contentious Politics. Cambridge, UK, and New York, NY: Cambridge University Press, 2005.

Bunck, Julie Marie, and Michael Ross Fowler. *Bribes, Bullets, and Intimidation: Drug Trafficking and the Law in Central America*. University Park, PA: Penn State University Press, 2012. http://muse.jhu.edu/.

Bureau of Democracy, Human Rights, and Labor, United States Department of State. "Country Reports on Human Rights Practices for 2011: Costa Rica." Accessed August 18, 2013. www.state.gov/j/drl/rls/hrrpt/2011humanrightsreport/index.htm? dlid=186503#wrapper.

"Country Reports on Human Rights Practices for 2011: El Salvador," n.d. www.state .gov/j/drl/rls/hrrpt/humanrightsreport/index.htm?dlid=186513.

Call, Charles T., ed. *Constructing Justice and Security After War*. Washington, DC: United States Institute of Peace, 2007.

"Democratisation, War and State-Building: Constructing the Rule of Law in El Salvador." *Journal of Latin American Studies* 35, no. 4 (November 2003): 827–62.

"War Transitions and the New Civilian Security in Latin America." *Comparative Politics* 35, no. 1 (October 2002): 1–20.

Calleros, Juan Carlos. *The Unfinished Transition to Democracy in Latin America*. New York, NY, and London, UK: Routledge, 2009.

Campbell, Maia Sophia. "The Right of Indigenous People to Political Participation and the Case of Yatama v. Nicaragua." *Arizona Journal of International and Comparative Law* 24, no. 2 (2007): 499–540.

"Canadian Gold Company Threatens Costa Rica with $1bn Lawsuit | MIN-ING.com." Accessed June 10, 2013. www.mining.com/canadian-gold-company-threatens-costa-rica-with-1bn-lawsuit-60920/.

Canales Ewest, Gisella. "A 20 años de La Piñata." *La Prensa*. April 24, 2010, sec. Nacionales.

Carothers, Thomas. *Promoting the Rule of Law Abroad: In Search of Knowledge*. Washington, DC: Carnegie Endowment for International Peace, 2006.

"The End of the Transition Paradigm." *Journal of Democracy* 13, no. 1 (2002): 5–21.

"The Rule of Law Revival." *Foreign Affairs* 77 (1998): 95–106.

Case of the Massacres of El Mozote and nearby places v. El Salvador, No. 252 Series C (Inter-American Court of Human Rights 2012).

Caso de Edgardo Picado Araya y otros, (Sala Constitucional – Corte Suprema de Justicia de Costa Rica 2003).

Caso López Lone y otros vs. Honduras, (Corte Interamericana de Derechos Humanos 2015).

Casos de Edgardo Picado Araya y Jorge Méndez Zamora, (Sala Constitucional – Corte Suprema de Justicia de Costa Rica 2000).

Cawley, Marguerite. "Key Witness in El Salvador Case Says He Bribed Judges." *In Sight Crime: Organized Crime in the Americas*, May 8, 2013. www.insightcrime .org/news-briefs/key-witness-in-el-salvador-drug-trafficking-case-bribed-judges.

CEJIL. "CEJIL Urge Al Presidente Funes a Sancionar La Derogación Del Decreto 743." Accessed September 11, 2013. https://cejil.org/es/cejil-urge-al-presidente-funes-sancionar-derogacion-del-decreto-743.

Centro Nicaragüense de Derechos Humanos. "Derechos Humanos en Nicaragua 2013." Managua, Nicaragua: CENIDH, 2013. www.cenidh.org/recursos/33/.

"Policía Impide a Diversidad Sexual Celebrar El Día Internacional Del Orgullo Gay." Accessed July 12, 2013. www.cenidh.org/noticias/458/.

Chamberlain, Anthony B. *Privatization in Costa Rica: A Multi-Dimensional Analysis.* Lanham, MD: University Press of America, 2007.

Chu, Juo-Juo. "Global Constitutionalism and Judicial Activism in Taiwan." *Journal of Contemporary Asia* 38, no. 4 (2008): 515–34.

"'Cicig En Honduras Y Salvador Sería Inteligente': Shannon." *Diario La Prensa.* Accessed July 26, 2016. www.laprensa.hn/mundo/857088-410/cicig-en-honduras-y-salvador-ser%C3%ADa-inteligente-shannon.

Clayton, Cornell W. "The Supply and Demand Side of Judicial Policy-Making (Or, Why Be So Positive about Judicialization of Politics?)." *Law and Contemporary Problems* 65, no. 3 (2002): 69–85.

Close, David. "From Guerrillas to Government to Opposition and Back to Government: The Sandinistas since 1979." In *From Revolutionary Movements to Political Parties: Cases from Latin America and Africa*, edited by Kalowatie Deonandan, David Close, and Gary Prevost, 17–42. New York, NY: Palgrave Macmillan, 2007.

Nicaragua: The Chamorro Years. Boulder, Colo.: Lynne Rienner Publishers, 1999.

Close, David, and Kalowatie Deonandan. *Undoing Democracy: The Politics of Electoral Caudillismo.* Lanham, MD: Lexington Books, 2004.

COIMER & OP. "Estudio de Opinión Pública: Nivel Nacional." Consultores en Investigación en Mercados & Opinión Pública, 2009.

Collins, Cath. *Post-Transitional Justice: Human Rights Trials in Chile and El Salvador.* University Park, PA: The Pennsylvania State University Press, 2010.

Comision del la verdad para El Salvador. "From Madness to Hope: The 12-Year War in El Salvador." United Nations, April 1, 1993. www.derechos.org/nizkor/salvador/informes/truth.html.

Comisión para el Esclarecimiento Histórico (Guatemala). *Guatemala, Memoria Del Silencio: Informe.* 1. Guatemala: CEH, 1999.

Committee of Experts on the Follow-Up on the Implementation of the Inter-American Convention Against Corruption. "Republic of Honduras: Final Report." Organization of American States, March 22, 2013.

Consejo Nacional de la Judicatura. "INICIO," 2012. www.cnj.gob.sv/Transparencia/.

"Quienes Somos," April 4, 2008. www.cnj.gob.sv/index.php?option=com_content&view=article&id=56&Itemid=38.

"Reseña Histórica," April 4, 2008. www.cnj.gob.sv/index.php?option=com_content&view=article&id=55&Itemid=43.

"Constitución de la Republica de El Salvador," 1983.

"Constitución Política de Honduras," 1982.

"Constitución Política de la República de Nicaragua," February 2007.

Cordero, Luis Alberto, Ruben Hernandez Valle, Carla Morales, and Daniel Zovatto. *Cultura de la constitución en Costa Rica.* Doctrina Jurídica 468. Mexico:

Universidad Nacional Autonoma de Mexico, Fundacion Arias Para la Paz, Institution Internacional para la Democracia y la Asistencia Internacional, 2009.
"Court Shuts down Crucitas Gold Mine Citing Environmental Harm | AIDA." Accessed June 10, 2013. www.aida-americas.org/en/project/crucitasshutdown.
Couso, Javier A. "Judicial Independence in Latin America: The Lessons of History in the Search for an Always Elusive Ideal." In *Institutions & Public Law: Comparative Approaches*, edited by Tom Ginsburg and Robert A. Kagan, 203–24. New York, NY: Peter Lang, 2005.
"The Judicialization of Chilean Politics: The Rights Revolution That Never Was." In *The Judicialization of Politics in Latin America*, edited by Seider, Rachel, Line Schjolden and Alan Angell, 105–29. New York, NY: Palgrave Macmillan, 2005.
"The Politics of Judicial Review in Chile in an Era of Democratic Trasition, 1990–2002." In *Democratization and the Judiciary: The Accountability Function of Courts in New Democracies*, edited by Gloppen, Siri, Roberto Gargarella and Elin Skaar, 70–91. London, UK: Frank Cass, 2004.
Cruz, Eduardo. "El 'padrino' de la justicia." *La Prensa*. May 13, 2012, sec. Portada.
"Justicia de Ortega vuelve con chantajes a Alemán." *La Prensa*. June 24, 2010, sec. Nacionales.
Custodio, Ramon. "The Human Rights Crisis in Honduras." In *Honduras Confronts Its Future: Contending Perspectives on Critical Issues*, 65–72. Boulder, CO: Lynne Rienner Publishers, 1986.
Dakolias, Maria. "A Strategy for Judicial Reform: The Experience in Latin America." *Virginia Journal of International Law* 36, no. 1 (1995): 167–231.
Diamond, Larry. *Developing Democracy: Toward Consolidation*. Baltimore, MD: The Johns Hopkins University Press, 1999.
Díaz Rivillas, Borja, and Sebastián Linares Lejarraga. "Fortalecimiento de La Independencia Judicial En Centroamérica: Un Balance Tras Veinte Años de Reformas." *América Latina Hoy* 39 (2005): 47–96.
Domingo, Pilar. "Judicial Independence: The Politics of the Supreme Court of Mexico." *Journal of Latin American Studies* 32, no. 3 (2000): 705–35.
"Judicialization of Politics or Politicization of the Judiciary? Recent Trends in Latin America." *Democratization* 11, no. 1 (2004): 104–26.
"Judicialization of Politics: The Changing Political Role of the Judiciary in Mexico." In *The Judicialization of Politics in Latin America*, edited by Rachel Sieder, Line Schjolden, and Alan Angell, 21–46. New York, NY: Palgrave MacMillan, 2005.
Domingo, Pilar, and Rachel Sieder. *Rule of Law in Latin America: The International Promotion of Judicial Reform*. London, UK: Institute of Latin American Studies, 2001.
D'Souza, Radha. "The 'Third World' and Socio-Legal Studies: Neo-Liberalism and Lessons from India's Legal Innovations." *Social & Legal Studies* 14, no. 4 (2005): 487–513.
Dugard, Jackie. "Judging the Judges: Towards an Appropriate Role for the Judiciary in South Africa's Transformation." *Leiden Journal of International Law* 20, no. 4 (2007): 965–81.
"El Salvador's Gangs: The Year of Living Less Dangerously." *The Economist*, March 9, 2013. www.economist.com/news/americas/21573109-unusual-armistice-has-lasted-longer-many-predicted-year-living-less-dangerously.

Epp, Charles. *The Rights Revolution: Lawyers, Activists, and Supreme Courts in Comparative Perspective.* Chicago, IL: University of Chicago Press, 1998.

Epstein, Lee, and Jack Knight. *The Choices Justices Make.* Washington, DC: CQ Press, 1997.

Epstein, Lee, Jack Knight, and Olga Shvetsova. "The Role of Constitutional Courts in the Establishment and Maintenance of Democratic Systems of Government." *Law & Society Review* 35, no. 1 (2001): 117–63.

Erdos, David. "Postmaterialist Social Constituencies and Political Triggers: Explaining Bill of Right Genesis in Internally Stable, Advanced Democracies." *Political Research Quarterly* 62, no. 4 (2009): 798–810.

Ewick, Patricia, and Susan S. Silbey. *The Common Place of Law: Stories from Everyday Life.* Language and Legal Discourse. Chicago, IL: University of Chicago Press, 1998.

Feeley, Malcolm M. *The Process Is the Punishment: Handling Cases in a Lower Criminal Court.* Paperback. New York, NY: Russell Sage Foundation, 1992.

Ferejohn, John. "Judicializing Politics, Politicizing Law." *Law and Contemporary Problems* 65, no. 3 (2002): 41–68.

Finkel, Jodi. *Judicial Reform as Political Insurance: Argentina, Peru, and Mexico in the 1990s.* Notre Dame, IN: University of Norte Dame Press, 2008.

"Judicial Reform in Argentina in the 1990s: How Electoral Initiatives Shape Institutional Change." *Latin American Research Review* 39, no. 3 (2004): 56–80.

Frühling, Pierre. "Maras and Youth Gangs, Community and Police in Central America." Swedish International Development Agency, 2008. www.Sida.se/publications.

Fukuyama, Francis. *The End of History and the Last Man.* New York, NY: Avon Books, 1992.

Fundación para el Debido Proceso Legal. *Controles y Descontroles de la Corrupción Judicial: Evaluación de la corrupción judicial y del los mecanismos para controlarla in Centroámerica y Panamá.* Washington, DC: Due Process of Law Foundation, 2007.

FUNDE. "SolucionES." Accessed September 11, 2013. www.funde.org/categories/soluciones.

Garoupa, Nuno, and Tom Ginsburg. *Judicial Reputation: A Comparative Theory.* Chicago, IL: University of Chicago Press, 2015.

George, Alexander L., and Andrew Bennett. *Case Studies and Theory Development in the Social Sciences.* BCSIA Studies in International Security. Cambridge, MA: Harvard University Press, 2005.

Ginsburg, Tom. *Judicial Review in New Democracies: Constitutional Courts in Asian Cases.* Cambridge, UK, and New York, NY: Cambridge University Press, 2003.

Ginsburg, Tom, and Tamir Moustafa. *Rule by Law: The Politics of Courts in Authoritarian Regimes.* Cambridge, UK: Cambridge University Press, 2008.

Girod, Desha M., Stephen D. Krasner, and Kathryn Stoner-Weiss. "Governance and Foreign Assistance: The Imperfect Translation of Ideas into Outcomes." In *Promoting Democracy and the Rule of Law: American and European Strategies,* edited by Magen, Amichai, Thomas Risse and Michael A. McFaul, 61–92. Governance and Limited Statehood. New York, NY: Palgrave MacMillan, 2009.

Gomez, Joyce. "Banana Industry Is the Principal Debtor of the Former Anglo Bank | Costa Rica News." Accessed June 23, 2013. www.costaricanewssite.com/banana-industry-is-the-principal-debtor-of-the-former-anglo-bank/.

Grann, David. "A Murder Foretold: Unravelling the Ultimate Political Conspiracy." *The New Yorker*, April 4, 2011. www.newyorker.com/reporting/2011/04/04/110404fa_fact_grann?currentPage=all.

Halpern, Stephen C., and Charles M. Lamb. *Supreme Court Activism and Restraint*. Lexington, MA: D.C. Heath and Company, 1982.

Hammergren, Linn A. *Envisioning Reform: Improving Judicial Performance in Latin America*. University Park, PA: The Pennsylvania State University Press, 2007.

The Politics of Justice and Justice Reform in Latin America: The Peruvian Case in Comparative Perspective. Boulder, CO: Westview Press, 1998.

"Twenty-Five Years of Latin American Judicial Reforms: Achievements, Disappointments, and Emerging Issues." *Whitehead Journal of Diplomacy and International Relations* 9 (Winter/Spring 2008): 89–104.

Helmke, Gretchen. "Checks and Balances By Other Means: Strategic Defection and Argentina's Supreme Court in the 1990s." *Comparative Politics* 35, no. 2 (2002): 213–30.

Courts under Constraints: Judges, Generals, and Presidents in Argentina. Cambridge Studies in Comparative Politics. New York, NY: Cambridge University Press, 2005.

"The Logic of Strategic Defection: Court-Executive Relations in Argentina Under Dictatorship and Democracy." *American Political Science Review* 96, no. 2 (2002): 291–303.

Hendrix, Steven. "Innovation in Criminal Procedure in Latin America: Guatemala's Conversion to the Adversarial System." *Southwestern Journal of Law and Trade in the Americas* 5, no. 2 (1998): 365–420.

Hernandez Pico, Juan. "La Revelación Parcial de Los Poderes Ocultos." *Política Y Sociedad*, no. 41 (2003): 9–24.

Herrera Cáceres, H. Roberto. *Análisis sobre los principios avances, obstáculos y desafíos que el poder judicial presenta en la lucha contra la corrupción en Honduras*. Tegucigalpa, Honduras: Consejo Nacional Anticorrupción, 2007.

Herron, Erik S., and Kirk A. Randazzo. "The Relationship Between Independence and Judicial Review in Post-Communist Courts." *Journal of Politics* 65, no. 2 (2003): 422–38.

Hilbink, Lisa. "Agents of Anti-Politics: Courts in Pinochet's Chile." In *Rule by Law: The Politics of Court in Authoritarian Regimes*, edited by Tom Ginsburg and Tamir Moustafa, 102–31. Cambridge, UK: Cambridge University Press, 2008.

Judges Beyond Politics in Democracy and Dictatorship: Lessons from Chile. Cambridge Studies in Law and Society. Cambridge, UK: Cambridge University Press, 2007.

"The Constituted Nature of Constituents' Interest: Historical and Ideational Factors in Judicial Empowerment." *Political Research Quarterly* 62, no. 4 (2009): 781–97.

Hirschl, Ran. "The Political Origins of Judicial Empowerment Through Constitutionalization: Lessons from Four Constitutional Revolutions." *Law and Social Inquiry* 25, no. 1 (2000): 91–147.

"The Realist Turn in Comparative Constitutional Politics." *Political Research Quarterly* 62, no. 4 (2009): 825–33.

Towards Juristocracy: The Origins and Consequences of the New Constitutionalism. Cambridge, MA: Harvard University Press, 2004.

"Historia | ACOJUD.org." Accessed June 12, 2013. www.acojud.org/historia/.

Hofnung, Menachem. "The Unintended Consequences of Unplanned Constitutional Reform: Constitutional Politics in Israel." *American Journal of Comparative Law* 44 (1996): 585–604.

"Honduras: Corte Suprema Rechaza Reponer Exmagistrados." *La Prensa.* February 18, 2013, sec. Honduras. www.laprensa.hn/Secciones-Principales/Honduras/Tegucigalpa/Honduras-Corte-Suprema-rechaza-reponer-exmagistrados#.UfAN721N-aM.

Hoque, Ridwanul. "Taking Justice Seriously: Judicial Public Interest and Constitutional Activism in Bangladesh." *Contemporary South Asia* 15, no. 4 (2006): 399–422.

"Hotel Punta Teonoste." Accessed July 15, 2013. www.puntateonoste.com/en.

Human Rights Watch. "Nicaragua." Accessed July 12, 2013. www.hrw.org/americas/nicaragua.

"World Report 2012: Guatemala." Accessed December 29, 2012. www.hrw.org/world-report-2012/guatemala.

"World Report 2012: Honduras." Accessed December 30, 2012. www.hrw.org/world-report-2012/world-report-chapter-honduras.

Huneeas, Alexandra, Javier A. Couso, and Rachel Sieder. "Cultures of Legality: Judicialization and Political Activism in Contemporary Latin America." In *Cultures of Legality: Judicialization and Political Activism in Latin America,* 3–21. Cambridge Studies in Law and Society. Cambridge, UK, and New York, NY: Cambridge University Press, 2010.

Huntington, Samuel. *The Third Wave: Democratization in the Late Twentieth Century.* Julian J. Rothbaum Distinguished Lecture Series. Norman, OK: University of Oklahoma Press, 1993.

"In View of Situation in Honduras, IACHR Stresses Importance of Principle of Independence of the Judiciary," January 3, 2012. www.oas.org/en/iachr/media_center/PReleases/2013/003.asp.

Inclán Oseguera, Silvia. "Judicial Reform in Mexico: Political Insurance or the Search for Political Legitimacy?" *Political Research Quarterly* 62, no. 4 (2009): 753–66.

Instituto Interamericano de Derechos Humanos. *Acceso a la justicia y derechos humanos en Nicaragua: Módulo autoformativo.* San Jose, Costa Rica: Instituto Interamericano de Derechose Humanos, 2009.

Inter-American Dialogue. "Security and Human Rights in Honduras." Accessed July 26, 2013. http://centralamericasecurity.thedialogue.org/events/security-and-human-rights-in-honduras.

International IDEA. "Voter Turnout Data for El Salvador (Parliamentary, Presidential)," October 5, 2011. www.oldsite.idea.int/vt/countryview.cfm?id=209.

Jackson, Vicki C., and Mark V. Tushnet. *Comparative Constitutional Law.* Foundation Press, 1999.

Jonas, Susanne. "Electoral Problems and the Democratic Project in Guatemala." In *Elections and Democracy in Central America, Revisited,* edited by Seligson,

Mitchell A. and John A. Booth. Chapel Hill, NC: University of North Carolina Press, 1995.

Jonas, Susanne, and Thomas W. Walker. "Guatemala: Intervention, Repression, Revolt, and Negotiated Transition." In *Repression, Resistance, and Democratic Transition in Central America*, edited by Walker, Thomas W. and Ariel G. Armony, 3–24. Wilmington, DE: SR Books, 2000.

Jubb, Nadine. *Regional Mapping Study of Women's Police Stations in Latin America*. Quito, Ecuador: CEPLAES, 2008.

Juhn, Tricia. *Negotiating Peace in El Salvador: Civil-Military Relations and the Conspiracy to End the War*. International Political Economy Series. New York, NY: St. Martin's Press, 1998.

Kapiszewski, Diana. *High Courts and Economic Governance in Argentina and Brazil*. New York, NY: Cambridge University Press, 2012.

"How Courts Work: Institutions, Culture, and the Brazilian Supremo Tribunal Federal." In *Cultures of Legality: Judicialization and Political Activism in Latin America*, edited by Javier A. Couso, Alexandra Huneeas, and Rachel Seider, 51–77. Cambridge Studies in Law and Society. New York, NY: Cambridge University Press, 2010.

Kapiszewski, Diana, Gordon Silverstein, and Robert A. Kagan. "Introduction." In *Consequential Courts: Judicial Roles in Global Perspectives*, edited by Diana Kapiszewski, Gordon Silverstein, and Robert A. Kagan, 1–41. Comparative Constitutional Law and Policy. New York, NY: Cambridge University Press, 2013.

Keck, Thomas M. "Activism and Restraint on the Rehnquist Court: Timing, Sequence, and Conjuncture in Constitutional Development." *Polity* 35, no. 1 (2002): 121–68.

Keller, Helen, and Alec Stone Sweet. *A Europe of Rights: The Impact of the ECHR on National Legal Systems*. Oxford; New York: Oxford University Press, 2008.

Kenny, Meryl. "Gender, Institutions and Power: A Critical Review." *Politics* 27, no. 2 (2007): 91–100.

Kmiec, Keenan D. "The Origin and Current Meanings of 'Judicial Activism.'" *California Law Review* 92, no. 5 (2004): 1441–77.

Knott, Tracy. "El Salvador Investigating 80% of Country's Judges." *In Sight Crime: Organized Crime in the Americas*, August 31, 2012. www.insightcrime.org/news-briefs/el-salvador-fight-judicial-impunity.

Lakhani, Nina. "Spanish Trial of Soldiers Who Killed Priests Raises Hopes of Ending Impunity in El Salvador." *The Guardian*, April 8, 2016, sec. World news. www.theguardian.com/world/2016/apr/08/spanish-trial-of-soldiers-behind-uca-atrocity-raises-hopes-of-ending-impunity-in-el-salvador.

Landes, William M., and Richard A. Posner. "The Independent Judiciary in an Interest-Group Perspective." *Journal of Law and Economics* 18, no. 3 (1975): 875–901.

Láscarez S., Carlos. "Proyecto Crucitas tuvo un viacrucis de 10 años." *La Nación*. de enero de 2015, sec. Sucesos. www.nacion.com/sucesos/juicios/Proyecto-Crucitas-via-crucis-anos_0_1466453373.html.

Lehoucq, Fabrice E. "Costa Rica: Paradise in Doubt." *Journal of Democracy* 16, no. 3 (July 2005): 140–54.

"Political Competition, Constitutional Arrangements, and the Quality of Public Policies in Costa Rica." *Latin American Politics and Society* 52, no. 4 (2010): 53–77.

Linz, Juan J., and Alfred Stepan. *Problems of Democratic Transition and Consolidation: Southern Europe, South America, and Post-Communist Europe.* Baltimore, MD: Johns Hopkins University Press, 1996.

Lohmuller, Michael. "Gang-Enforced Bus Strike Increases Pressure on El Salvador Govt," July 28, 2015. www.insightcrime.org/news-briefs/gang-bus-strike-increases-pressure-el-salvador-government.

Lutz, Ellen, and Kathryn Sikkink. "The Justice Cascade: The Evolution and Impact of Foreign Human Rights Trials in Latin America." *Chicago Journal of International Law* 2 (2001): 1–33.

Marinero, Ximena. "JURIST – Paper Chase: Spain Judge Garzon Defends 2008 Franco Probe." Accessed May 6, 2012. http://jurist.org/paperchase/2009/09/spain-judge-garzon-defends-2008-franco.php.

Martinez Barahona, Elena. *Seeking the Political Role of the Third Government Branch: A Comparative Approach to High Courts in Central America.* Saarbrücken, Germany: VDM Verlag, 2009.

Martinez Barahona, Elena, and Sebastian Linares Lejarraga. "Democracy and 'Punitive Populism': Exploring the Supreme Court's Role in El Salvador." *Democratization* 18, no. 1 (2011): 52–74.

Mata, Esteban A. "Congreso saca a magistrado de Sala IV con histórico voto." *La Nación.* November 16, 2012, sec. EL PAÍS. www.nacion.com/archivo/Congreso-magistrado-Sala-IV-historico_0_1305669499.html.

"Fernando Cruz Castro: 'Yo No Tengo Que Pedir Perdón Ni Dar Explicaciones.'" *La Nación.* November 16, 2012, sec. EL PAÍS. www.nacion.com/nacional/politica/Fernando-Cruz-Castro-perdon-explicaciones_0_1305669521.html.

"Sala Constitucional Frena Último Proyecto Del TLC." *Nacion.com.* September 12, 2008, sec. EL PAÍS. www.nacion.com/ln_ee/2008/septiembre/12/pais1698549.html.

McCann, Michael W. "Interests, Ideas, and Institutions in Comparative Analysis of Judicial Power." *Political Research Quarterly* 62, no. 4 (2009): 834–39.

McCleary, Rachel M. *Dictating Democracy: Guatemala and the End of Violent Revolution.* Gainesville, FL: University Press of Florida, 1999.

McCubbins, Matthew, and Thomas Schwartz. "Congressional Oversight Overlooked: Police Patrols versus Fire Alarms." *American Journal of Political Science* 28 (1984): 165–79.

Melton, James, and Tom Ginsburg. "Does De Jure Judicial Independence Really Matter? A Reevaluation of Explanations of Judicial Independence." *Journal of Law and Courts* 2, no. 2 (Fall 2014): 187–217.

Méndez, Juan E., Guillermo O'Donnell, and Paulo Sérgio Pinheiro, eds. *The (Un)Rule of Law & the Underprivileged in Latin America.* Notre Dame, IN: University of Norte Dame Press, 1999.

Miller, Mark C. "Judicial Activism in Canada and the United States." *Judicature* 81, no. 6 (1998): 262–65.

Møller, Jørgen, and Svend-Erik Skaaning. *The Rule of Law: Definitions, Measures, Patterns and Causes.* New York, NY: Palgrave MacMillan, 2014.

Moodie, Ellen. *El Salvador in the Aftermath of Peace: Crime, Uncertainty, and the Transition to Democracy.* Philadelphia, PA: University of Pennsylvania Press, 2010.

Moog, Robert. "Judicial Activism in the Cause of Judicial Independence: The Indian Supreme Court in the 1990s." *Judicature* 85, no. 6 (2002): 268–76.

Morán, Gloria Marisela. "Suspenden Exhumaciones Relacionadas a El Mozote." *ContraPunto Diario El Salvador,* April 17, 2015. www.contrapunto.com.sv/archivo2016/sociedad/derechos-humanos/suspenden-exhumaciones-relacionadas-a-el-mozote.

Morán, Otto. "Salvadoreños Perciben Más Corrupción." *La Prensa Grafica.* July 10, 2013. www.laprensagrafica.com/salvadorenos-perciben-mas-corrupcion.

Moustafa, Tamir. "Law versus the State: The Judicialization of Politics in Egypt." *Law and Social Inquiry* 28 (2003): 883–928.

The Struggle for Constitutional Power: Law, Politics, and Economic Development in Egypt. New York, NY: Cambridge University Press, 2007.

"Nacion.com, San José, Costa Rica [Sucesos]." Accessed June 23, 2013. www.nacion.com/ln_ee/2006/marzo/21/sucesoso.html.

North, D. C., and B. R. Weingast. "Constitutions and Commitment: The Evolution of Institutions Governing Public Choice in Seventeenth-Century England." *The Journal of Economic History* 49, no. 4 (1989): 803–32.

North, Douglass C., John Joseph Wallis, Steven B. Webb, and Barry R. Weingast. "Lessons: In the Shadow of Violence." In *In the Shadow of Violence: Politics, Economics, and the Problems of Development,* 328–50. Cambridge, UK, and New York, NY: Cambridge University Press, 2013.

Observer for Latin America of the International Commission of Jurists. *A Breach of Impunity: The Trial for the Murder of Jesuits in El Salvador.* New York, NY: Fordham University Press, 1992. www.icj.org/a-breach-of-impunity-the-trial-for-the-murder-of-jesuits-in-el-salvador-report-of-the-observer-for-latin-america-of-the-international-commission-of-jurists-una-brecha-a-la-impunidad-aunque-no-un-triun/.

O'Donnell, Guillermo. "Delegative Democracy." *Journal of Democracy* 5, no. 1 (1994): 55–69.

"Horizontal Accountability in New Democracies." In *The Self-Restraining State: Power and Accountability in New Democracies,* edited by Andreas Shedler, Marc F. Plattner, and Larry Diamond, 29–52. Boulder, CO: Lynne Rienner Publishers, 1999.

"Horizontal Accountability: The Legal Institutionalization of Mistrust." In *Democratic Accountability in Latin America,* edited by Scott Mainwaring and Christopher Welna, 34–54. Oxford, UL: Oxford University Press, 2003.

"Ployarchies and the (Un)Rule of Law in Latin America: A Partial Conclusion." In *The (Un)Rule of Law and the Underprivileged in Latin America,* edited by Juan Méndez, Guillermo O'Donnell, and Paulo Sérgio Pinheiro. Notre Dame, IN: University of Notre Dame Press, 1999.

O'Donnell, Guillermo, and Phillippe C. Schmitter. *Transitions from Authoritarian Rule: Tentative Conclusions about Uncertain Democracies.* Baltimore, MD: Johns Hopkins University Press, 1986.

Office of the High Commissioner for Human Rights. "Nicaragua Homepage." Accessed July 12, 2013. www.ohchr.org/EN/countries/LACRegion/Pages/NIIndex.aspx.

Okere, B. Obima. "Judicial Activism or Passivity in Interpreting the Nigerian Constitution." *International and Comparative Law Quarterly* 36, no. 4 (1987): 788–816.

Olsen, Tricia D., Leigh A. Payne, and Andrew G. Reiter. *Transitional Justice in the Balance: Comparing Processes, Weighing Efficacy.* Washington, DC: United States Institute of Peace, 2010.

Organizacián Mundial Contra la Tortura. "Violaciones de los derechos humanos en Nicaragua: Informe alternativo e informe seguimiento presentado al Comité contra la Tortura de la Naciones Unidas." OMCT, May 2009. www.omct.org/files/2005/09/3070/informe_alternativo_nicaragua_cat.pdf.

Organization of American States. "∷ Multilateral Treaties >Department of International Law >OAS∷" Accessed June 19, 2013. www.oas.org/dil/treaties_B-32_American_Convention_on_Human_Rights_sign.htm.

Ortiz, Dianna, and Patricia Davis. *The Blindfold's Eyes: My Journey from Torture to Truth.* Maryknoll, NY: Orbis Books, 2002.

Oviedo, Esteban. "Jefe de PLN Afirma Que Es Una 'llamada de Atención' a La Corte." *La Nación.* November 16, 2012, sec. EL PAÍS. www.nacion.com/archivo/Jefe-PLN-llamada-atencion-Corte_0_1305669534.html.

Oviedo Quesadao, Heidy Maria. "Principales efectos causados a un grupo de ex funcionarios del Banco Anglo Costarricense: (15 años despues del cierre)." Maestría en Criminología con mención en Seguridad Humana, Universidad para la Cooperación Internacional, 2010. www.uci.ac.cr/Biblioteca/Tesis/PFGMCSH20.pdf.

Partlow, Joshua, and Sarah Esther Maslin. "El Salvador's Gangs Call a Cease-Fire, but Many Doubt It Will Hold." *Washington Post,* April 3, 2016. www.washingtonpost.com/world/the_americas/el-salvadors-gangs-call-a-cease-fire-but-many-doubt-it-will-hold/2016/04/02/79222748-f5c2-11e5-958d-d038dac6e718_story.html?utm_term=.2f592265d6f6.

Peacock, Susan C., and Adriana Beltrán. "Hidden Powers in Post-Conflict Guatemala: Illegal Armed Groups and the Forces Behind Them." Washington Office on Latin America, September 4, 2003. www.wola.org/publications/hidden_powers_in_post_conflict_guatemala.

Pereira, Anthony W. "Of Judges and Generals: Security Courts under Authoritarian Regimes in Argentina, Brazil, and Chile." In *Rule by Law: The Politics of Courts in Authoritarian Regimes,* edited by Tom Ginsburg and Tamir Moustafa, 23–57. Cambridge, UK: Cambridge University Press, 2008.

Political (In)justice: Authoritarianism and the Rule of Law in Brazil, Chile, and Argentina. Pitt Latin American Series. Pittsburgh, Pa.: University of Pittsburgh Press, 2005.

Peruzzotti, Enrique, and Catalina Smulovitz. "Social Accountability: An Introduction." In *Enforcing the Rule of Law: Social Accountability in the New Latin American Democracies,* edited by Enrique Peruzzotti and Catalina Smulovitz, 3–33. Pittsburgh, PA: University of Pittsburgh Press, 2006.

Political Database of the Americas. "1993 HONDURAN PRESIDENTIAL ELECTION." Accessed February 22, 2013. http://pdba.georgetown.edu/Elecdata/Hon/93elec.html.

Popkin, Margaret. *Peace without Justice: Obstacles to Building the Rule of Law in El Salvador.* University Park, PA: Pennsylvania State University Press, 2000.

Popkin, Margaret, Jack Spence, George Vickers, Hemisphere Initiatives (Organization), Washington Office on Latin America, and Unitarian Universalist Service Committee. *Justice Delayed: The Slow Pace of Judicial Reform in El Salvador.* Cambridge, MA, and Washington, DC: Hemisphere Initiatives; Washington Office on Latin America, 1994.

Prillaman, William. *The Judiciary and Democratic Decay in Latin America: Declining Confidence in the Rule of Law.* Santa Barbara, CA: Praeger, 2000.

The Judiciary and Democratic Delay in Latin America: Declining Confidence in the Rule of Law. Westport, CT: Praeger, 2000.

Programa Estado de la Nación, ed. *I Informe Estado de la Justicia.* Pavas, Costa Rica: Programa Estado de la Nación, 2015. www.estadonacion.or.cr/justicia/.

Proyecto Interdiocesano de Recuperación de la Memoria Histórica (Guatemala). *Guatemala, Nunca Más: Informe.* 1. Guatemala, Guatemala: ODHAG, 1998.

Przeworski, Adam. "Some Problems in the Study of Transitions to Democracy." In *Transitions from Authoritarian Rule: Comparative Perspectives*, edited by Guillermo O'Dondell, Phillippe C. Schmitter, and Laurence Whitehead, 47–63. Baltimore, MD: Johns Hopkins University Press, 1986.

"The Games of Transition." In *Issue in Democratic Consolidation: The New South American Democracies in Comparative Perspective*, edited by Scott Mainwaring, Guillermo O'Donnell, and J. Samuel Valenzuela, 105–52. Notre Dame, IN: University of Notre Dame Press, 1992.

Quintanilla, Edmundo. "Support for the Administration of Justice in Nicaragua: The Rural Judicial Facilitators Program." The World Bank, 2004.

Ramseyer, J. Mark. "The Puzzling (In)Dependence of Courts: A Comparative Approach." *Journal of Legal Studies* 23, no. 2 (June 1994): 721–47.

Raventos, Ciska. "Construcciones y especulacciones en turno al 'descalacro financiero' del Banco Anglo Costarricense." *Ciencias Sociales* 68 (June 1995): 41–54.

Redacción. "Presidente de la Corte quedaría fuera del Consejo de la Judicatura – LaPrensa.hn." *La Prensa.* November 5, 2012, sec. Honduras. www.laprensa.hn/Secciones-Principales/Honduras/Tegucigalpa/Presidente-de-la-Corte-quedaria-fuera-del-Consejo-de-la-Judicatura#.Ue_8lm1N-aM.

"Retardación de justicia." *La Prensa (Nicaragua).* July 7, 2013, sec. Voces. www.laprensa.com.ni/2013/06/07/voces/149762-retardacion-justicia.

Ríos Figueroa, Julio, and Jeffrey K. Staton. "Unpacking the Rule of Law: A Review of Judicial Independence Measures." Political Concepts. Mexico City, Mexico: Committee on Concepts and Methods, International Political Science Association, September 2008.

Ríos-Figueroa, Julio. "Institutions for Constitutional Justice in Latin America." In *Courts in Latin America*, edited by Gretchen Helmke and Julio Ríos-Figueroa, 27–54. New York, NY: Cambridge University Press, 2011.

Rodriguez, Miguel Angel. *Di la cara: Una batalla por el estado de derecho.* Bogota, DC: Editorial Planeta Colombiana, 2006.

"Getting Costa Rica Right." *Journal of Democracy* 17, no. 2 (April 2006): 161–64.

Rose, Nikolas, Pat O'Malley, and Mariana Valverde. "Governmentality." *Annual Review of Law and Social Science* 2 (2006): 83–104.

Rosenberg, Gerald N. "Judicial Independence and the Reality of Political Power." *Review of Politics* 54, no. 3 (1992): 369–88.

The Hollow Hope: Can Courts Bring About Social Change? Chicago, IL: University of Chicago Press, 1991.

Ruhl, J. Mark. "Honduras: Militarism and Democratization in Troubled Waters." In *Repression, Resistance, and Democratic Transition in Central America*, edited by Walker, Thomas W. and Ariel G. Armony, 47–66. Wilmington, DE: SR Books, 2000.

Sala Constitucional, Corte Suprema de Justicia. "La Sala Constitucional en números 1989–2014," June 14, 2016. www.poder-judicial.go.cr/salaconstitucional/index .php/2016-06-27-17-08-39. On file with the author.

Salas, Luis. "From Law and Development to the Rule of Law: New and Old Issues in Justice Reform in Latin America." In *Rule of Law in Latin America: The International Promotion of Judicial Reform*, edited by Pilar Domingo and Rachel Sieder. London, UK: Institute of Latin American Studies, 2001.

Sánchez Fallas, Francisco. *La tramitación de los procesos penales.* San Jose, Costa Rica: Escuela Judicial, 2009.

Sanchez Urribarri, Raul A., and Songer, Donald. "A Cross-National Examination of the Strategic Defection Theory" Paper presented at the annual meeting of the American Political Science Association, Marriott, Loews Philadelphia, and the Pennsylvania Convention Center, Philadelphia, PA, Aug 31, 2006.

Scheppele, Kim Lane. "Constitutional Negotiations: Political Contexts of Judicial Activism in Post-Soviet Europe." *International Sociology* 18, no. 1 (2003): 219–38.

Schirmer, Jennifer. *The Guatemalan Military Project: A Violence Called Democracy.* Philadephia, PA: University of Pennsylvania Press, 1999.

Schulz, Donald E., and Deborah Sundloff Schulz. *The United States, Honduras, and the Crisis in Central America.* Thematic Studies in Latin America. Boulder: Westview Press, 1994.

Schumpeter, Joseph A. *Capitalism, Socialism, and Democracy.* New York: Harper & Row, 1942.

Schwartz, Stephen. *A Strange Silence: The Emergence of Democracy in Nicaragua.* San Francisco, Ca, and Lanham, MD: ICS Press; National Book Network distributor, 1992.

Scribner, Druscilla. "Courts, Power, and Rights in Argentina and Chile." In *Courts in Latin America*, edited by Gretchen Helmke and Julio Ríos Figueroa, 248–77. Cambridge, UK: Cambridge University Press, 2011.

Sección de Estadística, and Departamento de Planificación. "Anuario Judicial 2010." Poder Judicial, 2010. https://www.poder-judicial.go.cr/planificacion/ images/documentos/estadisticas/judiciales/Anuario_Judiciales_2010/index.htm.

Segal, Jeffrey A., and Harold J. Spaeth. *The Supreme Court and the Attitudinal Model Revisited.* Cambridge, UK: Cambridge University Press, 2002.

Seider, Rachel, Alan Angell, and Line Shjolden. *The Judicialization of Politics in Latin America.* New York, NY: Palgrave Macmillan, 2005.

Serrano Caldera, Alejandro. "The Rule of Law in the Nicaraguan Revolution." *Loyola of Los Angeles International and Comparative Law Journal* 12, no. 2 (1990): 341–468.

Shambayati, Hootan, and Esen Kirdis. "In Pursuit of 'Contemporary Civilization': Judicial Empowerment in Turkey." *Political Research Quarterly* 62, no. 4 (2009): 767–80.

Sieder, Rachel, Line Schjolden, and Alan Angell. "Introduction." In *The Judicialization of Politics in Latin America*, edited by Sieder, Rachel, Line Schjolden and Alan Angell, 1–20. New York, NY: Palgrave MacMillan, 2005.

Sikkink, Kathryn. *The Justice Cascade: How Human Rights Prosecutions Are Changing World Politics*. New York, NY: W. W. Norton, 2011.

Silva, Julia Maria. "El pacto Ortega-Alemán y la reelección." *La Prensa*. October 30, 2009, sec. Opinion.

Simon, Jonathon. *Governing Through Crime: How the War on Crime Transfomed American Democracy and Created a Culture of Fear*. Studies in Crime and Public Policy. Oxford; New York, NY: Oxford University Press, 2007.

Skocpol, Theda. *Protecting Soldiers and Mothers: The Political Origins of Social Policy in the United States*. Cambridge, MA: Harvard University Press, 1992.

Solis, Luis G., and Richard Wilson. *Political Transition and the Administration of Justice in Nicaragua*. San Jose, Costa Rica: CAJ, 1991.

Solomon, Jr., Peter H. "Judicial Power in Authoritarian States: The Russian Experience." In *Rule by Law: The Politics of Courts in Authoritarian Regimes*, edited by Tom Ginsburg and Tamir Moustafa, 261–82. Cambridge, UK: Cambridge University Press, 2008.

Stanley, William. "Business as Usual? Justice and Policing Reform in Postwar Guatemala." In *Constructing Justice and Security After War*, edited by Charles T. Call, 113–55. Washington, DC: United States Institute of Peace, 2007.

Stevens, Robert. "The Independence of the Judiciary: The Case of England." *Southern California Law Review* 72, no. 3 (1999): 597–624.

Stone Sweet, Alec. *The Birth of Judicial Politics in France: The Constitutional Council in Comparative Perspective*. New York, NY: Oxford University Press, 1992.

Super, Gail. *Governing Through Crime in South Africa: The Politics of Race and Class in Neoliberalizing Regimes*. Advances in Criminology. Surrey, UK: Ashgate, 2013.

Tate, C. Neal, and Torbjörn Vallinder. *The Global Expansion of Judicial Power*. New York, NY: New York University Press, 1995.

Taylor, Matthew M. *Judging Policy: Courts and Policy Reform in Democratic Brazil*. Stanford, CA: Stanford University Press, 2008.

Tezcür, Güneş; Murat. "Judicial Activism in Perilous Times: The Turkish Case." *Law and Society Review* 43, no. 2 (2009): 305–36.

The World Bank. "Crime and Violence in Central America: A Development Challenge," 2011.

"News & Broadcast – Improving and Modernizing El Salvador's Judicial System." Accessed September 11, 2013. http://go.worldbank.org/M5IHQZ4XF0.

Torres-Rivas, Edelberto. "Guatemala: Democratic Governability." In *Constructing Democratic Governance: Latin America and the Caribbean in the 1990s, Part IV: Latin America and the Caribbean*, edited by Dominguez, Jorge I. and Abraham F. Lowenthal. Baltimore, MD: The Johns Hopkins University Press, 1996.

Transparency International. "Corruption Perceptions Index 2015," 2016. www .transparency.org/cpi2015/#results-table.

"El Salvador." Accessed September 11, 2013. www.transparency.org/gcb2013/ country/?country=el_salvador.

Trejos Salas, Gerardo. "Informe del Presidente de la Comisión Legislativa encargada de estudiar las irregularidades que condujeron al cierre del Banco Anglo Costarricense." Accessed June 23, 2013. www.nacion.com/ln_ee/anglo/angloindi/minori .html.

Tribunal Supremo de Elecciones. "Elecciones, Estadísticas de Procesos Electorales." Accessed June 17, 2013. www.tse.go.cr/estadisticas_elecciones.htm.

Trochev, Alexei. *Judging Russia: The Role of the Constitutional Court in Russian Politics 1990–2006*. Cambridge, UK, and New York, NY: Cambridge University Press, 2008.

Ungar, Mark. *Elusive Reform: Democracy and the Rule of Law in Latin America*. Boulder, CO: Lynne Rienner Publishers, 2002.

Policing Democracy: Overcoming Obstacles to Citizen Security in Latin America. Baltimore, MD: The Johns Hopkins University Press, 2011.

United Nations Office on Drugs and Crime. "UNODC Statistics Online – Homicide Counts and Rates (2000–2014)." *UNODC Statistics*, May 18, 2016. https://data .unodc.org/#state:3.

Urueña, René. "Indicators and the Law: A Case Study of the Rule of Law Index." In *The Quiet Power of Indicators: Measuring Governance, Corruption, and Rule of Law*, edited by Sally Engle Merry, Kevin E. Davis, and Benedict Kingsbury, 75–102. New York, NY: Cambridge University Press, 2015.

U.S. Department of State. "Central America Regional Security Initiative." Accessed March 21, 2017. www.state.gov/j/inl/rls/fs/2017/260869.htm.

Valverde, Mariana. *Law's Dream of a Common Knowledge*. The Cultural Lives of Law. Pinceton, NJ, and Oxford, UK: Princeton University Press, 2003.

Vásquez, Martha. "Inscriben despojo a Punta Teonoste." *La Prensa*. February 14, 2013, sec. Portada.

"Propiedad sigue en problemas." *La Prensa (Nicaragua)*. January 22, 2014, sec. Nacionales.

Velasquez Rodriguez Case, No. 4 Inter-Am.Ct.H.R. (Ser. C) (Inter-American Court of Human Rights 1988).

Verner, Joel. "The Independence of Supreme Courts in Latin America: A Review of the Literature." *Journal of Latin American Studies* 16 (1984): 463–506.

Vidaurre Arias, Alma, and Lésber Quintero. "Empresarios cierran filas a favor de Punta Teonoste." *El Nuevo Diario*. February 16, 2012, sec. Nacionales. www .elnuevodiario.com.ni/nacionales/241945.

Villalobos, Carlos A. "Sala IV Resuelve Que El TLC Es Constitucional." *Nacion.com*. July 4, 2007. www.nacion.com/ln_ee/2007/julio/04/pais1155599.html.

Vondoepp, Peter. "Politics and Judicial Assertiveness in Emerging Democracies: High Court Behavior in Malawi and Zimbabwe." *Political Research Quarterly* 59, no. 3 (2006): 389–99.

Walker, Lee Demetrius, and Susanne Schorpp. "Judicial Politics of Presidential Reelection." Orlando, FL, 2013.

Walker, Thomas W. "Nicaragua: Transition Through Revolution." In *Repression, Resistance, and Democratic Transition in Central America*, edited by Walker, Thomas W. and Ariel G. Armony, 67–88. Wilmington, DE: SR Books, 2000.

Walker, Thomas W., and Christine J. Wade. *Nicaragua: Living in the Shadow of the Eagle*. 5th ed. Boulder, CO: Westview Press, 2011.

Waltman, Jerold L. "Judicial Activism in England." In *Judicial Activism in Comparative Perspective*, edited by Kenneth M. Holland, 33–52. New York, NY: St. Martin's Press, 1991.

Washington Office on Latin America. "Historic Breakthrough in the Case of Jesuits Murdered in El Salvador in 1989." Accessed March 21, 2017. www.wola.org/analysis/a-sample-blog/.

Weingast, Barry R. "The Political Foundations of Democracy and the Rule of Law." *American Political Science Review* 91, no. 2 (June 1997): 245–63.

Weingast, Barry R. "Why Developing Countries Prove So Resistant to the Rule of Law." In *Global Perspectives on the Rule of Law*, edited by James J. Heckman, Lee Cabatingan, and Robert L. Nelson, 28–51. New York, NY: Routledge, 2010.

Wenzel, James P., Shaun Bowler, and David J. Lanoue. "Legislating From the State Bench: A Comparative Analysis of Judicial Activism." *American Politics Quarterly* 25, no. 3 (1997): 363–79.

Whittington, Keith E. *Political Foundations of Judicial Supremacy: The Presidency, The Supreme Court, and Constitutional Leadership in U.S. History*. Princeton Studies in American Politics: Historical, International, and Comparative Perspectives. Princeton, NJ: Princeton University Press, 2007.

Widner, Jennifer. *Building The Rule of Law: Francis Nyalali and the Road to Judicial Independence in Africa*. New York, NY: W. W. Norton, 2001.

Widner, Jennifer, and Daniel Scher. "Building Judicial Independence in Semi-Democracies: Uganda and Zimbabwe." In *Rule by Law: The Politics of Courts in Authoritarian Regimes*, edited by Tom Ginsburg and Tamir Moustafa, 235–60. Cambridge, UK: Cambridge University Press, 2008.

Williams, Phillip, and Knut Walter. *Militarization and Demilitarization in El Salvador's Transition to Democracy*. Pittsburgh, PA: University of Pittsburgh Press, 1997.

Wilson, Bruce M. "Changing Dynamics: The Political Impact of Costa Rica's Constitutional Court." In *The Judicialization of Politics in Latin America*, edited by Sieder, Rachel, Line Schjolden and Alan Angell, 47–65. New York, NY: Palgrave MacMillan, 2005.

"Claiming Constitutional Rights through a Constitutional Court: The Example of Gays in Costa Rica." *I CON: International Journal of Constitutional Law* 5, no. 2 (2007): 242–57.

Costa Rica: Politics, Economics, and Democracy. Boulder, CO: Lynne Rienner Publishers, 1998.

"Institutional Reform and Rights Revolutions in Latin America: The Cases of Costa Rica and Colombia." *Journal of Politics in Latin America* 1, no. 2 (2009): 59–85.

Woods, Patricia J. "The Ideational Foundations of Israel's 'Constitutional Revolution.'" *Political Research Quarterly* 62, no. 4 (2009): 811–24.

World Economic Forum. "Global Competitiveness Report 2013–2014." Geneva, Switzerland: World Economic Forum, 2013.

World Justice Project. "WJP Rule of Law Index® 2015," 2015. http://data.worldjusticeproject.org/.

Yatama v. Nicaragua, No. 127 Series C (I/A Court H.R. 2005).

Zamora, Rubén, and David Holiday. "The Struggle for Lasting Reform: Vetting Processes in El Salvador." In *Justice as Prevention: Vetting Public Employees in Transitional Societies*, 80–118. Advancing Transitional Justice Series. New York, NY: Social Science Research Council, 2007.

Index